Countdown To Murder

Pam Hupp:
(Death "Insured")

Rebecca F. Pittman

DEDICATION

To Betsy Faria, Louis Gumpenberger, and Shirley Neumann.

To their families and friends who shared their stories with pain and happy memories.

To the dedicated prosecutors and officials who will not rest until all the layers are peeled back and the truth is revealed.

Acknowledgments

So many people gave of their time and insight for this book. Through copious hours of interviews with not only family and friends of Betsy Faria, but of members of law enforcement, the media, cyber techs, county officials, archivists, and myriad peripheral participants, a comprehensive book evolved covering the deaths of Louis Gumpenberger, Shirley Neumann, and Betsy Faria.

A huge heartfelt thank you to:

St. Charles County, MO Prosecuting Attorney Tim Lohmar; Litigation Assistant to Tim Lohmar Traci Johnson; Lincoln County, MO Prosecuting Attorney Mike Wood; Lincoln County Prosecuting Investigators Bill Wilcox and Mark Ehrhard; O'Fallon, MO Police Chief John Neske; Lincoln County Sheriff Richard Harrell; Cyber Expert Greg Chatten; Former State Farm Insurance Manager Mike Boschert; Collier County, Florida City Clerks' Office; Collier County, Florida Assessors Office; *Fox 2 News* investigative reporter Chris Hayes, *St. Louis Post-Dispatch* reporter Robert Patrick, and Melissa Massman with the Department of Corrections at Chillicothe Prison in Missouri.

My sincere thanks to those who shared their stories of Betsy Faria with me: Rita Wolf, Janet Swaney, Mariah Day, and Mike Boschert. These were interviews with Betsy's family, former boss, and best friend who still feel deeply her passing.

To Patti Bathe for her time in collecting photos of Pam Hupp from her High School Yearbook in Missouri, and for introducing me to this story to begin with. Thank you to Jayden Mayberry for her help in the reenactment of Betsy Faria's murder. And a big thank you to Dylann Leal with the Glenn A. Jones MD Memorial Library in Johnstown, Colorado for fixing the formatting issue with this manuscript.

Finally, thank you to all the people who took my calls and answered my random questions—from tennis court owners, oncologists, and pharmacists, to life insurance agents and assisted living facility managers—you contributed more than you know.

CONTENTS

Prologue

Prologue

With every murder, there comes a point when someone decides to end another person's life. Even with crimes of passion, where often the crime is a spontaneous one; someone's emotions hit "Tilt" and in a split second an irrevocable act is committed. There are other times, however, when the dark hours are filled with planning and a countdown begins. At some point, a decision is made to end another person's life. When do you decide that the victim will never see another birthday or fulfill the dreams they had put in place? The word entitlement doesn't even scratch the surface. Psychologist's ledgers are filled with convenient labels for these aberrations of mental conscience: sociopath, narcissist, borderline personality disorder, bi-polar, schizophrenic, psychopath, etc. Yet, many with these personality disorders don't go about killing. And when the ending of another's life falls into the category of "murder for profit," it's even more insidious. A price tag has now been placed as the value of a person's life.

The telling of the murders of two people (and possibly three or more) by the hands of Pamela Hupp is a tragic story of murder plots so devious, so evil and diabolical, that it pushes at the boundaries of disbelief. How could one woman spend her hours planning all the events that would culminate in multiple deaths? Was there a laundry list of things to do? Surely there was in the days leading up to Louis Gumpenberger's death. The countdown to Betsy Faria's murder may have begun the moment Pam found out Betsy had terminal cancer and saw a chance to insinuate herself into her friend's life; coming away $150,000 richer. And what about Pam Hupp's mother, Shirley Neumann? Had Pam pushed her over a third-story balcony for the benefits Pam told a detective were worth $500,000?

It is a story of ruined lives. The ripple effects from the actions of this one woman are wide and varied, and still impacting lives today. Trials and investigations are still in the works and this book is published with that in mind. It is still an on-going investigation and new evidence may alter the final results. The investigation into Pam Hupp's mother, Shirley Neumann's death, is still open. There are rumors of other victims, and it is being looked into at the date of this publication. With a Preliminary Hearing and a First-Degree Murder Trial in the upcoming months, the future sequel to this book will fill in all the latest activity on this bizarre case.

It was a rare gift for this author to have multiple interviews with Prosecuting Attorneys Mike Wood and Tim Lohmar, along with their investigative detectives and police officers. I was privy to inside information on a "you can or cannot publish this yet" basis. I am doing research into the possibility of another victim from Pam's time in Florida, and I'm deeply grateful to the Collier County Assessor's Office, and other public organizations that gave me so much of their time.

This is the most comprehensive account of all that's happened to date (as of this publication) with myriad interviews with law enforcement, prosecuting attorneys for two of Pam's victims, federal agencies, family and friends. My profound thanks to Chris Hayes with *Fox 2 News* and Robert Patrick with the *St. Louis Post-Dispatch* newspaper who covered these crimes from the beginning. The crime scene photos were furnished to me by the prosecuting attorneys and their law enforcement agencies.

This was not an easy book to write. After spending so much time in interviews with Betsy Faria's family and friends, I am acutely aware of the pain they are still carrying over her insidious murder. I wanted to write the most comprehensive book I could and present all the evidence put before me, yet remain cognizant of the fact that the telling and the photos would bring them more sorrow. It is why it was important to me to hear Betsy's story from those closest to her and capture it here in the book. I wanted Betsy Faria, Louis Gumpenberger, and Shirley Neumann to be so much more than just victims.

I am positing questions throughout the book to allow you to play armchair detective. They are for your consideration and debate.

One thing is for sure:

Pam Hupp will be a topic of conversation for many years to come. With an upcoming NBC mini-series in early 2022, starring Rene Zellweger as Pam Hupp, the story will only grow. My wish is that Betsy Faria, Louis Gumpenberger, and Shirley Neumann are spoken of more often. They deserve our memories and our fight for justice.

Rebecca F. Pittman
December, 2021

Betsy Faria

March 24, 1969-December 27, 2011

Chapter One
Sumac Drive

Four Christmas stockings, emblazoned with the family's names and depleted of their goodies, hung from the fireplace mantle. There was an extra stocking for Sicily, the family dog, hanging at one end. Opened Christmas cards from friends lay scattered on an ottoman, while family photos stood atop the hearth and mantle. A small tree was sandwiched into the corner near the television set. Shopping bags, still holding holiday gifts, sat on the floor, incongruously splattered with blood.

It was less than three days since the last New Moon. Only a sliver of light illuminated the night of December 27, 2011. The Waxing Crescent shed just 9% of the glow of a full moon, keeping most of the lunar face in darkness. It glinted feebly off frosted grass blades and left houses and trees in nondescript silhouettes.

The sun had set at 5:02 p.m. that day in Troy, Missouri; a small town one hour north of St. Louis. Two hours later a car's headlights made its way up Highway H, turned onto Waterbrooke Drive, and then left onto Sumac. The few homes flanking the house bearing the numerals 130 had settled in; the LED-glow of TV screens playing across windows. Sumac was a dead-end cul-de-sac, still showing signs of vacant lots waiting for construction. The entire backside of the corner house was an empty expanse; broken only by a hopeful road with delegated lots for purchase. Kiddy-corner from the house sat another vacant lot. Only a few residences were within ear-shot of the night's unfolding of events. And only one living person knew what happened between the sparse minutes of 7:04 and 7:21 p.m. that fateful evening.

A Waxing Crescent Moon—how like the murder of Betsy Faria this was. So many shadows, so much left in darkness as the twists and turns of this bizarre case played out for years. In the end, several lives were lost, and untold others wounded in the form of collateral damage. It would take the dogged determination of a defense lawyer in one county, a dedicated PA and police force in another, and those who continually questioned, "Have you looked at Pam Hupp?" to finally shed light onto a series of events of which nightmares are made.

The yellow crime scene tape surrounding the home at 130 Sumac Drive seemed garish alongside the front lawn candy canes and tilted inflatable snowmen on neighboring lawns. It was only three days after Christmas, December 28, 2011. The morning air was crisp—a mere 28 degrees that would climb to only 37 before the day ended. The light frost on the grass surrounding the house yielded no clues. The police report stated "the ground covering had no visible shoe impressions in the frost, and the tall grass/weeds along the perimeter of the vacant lot do not show any visible signs of trampling."

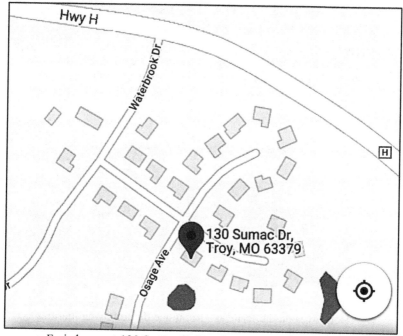

Faria home at 130 Sumac Drive. Courtesy of Google Maps

In the subdivision of Waterbrooke Estates, just two streets over from Highway H, it was that anticlimactic time when all the presents have been opened and the anticipation and preparation for the year's biggest holiday now lay in scattered wrapping paper and discarded bows, strewn across living room floors. For some, it's a melancholy time once the excitement has ended. Others look forward to yet one more holiday before the calendar flips to a fresh start: New Year's Eve. For Russ and Betsy Faria, their family and friends, it would mark the most-devasting time of their lives.

Crime scene tape blocking 130 Sumac December 27, 2011.
Russ's Ford Explorer and the Silver Nissan are in the driveway.

Detectives on the scene at 130 Sumac the following morning,
December 28, 2011.

Corner of Osage and Sumac Drive

Neighbors stared as one police car after another arrived, along with Crime Scene units and a fire truck. It had started the evening before when the telltale blue-and-red flashing lights penetrated, unwelcome, the windows of Sumac Drive residents around 9:45 p.m. What was happening at the Faria home? Door-knocking detectives would soon learn that few in that quiet neighborhood knew the Faria's. The couple had only lived there for two years. Detectives Mike Merkel, Mike Reiter, and Brett Mitchell scribbled reports as one neighbor-after-another claimed they heard nothing the night before—not even a dog barking. It had been a time to kick back after resuming their normal routines following Christmas weekend. They were still probing stockings for chocolates and playing with the new technology Santa had brought them. One neighbor stated he got home around 10:00 p.m. and noticed the police cars outside the residence at 130 Sumac, but he didn't see anything else and did not know the Faria's. One woman questioned said she had known Betsy Faria for the past two years and talked to her from time to time. The last time she had spoken to her was Christmas Eve. She had nothing further to offer.

Then what had prompted a frantic 911 call to the Lincoln County dispatcher at 9:40 p.m. on a quiet Tuesday evening, only two days after Christmas?

Dispatcher (D): "911, what's the location of your emergency?"

Russ (R): (heavy breathing)

D: "Ok, Mam, Hello?"

R: "Hello"

D: "I need you to take a couple of deep breaths so I can see what's going on. What is the address where you need us to come?"

R: "1-1-1-130 Sumac."

D: "Ok, what is the number you are calling from in case we get disconnected?"

R: "I don't know this number. I know my cell phone number." [Russ was calling from the home's land line]

D: Ok what is that number?"

R: "It's…it's _____."

D: "I'm sorry, repeat the last 4."

R: "_____."

D: "Ok, who am I speaking with?"

R: "My name is Russell Faria."

D: "Russell, what's going on there?"

R: "I just got home from a friend's house and my wife killed herself. She's…she's on the floor!"

D: "Ok, Russell, I need you to calm down honey, ok? I need you to calm down. Take a couple of deep breaths. We're going to get somebody on the way there, ok? What did she do?"

R: "She's got a knife in her neck and she slashed her arms!"

D: "Ok, Ok…calm down honey. Is she breathing at all?"

R: (Sobbing) "No!"

D: "Is there anyone we can call for you?"

R: "Call…call my mom." [Russell gives her his mom's name & phone number]

D: "How old is your wife?"

R: "My wife..she's…she's 42."

D: "And you're for sure she's not breathing now?"

R: "She's dead."

D: "Russell, how long were you gone today?"

R: "I left around five. I just got back. She went to her mom's and her friend was bringing her home. I don't know what time she got home."

D: "And you said she had been depressed lately?"

R: "She's got cancer."

D: "Russell, where's the knife now?"

R: "It's still in her."

D: "I'm sorry, I didn't understand what you said, hon."

R: "It's still in her."

D: "It's laying right next to her?"

R: "No, it's in her neck!"

D: "It's in her neck, ok."

R: (sobbing) "Oh my God! Why would she do this to me? Why would she do this?"

D: "Russell, they are on their way, hon. They'll be there shortly. Is there anybody else there in the house with you?"

R: "No. There's nobody else here." (Screaming)

D: "Russell, take a couple of deep breaths, ok, honey?"

R: "What am I going to do?"

D: "Is she on any medications?"

R: "She's on medication for her chemotherapy. (Unintelligible)

D: "Ok. Can you do me a favor? What I need is I need you to get those medications for the paramedics, ok?"

R: "I think they are here on the table."

D: "We have everybody coming to you. Russell, I need you to take a couple of deep breaths and try to get the medications together, ok?"

R: "No no no no"

D: "Russell, where are her medications?"

R: "I think they are here on the table."

D: "On the table?"

R: (Unintelligible) "I don't think these are it."

D: "Where is she in the house?"

R: "She...she died on the living room floor."

D: "Where are you right now?"

R: "I'm in the kitchen. My God oh My God, God, oh my God."

D: "Russell, they're on their way, ok?"

R: "Please God, OH, please God!" (sobbing)

D: "Russell, take a couple of deep breaths, please. I don't need you hyperventilating, ok?"

R: "My God, what am I going to do?"

D: "What is her name?"

R: "Her name is Betsy."

D: "Betsy."

R: "Yes, Betsy. No! Oh my God, no! She went to her friend's house and her friend dropped her off at her mom's house. She was at her mom's house and her friend was going to bring her home from her mom's house."

D: "They are on their way, hon."

R: "What am I going to do?"

D: "Just wait for them to get there, ok?"

R: "What am I going to do?"

D: "Russell, do you think she's beyond help right now?"

R: "I think she's dead! OH GOD!"

D: "Ok, take a couple of deep breaths...if you need to step outside..."

R: "No no no! I don't want you to go!"

D: "Do you have dogs outside?"

R: "My dog's on a chain in the backyard." (Unintelligible)

D: "Ok Russell, I got a couple of officers who are out there right now. Can you do me a favor and open your front door?"

R: "It's unlocked...it's unlocked."

D: "Ok, can you go meet them at the door?"

R: "It's unlocked...it's unlocked."

D: "Russell, are the officers inside with you right now?"

R: "Oh God, they are here."

D: "Ok, good luck to you honey. I'm going ahead and hang up and try to call your mom, ok?"

R: "Ok."

D: "Bye bye."

Deputy Chris Hollingsworth was the first officer to arrive on the scene, logging it as approximately 9:40 p.m., December 27, 2011. [As Russel's 911 call to Lincoln County Dispatcher Tammy Vaughn came in at 9:40:10, Deputy Hollingsworth must have arrived shortly after 9:40 p.m.] He was responding to the report of a possible suicide. The Lincoln County Dispatcher had advised that the victim's wrists were cut and that a knife was sticking out of her neck. Deputy Hollingsworth reported:

"Upon arrival, I knocked, opened the door and made contact with Russell Faria (husband) near the front of the couch, closest to the front door and to the head of the female. I observed Russ to be visibly upset with a minimal amount of tears coming from his eyes.

Russell appeared to be going into a state of panic by having a hard time breathing and talking. I observed a female subject, later identified as Betsy Faria (wife), laying with her abdomen flat on the ground, but her torso was twisted in such a fashion that she was resting on her right shoulder and the right side of her head (head to the North, feet to the South). Her body was resting in what appeared to be a pool of blood on the living room floor. I observed a large laceration on the right wrist of Elizabeth, and what appeared to be a black in color knife handle, sticking out of the left side of Elizabeth's neck.

"Believing this was a crime scene and not a suicide, I immediately requested Russell exit the residence. I had Russell sit in the chair on the front porch, fearing he may pass out, due to the way he was breathing and speaking.

"Corporal Pirtle and paramedics arrived on the scene [at 9:51 p.m.]. Corporal Pirtle advised that the lead medic, Mike Quattrocchi, stated the victim was 'stiff.' [It was added later that she was "stiff and cold."] Corporal Pirtle advised medical personal to exit the residence and he then conducted a protective sweep. Corporal Pirtle did not locate anyone else in the residence.

"I requested the medics give Russell a blanket due to the low temperature outside [28 degrees]. I requested Russ sit in the rear of the patrol vehicle to keep warm as I sat in the front seat." Deputy Hollingsworth goes on to say he put Russ in the back seat as the passenger side front seat contained his gear and was partially blocked by his patrol car computer. He told Russ he was not under arrest; it would just be warmer in the car. Russ asked to smoke a cigarette and agreed to sit in the car.

A crime scene log was begun and Corporal Pirtle advised that other law enforcement would be showing up, including detectives from the Lincoln County Sheriff's Office and the Criminal Investigation Division. Corporal Pirtle then secured the scene with crime scene tape.

"While in the patrol car, I began asking Russell regarding his wife," Hollingsworth reported. "I asked Russell if his wife had any medical issues or is on any medication. Russell advised his wife has breast cancer, and had her breasts removed two years ago. Russell advised Elizabeth still goes to chemotherapy, which she went to today [December 27], and is on multiple medications. Russell also stated his wife was on depression medication. Russell stated he works from home and left at approximately 1700 hours (5 p.m.). I asked Russell when was the last time he had spoken to Elizabeth. Russell stated he called Elizabeth when he got into the city limits of Troy (Lincoln County), at approximately 1730 hours (5:30 p.m.), due to the bad phone reception on Highway H. Russell stated that he asked Elizabeth if she wanted him to pick her up from her mother's house in Lake St. Louis (St. Charles County) where she had stayed the night from 12-26-2011 to 12-27-2011. Russell stated Elizabeth said, 'No, she would have her friend Pam Hupp bring her home after they were finished playing the game *UPWARDS*.' Russell stated Elizabeth wanted to talk to him about something when they got home. Russell stated Elizabeth would not tell him over the phone what it was, but it was supposed to be something "good." Russell also stated he was going to pick up dog food, then he was going to his friend Mike's house, in the Rolling Meadows Subdivision in O'Fallon. Russell stated he normally visits Mike's house on Tuesdays.

"It should be noted that during this conversation, Russell appeared to be calm, laughing at times."

Russ exited the patrol car to smoke another cigarette and while he was doing so, the deputy cleared his gear off of the front seat. He noted that Russ was crying as he mentioned he didn't know how he would tell his daughters about their mother's murder. He sat down in the front seat of the patrol car.

"I asked Russell when he left his friend Mike's house? Russell stated that he left at approximately 2100 hours (9:00 p.m.) to head home. Russell stated prior to going home he stopped at Arby's drive-through for dinner and U-Gas on the Wenztville Parkway for cigarettes. Russell stated he got home at approximately 2145 hours (9:45 p.m.), put the dog food down by the door and observed Elizabeth on the floor of the living room. [Russ couldn't have arrived home at 9:45, as his 911 call came in at 9:40, after he entered the house and found Betsy. It was later amended that he got home around 9:37 p.m.] Russell stated he fell to the floor near Elizabeth for a few minutes. Russell stated he got up and used the house phone to call 911. I asked Russell if his dog was an indoor dog or an outdoor dog. Russell stated the dog is an inside dog. I asked Russell if the dog was outdoors when he got home. Russell stated "Yes." I asked if it was usual for the dog to be outside for extended periods of time. Russell stated, "No, the dog usually goes out and comes right back inside."

Detective Merkel and Detective Harney arrived and took control of the crime scene.

Detective Mike Merkel stated, "I entered the residence and observed the deceased subject. It appeared as if she did have a knife protruding from her neck, as well as numerous lacerations to her left arm. Based upon my training and experience, these wounds were consistent with defensive wounds which could be incurred during an assault. Detective Harney arrived on the scene a short time later and we made contact with Russell. Russell was advised of the current situation, in brief, and asked to allow us to escort him to the Sheriff's Office to gather more information. Russell was then placed in the front seat of an unmarked detective's vehicle and escorted to the Sheriff's Office."

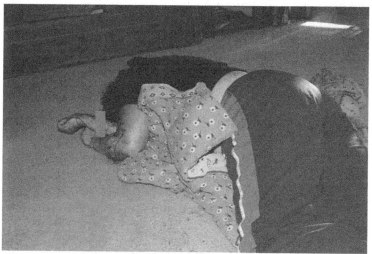

Crime scene photo of Betsy Faria.
Photo courtesy of PA Mike Wood.

As neighbors gawked from the sidewalk and windows at the house on the corner (now encased in crime scene tape), inside the residence forensic teams and detectives were processing anything of evidentiary value. Betsy Faria had not been moved from her final resting place. This vibrant, beautiful woman who had appeared in so many family photos, flashing her brilliant smile, was now photographed from every angle, the glaring flashes from police cameras a harsh invasion of her private life.

Flash! The living room area where Betsy lay. *Flash!* Betsy's purse by the couch. *Flash!* A pair of men's black leather gloves and a plaid throw blanket atop the love seat. *Flash!* The dining room table with a black handbag and several prescription bottles for Betsy: Oxycodone, Sulfamethoxazole (TMP), Docusate Sodium, and Gabapentin. *Flash!* A green cloth with unknown stains in the kitchen top drawer beneath the toaster oven. *Flash!* A blood smear on the master bedroom light switch. *Flash!* A pair of bloodied men's slippers tossed atop a pile of other shoes in the master bedroom closet. On-and-on the camera froze the minute details of that early morning of December 28, 2011. During the initial crime scene investigation, 704 crime scene photos were taken, 83 articles of evidence were seized, and 4 latent prints collected by CSI Tiffany Fischer—two of which were Russ Faria's palm prints from the sliding glass door leading to the back deck.

View from back deck sliding door. Crime scene tape is attached to the glass where they lifted two palm prints belonging to Russ Faria.
Photo courtesy of PA Mike Wood.

The official report gave the following description of the family room where Betsy Faria lay:

"The family room consists of a fireplace, sofa, love seat, chair, ottoman, and entertainment center. Numerous Christmas décor was observed throughout the room, including a Christmas tree along the north wall and opened Christmas presents on the floor in front of the chair. The room was clean, yet unorganized, and appears to be 'lived in.' A floor mat was observed upon entry to the family room, atop the carpet. A pair of white slip-on 'DC SHOE CO' ladies shoes was observed atop the floor mat and edge.

Crime scene photo. The loveseat to the left had blood stains on the fabric. Betsy Faria's body is blurred in the foreground.

Betsy's shoe on floor mat. Photo courtesy PA Mike Wood.

"A grey/khaki fabric sofa was angled along the east half-wall of the stairwell. An end table was aligned against the left arm rest, consisting of a lamp, numerous personal items, remotes, outdated receipts, etc. The end table and contents atop the table do not appear disturbed. A throw blanket was observed atop the back of the couch, a throw pillow was against the left arm rest and a second throw blanket was observed laying atop the right arm rest and cushion. A 'UNIDEN' cordless phone was observed face down atop the right arm rest of the couch. Redial of the 'UNIDEN' phone displayed "911." A white purse with black and white print was observed atop the floor, against the right arm of the couch. The contents of the purse contained the victim's wallet with a Missouri Driver's License, identifying the victim as:

Elizabeth Faria K.   W/F

Couch flanking stairwell. The UNIDEN phone is seen laying atop the couch. It was originally found on the right armrest of the couch where Russ laid it after his 911 call. The hallway to the front door is to the left and the kitchen half-wall is to the right. A crime scene tech has placed the foam cushions from the loveseat against the couch after their blood-stained covers were removed.
Photo courtesy of PA Mike Wood.

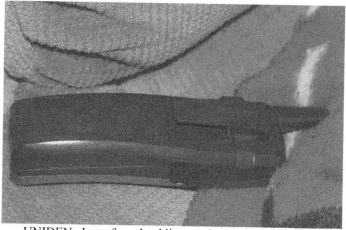

UNIDEN phone from land line used to make the 911 call.
Photo courtesy of PA Mike Wood.

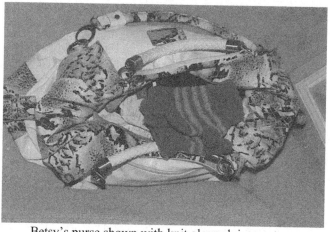

Betsy's purse shown with knit gloves lying on top.
Photo courtesy of PA Mike Wood.

"A brown fabric love seat was situated in the southwest corner of the family room. The left, north front corner (foot) of the loveseat is 1'8" from the baseline against the hearth of the fireplace. The loveseat feet seem to be in their normal position, indicated by the deep carpet depressions. A pair of men's black leather gloves and a plaid throw blanket was observed laying atop the back of the loveseat. Two throw pillows are propped against the right arm rest and a black handled knife was located between the two pillows. The knife handle was situated in the corner of the love seat, angled, and the knife blade was pointing towards the center of the seat cushion. Multiple patterns of red, blood-like substance were observed on the fabric on the back of the loveseat, seat cushions, and skirt. The blood patterns were photographed with scale and the sections of the fabric were removed."

Love seat where Betsy had been lying during the attack. A pair of men's black leather gloves are sitting atop the couch at the left. It is believed Betsy had been lying on her right side with her head on the two pillows to the left when she was attacked. Photo courtesy of PA Mike Wood.

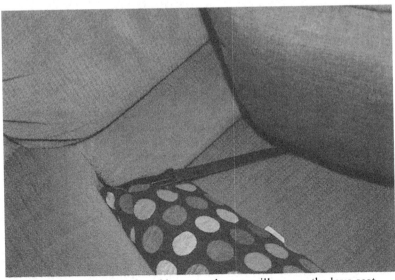

Black-handled knife found between the two pillows on the love seat, pointing down. Photo courtesy of PA Mike Wood.

Christmas stockings still hung from the mantle, and a small tree sporting carefully placed ornaments seemed an incongruous backdrop to the gruesome finding of a woman lying on the floor amid sacks of recent purchases and a snowman-adorned gift bag. It was evident that the attack had occurred on the loveseat, as it was the only piece of furniture showing bloodstains. The area rug in front of it was flipped half-way over, as if Betsy had rolled from the couch onto the floor. Nothing seemed to indicate a struggle; not even items on the small tables about the room had tumbled over. The amount of blood found on the loveseat's fabric seemed minor compared to the egregious wounds inflicted upon the victim.

Crime scene photo of love seat with blood stains, the carpet runner flipped back, cell phone, and the edge of the blanket still wrapped around Betsy's body (1). The kitchen is a few feet away from the head of the love seat where the two small pillows are seen. The pantry door can be seen in the middle of the photograph.
Photo courtesy of PA Mike Wood.

Crime Scene Investigators have long known that the body of a victim has clues to impart. In Betsy Faria's case, there were several very telling elements as to how she died and if one or more perpetrators were involved. The placement of the "unrolled" comforter on the floor spoke as to whether she ever stood up during the attack, and just how far she got. The stains on the couch and on her cell phone tell a story, as does the blood patterns on the carpet. Yet, to this author, there was one very telling aspect of Betsy's body. Russ mentioned it on his 911 call—Betsy's tongue was protruding. After much research, it became apparent that the only forms of death resulting in the victim's tongue protruding are those involved with loss of air: hanging, drowning, suffocation, and burning. Burn victims typically die of smoke inhalation rather than succumbing to burns. Knowing that, I looked at the autopsy report that Detective Bill Wilcox supplied me, and there it was: Betsy's trachea had been cut clean through, severing her windpipe and cutting off her air flow. Once the knife was stuck into her neck—and it is believed that may have been the first wound inflicted as she lay on the couch—she would have had only minutes to live. Betsy's still form had given investigators a big clue: it would have only taken one person inflicting a knife wound to the neck to kill her. The theory of the murderer needing an accomplice was closer to being resolved.

The autopsy report concerning that one wound is as follows:

"All of the stab wounds in the neck track backward and rightward via the skin and tissue with penetrating injuries noted to the thyroid, trachea and right jugular vein...beneath the right lateral aspect of the neck beneath the exit stab wound below the right ear."

The report shows that the large kitchen knife went all the way through her neck and exited on the right side below the ear. That accounts for all the blood pooling beneath Betsy's head. It also shows the knife entered from the left side, just as it would have if she was attacked while lying on her right side on the couch.

A reenactment was performed by this author using a woman approximately Betsy's height and strength, using a similar love seat, cushions, and runner carpet in the exact positions as the crime scene photos. When the female lunged from the couch as if to get away from a sudden attack, her left foot hit the carpet runner and it flipped back exactly as seen in the crime scene photo. She hit the floor and half-rolled, half-crawled before lying still, again just as seen in the photo evidence. The blood stains on the carpet show two distinct places where Betsy may have put her bloodied forearm down as she fell across the floor. The blanket remained still tucked around our female actor with the tail of the blanket reaching toward the loveseat as if she had rolled out of it, as seen in the photos. Our conclusion was that Betsy was attacked first by a knife going into her neck to keep her from screaming, to sever her airway, and to incapacitate her. She was quickly stabbed in her left arm and head as she bolted from the couch. The blood on the far right of the couch would align with damage already done to her arm, and a smear at the back of the right couch cushion could be where her hand pushed off, or her arm hit it as she lunged from the couch.

During the reenactment, the only scenario that resulted in Betsy's cell phone landing where it did by the carpet runner was when it was held in the left hand of the female. Laying it on the blanket or couch found it falling straight down, not off to the left. It appeared it was flung as the female lunged from the couch. Betsy was expecting a phone call from her daughter Leah, and may have been holding it as she lay on the couch. Blood found on the phone points to Betsy already bleeding as she sat up to lunge from the couch. *[This reenactment does not reflect any findings other than those of the author and is not meant to represent the conclusions of law enforcement.]*

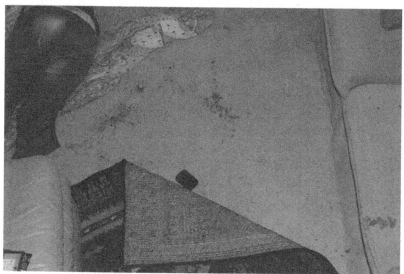

Close-up of flipped carpet runner and Betsy's cell phone. Betsy is lying to the left, the blanket tail toward the loveseat.
Photo courtesy of PA Mike Wood.

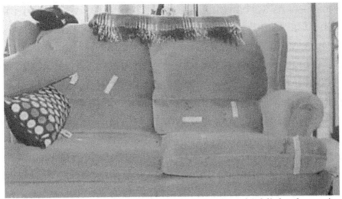

Crime scene photos of love seat. The scale markers highlight the various small blood stains. A pair of men's black leather gloves are at the top left.

Photos are courtesy of PA Mike Wood.

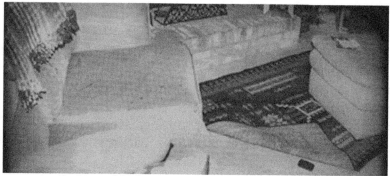

Position of the loveseat near the fireplace showing the
flipped hearth rug and cell phone.

Officer Amy Pratt continued the detailed description of the crime
scene in the family room:

"A height adjustable style table was observed adjacent to the
right arm of the love seat. Two remotes were atop; the table nor
contents appeared to be disturbed. A small dog treat and a portion
of another were on the floor beneath the table. A 'T-ZONE
VIBRATION' machine was abutted against the back of the loveseat
and did not appear to be disturbed.

"A brick fireplace with a white wood mantle was medial along
the west wall of the family room... Numerous photo frames, floral
décor, and a candelabra sit atop the hearth. Photo frames sat atop
and stockings were hung to the wood mantle. None of the décor had
been disturbed and a visual examination for blood evidence was met
with negative results. An area rug is positioned in front of the
fireplace hearth, with the southwest lower corner folded over. A tan
ottoman was sitting atop the area rug, northwest, slightly angled,
with personal cards and letters addressed to the victim. A red, blood-
like stain was observed on the side of the ottoman facing the east
wall. A sterile cotton swab, moistened with distilled water, was used
to obtain possible trace evidence, and seized. A 'MOTOROLA'
purple cell phone was observed face down atop the carpet, adjacent
to the area rug. The cell phone exhibits red, blood-like stains and
was powered on and rings during the investigation.

An entertainment center was observed situated in the northwest
corner, angled...

"A rocker style chair was situated in the northeast corner of the
family room, angled, facing the southwest corner. A 'DOLLAR

GENERAL' bag, containing toilet tissue, was observed atop the seat cushion of the chair. A throw blanket and a black 'HARLEY DAVIDSON' coat was atop the back of the chair. A gray 'KOHLS' Department Store bag containing new unwrapped Christmas presents sits atop the carpeted floor, parallel to the chair. The bag exhibits red, blood-like stains. A decorative snowman gift bag containing new unwrapped Christmas presents sits adjacent to the 'KOHLS' bag, parallel to the chair. The bag exhibits unknown stains.

Crime scene photo showing gift bags (center bottom) and bag with toilet tissue on the rocker style chair (right). Betsy's body has been blurred (lower left bottom).

The Kohl's bag (top right) showed blood spatter, possibly cast-off.

Betsy Faria, who had always been larger than life, with her trademark smile and piercing blue eyes, was now relegated to the dry statistics as Officer Pratt's investigative report continued:

Betsy Faria. Photo courtesy of Mariah Day.

"The victim was located in the family room, center of the family room floor. The victim was clad in blue sweat pants, black t-shirt, black underwear, black bra, and green and white socks. The victim was lying mostly on her right side atop the family room carpet and a multi-colored comforter, partially wrapped between her and the floor. The victim was positioned mainly on the right side with the left side elevated. The right arm was tucked underneath the torso, bent at the elbow and pointing upwards, with the forearm resting on the left wrist and floor. The right palm was face-up with the fingers slightly curled inward. A deep cut was observed on the right forearm. The left arm was perpendicular to the shoulder, bent at the elbow with the forearm resting against the floor, beneath the right forearm. The left palm was facing downwards with the fingers curled under. The left wrist is not visible, obscured by the right arm.

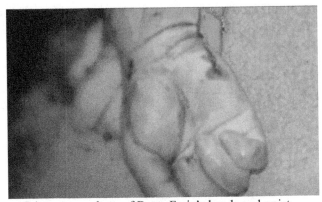

Crime scene photo of Betsy Faria's hands and wrist.

"The victim's legs are parallel to each other, with the feet pointed toward the west and the head towards the east. The left leg was partially bent at the knee, with the right leg fully extended. The victim's right foot was approximately 1'5" from the fireplace hearth. The victim's socks were partially removed from the feet. The heels of the victim were visible. The victim's head was approximately 8' 9" from the fireplace hearth, and approximately 9' from the north wall.

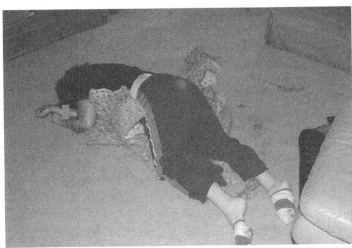

Betsy Faria. Her feet are near the ottoman which showed blood spatter. The knife is still in her neck, the black handle hidden here by her hair and dark shirt. Photo courtesy of PA Mike Wood.

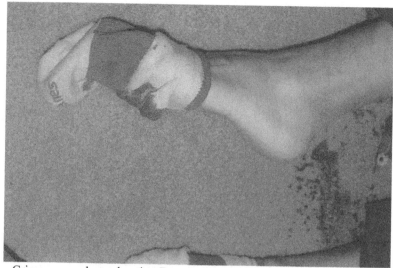

Crime scene photo showing Betsy's socks half-way off her feet. The blood found on the socks would later give the investigation team a huge clue.
Photo courtesy of PA Mike Wood.

"The victim's face was covered with dried and coagulated blood. A black handled knife was protruding from the left side of the victim's neck. Numerous wounds were observed on the left upper arm and forearm, with dried blood adhered to the skin. A long swipe of blood was observed on the back of the victim, above the waistline, extending from the left side torso to the small of the back.

Close-up of black knife handle in the victim's neck. The pattern of the blood found on the handle would be yet another important clue.

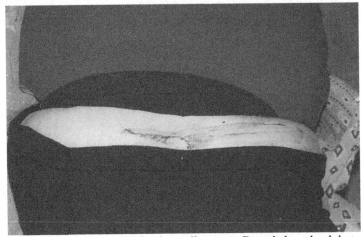

Long smear of blood running horizontally across Betsy's bare back between her shirt and her pants. Could it have been from a knife being laid there for a moment, or from wiping a blade off? It is the shape of a knife, with a pointed blade tip (1). Photo courtesy of PA Mike Wood.

"Upon the arrival of the Coroner, R. Shramek [who arrived at 8:24 AM the morning after the murder and departed at 11:49 AM], the victim was processed for possible trace evidence. Trace evidence lifts were applied to the back of the victim, and to the carpeted floor to the right and left of the body. A blood pattern similar to that of a dog print was observed on the pants on the left buttock of the victim. The blood pattern was photographed using a scale for evidentiary value. The hands, feet, and the knife handle were bagged for trace evidence using TYVEC evidence hand bags. A bracelet was observed on the victim's left wrist. The victim was examined and numerous wounds were found on the front and back of the torso. The victim's t-shirt was bunched and twisted at the left shoulder. Wounds were observed on the victim's face and sides of the head. The victim's eyes were closed, and the mouth was closed with the tongue partially protruding outward. Rigor and Livor mortis were evident. The victim was transported to the Medical Examiner's Office in St. Louis for autopsy at approximately 1149 hours [11:49 AM].

"The carpet that the victim laid upon had numerous blood stain patterns and blood spatter around the perimeter of the body and beneath. The section of carpet from beneath the victim and surrounding area was cut and removed for further analysis."

Crime scene photo after carpet area and cushion sections have been removed. The blood still showing on the floor is on the remaining padding beneath the carpet. The dining room table is seen at middle top. On that table was found Betsy's cancer bag that she retrieved from the Nissan after arriving home that night, and several prescription bottles listed earlier. It was here Russ told the dispatcher he looked for his wife's medication, and then said, "These are not the ones." Photo courtesy of PA Mike Wood.

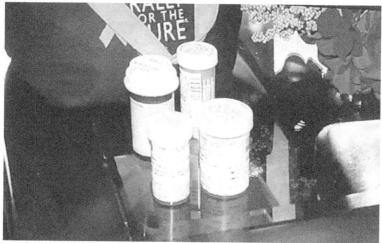

Photo of Betsy's cancer bag and four prescription bottles sitting atop the dining room table behind the love seat where Betsy was attacked.

The crime scene seemed inexplicable. Not even a standing family photo on the hearth had fallen to the floor, so near where the feet of Betsy Faria would have been while lying on the love seat with a multi-colored comforter over her. Not one item turned over or upended, other than the flap of the hearth area rug where she fell. Even the men's gloves sitting atop the couch were in place and the comforter hanging over the edge was barely disturbed. There were no forced entries found, the dog was chained outside, and it all looked so natural. So peaceful. Except for the woman lying prone on the family room floor with a knife protruding from her neck and deep slashes to her face, wrists, and forearms. The coroner would later determine that Betsy Faria had been stabbed 56 times. How does an attack like that happen and leave no signs of a struggle or of a bloodier crime scene? The answer to the latter question would come during the autopsy—most of those 56 stab wounds had been inflicted post-mortem—but why? The gash to her right forearm had gone clear to the bone and had been done after she was already dead. The lack of blood that would have emanated from a wound that size proved her heart was not beating at the time. The answer to the first part of the question would have a more insidious meaning. Betsy must have known her attacker and felt safe lying there, cuddled beneath the warmth of a blanket on a cold December evening, facing the television.

Crime scene photo of Betsy Faria, courtesy of PA Mike Wood.

Chapter Two
Betsy Faria: "A Force of Nature"

Elizabeth Faria was known to everyone simply as "Betsy." At 5' 3" tall, she could still command a room with her bright smile and huge personality. She has been described as "a force of nature." It was no surprise then that Betsy fell in love with entertaining. Her field of choice became DJing for parties, weddings, and special events. "Party Starters" soon became the vendor to hire if you wanted a party guaranteed to get your guests out on the dance floor. Betsy ran the burgeoning business from home, while at times holding down other jobs, such as an agent for State Farm Insurance. She was well-liked, with so many friends that she was never at a loss for a ride to chemo during her cancer treatments, or for a tennis match partner. She loved her two daughters, Mariah and Leah Day, her husband Russ, mother, sisters, and extended family. It was hard to find a photo of Betsy where she wasn't smiling.

Betsy Faria's death hit like a thunderbolt to her family and friends. Only an hour before her murder on December 27, 2011, she had been playing a friendly board game with her mother Janet Meyer and friend Bobbi Wann at her mother's apartment in Lake St. Louis. Her daughter Mariah had been lying on the couch nearby. Pam Hupp arrived around 5:30 p.m. to give Betsy a ride home.

"On the day Pam Hupp picked up my mom," Mariah Day said, "I was sick with the flu. Russ had taken me to the hospital the day before. I was lying on the couch while Mom, Bobbi, and my grandmother were sitting at the dining room table playing *UPWORDS*. I don't remember what Pam was wearing that night. I think Pam was sitting at the table with them, or she was standing up. She definitely wasn't sitting in the living room with me. It's a small

31

apartment. Pam is always strange and stand-offish, so it's hard to say if she was anxious that night. My mom asked me if I wanted to go stay the night with her. I don't know if Pam said anything. I said 'No,' because my boyfriend was 'coming over later that night.' I don't know if I had gone with her that night if I could have saved her, or if I would have been gone too."

Mariah Day is an amazing young woman who has been through a lot. She was only 17-years-old when her mother was murdered. The youngest of two daughters, Mariah was suddenly thrown into a maelstrom of police interviews from the moment she was alerted by a knock on the door the morning of December 28, 2011, and told her mother was dead. There was hardly any time to grieve Betsy Faria's passing. Today, Mariah is a mother of a two-year-old and expecting again. Her voice filled with emotion during this author's phone interview with her.

"I am actually pregnant with my second child. The due date is actually my mom's birthday. I found out the week that Pam Hupp got charged and all that, so I'm taking it as a sign. I don't know if it's a boy or a girl, but everyone is hoping for a girl. I already have a boy. He's two.

Mariah Day with her mother, Betsy Faria. Photo courtesy of Mariah Day.

"My mom was very unique. She had a very interesting parenting style," Mariah said. "She wanted to be more our friend than our mom. It could be frustrating for me, because I sometimes wanted her to parent me more than be my friend, but I was kind of like a rude teenager when she passed away, because I was 17-years-old. It took me awhile to get over a lot of regrets. There were times she was a friend to my older sister, but parenting me more, and it could feel one-sided. My sister could go out and do more things because she was older, and I couldn't because I was younger."

It is a typical situation between mothers and teenage daughters; headbutting is in the fine print. It's evident in Mariah's memories of her mother that they were very close.

"We went on a family cruise my sophomore year," Mariah continued, "so I want to say it was like 2009. It was a Halloween cruise so we got to dress up on Halloween and then they always had an elegant night on cruises. That was fun.

2009 Cruise. Leah, Mariah, Russ & Betsy.
Photo courtesy Mariah Day.

"Mom loved to travel. Her favorite place to go was Branson, Missouri. She always said she would retire there. She had a timeshare there that included places all over the country. She just loved Branson. They have these cool shows, and we would always go see a show called *The Legends*. It's people who impersonate Elvis Presley and famous people like that. We used to go there every time we would go down to Branson. It would always be different. They didn't have the same impersonators.

Legends in Concert. Courtesy of the Branson Travel Office.

"Traveling is a lot of my fondest memories with my mom, and going to her DJ shows. She always kept us busy on the weekends. She would bring us there. We would go to different pool parties in the summertime or weddings. She would always have us get out there and dance to get the party started. We were the little assistants. We learned it from her.

"Christmas or Thanksgiving were her favorites holidays…any holiday that brought the family together, because she loved when her family was together." Mariah said. "She was not a very good cook [laughing]. She had a few special dishes she could make. She had this one really good Chicken and Rice recipe, and this thing called 'Gooey Butter Cake.' It's like a St. Louis staple."

Betsy was diagnosed with breast cancer in January of 2010. Later that year, Betsy was given the good news that the cancer appeared to be in remission after rigorous chemo treatments. Russ and Betsy planned a Celebration of Life cruise with adult family and friends just before Thanksgiving, 2011, to celebrate. However, in October, 2011, a month before the cruise, Betsy was told the cancer was not only back, but had spread to her liver. Although the news was devastating—she was given only 3 to 5 years to live—it was decided that the cruise would go on as planned. Betsy had a lifelong dream of swimming with the dolphins, and Russ made sure that dream was fulfilled.

Betsy swimming with the dolphins, Nov. 2011.

Friends and family gathered around the Faria's on the cruise that would be Betsy's last. Her daughter Mariah Day told this author that her mother was planning to take her on a Spring Break cruise in March, 2012. Betsy died three months before the promised trip. According to Mariah, Betsy also had a New Year's Eve DJ party scheduled four days after her murder.

Betsy and Russ Faria aboard the Cruise ship.

Julie Swaney, Betsy Faria's sister.
Photo courtesy of Julie Swaney.

Julie Swaney has so many wonderful memories of her late sister. Julie is Betsy Faria's older sister. She lives in Creve Coeur, Missouri, a bedroom community of St. Louis with an exotic name that smacks of Cajun. Speaking with her is a delight. Her infectious laugh bubbles up frequently during the conversation and you get a sense of the zest for life these sisters shared. A hardworking entrepreneur with a large heart, Julie is there for her family and was a big part of her nieces, Leah and Mariah's lives. They both lived with Julie at times after Betsy died. Leah was there when the police knocked on the door with the news that was hard to take in. This author's interview with Julie gave me a glimpse into Betsy's personality, her verve, determination to beat cancer, and an immense love of family.

"Betsy was very unique in that she never let too much time pass with her friends," Julie said. "Her friends were important to her. I still hear from all of her friends: 'Betsy never missed my birthday; she never missed a grandson's soccer game...she came to this... she came to that.' I don't know how the girl had enough time in the day. If it was important to someone else, it was important to Betsy. Her daughters were the most-important people in her life. The crazy trials have come along, and all the negativity that was out there...the bottom line is, she loved her daughters. The girls didn't do anything most normal teenagers don't do. I'm a proud Aunt. Mariah and Leah have been through a lot, and they've come a long way. They still hurt and grieve her loss, but they've found their way, and they are happy and love the people in their lives. They are good humans.

"Betsy loved to travel," Julie remembered, "she loved music, she loved her DJing business, she loved to laugh, she loved to spend time with her friends, she loved to play tennis. She was playing tennis even when she wasn't supposed to be playing tennis after she had her mastectomy and after she had her reconstructive surgery. She kept playing tennis. (The laugh bubbles up) The doctors would tell her to take it easy, and her answer was, 'Well, I really love to play tennis.' She was going to do what she wanted to do and spend her time doing the things she loved. Even though she died young, many of us have said, 'She probably did everything she wanted to do in her 42 years and not many people can say that.'

"She didn't have a fear factor. She would try anything. She was outgoing. She did everything with a smile on her face. The last ten years have been extremely difficult but if you walk around with a bad attitude, that's just going to bring everyone else down.

Appreciate what you have, and the people in your life. Time is short and you never know when it's going to be taken away.

Betsy Faria and her sound system. Photo courtesy of Mariah Day.

"Betsy and I are a couple of years apart," Julie said. "I'm a couple of years older. When I was a senior in High School, a friend of a friend was getting married, kinda young. They didn't have a lot of money and they wanted to have music at their wedding reception but couldn't afford much, so they literally paid Betsy and I to do the music. This was back in the day when it was like a little stereo thing, like a record player stereo back in the 80's, so we literally dragged our stereo system from our house up to this rental hall. (Laughing.) We played the music for this wedding reception for this young couple. I thought it was stressful. It was a lot of work picking out all the songs and having them cued up. I love music too and I've been singing for years, but the DJing was like a whole 'nother thing and I'm not into the electronics and all that. But Betsy fell in love with it. First job she ever had was with me because a friend needed a DJ at her wedding reception. She did fantastic with it. She would have four or five events in one night. She would just contract out or hire other DJ's. She sent them with the equipment and said, "Here you go, here's the list of songs." She had a real knack for it. She was very gifted with it. I've never seen a DJ do even half a job she did. She had this innate ability to pick the right song at the right time and just get everyone out on the dance floor. She could get you out on the dance floor whether you wanted to be there or not. She was dancing and then grabbing people out of their seats and getting them on the floor. She was a very confident person.

"Betsy loved cruises…she loved the beach. Two of her favorite songs were "Girls Just Wanna Have Fun" and "We Are Family." She loved a lot of 80's music and dance songs.

"A Force of Nature." Photo courtesy of Mariah Day.

"When Betsy died, two police officers came to my house. Leah was staying with me at the time, so we both got the news at the same time," Julie stated, the memories still painful. "That wasn't an interview, it was just to say 'Here's what happened and you probably want to go see your family.' It wasn't the best Christmas; it wasn't the best holiday season. It was sad because we were all aware Betsy had cancer again. We were trying to put on our best faces and do the family time thing and spend time together. We all knew she was facing a kind of death sentence after the cancer spread to her liver. Her last doctor's appointment told her she might have three years. So, although it wasn't the best holiday season, we certainly didn't expect what happened.

"I didn't even understand what the police officers were saying to me that morning. I thought they were saying she was sick and in the hospital. It didn't sink in for me for hours after they came to my house. It's unfathomable for someone to die in that manner. They said that she was "hurt." I asked, 'Is she in the hospital?' And they shook their heads, no. I think they keep the information low to see what you're going to say or to get information out of you. I just kept asking questions, like, 'Is she really hurt, is she going to be okay?' They keep shaking their heads, no. I finally asked, 'Was there a weapon, like a gun involved?' And they shook their heads, no. So, I didn't know what the heck was going on. I knew she was hurt and that it was not good. I didn't register anything after that. I just wanted to go see my family. It was horrible. Leah was bawling and falling on me and I was trying to ask the detectives questions. My husband had already gone to work. I knew it wasn't good when I have two police officers knocking on my door at 6:30 in the morning before work."

Rita Wolf was Betsy's Faria's best friend. Rita is an attractive woman with long brown hair and an engaging manner of speaking. Her keen eye for detail and her closeness to Betsy Faria as one of her closest friends offered an invaluable insight to the overall situation. Rita works from home in medical sales and raises two rambunctious boys. Rita began her phone interview with this author by stating, "We all want real justice for Betsy, but with all that the families have been through, why open another can of worms? [Referring to the new charges in the Betsy Faria case.] It is good that her daughters are finally opening up.

"Betsy was a rebel to the core," Rita recalls fondly. "Not afraid to try anything new. We would sneak into the tennis courts. Did that scare me? No, because I knew the worst that would happen is that we would be told to leave. Would I do something that would get me thrown in jail? Oh, hell no! When we were younger, we would "trampoline hop" where you would go into neighbor's back yards and jump on their trampolines. We sneaked into the pool at Lake Saint Louis and I'll never forget the year that we technically got caught but Betsy and me got away, and all the other girls got arrested.

Betsy Faria (l) and Rita Wolf in their High School days.
Photo courtesy of Rita Wolf.

"Betsy knew her cancer had progressed farther than her family knew," Rita continued. "Betsy loved Russ. Betsy and Russ loved each other and there is no way in hell Betsy would want Russ to go to jail. From witnessing them together, I will tell you this: Betsy did not dislike, nor was she afraid of, her husband. I think that the prosecution tried to convince the family to hate this poor man they had adored at one point. That part makes me sick... that they destroyed all of that. Especially for the daughters.

"Betsy died, and the way I found out was horrible," Rita said, her tone changing. "It was on the News the next day at 5:00. Betsy's sisters didn't have my contact information and had no way of getting hold of me. The report said she died of mysterious causes, and I assumed cancer killed her. I thought, 'I just talked to her yesterday!' When I couldn't reach Betsy's sisters on *Facebook*, I got in my car and drove to Janet's [Betsy's mother] house, apartment, or condo, or whatever it is. Pam Hupp had already been there and left. All of Betsy's sisters were there, and some of their husbands were still there. Mariah and Leah were still there with Janet and we were just sitting there talking.

"I just hope we get to the truth. Betsy deserves justice. I think Betsy's story needs to be told many times. She was a wonderful human being and she is dearly missed."

Leah and Mariah Day with their mother Betsy Faria at a "hat day" gathering shortly after Betsy found out she had breast cancer.
Photo courtesy of Mariah Day.

Mariah as a little girl dancing with her mother Betsy.
A moment of joy frozen in time. Photo courtesy of Mariah Day.

As day dawned in Troy, Missouri and surrounding counties on that cold morning of December 28, 2011, things began to happen quickly. Like a stain spreading out from ink dropped into a glass of still water, the detectives fanned out to knock on various doors. They went out in groups of two, like fishers among men, only their nets were set to gather information rather than souls. While one group knocked on the door of Julie Swaney at 6:30 a.m., a doorbell was shrilling through the home of Pamela Hupp—the last person to reportedly see Betsy alive the previous night. As for Russ Faria, his nightmare was underway at the Lincoln County Sherriff's Office.

Chapter Three
A Narrow Dragnet

Russell Faria sat in a small interrogation room at the Lincoln County Sheriff's Office in Troy, Missouri, in the late evening hours the night of Betsy's murder. The emotion he had shown during his frantic 911 call to beg for help upon finding his wife's dead body had not abated. He wailed and repeatedly cried out "Oh God!" and "No, no, no, no!" He asked the detectives if he could have a drink and a cigarette. Wrapped in a white medic's blanket, the security video camera recorded Russ during the hours-long interview. As the two detectives gently questioned Russ, he would go in-and-out of clarity as waves of reality flooded over him; sinking him one moment, and allowing him to surface to answer questions the next. When left alone in the room, he would wail, slump over the small table (head on his arms), or rock back against the wall, racked with shuddering sobs and pleadings to God. It was still dark out and his house was under siege by crime scene investigators.

The detectives encouraged him to pull himself together. They needed his help and his focus. Sniffing, and with a huge intake of breath, he began to recount the night's events:

"I came in through the front door," Russ said in reply to the detective's question as to which door he entered his home. "I was putting the dog food down and taking my jacket off when I saw Betsy. And I fell down and I was looking at her and she wasn't moving (sniff) and I thought she killed herself."

The detective asked, "What made you think that?"

Russ answered, "Because I saw her arms slashed...her arm was slashed and it was slashed crossways, and it was very deep, and I saw a knife."

The questions continued. Russ said he had finally gotten up from the family room floor and stumbled to the kitchen where he "fell on the floor because I couldn't breathe." The detectives seemed concerned about Russ repeatedly saying he thought his wife had killed herself. What Russ didn't know was that reports were coming in from crime scene investigators at the home that Betsy's body had multiple knife wounds that did not resemble a suicide. The two detectives, Patrick Harney and Mike Merkle, kept that information to themselves for the time being and again asked about his suicide theory.

Russ responded that Betsy had tried to kill herself before with a knife, seven years earlier during an argument. As Russ tried to wrestle the knife away from his wife, his arm had been cut deeply enough to require stitches. There were other times, when Betsy had sunk into a darker mindset, despondent over her cancer prognosis. She had even been taken in for a psychiatric review after leaving a suicide note on her pillow once, and according to Betsy's sister, Pamela Welker, Betsy had made an ominous comment to a police officer who had stopped her on a bridge. It was enough for him to order her hospitalized.

Russ related to the detectives that he worked from home, using a network of computers. His current employer was Enterprise Leasing. Russ was an IT guy; a degree he acquired after Betsy encouraged him to go back to school.

After hours of answering questions, interrupted with Russ's wails as images of Betsy's mutilated body surfaced again in his mind, a new set of detectives took over. They were with the Major Case Squad. It was now the wee hours of morning. Russ was not afforded the same break. He settled in for round two of the interrogation. This time, they would go over Russ' movements the evening before (the night of the murder) in minute detail.

At 5:00 PM that day, Russ had finished working from home and got ready for his weekly Game Night with his friends at Mike Corbin's house near Lake St. Louis in O'Fallon. He called Betsy.

Detective: "When was the last time you called Betsy?"

Russ: "A little after 5. I called her before I left the house."

Russ said that as he left the house, he left the foyer light and front porch light on for Betsy after speaking with her on the phone and learning she would not be riding home with him.

"And what was the nature of the conversation that you had with her when you talked to her around 5 o'clock?"

Russ: "I asked her if she needed a ride on my way home and she said, 'No,' that her friend was going to bring her home…that her friend Pam was going to come pick her up after running some errands.'"

Detective: "Do you know Pam's last name?"

Russ: "Yeah, it's Hupp…H-U-P-P."

Detective (scribbling notes into a notebook): "What do you know about her friend? Is there anything that would be hinky about her…what do you think of her? Do you consider her a friend of yours as well?"

Russ: "Yeah, she's a good person. She's very friendly."

They picked up Russ' last conversation with Betsy again. What else was said?

Betsy had told him on the phone that she had some news to talk to him about. "I said, 'Well is it good or bad, and she said, 'Well, it's good so don't worry.' And I said, 'Well, okay, I'll see you at home later and I love you,' and that was the last time I talked to her."

Russ had also texted Betsy around noon that day. According to cyber expert Greg Chatten, he was able to remove from Russ and Betsy's cell phones their texting history. Russ had texted 'Going to game and then come get you. Will call when on way. Should not be too late.' Betsy had texted him back, 'Okay, great honey.' She later texted him to buy dog food as they were out. Betsy also texted him later that day after her chemo treatment to say, 'Pam Hupp wants to bring me home to bed.' She mentioned that her white blood count was low. Russ double-checked: 'She is bringing you?' Betsy texted back: 'Yes, she offered and I accepted. Didn't get much sleep. Mom snored.' Betsy had spent Monday night at her mother's apartment to be closer to her chemo treatment the next day. She often did that. Betsy's mother, Janet Meyer, lived only five minutes from Mike Corbin's house where Game Night was always played. Yet, it was Pam Hupp that drove Betsy home the night she was murdered.

Russ told the detectives his movements after the phone conversation between he and Betsy at 5 o'clock: He hung up the phone and began his trip to Mike's house for Game Night. "I stopped for gas [at Conoco in Troy] before I got on the highway and filled up the truck, and I got on the highway, and I knew I had to get cigarettes...I was out of cigarettes and the dog was out of food. I called my mom on the way [at 5:22 p.m.] and said 'I have some errands to run before I go over to my friend Mike's house, so I'm not going to be over for dinner tonight,' so she wouldn't expect me." Russ also grabbed a couple of bottles of Snapple iced teas while buying the other items.

Everyone was familiar with Russ's Game Night with his friends. They gathered for a role-playing game called *Rolemaster* every Tuesday night. He arrived at Mike's house around 6:00 p.m. Mike's girlfriend was there and a couple of other players. One of the usual players couldn't make it that night, so they decided to watch a movie instead.

Russ: "We watched some movies. We watched the new *Conan* and then we started watching this new movie called *The Road*, but it was boring."

Russ's friends would later testify that Russ fell asleep during that movie. They also admitted they had smoked some pot. Russ left Mike's house about 9:00 p.m. and headed the almost 25 miles home. He was hungry...pot will do that, plus he had missed dinner with his mother, so he pulled into an Arby's drive-thru restaurant at 9:09 p.m., not far from Mike's house, and bought two Junior Cheddar Melt sandwiches.

Detectives: "So, you pulled into Arby's a little around 9 o'clock and got your sandwiches, and then what did you do?"

Russ: "I went home."

Detective: "What time did you get home?"

Russ: "I'd say probably around 9:45." [It was about a 27-minute drive from Mike Corbin's house to Russ' home.] Russ also stated he had gotten a strange call from an unknown person around 8-8:30 p.m. on his cell phone. They did not leave a message. Was someone trying to ascertain where he was at the time or if he was home yet?

Russ had placed the 911 call at 9:40:10. His timeline was standing up, even if his guestimate of his arrival time was a few minutes off. The detectives seemed calm; simply gathering information. Russ assumed it was all part of their need to get a feel for the whereabouts of people close to Betsy. He had described what he remembered Betsy wearing the last time he saw her. He described what he had on that day as he worked on computers in their basement on Sumac Drive. He had not changed his clothes after arriving home and finding Betsy. No big deal.

But things were about to change.

Detective: "Does anyone other than you know that Betsy is gone? Did you call anybody else?"

Russ: "I called the police first…I called 911."

Detective: "And if it comes back that it's not suicide, you don't know of anybody that would want to harm Betsy?"

Russ: "No. Everybody loved Betsy. She was a positive soul. She always brought smiles to people. (Sniff) She made me smile all the time. She made me so proud. I was happy to have her in my life."

Detective: "The hang-up, and you probably know this as well as I do, it's not typical for someone that's going to commit suicide to do it by the way that she done [sic] it. That's what concerns us."

While the Detective's voice maintained its calm, low-key tone, his message and insinuation had changed. Russ, confident in his alibi, and feeling he was just there to provide information, felt the air change in that tiny, sparse interrogation room. Something was different.

What Russ didn't know was, as the sun rose on December 28, 2011, as he sat in that windowless room not knowing if it was day or night, the police were fanning out to interview other people close to Betsy. Death notifications were being made as well. After Russ alerted the detectives hours earlier that a woman by the name of Pam Hupp had driven his wife home the night she was murdered, they made a beeline to the Hupp residence, arriving shortly after 6:30 a.m.; just about the time another set of officers was giving the bad news to Betsy's family.

An Interview with Pam Hupp

When Detectives Stephanie Kaiser and Perry Smith rang the doorbell of Pam Hupp's home in O'Fallon, Missouri at 6:42 AM, December 28, 2011, they were met at the door by a woman standing about 5'6" in height, in her 50's, overweight, with a broad nose and a perpetual grin that spread across her lower face. She identified herself as Pam Hupp and said she had just gotten out of the shower. Her short blond hair was still wet as she invited the two detectives into her dining room where they pulled up chairs.

Upon hearing that her friend Betsy was dead, Pam's breezy countenance melted and she appeared shocked to hear the news. With a quivering voice and muffled sniffles, she spelled her name for the detectives—H-U-P-P. First name, Pam...Pamela. The detective's small voice recorder whirled.

Detective Kaiser asked Pam, "What you told us a few minutes ago, you've known Elizabeth [Betsy] ten years as friends?"
Pam: "Probably ten years, almost eleven, yeah. (Deep sigh) She did my daughter's wedding, she's a DJ, and we saw each other almost every day."

Pam filled them in on the more mundane details of her life. She was 53-years-old. She was married to Mark Hupp, her second husband. Her daughter Sarah was a teacher in the Pattonville School District, and her son, Travis, lived just down the street. She was also quick to point out that she had undergone back surgery several years ago, resulting in a loss of feeling in her right side and the need of a cane to walk.

Pam spoke of Betsy's breast cancer and how it had spread to her liver. The day Betsy died Pam had visited her at the Siteman Cancer Center in St. Peters where Betsy underwent her chemo treatment. Pam had first stopped at Betsy's mother's apartment around 1:30 p.m. to pick Betsy up for the 2:00 p.m. chemo appointment. Janet told Pam, "They've gone already." Unbeknownst to Pam, the chemo appointment had been moved up. Bobbi Wann, a dear friend of Betsy's mother, was visiting from another state and had taken Betsy to the treatment.

Bobbi was Betsy's babysitter in her youth and the two wanted some one-on-one time. Betsy messaged Pam via text to tell her not to come. Her friend Bobbi was taking her to the chemo appointment and they wanted some alone time. Pam said she never received the text. But, when Greg Chatten, the cyber forensic expert working on the case, went through Pam's and Betsy's cell phone records, it showed that not only did Pam receive the message asking her *not* to come, but that Pam even replied via text, "Bummer."

Pam didn't mention that part to the detectives, nor did she relate the circumstances of that afternoon, other than to say she texted Betsy at 1:19 p.m. Despite being told to stay away for Betsy's chemo treatment that day, Pam drove to Janet's house to intercept Betsy

49

and take her at 1:30 p.m., but Betsy and Bobbi had already gone. No matter. Pam drove to the cancer center anyway and sat with Bobbi and Betsy throughout the treatment until Betsy finally took Bobbi to dinner. Pam had to finally leave them alone and go home to have dinner with her husband. She was back at Janet's house to take Betsy home at 5:30 p.m..

This was the first time Pam had not been the one taking Betsy to her chemo treatment for some time. Though asked not to come, Pam showed up anyway. Bobbi Wann said Betsy seemed 'surprised' to see her there. According to Russ and family members and friends, Pam had suddenly popped back into Betsy's life the year before after being out of touch for ten years. With an almost fierce territorial claim, Pam was there to offer rides for her friend's cancer treatments, to go on walks with her, and to basically become Betsy's biggest supporter. It seemed wherever Betsy was, Pam was nearby.

Pam told the detectives as her hair dried, that she left the Siteman Cancer Center after Betsy's treatment the day before and headed home to have dinner with her husband, Mark Hupp. Betsy took Bobbi to dinner at the Lion's Choice restaurant in Lake Saint Louis, and then they headed back to Janet Meyer's apartment in the same town to await Pam's arrival. Pam had insisted on giving Betsy a ride back to her home in Troy. It was clearly out of Pam's way—a good thirty minutes one way, and Russ was only five minutes away at Game Night by the time the two headed home. In the meantime, while waiting for Pam, Betsy, her mother Janet, and Bobbi played their favorite word game, *UPWARDS*. Betsy told Russ in their text messages that Pam had asked to give her a ride home. Pam told detectives Betsy had asked *her* to give her a ride.

As the two detectives interviewed a grieving Pam Hupp, she continued her recounting of the previous day. "She said to pick her up between five and six and she would be ready to go." Pam's voice continued to gain a little control over her earlier emotions as she continued. "She said she didn't have any more clothes. She had been there I guess all weekend, or something at her mom's house."

Detective Smith asked, "How come she was staying the weekend at her mom's house?"

Pam: "A lot of it, she didn't like the drive, and a lot of it, she didn't like going home." Little did the detectives know, this statement would be the first brick in the wall of evidence against Russ Faria that Pam was building.

Detective Smith: "Why didn't she like going home?"

Pam: "A lot of it, was her husband. They had been separated, gosh, six or seven times in the years that I've known her. He's not the most...he's kinda not nice verbally to her, so he makes us uncomfortable sometimes."

Detective Smith: "Have you heard him not be nice to her sometimes?"

Pam: "Oh yeah! He makes comments about how much money he'll have after she's gone cuz she's got...this is what she said, I don't know for sure, because I've never seen their financials...but he's got life insurance on her at work, she's got life insurance..."

Pam went on to embellish her story about the Faria marriage; the pace of her dialogue picking up momentum as she dug a deeper hole for Russ. She told them about the "good news" Betsy was going to tell Russ when he got home from Game Night. According to Bobbi Wann, the friend who had taken Betsy to chemo the day of her death, Betsy wanted to move into her mother Janet Meyer's old house that was due to be foreclosed on in February, 2012. Betsy's plan was that she, Russ, and their two daughters, Mariah and Leah, could live in the bottom half of the home, and her mother Janet and Bobbi Wann could live upstairs. Currently, Janet's daughter Mary and her family were living in the house. The payments were behind. Janet was renting the apartment in Lake St. Louis where she was living at the time of Betsy's death.

According to the police interview of Bobbi Wann, she said Betsy was sick of Troy. She wanted to live in Lake St. Louis where she was closer to her friends, her chemo treatment, and her tennis club. Troy was a very rural area, "out in the middle of nowhere," according to one source. Bobbi stated that she and Betsy and Pam had discussed putting the idea to Russ that night when he got home from Game Night. Betsy and Pam were going to write down what they were going to say to him. Betsy was nervous he would be angry about the idea, because they had only lived in the Troy home for two years and he didn't want to move again. It was their first real home after living in a trailer park and ten years of marriage. Russ' plan was to live in the house in Troy for another twenty years, and then move to Florida. But Betsy didn't want to live in Florida. Bobbi said, "Whether Russ agreed or not, she was out of there. She just couldn't take it anymore." Betsy's plan was to tell Russ they could even rent out the house in Troy and make extra money.

Bobbi also told police that Betsy wasn't feeling well that night at *UPWORDS*. "It seemed she was coming down with a cold," she said.

Pam went on to tell the detectives at her dining room table about the "good news" Betsy was going to tell Russ and how nervous she was about Russ' reaction. "She said, 'Alright, we'll tell him, but I'm telling you right now, that he's going to get very angry.'"

Detective Smith: "So, she already approached him with the idea?"

Pam: "She was going to approach him when he came home."

The detectives recorded the interview and scribbled notes. Pam was just warming up.

Pam: "The last weekend she was with him, he started playing this game of putting a pillow over her face, to see what it would feel like, I don't know if she said 'This is what it's going to feel like when you die,' or whatever, and then act like he was kidding. She was very upset."

Detective Smith: "She said he was actually putting a pillow over her face?"

Pam: "Yeah."

Detective Smith: "Did she sound scared?"

Pam: "Oh yeah! *Very* scared!"

Pam lamented that she felt guilty for leaving Betsy there knowing Russ was going to be angry about the news Betsy was going to tell him.

Pam continued on, brick after brick, adding to the wall that would become a prison for Russ Faria.

Pam related that Betsy and Linda Hartman, a cousin from England, had gone to Branson, Missouri, the weekend prior to Betsy's death. According to Pam, they were going to plan out how they were both going to leave their husbands and live in Branson. Pam said she was supposed to join them that weekend but her husband said, 'No." She said Linda was currently living in the South County area of Missouri.

The detectives asked about the previous night and a timeline for Pam picking Betsy up to take her home from her mother's house in Lake St. Louis.

With admirable precision, Pam Hupp relayed the concise events of the prior evening. She had arrived at Janet Meyer's apartment about 5:15-5:30 p.m. Pam said she was driving a gray 4-door 2004 Honda Accord. She waited while Betsy, her mother, and Bobbi finished playing a game of *UPWARDS*. They left Janet's home around 6:30 p.m. and drove roughly thirty minutes to 130 Sumac Drive in Troy. Upon arriving at Betsy's home, Pam said there was a silver Nissan parked in the driveway. According to Pam, Betsy said the Nissan was the car Russ was supposed to be driving that night.

Pam next described the dark house. According to her, there was no light on and the front door was unlocked. She said Betsy remarked that "Russ thought I was going to be home earlier." [As it was winter, the remark was presumably to account for no lights being left on for her and Russ leaving the door unlocked as he departed for Game Night at 5:00 p.m. Russ said he did leave the foyer light and front porch lights on for Betsy.]

Pam said Betsy turned on the "front light and living room light." Yet, in the next sentence, Pam said she followed Betsy into the house and *she* turned on the living room light, and the kitchen light. Pam next called her husband Mark at 7:04 p.m. to let him know she had arrived at Betsy's home alright—"I don't like to drive at night"—and while she had him on the phone, suddenly handed it to Betsy who blurted out "Merry Christmas and Happy New Year!" in her usual bubbly voice. Pam then told him she was heading home.

But Pam did not leave immediately. In fact, her story would change multiple times concerning her movements that night. When first asked if she went into the Faria's home upon delivering Betsy that night, she replied, "Ummm…No." She then changed her story later in the interview to say, "I did go in to turn on a couple of lights." It evolved again to her following Betsy into her bedroom to show Pam the jewelry armoire Russ had given her as a Christmas present. Oddly, Pam found it necessary to say that the armoire was scratched and broken and "looked used."

Finally, she admitted to staying 15-20 minutes because Betsy didn't want to be alone and Russ would be home soon. She also said Betsy asked her to stay and watch a movie with her, but Pam said she was tired and needed to get home. Pam also said she suggested to Betsy that she go to bed, but Betsy wanted to lie on the sofa and watch TV. She said that when she left Betsy, she was wrapped up in a blanket, lying on the sofa, watching TV.

Pam relayed that the first thing Betsy did upon entering the house that night was to turn on a couple of lights and let the dog, Sicily, out the back sliding glass door. Pam told detectives that the dog was vicious and would attack the front door when people arrived at the house. She said the dog "would jump on you" and she was afraid of the chow mix.

Jewelry armoire Russ gave Betsy for Christmas only two days before the murder. It was chipped on top and one of legs was broken off and lying on the floor of their bedroom. Photo courtesy of PA Mike Wood.

Pam said she left Betsy lying on the couch and headed home. She said she called Betsy at 7:27 p.m. to let her know she was home, because Betsy knew Pam didn't like driving at night and often got lost in Troy. Betsy did not answer the call. Pam said she texted her son, who lived just down the street in a condo when she arrived home, then texted Betsy. No response. She next called Betsy's mother, Janet Meyer, at 8:52 p.m. to say she was worried Betsy wasn't returning her phone call because Betsy may have been mad at her for not staying to watch a movie. Pam calls Betsy again at 9:07 p.m. and receives no answer. That was about the time Russ was ordering his two Arby's Junior Cheddar Melts, twenty-some minutes from home.

Author's Note: It would later be found through cell phone data that Pam's timeline of her text messages to her son Travis came *after* her last call to Betsy…exactly two minutes after, at 9:09 p.m. Pam said she texted her son when she arrived home, then texted Betsy and then called Janet. Pam's order of calls and texts don't line up. Pam's call log that night is as follows:

Pam's Outgoing Cell Phone Records 12/27/2011:		
Mark Hupp:	0824 AM	8:24 AM
Betsy Faria:	1319 PM	1:19 PM
Mark Hupp:	1904 PM	7:04 PM
Betsy Faria:	1927 PM	7:27 PM
Janet Meyer:	2052 PM	8:52 PM
Betsy Faria:	2107 PM	9:07 PM
Travis Hupp:	2109 PM	9:09 PM
Travis *to* Pam:	2109 PM	9:09 PM
Travis Hupp:	2110 PM	9:10 PM

Pam described to the two detectives how she got home after dropping Betsy off. She said she watched some TV with her husband Mark and took a shower. Possibly to head off the next question of why she took a shower last night and another this morning, Pam offered, "I don't like messing around with somebody who's been sweaty all day." That didn't answer the question of why *she* needed two showers.

Bobbi Wann made an interesting statement to the detectives that interviewed her the morning after Betsy's death. She said that

Betsy's mother had mentioned the previous night as Pam called her, that she found it odd that Pam would call Betsy after she left her when she knew Betsy was tired and might even be sleeping. Why did Pam keep bothering her?

Next, as detectives worked to keep up during that first interview with Pam, the morning after Betsy's murder, Pam related something that happened the previous week as Pam accompanied Betsy to the West James Tennis Club in Lake St. Louis. It was a tennis club offering six indoor courts and restroom facilities. According to Pam, she watched her good friend play tennis. Afterwards, Pam said Betsy told her that she had sent Pam an email that she was anxious for Pam to read. Pam made the email letter sound ominous. She said Betsy told her that the email included something Russ was saying to her that was disturbing. Pam brought it up twice during the detective's interview at her home, sniffing as she did so, voice filled with emotion. Apparently, Pam had never received it. She said Betsy had tried to print it out for Pam, but that Pam's old printer wouldn't hook- up to Betsy's laptop. Betsy said she would email it to her. "I really hope you find that letter," Pam pleaded with them brokenly. She corrected her statement to say "document," not an email.

And now, the bombshell. Pam told the detectives that Betsy was afraid Russ would soon learn that she had changed her life insurance policy, making Pam the beneficiary of $150,000 that had been in Russ' favor. The second $100,000 policy would go to Betsy's cousin Linda Hartman. Pam said all this was in the email Betsy was going to send her, plus the information that Russ had started putting a pillow over her face the weekend before.

In one police interview, that lasted from 6:42-9:06 a.m., Pam had loaded the deck against Russ. The detectives heard about the Silver Nissan sitting in the driveway that supposedly Russ was driving that night, and a dark house with an unlocked door. They heard about the "good news" Betsy was fearing would set Russ off upon hearing it when he came home that night from Game Night. Afterall, Betsy's mother's house was scheduled to be foreclosed on in just a couple of months. They would have to move fast.

They were told Russ had begun playing an insidious game of putting a pillow over his wife's face and telling her 'This is what it's going to feel like when you die.' And now the explosive news that Russ had been taken off Betsy's life insurance policies—the very

56

policies from which Pam said Russ was anxious to benefit in the first few minutes of her interview with detectives. Their heads must have been swimming. How could there be any more damning evidence than this? Russ' wife was afraid of him, and he was about to get a double dose of "bad news" the night she died.

The two detectives rose and turned off the recording device. But if they thought Pam Hupp had run out of bricks, they were sadly mistaken. She suddenly remembered something else. They took their seats again at the dining room table and started the recorder.

"In the last couple of weeks," Pam said, almost eagerly, the week before Christmas, she went on, she and Betsy were at the gym. Betsy supposedly reached for a Gatorade bottle in her gym bag and took a sip. She made a face and spit it out, saying it didn't taste right. Was Pam implying poison? By Russ' hand? A Gatorade bottle with missing liquid was found by crime scene techs in the Faria refrigerator. It was not listed on the evidence log and may have seemed inconsequential. Yet, Pam seemed to include a kernel of truth in all of her fabrications. Had she left the bottle there with perhaps something added to it in hopes the investigators would find it? It wouldn't be any different than the other staging, such as Russ's bloodied slippers and light switch. Pam also related how Russ degraded Betsy, even showing his disdain for the times Betsy wet the bed due to chemo issues. According to Pam, Russ said the bed smelled. Pam said he was a heavy drinker. It went on-and-on.

Gatorade bottle with liquid missing in the Faria refrigerator.
Crime scene photo courtesy of PA Mike Wood.

Pam also did a run-down of the Faria vehicles that were usually at their home. She said there was a PT Cruiser, a Silver Nissan Maxima, a Ford Explorer, and a motorcycle. The only car she saw the night she took Betsy home was the Silver Nissan in the driveway, she told them. She and Betsy did not look in the garage while they were there.

Pam mentions again that Betsy thought Russ was driving the Nissan that night. She seemed fixated on the Nissan and relaying that information to the detectives. She also repeated that Betsy said Russ expected her home earlier and that's why the door was unlocked.

If Pam had made it a point to repeat the missing email from Betsy to the detectives, and to mention the Silver Nissan three times during the interview, she also zoomed in on the fact that Betsy did not have her purse with her "all weekend." "She didn't have her purse, and didn't bring it with her," Pam said ominously. "She said she didn't have her purse all weekend." The truth was that Betsy spent Christmas weekend with Russ. She had only spent Monday night with her mother to be closer to her chemo appointment on Tuesday. Betsy had admitted she left her car and house keys at home, and Russ stated he had left the door open for her. It was Tuesday night that Pam picked her up and brought her home. And Pam Hupp was the last known person to see Betsy alive.

Pam told police that Betsy had gone out to the Nissan to retrieve her chemo bag "because she did not have her car all weekend." Oddly, Pam casually mentioned that Russ had always been nice to her [Pam]. That statement concerning Russ would change later.

As Pam spilled out the ominous details of the Faria's marriage, the information was being relayed back to the Lincoln County Sheriff's Office to that small interrogation room where Russ still sat huddled in disbelief. How could he have gone from watching movies with his friends to coming home and finding his beloved Betsy lying on the family room floor with a knife protruding from her neck? He had only spoken to her hours before. But if he thought the reality he was living at this moment was surreal and frightening, it was about to turn into an unrelenting nightmare.

Chapter Four
The Interrogation

The interviews and reports continued to pour in on that busy Tuesday morning following the murder of Betsy Faria. Bits and pieces of testimony filled ledgers as detectives knocked on various doors. As Betsy's body was undergoing an autopsy, Russ was still being questioned in that small, claustrophobic room at the Lincoln County Sheriff's Office. DNA swabs were taken from Russ's mouth, feet, and hands once his Miranda Rights were read to him. His left and right palm prints were taken. Similar prints had been found on the sliding glass door at his home by crime scene investigators. He went through it all in a fog of pain and disbelief.

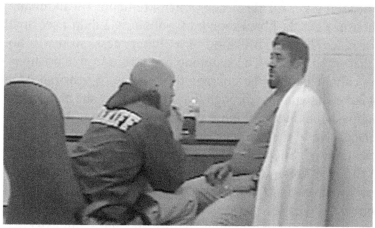

Russ Faria during the police interrogation looking dazed. Photo from video camera at the Lincoln County Sheriff's Office, 12/27/2011.

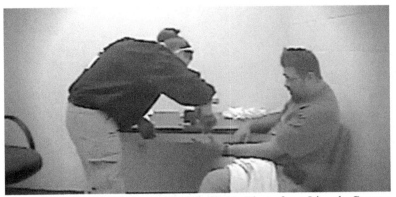

Russ Faria having his hands swabbed for DNA. Photo from Lincoln County
Sheriff's Office video camera, 12/27/2011.

Russ' voice was low and husky from stress and the hours of
answering questions. He had one of those faces that could come off
as gentle and kind one second, but as rough as his Harley the next.
Today, he simply looked broken.

There were others dealing with unspeakable pain as they
acquiesced to police requests. Betsy's daughter, Mariah Day, from
Betsy's first marriage to Tremis Day, was asked by detectives to go
through the house where her mother died.

"I did the walkthrough through the house with the police to see if
anything was out of place or missing," Mariah told this author in a
phone conversation. "It was the 28th, the same day we were told she
was dead. It gives me flashbacks when I remember walking through
the house. I get flashbacks randomly about it. I didn't see anything
out of place. My Mom is kind of a clutter mess, so it was normal
that there was clutter. The shopping bags were from Christmas."

One cannot fathom the courage this young 17-year-old daughter
must have shown to go through that home where she and her sister's
Christmas stockings still hung with their names on them above the
fireplace. Now the carpet padding was blood-stained and the
loveseat gutted. She had just seen her mother the night before.

On the ride home the night Betsy was murdered, Betsy made a
phone call from Pam Hupp's car to her friend Laurel Moran with
whom she played tennis every Wednesday. Betsy placed the call at
6:58 p.m., roughly two minutes before she and Pam arrived at the
Faria home. She told Laurel she could not play the next day as her

white blood cell count was low. Pam would have overheard the call. For Betsy to miss a chance at tennis meant one thing—she was pretty weak.

A search warrant and seizure of home and vehicles was ordered for the house at 130 Sumac Drive. Everyone in the law enforcement agency seemed to have been involved in one form or another. From fire department personnel to crime scene forensic experts, they filed in and out of the house. One thing they all agreed upon: Betsy Faria had been dead for well over an hour when Russ placed that 911 call. Eventually, her time of death would be estimated at around 7:21 p.m., the exact time that Pam Hupp left the Faria residence in Troy to drive home to O'Fallon, Missouri. First responders stated that her body was "cold and stiff." Her tongue was protruding partially from her mouth. The preliminary report also had some shocking news. It appeared Betsy had been stabbed over 25 times. That number of wounds would double during the autopsy.

Russ' 1999 Ford Explorer would not be thoroughly searched until December 30, 2011. The evidence taken were receipts and paper napkins, an unknown computer tower in the back seat, and the seat cover and floor mat from the driver's side. The receipts were listed coming from Greene's Country Store, and Arby's. A black Palm brand electronic device was held for computer analysis, as well as CDRs. A box of Edgefield cigarettes was in the car, one pack missing; two bottles of Snapple—one opened. DNA swabs were taken of the exterior door handle and panel, window frame, door locks, window locks, arm rest, steering wheel, and gear shift.

Cigarettes, Snapple tea and Arby's in Russ' front seat.
Photo courtesy of PA Mike Wood.

The day after Betsy's death the Faria's home was searched and evidence gathered. Bags of evidence were collected, hairs gathered, fingerprints dusted, and every inch of space looked at for sinister implications. The list of items leaving the scene in brown paper bags with "evidence" seals was formidable:

- Betsy's cell phone: Purple Motorola with blood stains
- Silver One men's slippers with "blood-like stains"
- Black handled Master Chef knife
- Yellow baseball hat w/circle logo w/unknown stain
- Green cloth found in kitchen drawer w/unknown stains
- White switch plate w/bloodstains
- Cotton swab evidence from sink knob, sink drain, shower knob, and shower drain.
- Natural Wear Black bra with bloodstains
- Black T-Shirt w/bloodstains & "Defects in Material"
- Pair of black leather gloves
- Black handle knife w/8" blade
- Brown wood handled knife
- Black handle knife
- Black leather-like dog collar w/tags & chain
- Rx bottles
- Fabric from loveseat, cushions back & skirt, plus seat covers
- Grey Kohl's Dept. Store bag w/blood stains
- Decorative Snowman Gift Bag
- Harley Davidson coat
- Various bath towels
- Dark Brown Bath Rug
- Athletic Blue Pant w/white stripe [Russ']
-Trace evidence from back of victim, right side of body & floor, left side of body & floor
- Inked paw pads from dog
- Tin with pulled dog hairs
- IBM Thinkpad
- HP Laptop
- Black backpack with IBM Thinkpad
- Icon briefcase bag w/HP Laptop
- Computer Tower & Gateway Hot Pink Computer Tower
- HP Compaq Computer Tower
- Other digital devices & CD's, writeable disks

- Sony camera case & Fuji Film camera
- Master Chef Butcher Block w/6 knives, 1 scissors
- Northwest Territory Size 11 Men's slippers
- Cut carpet from the living room floor
- Metal tin containing trace evidence
- Items 82-88 on the evidence sheet had a black X through them

The following day, December 29, 2011, more items were collected:
- Comforter and original packaging
- Victim's pants and shirt from the Medical Examiner (ME)
- Hand covers (used to bag the victim's hands)
- Women's socks & foot covers
- 4) envelopes containing physical evidence from body
- Sexual Assault Kit
- ME Property Sheet
- DVD of crime scene

On January 3, 2012, 19 other items were seized:
- 9) Kitchen floor samples
- 7) Cabinet facings
- 1) Orange & White Mop Head—Laundry Room
- 1) Kitchen drain trap w/liquid substance
- Crime Scene photos

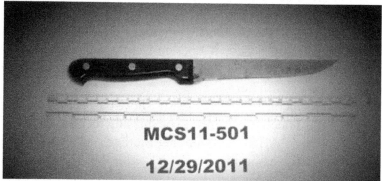

MCS11-501

12/29/2011

Knife used in Betsy Faria's murder.

As crime scene specialists swarmed Betsy's home on day two of their search, detectives were making a second call at Pam Hupp's home. This time, her husband Mark Hupp was there.

Mark Hupp was reserved. He was the polar opposite of his wife, Pam. He was able to only answer two questions before she took over the conversation. He said he did not answer the phone call Pam placed to him upon her arrival at the Faria home at 7:04 p.m. December 27, 2011, because he had left his cell phone in his truck. He missed hearing Betsy's cheerful greeting of "Merry Christmas and Happy New Year!"

The detectives asked Pam for her cell phone, and she handed over a pink ATT Pantech with a missing back panel. She was then asked what she was wearing when she drove Betsy home. She replied khaki-colored slacks and a red t-shirt, and gray-and-pink Nike tennis shoes, size 8.5, and a white coat. The coat is conveniently draped around the back of a dining room chair where they are all seated. She says it is brand new—a Christmas gift from her daughter. She is asked to gather the other articles she just mentioned. Pam retrieves the khaki slacks, neatly folded from her bedroom closet, and pulls the red t-shirt from a hamper. She hands over the Nike shoes, as well.

Pam allows the detectives to photograph her face, neck, hands, and feet. They take buccal swabs (inside the mouth). Wanting to appear helpful, she even offers them her bra and later alerts them as to her trash day, in case they want to look through it.

Pam mentions the Winghaven Library that she and Betsy visited four days before her death. She said Betsy took her to lunch, paying for it with a debit/credit card. She also brings up that she and Betsy usually have Christmas lunch together. According to Russ's timeline of Christmas day, it does not appear the friends shared lunch this year. Once again, Pam brings up that Betsy did not have her purse or keys with her.

If there were inconsistencies already showing up in Pam Hupp's interviews, the detectives seemed to be missing them. Pam told them the night she picked Betsy up from her mother's apartment, Betsy's daughter Mariah was on the couch sick with the flu. According to Pam, Mariah asked for a ride and Pam said she told the girl, "No…it's out of our way and you're sick and you shouldn't be around your mother when she's weak from chemo." Mariah had a different story. She said she never asked Pam for a ride. As stated earlier, Betsy asked Mariah if she would like to come home with her and watch a movie and Mariah declined, saying her boyfriend was coming to pick her up. So, which was it? There would be many, many conflicting versions of events if Pam was doing the telling.

It was stated that Betsy's cell phone continued to ring eerily during the crime scene investigation at the house. It lay face down on the blood-stained carpet. The comforter found half-way wrapped around Betsy's body had been taken with her to the Medical Examiner's. The knife was left in her neck as to not disturb the evidence. It had been photographed from every angle and close-ups taken. There was an odd fabric-like pattern in the blood stain on the black handle. 186 autopsy photos were taken.

The Medical Examiner's initial report was disappointing. Short and succinct, it read: "Due to the nature of her injuries, it would not be possible to determine a time of death or point to a single cause of death. The stomach contains a large amount of tan solid and liquid gastric material." It also mentioned a 'purple contusion on the neck.'

Typically, stomach contents can be helpful in determining a time of death. It was known that Betsy had dinner with Bobbi Wann in the late afternoon. Was her mother questioned as to whether Betsy ate anything at her home while playing *UPWORDS*? If the stomach contents had made it to her intestines, that would help in narrowing down time of death, yet the intestines were not mentioned in this report. Any idea of what the tan solid and liquid gastric material was? Was a toxicology report done to establish if any medications were found in her blood stream? Had anyone given her a sedative prior to her death? A later report stated ingredients listed in Benadryl were found in her bloodstream. A call to an oncologist confirmed that they do sometimes include the drug in the IV infusion during chemo treatments.

Reports showing many of the knife puncture wounds did prove one thing: many, many of them had been inflicted after Betsy's heart had already stopped pumping. There was no blood seeping from the wounds. The deep laceration to her wrist went to the bone, yet there was no blood coming from such a grievous cut. There was very little blood found on the couch. Most of it pooled on the carpet beneath and around Betsy's head. These findings, along with the interviews, 911 call transcript, crime scene reports, log-ins, etc., were in the Major Case Squad Investigation, which lasted approximately four days.

At the Lincoln County Sheriff's Office, Russ continually answered questions, his energy flagging as the hours wore on and on. They began hammering home the new evidence coming in from the crime scene investigators and Pam Hupp's helpful testimony. Blood had been found on a pair of men's slippers in the Faria's master bedroom closet. Russ looked surprised. He told them he didn't even go to the bedroom when he found Betsy lying on the family room floor. He had only gone to the kitchen and called 911. Besides, he never put those slippers in the closet when he wore them. That's not where they were kept.

Finally, the two detectives asked if Russ would take a polygraph test. He said, 'Sure.' They drove him to the Lake St. Louis station to have it conducted. In a small room, facing a man with a laptop that had it's back turned toward Russ, he answered the polygraph examiner's questions. Something seemed off about it.

When they brought Russ back to that same sparse room at Lincoln County, they told Russ how he'd done on the polygraph test.

Detective: "Alright. How do you think you did?"

Russ: "I had to pass."

Detective: "You had to pass? Okay. Remember when I was talking to you before the polygraph examination? And I said in order for you to pass this test, you're going to have to be one hundred percent honest with me."

Russ: "Yes."

Detective: "You were not honest. I do this for a living. You were not one hundred percent honest with me. I don't want to drag this thing out forever, ok? The fact of the matter is, you stabbed Betsy."

Russ: "No, I did not! I wasn't even there."

Detective: "You were there."

Russ: "No I was not. I found her like that when I came home."

The detectives bored into him with all the accusations they had been saving up. What about the news Betsy shared with him that she wanted to move into her mother's house?

Russ: "She never mentioned that to me."

Detective: "Well, that was the news she wanted to share with you when you got home."

Russ: "I never got a chance to hear it. The first time I heard about it was when you told me."

Detective: "How many times did we practice putting a pillow over her face and suffocating her and telling her this is what it will feel like to die?"

Russ: "I never did that."

Detective: "Why would her friend tell the police that you did that and that she was scared?"

Russ: "She had no reason to be scared of me. She's never been scared of me."

Detective: "The fact of the matter is, it's a sloppy crime scene. There's blood on your clothes, in your residence, in your bedroom."

Russ: "I didn't even go to my bedroom."

The inquisition went on for another forty minutes. Somehow, they would break this man down who had been without sleep for 36 hours. He sat in a chair turned sideways from the small table, his body slumped against its back, head against the wall. The white blanket was gone. He still wore the orange t-shirt with Rhode Island emblazoned on it, and his faded jeans. His eyes were bleary from lack of sleep and shock. What more incredible things could they possibly tell him? Not once did he yell, or break down. That is until they took their final shot.

Detective: "You got home. You got in a fight. You pulled a knife and you stabbed your wife multiple times and you killed her."

Russ: "No! I did not do this!" His voice was finally rising as he felt the net tighten around him.

Detective: "It's what everything points to. I'm telling you what happened."

Russ: "I didn't' do this!"

The barrage continued as they tried to wear him down. He continued to state "I did not do this! I know what I know, and I did not do it!"

Detective: "We know how she died. We know who did it. And the only thing that we have to figure out is the 'why'."

Russ: "I did not kill my wife."

Detective: "God is in this room, Russ…"

Russ: "And God knows I did not do this!"

Finally, it was time to play the trump card the detectives had been holding.

Detective: "She was stabbed over 25 times, Russ."

Russ: "Oh my God, NO!" He slumped over, his right elbow resting on the table as his hand cupped his forehead.

Detective: "25 times! And they're not done yet. They're still counting. A burglar doesn't do that, Russ. A stranger doesn't do that, Russ. Someone who loves that person does that. Somebody who goes into a blind rage does that."

By then the coroner had completed his examination of Betsy's body and found she had been stabbed 56 times. The knowledge that Betsy had so many wounds was the reason the detectives had doubted Russ' 911 call, saying he thought his wife had committed suicide. How could a man see so many wounds, some in her back, and think she had taken her own life? They had kept that knowledge to themselves as they put him through the long relentless interrogation, waiting for him to fall into a trap.

Russ finally grasped the danger he was in. With an authoritative voice that had been missing, he announced, "I want a lawyer. I want a lawyer right now. I want a lawyer!"

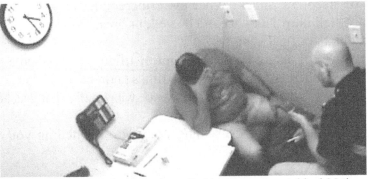

Russ' reaction when the detective tells him Betsy was stabbed 25 times.
Lincoln County Police video.

In the photo above, you can see the clock. It reads 4:28. With Russ demanding to speak to a lawyer, his long ordeal in the that small windowless room was over. He called his attorney Robert Beeny and was formally released at 4:30 p.m. from the Lincoln County Jail where he had been held under a 24-hour-hold. He had made three phone calls while there…all to his mother Luci. It was to her house that he was driven that afternoon, as his home was still a crime scene. The detectives had no choice but to let him go once he asked for a lawyer. They were not, however, finished with him.

Chapter Five
An Arrest

Brandon Sweeney, one of the Game Night friends, testified to detectives that Russ was driving his dark blue Ford Explorer the night Betsy died, not the Silver Nissan Pam was so eager to point to. In fact, the Nissan had belonged to Betsy's daughter, Leah. It had been taken back as a punishment for some things Leah was going through. It was not a car Russ drove. As the Game Night gathering broke up at the same time, several people took off for home, and Brandon said Russ left at 9:00 p.m., the same time he did. He saw his car lights as they drove off.

Game Night friends leaving the Court House after Russ' trial.
Left to right: Brandon Sweeney, Mike Corbin, Marshall Bach,
& Angelina Hulion.

During the investigator's research into the Faria's background, they looked at their past insurance history. There was a claim on 8/21/2008 that Betsy's car had been involved in an accident where it was claimed the car hit a deer. The insurance claim was deemed fraudulent, as the coverage had only been upgraded two days before the accident, changing it to full coverage. Insurance forms also showed that Betsy had been a smoker.

Further research showed Betsy had changed beneficiaries on her life insurance policy of $150,000 from Russ Faria to Pamela Hupp on 12/23/2011. The form was received at State Farm one day after Betsy was murdered. According to State Farm records, on January 25, 2012, "State Farm reached out to Detective McCarrick" who had taken over the case the same day the Major Case Squad disbanded on December 31, 2011. He was now in charge of Betsy's murder case. State Farm was told by the detective that Mr. Faria is currently "in custody" and Pam Hupp was not a suspect in the case. He said to go ahead and honor the payment. They did, and Pam received the $150,000 pay-out.

Winghaven Library in St. Charles County where Pam and Betsy had the insurance beneficiary form witnessed by a librarian.

As with many of Pam's statements to detectives, the insurance policy transactions were no different. Pam told the detective she was not sure if Betsy mailed the change of beneficiary form after she and

Pam signed it in front of librarian Lauren Manganelli (who acted as a witness to the signatures) at the Winghaven Library, four days before Betsy's death. Yet, on January 17, 2012, a little over two weeks after Betsy's death, Pam told State Farm she and Betsy had gone *straight* to the Post Office to mail the form after leaving the library as "Betsy wanted to be sure the form was postmarked on that day." It is interesting, looking back, that Pam wanted it postmarked that Friday, and Betsy died Tuesday, with a Christmas holiday in-between, when Post Offices are closed for the holiday. What was the urgency? It was brought out during motions in Russ's first trial that Betsy told Bobbi Wann and Pam Hupp at her chemo treatment that day that she had the other insurance policy laying out at home and was going to change the beneficiary on that to one of her sisters. Yet when police searched the Faria home after the murder, they found no insurance documents in the house.

With the life insurance money looking a bit problematic, Detective Kaiser asked Pam to take a polygraph test. She said, "Yes."

At first, Pam had agreed to undergo a polygraph, helpful as always. Then suddenly, she hired an attorney and some issues arose: It seems Pam sustained head injuries while at work in 2009. Apparently, she tripped and fell into a metal filing cabinet, whereafter she filed for Workman's Comp. When that news was relayed to the detective, she was asked to get some form of a note from her doctor detailing why she should, or could, not take the lie detector test. Pam scribbled off a note to her doctor asking for a disclaimer. The note Pam wrote was succinct and evasive:

"Dear Dr. Fischer, could you please write Detective Kaiser a letter stating that I was not able to do a polygraph due to medical reasons. Don't need any more detailed than that."

Interestingly, Dr. Ronald Fischer had recently seen Pam in his office at St. Luke's Medical Group, where he specialized in physical medicine and rehab, on January 3rd, after not seeing her for months. But, if nothing else, Pam could persuade a lion to go on a vegetarian diet, and so, Dr. Fischer dutifully constructed a brief statement.

"Pamela Hupp is unable to undergo a polygraph due to her medical condition."

That put an end to it. Pam Hupp did not take a polygraph. Her visit to Dr. Fischer was on the day of Betsy's funeral on January 3th, 2012. It would be a day to remember.

So, why weren't detectives looking harder at Pam Hupp? They had taken DNA samples while at her home the day after Betsy's murder, but never processed them. Nothing was looked at in her car; in fact, Rita Wolf, Betsy's friend, said Pam had that same car demolished years later. There is nothing to test now. Russ's daughters were constantly asking the detectives, "What about Pam? Why aren't you looking closer at her?"

Pam's daughter, Mariah Day, pointed out in a phone interview, "Mom often laid on the couch to watch TV. From what I know about that night, Pam and my mom were supposed to go back and watch a movie. I heard them discuss it at my grandmother's house that night. From what I understood, they were going to go to Mom's and hang out. Pam wasn't just going to drop her off. Mom didn't seem too excited that Pam was there to drive her home, and then Mom asked me if I wanted to go."

Back in the interrogation rooms, the insurance payout and skipped polygraph weren't the only flags waving concerning Pam Hupp over the following months. Pam changed her story about when she last saw Betsy the night she died. As she sat across from Detective McCarrick on June 25, 2012, he read from her interview notes taken the morning after Betsy's death. "You last saw Betsy lying on the sofa?"

Pam, gesturing with her hands, legs crossed, flip flops motionless, replied, "She may have been on the couch, but today it makes sense that she may have walked me to the door."

Pam would later change her story about the phone call she made to Betsy that night after she left. Originally saying she called Betsy to let her know she had gotten home safely; she amended that statement after cell phone towers put her still in Troy at 7:27 p.m. when she called Betsy. She could not have possibly driven the 30 minutes home since leaving Betsy at 7:21. On the stand during Russ' trial, Pam said that she meant she had pulled over at the highway interchange after getting off Highway H to say she was "home free," meaning, she was now in familiar territory and headed home. She would later beef up the story of pulling over about two miles from Betsy's house to make that call and stated she sat there about 15 minutes waiting to see if Betsy was mad at her for not staying and watching a movie with her. Detective McCarrick rarely seems chagrined with Pam's changing stories.

Pam Hupp being questioned by Detective McCarrick in
June of 2012, repeating her memories of the night Betsy died.

And what about the ominous statements that Betsy had left her purse home all weekend because Russ told her to? A weary Russ replied that he never told Betsy to leave her purse home. They were going out to some Christmas festivities with family and Betsy left it there. She didn't need her house keys because he was going to give her a ride home from her mother's Tuesday night after her chemo, but Pam took her home instead. Betsy's daughter, Mariah Day, said her mother was always forgetting her purse. She often carried her chemo bag or laptop bag instead. It was no big deal. But Pam kept hammering home the purse and house keys being left behind.

The house keys. Who was telling the truth, Russ or Pam? According to Rita Wolf, Betsy's best friend, Betsy had told her herself:

"The day of chemo on the day Betsy died," Rita told this author, "Betsy did not want Pam to come get her. Betsy did not want to talk to Pam that day. Betsy never told me why. She did not want Pam to come be with her or take her anywhere that day. We were just talking about what we had found on the Internet and what kind of vacation did we want to do? Maybe just go to Branson or even to Waikiki. She had some time shares in Waikiki, Hawaii, and we were talking about where do we want to go, and my kids were going to come along so we were nixing the whole Hawaii thing and it was possibly going to be a cruise.

"I talked to her on the phone around 5 o'clock, or 5:54, somewhere in there on the day she died. We were on the way to my nephew's birthday dinner at the Olive Garden and we were meeting my sister and her husband and three kids, my aunt, and her daughter and kids…a whole group of us. There was like twenty of us. I had called Betsy back because she had called me earlier in the day and it was right around 5 o'clock-ish. We talked and she was at her mom's and they were playing a game. All of a sudden, Betsy blurts out, 'Oh crap! I left my keys at home! I'm going to have to call Russ and make sure he leaves the door open for me.' Her house was left unlocked all night." When asked if she knew whether or not Pam overhead that phone conversation on Betsy's end, Rita did not know.

It's interesting that Betsy told her friend Rita that she didn't want to see or talk to Pam the day of the murder. Had she changed her mind about making Pam the beneficiary a few days earlier? Had Pam pressured her into it and she was having second thoughts? Was she planning to change the policy yet again?

The *St. Louis Post-Dispatch* ran the following obituary shortly after Betsy Faria's death:

Faria, Elizabeth Betsy Meyer 42, of Troy, MO. December 27, 2011. Loving wife of Russell Faria. Beloved daughter of Kenneth (Judy Geiger) Meyer and Janet Meyer. Loving mother of Leah Day and Mariah Day. Dear sister of Mary Rodgers, Julie (Les) Swaney, and Pamela (Scott) Welker. Daughter-in-law to Luci and Richard Faria. Sister-in-law to Joshua and Rachel Faria. Aunt of nine and great-aunt of one. Services: Services will be 10:30 am, Tuesday, January 3 at St. Patrick Catholic Church, Wentzville, MO and 7 pm Tuesday at Morning Star United Methodist Church, Dardenne Prairie, MO. Visitation will be Monday, January 2, from 1-8 pm at the Pitman Funeral Home, 1545 Wentzville Pkwy, Wentzville,

MO. Interment will be private. Memorials may be made to Susan G. Komen Foundation or Caring Bridge, in care of Pitman Funeral Home, P.O. Box 248, Wentzville, MO 63385. Share your condolences and memories at: www.pitmanfuneralhome.com

Preceding Betsy's funeral, Pam had spent time with Betsy's grieving mother, Janet Meyer, almost daily. It was reported that Pam even had matching necklaces made for herself and Janet—a delicate strand with a small diamond. To all appearances, Pam was as grieve-stricken as the rest of them. But then, the information about the insurance proceeds came out.

According to the family, the first time they knew that Pam had been made the beneficiary of Betsy's life insurance proceeds was when they went to State Farm to look into the money. They needed some of it for Betsy's funeral. "We were shocked to find out Pam got the money," they said. When they went to Pam to ask for enough for Betsy's funeral expenses, reportedly Pam told them that she would not give them any. She said since Russ killed her, it wasn't right that Betsy should pay for her own funeral. It was after that, that Pam stopped coming by Janet's apartment or seeing the family. They would soon learn that there was a lot more to come where the insurance proceeds were concerned.

State Farm Change of Beneficiary form with Pam Hupp's signature at bottom, along with her birthdate.

The funeral of Betsy Faria was a painful one. Russ was there, and after his grueling two-day interrogation, and newspaper headlines covering the case, he must have felt all eyes were upon him. Everyone was still trying to understand how this lively 42-year-old DJ, wife and mother, was dead from a maniacal attack with a knife. They had come to grips with her prognosis of terminal cancer, but this? It had to be a nightmare from which they would all awake.

Russ had barely hung up his suit from the funeral, when the next day, on January 4th, 2012, he was formally arrested for the murder of his wife, Elizabeth "Betsy" Faria. The charge was First-Degree Murder and Armed Criminal Action. Without preamble, he was jailed and his own personal nightmare begun.

Russ was booked and his file added to, beginning with some basic statistics: Russell Scott Faria: 5'10" tall, 200 pounds, with brown eyes and brown hair. 41-years-old. Build: Large.

With his dark hair combed at an angle, he looked straight-forward as he was photographed in an orange jumpsuit in front of the police height marker. Although he was logged in at 5'10" tall, the photo suggests he may have been a few inches shorter. With a neatly-trimmed beard and mustache, his gaze was neither sinister nor pained—simply a blank canvas that was hard to penetrate. Shock? Perhaps. Exhaustion. Certainly. He had just buried his wife the day before.

This would be more than his attorney Robert Beeny could take on. He now needed a criminal defense attorney. A good one. He found that and more in a compassionate and determined counselor—Joel Schwartz.

Russ Faria, booked into the Lincoln County Jail on January 4, 2012 for the murder of his wife, Betsy Faria.

Chapter Six
The Woman Behind the Curtain

Russ Faria was behind bars. Jails and prisons are known for their relentless noise of clanging doors, shouting, and the murmurings of restless cellmates that go on into the wee hours of the morning. What was going on in Russ' mind as he looked about himself at his new home? A small room with a bed, toilet, sink, and wafer-thin mattress and pillow. Doubtless, he was still in shock. It had happened so fast. It had only been eight days since his Betsy was murdered and his world had spun out of control. Surely, they would find they had made a mistake. How could he have failed the polygraph? Something nagged at him still about the lie detector test and the detective's words afterwards. What had he said? "You were not 100 percent honest. I do this for a living. You were not one hundred percent honest with me. I don't want to drag this thing out forever, ok? The fact of the matter is, you stabbed Betsy." Had the detective actually said, "You *failed* the polygraph?" No...he had skipped right to the accusation that he had murdered Betsy.

News of Russ' arrest shocked his family and friends. His Game Night buddies were incredulous. The man had sat eight feet from them the entire night; until he left at 9 p.m. How could he barely walk into his home, stab his wife 56 times, clean-up, and call 911 in under three minutes? The police wondered that to, and began tracing Russ' movements that night, according to his testimony. They timed leaving Mike Corbin's house, Russ' stop at Arby's and arriving at 130 Sumac Drive. Even though they drove faster than Russ did that night to give his timeline less girth, they had to admit, it could be done exactly as he said, so a new theory was posited. They claimed Russ ran errands and made sure he was on security video and had receipts. Then, he went home and murdered Betsy. One of the Game Night buddies must have helped Russ out. Brandon Sweeney must have kept Russ' cell phone to verify his locations, gone to Arby's himself, driven to Russ' home and slipped Russ the drive-through receipt, handing him back his phone. Is that why Russ used the house's landline to call 911 instead of his cell phone? Is that why he canceled dinner with his mom? Pam had testified Betsy said, that "Russ expected her home earlier."

If detectives were looking to find evidence against Russ, they found a gold mine in Pam Hupp. The woman showed up repeatedly to add to her story—all of it implicating Russ. So, who was this woman so eager to help the investigation into Betsy Faria's murder?

Pam Hupp (l) Riverview Gardens High School Senior photo. Pam (4th from left) in her cheerleading team photo the same year.
Photo's courtesy of Riverview Gardens HS and Patti Bathe.

Pamela Marie Neumann was born on October 10, 1958, to Shirley and Victor Joseph Neumann Jr. She grew up in Dellwood, Missouri, a St. Louis suburb. At Riverview Gardens High School Pam stood out for her athletic ability, joining gymnastics and cheerleading. Her high school photos are unmistakable. With her distinctive smile and broad nose, it's as if her face simply filled out over the years while maintaining its most-recognizable features.

Friends at the time described Pam as very outgoing with a personality that was hard to ignore. Talkative, confident, and outgoing, her picture appeared several times throughout the Riverview Gardens High School yearbook. Her figure was hard to ignore. She was slender yet curvy and held herself erect. As for her grades, it was stated she was obviously very intelligent, with a quick mind and impressive memory for detail. But her Achilles' heel was boys. Pam loved boys, and her grades suffered for it. Why do homework when there were more interesting things to pursue?

Pam Hupp (l) and (middle) 1977 Gymnastic Team at Riverview Gardens High School. Pam w/Prom Date, 1977, below. Photo's courtesy of Riverview Gardens High School and Patti Bathe.

It was during Pam's high school year that she met and dated a young man who also exceled at Riverview. He was on the golf and soccer teams, and made the National Honor Society. Pam's opposite, he was soft-spoken with an easy-going manner that won him friends. He became Pam's Senior Prom date, and it changed their lives.

Three months after that glitter-filled night, the pair "had to get married." Pam had been raised as a strict Catholic, and that may have played a part in the decision for the two to set up house. A beautiful baby girl, Sarah, bounced into the world six months later. Pam was now a mother at 18, a time when a young woman is usually exploring career paths, travel, parties, college, boys, and *freedom*. The small apartment and a crying baby provided none of those.

The marriage lasted six years. Not much is known about those growing years, and Pam's husband has wished to remain anonymous. Shortly after the divorce, Pam married Mark Hupp, a quiet, likeable guy who was also athletic. Mark played minor-league baseball for the Texas Rangers. He did not make the pick for the pros, so he settled on his love of building things and cabinetry. It was that love that saw him flipping houses during his marriage to Pam.

Pam was once again expecting, and this time, gave birth in 1969, to a healthy baby boy they named Travis. In 1982, Pam and Mark moved to Naples, Florida; an exotic location about as far removed from Missouri landscape as one can get. Naples is known for its wealth and beaches. It has been said there are more millionaires per square mile in Naples than anywhere else in the United States. Larry Bird of the Boston Celtics was only one of many celebrities who called Naples home. Known for its upscale restaurants, boating marinas, the smell of gardenia bushes, and high-rise condominiums with beachfront views, about the only thing that ever blighted this idyllic setting was the occasional "red tide" that caused dead fish to roll up onto the white beaches.

The Hupps lived at two residences while in Naples: 9787 Sussex Street and 3413 Timberwood Circle. Sussex was a well-groomed street with nice houses. A recent photo of the house shows an indoor swimming pool. The Timberwood address was a condominium complex with groupings of four condos per unit. It's surrounded by a parking lot rather than manicured lawns. The Hupps also owned two vacant lots that they sold; one for $25,000. They lived in Naples from 1982-2001.

A recent photo of Mark and Pam's Hupp house at 9787 Sussex Street in Naples, Florida. Photo courtesy of Zillow.

Indoor swimming pool at 9787 Sussex St. in Naples, Fl. Current photo of pool that may not have been there at the time of the Hupp's ownership. Courtesy of Zillow.

Pam and Mark sold the Sussex Street house on August 16, 2001, for $209,000. They sold the Timberwood Circle condominium two months later in October, and returned to Missouri in 2001, settling in O'Fallon. Pam went to work for State Farm Insurance as an agent. She held several jobs in life insurance and was reportedly fired from two agencies for "forging signatures." While at State Farm around 2003, she met a bubbly woman ten years her junior, named Betsy Faria. It seems that Pam's reputation for strange behavior begins here, although rumors of prior mysteries surrounding her would surface.

Mike Boschert was the manager at State Farm Insurance when Betsy Faria and Pam Hupp worked together. Mike is an articulate man with a strong work ethic and desire to help others. While at State Farm during 2002-2003, he had an opportunity to observe Pam and Betsy as co-workers. His insight into their personalities is a unique glimpse into the psyche of both women.

"Pam worked for me at State Farm Insurance," Mike began in a phone conversation with this author. "She was an awesome employee. At the time, I thought she was heaven-sent. She was my right arm. Betsy was there before Pam came along. They became friends. Betsy worked for me and then left. She then came back when Pam was there for a little bit and then I left. Pam left and went to work at other offices. They stayed friends afterwards.

"Betsy was a super girl. She was nothing but nice. She would do anything for you. She went to nice schools, had a luxurious life, but probably made some choices that weren't the best for her. She was living in a trailer; not that living in a trailer is a bad thing. She had some financial issues that weren't normal for someone with her background.

"Funny story about Betsy," Mike continued. "In 2002, it was my first time ever being a boss and Betsy was like one of my second hires, my first producer. She seemed like a nice girl. I hired Betsy and on day two she came into my office, closed the door and just started bawling. She just had some stress in her life and she just needed to let it out, which she did. She just was crying about Russ and the kids, and so on, and she just got it out and went on about her day like nothing had happened. I was sitting there like a deer in headlights, going 'Oh my God, what just happened?' [Mike was chuckling fondly over this memory of Betsy.] She worked through that and everything was fine. She was usually always gregarious, happy, and outgoing, so it surprised me when that happened. She was always positive and just a good lady.

"Pam never told me exactly what, but there was a big red flag with her while she was working for me. She always had something that she would say, and then when asked what she meant by it, say, "Oh, I can't talk to you about that." It was like she was hinting that she was a spy, or a CIA operative, and she would drop little things and then say, "I can't talk to you about that. I just can't explain that." It was very weird.

"I left State Farm in 2003," Mike continued. "Right after I left State Farm, the O'Fallon Police called and said, 'Hey, some of your former employees' cars were keyed; can you come out and help us figure out what happened?" I said, 'Absolutely, sure, be happy to.' When I got there, it was obvious he was trying to pin it on me...that I did it. 'No! I did not do that!' That was really weird. Pam was still working there; in fact, one of the other workers told me Pam left early the day the cars were keyed. To me, it pointed very much to Pam, I guess. I don't know for sure. The cars were all sitting in the State Farm parking lot. [It was later reported that cars in Pam's neighborhood were also keyed that same day.]

This author asked Mike if he could think of any reason Pam would key the cars, if it indeed was her? Was she mad at someone? Was she about to quit? Mike responded: "None of the above. The more I ruminated through my mind, and hearing stories from other people, I think Pam just liked being the center of attention. I was terminated from State Farm as an agent, which was hurtful, and I do think with 20/20 hindsight now, that there was probably a lot she was doing to probably hurt my reputation.

"Another weird story, in 2002," Mike said, "in the course of a day, we're all sitting there talking, and an employee mentions that she's selling her house and she got a free roof from insurance for hail damage. She got the insurance money, but she said she wasn't going to put the roof on. In the insurance business, that's not the right thing to be sharing, let alone doing. It was an awkward conversation. Two weeks later, I get a phone call from a guy who says he received a letter from me, and he says 'I bought this house from your employee and it looks like insurance fraud. You should probably talk to an attorney.' He went on to explain the roof had hail damage, and I said, 'Sir, I don't know what you're talking about.' He said, 'I got a letter on your letterhead, signed by you.' I said, 'No, I didn't send that. Can you send it to me?'

I still have the letter," Mike said. "I've always wanted to do some kind of forensics on it for fingerprints to see if it was sent by Pam, which would be my guess. Again. I don't know. The signature was my signature. I don't know if it was a copy and paste job, I don't know. I don't know if someone could copy my signature that well. It looked like a copy."

This author then asked Mike: "Did you get the sense with the car keying incident that Pam could have been setting you up, as in 'Here's the disgruntled employee leaving' kind of thing?'" Mike reiterated his story as an answer: "It was the day after I was terminated. I left the office. I'm at home and I get the call from the police officer saying 'Your employees' cars were keyed today, can you come in?' It adds to the drama. It feels very much like the Gumpenberger thing [a murder Pam was arrested for in 2016] where she thought in her mind, 'I'm going to get this guy and bury him.'

"I told people how hard I worked. I used to say I was always doing 57 in a 55-mile-an-hour speed limit. It was nothing I did. They had to have more stuff on me and they wouldn't share with me what it was. My guess is Pam was probably telling them things that weren't true. I just don't know. I trusted her. Every day we would sit and talk about the day, the week, how the agency was doing, what we needed to do, who was the weakling, what needed to happen. She was on the edge of knowing everything there. That can be dangerous.

"State Farm looked into Betsy making Pam her beneficiary on her life insurance policy pretty extensively. I have no idea why Betsy would do that," Mike related.

"One other story… when I was with State Farm in early 2003, Pam came to me and said she had like $75,000-$80,000 and needed to do something with it. At the time I was a certified representative and I could sell mutual funds, annuities, and different things, and we talked through what she could do with it for tax reasons. She ended up buying an annuity for about $75,000. She said she got the money from selling her part-ownership in a golf course in Florida, which is where she moved from. I've always questioned in my mind two things: 1) Did she really own a golf course down there or where did that money come from? Was there a life insurance policy down there and someone was killed, I don't know? 2) She was at the time in her early 40's. If you were given $75,000 income, you probably have some bills you want to pay, a car you would want to buy…you wouldn't just want to chuck that all away into an annuity that you couldn't touch until you're 59 ½. I just thought that was weird. If she cashed it out early, there were penalties involved. Annuities go tax free. You can say 'Give me $700 a week for the rest of my life.' You do assign a beneficiary to that should something happen to you. I have heard she may have been involved in some other State Farm agencies and some fraud issues.

"I saw Betsy a year before she died. She owned a company called Party Starters and she was the DJ at a wedding I went to. It was great to give her a hug and catch up.

"I met Mark Hupp maybe once or twice, not at length. Just enough to say, 'I enjoy working with your wife...nice to meet you.'

"Betsy was super special. It is just really sad to see what happened to her."

By 2010, Pam had stopped working and had filed for disability benefits for back, leg, and neck pain. She was turned down. She was no longer working at State Farm. She and Mark co-owned a house flipping business. Her work history also shows she worked from home running a business called The Sensory House in November 21, 2010, possibly after being turned down for disability. Pam is listed as the Registered Agent. It has a DUNS number but no website shows up for this. While in Naples, Florida, Pam ran a company called Medical Billing Review from the condo on Timberwood Circle. Again, a DUNS number is given the business. When one does a background check, a statement beneath the business name of Medical Billing Review says 'Fictious Name.' Pam Hupp is listed as the owner. Neither business could be found as registered entities other than with Duns and Bradstreet. You need a DUNS number because it is required for receiving your business credit report from Dun and Bradstreet and for applying for any grants or cooperatives from the federal government. It's free to obtain a DUNS number or you can pay $229 to expedite the process. Were the DUNS numbers set-up for the purpose of obtaining grant money or federal aid after disability fell through?

The question of Betsy Faria and her life insurance policy is one that lingers. Rita Wolf, Betsy's best friend shed some light on what Betsy was looking at as a way to leave something for her daughters after her death.

"At the time, I did not know she had put the life insurance into Pam's name," Rita told this author concerning Betsy. "Years before,

Betsy had come to me and asked if Brian and I would be the beneficiaries of her life insurance. The reason she came here was because I had just met with an attorney who came to my home, that my husband had met at the Chamber of Commerce. She offered to come to our home for free and educate me on the difference between a trust, a will, power of attorney, and a couple of other things. It was basically to educate me on the importance of setting up a trust for my kids and not just a will. Betsy and I were talking on the phone one day, and this was long before she died, three to six months or so, and she sounded frustrated, and I said 'What's wrong?' She said, 'Oh, it's nothin'. I just tried to figure out what to do with my life insurance, and I said 'What do you mean?' and we talked about it on the phone briefly. I said, 'Well, this attorney was just at my house, why don't you come over and I'll sit down with you and go over what she went through with me. Betsy came to my house and we sat down with a yellow legal pad that I had, and we wrote out all the things that Betsy would want to do with one of her life insurance policies. She had shared with me that she had two or three different ones and one of which she was going to make sure the girls got when she died.

"I told her, "Listen...you don't need Brian or I to be the beneficiary. What you need is to just set up a trust and you can put all of your money into the trust and designate pay-outs... like awarding your daughters different amounts at certain milestones in their life. You can have X amount of dollars set aside for a car for them, etc. We went through it, line-by-line. Betsy said, "How much do you think I should set aside for their wedding?" We just sat there at my dining room table and allocated certain money for certain things the girls would need, and she said she really didn't know you could do that. We were just jotting it all down to see what it would look like. We weren't filling out forms.

"A lot of people said, 'Well, she sold insurance, how could she not know that?' And I said, "Listen, I love my best friend. She's one of my best friends, but Betsy only paid attention long enough to pass the test, if that makes sense. She was that girl who flew by the seat of her pants. She always lived on the edge and enjoyed life. It did not surprise me in the least that she did not know that...how to set up a trust and what was involved in a trust. So, when she left my house that particular day, she said she was going to sit down with her sisters and she was more than likely going to have either Pam (Welker) or Julie (Swaney) be the executors, if you will, of her will or estate. I told her that when you set up a trust, you can certainly set up an executor, and that's what she was going to do.

"Well then, fast-forward, and shortly before she died, I couldn't tell you the date, it could have been 3 weeks or two months, we talked about the life insurance on three separate occasions, and the very last conversation I had with her about the life insurance was, I was asking her, 'Did you get it worked out?' and she said, 'Yeah, I'm pretty sure I'm going to have my sister be the person and I'll get it worked out,' and that was it. So, when she died, the Major Case Squad was actually at my house when this happened, and Mariah (Betsy's daughter) texted me and said, 'Pam got the life insurance.' And I texted her back and I said, 'Oh good. Your mom told me she was going to have one of her sisters do it.' She said, 'No, no! Not Pam, my aunt...Pam Hupp!' I texted, *What? That doesn't even make sense!*' Mariah texted, 'I know it! It pisses me off.' Mariah and I texted back and forth for a few minutes. Nobody knew that Betsy had changed her life insurance policy and put it into Pam's name until a day or two after Betsy's death."

Rita had a strange story of a different sort to relate about Pam Hupp during our phone conversation:

"The first time I ever met Pam in my life, Betsy brought her to my house," Rita told this author. "We're standing at my counter or sitting in the bar stools at this low counter, just sitting with our elbows on the counter, and talking and laughing. I don't know how we got on the subject, but Pam was telling us a story about a dog she had that got injured and how they created this little wheelchair-like thing so that the injured dog could get around. The back legs sit in the wheelchair, and the front legs now can run around. She tells this very elaborate story, and I think she told it because at the time I had two dogs and she was loving on my dogs, and then she decides to tell this elaborate story about this injured dog in the wheelchair.

"About a month to six weeks goes by. My mother's dog jumps off the couch and injures its back and can't walk. My mom is crying...she's in a panic, takes the dog to the emergency vet. The vet says the back is not broken but it's a really bad situation. I tell my mom, 'Don't put her to sleep yet or anything. Let me get ahold of Betsy and have her call her friend, Pam. Pam has one of these wheelchair things and she's no longer using it. This is a very elaborate story that Pam had told us about this dog wheelchair. Betsy connected me, and it was she, Pam and I on the phone, and Pam said, 'I have no idea what you're talking about.' I said, 'Pam, you were just at my house a month or so ago, and you told us this very long story about your dog in the wheelchair because it hurt its back, and that you still had this wheelchair thing at your house.' Pam said, 'You must be talking about somebody else.' Betsy says, 'No Pam, that was you.' We get off the phone with Pam, and Betsy calls me and says, 'I'm so sorry, I don't know what the problem is.' At this point in time, Betsy was starting to not want to hang around with her so much. My mom had to have this poor dog put down. Pam cannot tell the truth to save her life. I don't think we'll ever hear the truth from Pam," Rita said.

In 2010, Pam re-connected with Betsy Faria, whom she had been out of touch with for many years. Betsy was dealing with breast cancer. Betsy and Pam decided to help another family who were also dealing with cancer. The pair went door-to-door with flyers to ask for donations for the wife, a Mrs. Murphy, suffering with the illness. The odd part was, the family in question knew nothing about it. There was no evidence that Betsy knew the fundraiser was questionable. Her friends recalled that she said she was excited to be helping a struggling family, even though she herself was dying. One of those friends, Kathleen Meyer, said, "This was going to be a legacy for her to leave; something like this behind in her memory."

What happened to the money they raised? One rumor has it that they collected $10,000 for this woman who Pam said was a friend and needed financial help. It was not a legitimate fundraiser in the sense that there was a tax write-off or organized foundation. It was just two women knocking on doors with a flyer.

After Nora Murphy succumbed to cancer two years later, Chris Hayes with *Fox 2 News* reached out to her husband at a later date to ask about the fundraiser. Mr. Murphy had never heard of it. He was shocked when Chris handed him the flyer Pam had handed out. "This is our Christmas card photo," he said, brokenly, clearly hurt and astounded. The flyer had said that year would be Mrs. Murphy's last Christmas. She lived for two more Christmases before her death. Her husband said seeing that sentence pained him as well. Eerily, the story about Nora Murphy was similar to Betsy Faria's. Pam had regularly taken Nora out as she underwent chemo. But she never said anything about a fundraiser being undertaken for her, apparently oblivious to the fact it was going on. Nora's husband, James stated that he thought Pam was taking a big risk, as someone could have spoken to him or Nora about it, but no one did.

Pam's taking advantage of people dying was not her only means of getting what she wanted. There was also a rumor that she undercut her own daughter out of a house sale. When Sarah excitedly showed the listing ad for a house for which she putting in a bid, Pam underbid her and got the house.

Chapter Seven
A Knight on A White Horse

Two days after Russell Faria was arrested, the state of Missouri learned of the strange case now unfolding in Lincoln County. In bold headlines, *stltoday.com* proclaimed: *"Marital problems lead to stabbing death of Lincoln County woman."* The small case that had only garnered local attention in and around Troy was now being discussed over St. Louis breakfast tables and in area bars. It would soon make national news as strange events continued to happen.

Russ was in jail; probably for a long time. Criminal cases can take years to see a trial day. His cousin, Mary Anderson, hired Joel Schwartz to defend Russ. Little did she know, she had chosen a champion who would go to the mat for the hapless man behind bars. Joel Schwartz and his co-counsel, Nathan Swanson, went over Russ Faria's and Pam Hupp's alibis with a fine-tooth comb. Along the way, they found shocking evidence of another sort. Just what had been going on with this investigation?

Criminal Defense Attorney Joel Schwartz.

Joel Schwartz received a B.A. in 1984 and his J.D. in 1987 from the University of Texas in Austin. He was admitted to the Missouri Bar in 1989 and has been practicing in the area of Criminal Defense for 20 years. He is a member of the Missouri Bar, the Eastern and Western Districts of Missouri, the Central and Southern Districts of Illinois, the Southern District of Iowa, and Eastern and Western Districts of Michigan. Mr. Schwartz has represented individuals in Missouri, Illinois, Iowa, Nebraska, Michigan, Kansas, Arizona, Texas, Colorado, and California.

Joel has the youthful face of a man many years younger. With his tousled curly hair and chiseled jaw, he is known for his professional, polished demeanor and imposing dialogue. Seldom at a loss for the correct word, he enunciates clearly while using head gestures and pregnant pauses to underscore his meaning. His deep conviction that Russell Faria was innocent never wavered.

Nathan Swanson, Criminal Defense Attorney.

Nathan Swanson received his B.A. from the Colorado College in 2004, and his M.A. from King's College, London in 2006. He graduated from the University of Denver Sturm College of Law in 2009. While at DU, Nathan served as a student attorney with the Civil Rights Clinic, representing those incarcerated in the Supermax prison, located in Canon City, Colorado. He was admitted to the Colorado Bar in October, 2009, and to the Missouri Bar in April, 2010. His primary area of practice is criminal defense.

Nathan is a breath of fresh air when one watches him during televised interviews. Relaxed and candid, he foregoes the wooden countenance of many attorneys aware of the camera trained upon them, and instead, engages with the interviewer with humor and facial expressions that put you at ease. You sense a man who cares deeply about integrity and who openly portrays shock at the evil machinations of others.

This daring duo took on the Russ Faria murder case. Pouring over depositions, audio and video tapes, interviews, photographs, and police reports, they saw an investigation that simply did not make sense. "Hinky" doesn't come close to the feelings unfolding as each new piece of evidence was dissected. How in the world was this man behind bars and facing life in prison? It was time to compare the alibis of the two major suspects side-by-side. And if the Lincoln County Sheriff's Office had passed on calling Pam Hupp a suspect, these two attorneys had no trepidation in doing so.

Russ Faria's Timeline and Alibi Corroboration

Joel Schwartz and Nathan Swanson looked closely at Russ Faria's movements the night Betsy was murdered. They looked at the surveillance video of the stores Russ visited that night and his cell phone records and location history; all the evidence the police had looked at while deciding if they had enough to warrant an arrest. This is Russ's timeline on December 27, 2011:

5:00 PM: Russ finishes work in his basement.
5:15-5:45 PM: Calls Betsy to ask if she wants a ride home.
Gets gas at Conoco on the way out of town.
Stops for Snapple Iced Tea and Cigarettes at U-Gas in Wentzville. (Receipt)
Stops for dog food at Greene's Country Store. (Receipt)
5:45 PM: Calls his mother to tell her he won't be there for dinner.
6:00 PM: Arrives at Mike Corbin's house in O'Fallon for Game Night. Watches two movies.
9:00 PM: Leaves Mike's house and heads home.
9:09 PM: Stops at Arby's in Lake St. Louis. (Receipt)
9:37 PM: Arrives home.
9:40 PM: Calls 911.

Russ getting gas at Conoco on his way out of town. Police evidence photo.

Surveillance video from the two stores Russ stopped at that night.
Police evidence photos.

Arby's receipt found in Russ's SUV. Arby's, Lake St. Louis showing
pick-up at 9:09 PM.

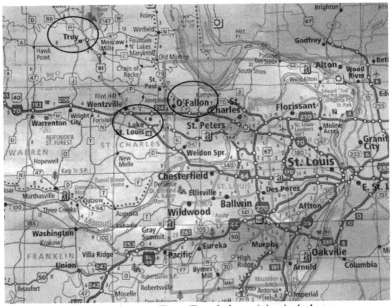

Map of St. Louis area. Troy (Russ's home) is circled at top,
Lake St. Louis (Betsy's mother's house) middle left, and O'Fallon (Game Night
& Pam's Hupp's house) is circled middle top. The city of St. Louis is shown
middle right.

Russ is shown in each surveillance video as wearing his Harley
Davidson jacket, a yellow hat with circular logo, and an orange t-
shirt with a Rhode Island logo. His hands are bare. The crime scene
at 130 Sumac Drive shows a pair of Harley Davidson men's black
gloves sitting atop the sofa where Betsy died. It does not appear Russ
was wearing them that night. He testified he came into the house,
dropped the bag of dog food on the floor, and took off his jacket. It

was then he saw Betsy lying there. The dog food and jacket were found where he said he put them. And the UNIDEN phone that he used to called 911 was lying on a couch arm near the door.

Russ was taken from the house after police arrived only moments after he placed that call. He was first asked to sit on the front porch, and finally in an unmarked squad car due to the cold temperatures. Video of him in the interrogation room only minutes later show him wearing the same clothes as seen in the gas station and store videos. There was no blood found on his clothes or body.

A still shot from the police video during Russ's interrogation on 12/27/2011. He is wearing the orange Rhode Island t-shirt seen in his alibi videos.

Pam Hupp's Timeline and Alibi Collaboration

Russ had stated he worked all day with computers from his basement at his IT job, wrapping up at 5:00 PM. We do not know Pam's whereabouts the day Betsy died until her cell phone records and witness reports place her whereabouts.

1:19 PM: Texts Betsy to say she will be by to pick her up for chemo. Betsy tells Pam not to come. Bobbi Wann is taking her. Pam texts back, "Bummer."

1:30 PM: Pam shows up at Janet Meyer's apartment where Betsy had spent the previous night to give Betsy a ride to chemo. Janet tells Pam, "They've already gone."

2:00 PM: Pam arrives at Siteman Cancer Center in St. Peters.

Late afternoon: Pam goes home to have dinner with husband in

O'Fallon. Betsy is with Bobbi Wann at Lion's Choice restaurant.

5:15-5:20: Pam arrives at Janet's to give Betsy a ride home to Troy. Waits an hour while Betsy, Janet, & Bobbi play game.

6:30 PM: Betsy and Pam leave Janet's house for Troy.

6:38 PM: Betsy calls her friend to cancel tennis the next day.

7:00 PM: Betsy and Pam arrive at 130 Sumac.

7:04 PM: Pam calls her husband Mark Hupp. Puts Betsy on phone.

7:27 PM: Pam calls Betsy's house and receives no answer. She is supposedly on the road, heading home. Cell phone tower data place her still within a few miles, or, at the very least, still at Betsy's house.

Pam arrives home. Says she texts her son (does not show up in phone data). Watches TV with Mark Hupp. Showers before bed.

8:52 PM: Pam calls Janet (Betsy's mom) to say she's worried Betsy isn't responding to her.

9:00 PM: Janet calls Betsy. No answer.

9:07 PM: Pam calls Betsy again. No answer.

9:09-9:10 PM: 3 texts between Pam and Travis Hupp.

When detectives interviewed Pam Hupp the following morning, oddly, they did not ask her what time she got home. Once Pam began answering questions, she steered the conversation. The tape-recorded session is filled with a run-on monologue, mainly against Russ. According to her husband Mark, whom they interviewed the next day, he did not answer the phone when Pam called him at 7:04 p.m. because he had left his cell phone in his truck. He was not asked what Pam was wearing when she got home that night, whether she went straight upstairs to shower, when they watched TV, or what they watched, etc. There is a distinct difference between Russ' alibis (complete with receipts, video verification, and witnesses) and Pam's, where we mostly know nothing of her movements before she stopped at Janet's at 1:30 p.m., and a time lapse of over an hour between leaving Betsy's home shortly before 7:27 p.m. and calling Janet Meyer at 8:52 PM.

Pam's only statement concerning her whereabouts before stopping at Janet's at 1:30 p.m. that day was that she "was running errands." Bobbi Wann, the friend who took Betsy to chemo that day, said, "They took her early [for chemo]. The appointment was for 2:00 but they took her at 1:30. Betsy was very *surprised* to see Pam Hupp walk in. She had asked her not to come. After chemo, Betsy took me out to eat at Lion's Choice. During chemo at the hospital, we had discussed that she and Pam would write down what they were going to say to Russ, and then talk to him when he got home from the card game. Whether Russ agreed or not, she was out of there," Bobbi said. "She couldn't take it anymore."

Bobbi was referring to Betsy "good news" about her idea to move into her mother's home in Lake St. Louis and rent out the Troy house she now occupied with Russ. There is never any mention of whether or not she and Pam wrote anything out to tell Russ, and Pam left before Russ got home. Pam would later say that she felt guilty for leaving her friend home alone with a man who was going to get angry about Betsy's idea.

Pam's actions upon arriving at Betsy's home at 7:00 p.m. that night varied throughout interviews. The final timeline is as follows:

7:00 PM: Arrive at 130 Sumac with Betsy in the car. Notices the Silver Nissan in the driveway. The house is dark. Door unlocked.

Betsy enters first and turns on foyer and living room light. Lets Sicily (the dog) out the back door. Does not mention if Betsy puts the dog on a chain. Dog was found chained and outside when police arrive. Betsy goes out to Nissan to retrieve her chemo bag. Pam states it was *she* who turned on the living room light and then the kitchen light. Follows Betsy to master bedroom where Betsy shows her a standing jewelry armoire that Russ gave her for Christmas. (Police evidence report states there was a black chemo bag with pink ribbons found in the master bedroom on the floor by a small pile of clothes.) They return to family room. Betsy lies on couch covered in a blanket and asks Pam to stay and watch a movie. Pam declines, stating she's tired and needs to get home to Mark.

Pam leaves, first stating that Betsy was on the couch watching TV when she left, but changes her story to that she now remembers Betsy walking her to the front door.

7:27 PM: Pam calls Betsy to say she is "home free." No answer.

There is a big discrepancy in the different interviews between Russ and Pam concerning the house on Sumac. Russ testified he left the foyer and porch lights on for Betsy, and the front door unlocked. It was December and on the night of the 27th, the sun set at 5:02 p.m. As that was the time Russ quit work that day and was getting ready to leave, it may have already been dark and he left lights on. Yet Pam stated the house was "dark." She told Janet Meyer when she called her, after not getting a response from Betsy after leaving her that night, that she [Pam] hadn't wanted to go into the house because it "was dark and the door was unlocked." Russ was certain he had left the foyer and porch lights on.

Interesting Evidence

One of the interesting findings in the police evidence reports was that "no latent prints were found on the light switch or knife handle." The light switch they were referring to was the one in the master bedroom with blood smears on it. The knife handle was the one found in Betsy's neck. How can there be no prints on either one? Had they been wiped down and then the blood added? Had Russ' slippers simply been dipped in the blood pooling on the carpet floor beneath and around Betsy's body?

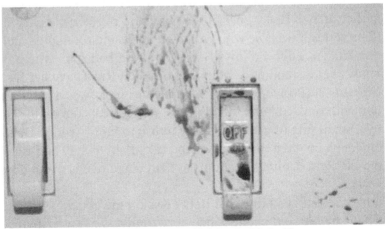

Master bedroom light switch with bloody fabric-like smear.
Police evidence photo.

The definition of a latent print is: an impression of the friction skin of the fingers or palms of the hands that has been transferred to another surface. The permanent and unique arrangement of the features of this skin allows for the identification of an individual to a latent print. It is also a print that is invisible to the naked eye.

Detail of fabric-like blood-stain on black knife handle in Betsy's neck. Police evidence photo.

MCS11-501

12/29/2011

#303/#306

Russ' bloody slippers found in master bedroom closet. Police evidence photo.

Russ's slippers as they were found atop other shoes
in the master bedroom closet. Police evidence photo.

Not finding latent prints on the light switch plate or the knife
wasn't the only odd thing; it was the smearing of the blood on the
two items. It had a distinct fabric pattern rather than a fingerprint
imprint. That small detail would surface later and show the
incredulously evil machinations at work that night.

Russ' Polygraph

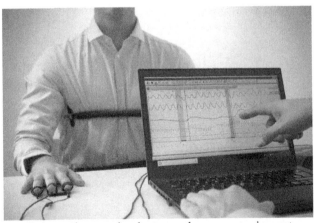

Polygraph test using laptop and sensory equipment.

Russ had been taken to the Lake St. Louis Police Department on
December 28, 2011, for a polygraph test, after he had gone through
10 hours of interrogation and been up for a total of 36 hours. He had
also smoked pot with his friends at Game Night. Russ would later

say that all he remembered was a man seated across from him with a laptop that was turned away from him. "I don't even know if it was turned on," Russ stated.

Joel Schwartz knew there was such a thing as a 'faux polygraph' test. While not illegal, it was part of the procedure to disclose that fact to counsel. Joel had not received word concerning the test. He asked the detectives for the results. He asked to see audio or video of the lie detector test and was told that the video camera had been inoperable that day. No paper graph, no evidence at all that a true test had been administered. Only a succinct report stating "there were significant, consistent physiological responses indicative of deception." There was also Russ' consent form in the file giving them permission to administer the test. That was it. No heart rate, perspiration markers, or other indicators noted during such a test were made available. When Russ requested a second test, and his Game Night buddies asked for one as well, they were declined by the Lincoln County Prosecutor, Leah Askey.

Pam's Polygraph

As mentioned earlier, Pam Hupp wiggled out of taking a polygraph test, claiming previous head injuries that would limit her cognitive responses. Joel Schwartz talked to the doctor who had provided Detective Frazier with a note excusing Pam from the test. Dr. Fischer, during a deposition with Joel Schwartz, before Russ' first trial, admitted that "She [Pam] said she didn't think she could do it [take the test]. Apparently, the police thought she couldn't do it," the doctor pointed out. This was after the doctor had written the short note to the detectives stating, "Pamela Hupp is unable to undergo a polygraph due to her medical condition."

Schwartz pressed, asking if there was any medical condition that would preclude Pam from taking a polygraph test? Dr. Fischer's answer was, "I would say there is not any condition that would prevent her from doing it."

"There is nothing about her condition that would actually keep her from telling the truth?" Schwartz asked.

"As far as I'm aware, there is nothing that would limit her," Dr. Fischer replied.

Joel Schwartz presented this information to Pam Hupp during her

March 20, 2013, deposition in preparation for the trial against Russell Faria. With her usual calm, she replied she knew nothing about a note from Dr. Fischer. When asked whether or not she had asked the doctor to write a note for her to back-up her story to detectives that she should not take the test, Pam replied, "I don't think I said anything."

"If you did," Schwartz pressed, "it certainly would have said, 'Write something saying I can't take a polygraph due to medical reasons?'"

"Absolutely not," Pam replied. She was unaware that Schwartz had a copy of her note, faxed to him from Dr. Fischer. He would bide his time for now.

During this same deposition, nine months before Russ' trial for first-degree murder, Joel Schwartz hit Pam with the questions no one had. He circled around to their previous conversation about her reason for declining the polygraph.

"What's your disability?" he asked, honing in on her refusal to take the lie detector test.

"I'm not sure what they classify it as," Pam said, unflappable as always. "I know I have drop foot and balance problems."

She recounted to the attorney how she had tripped and fallen into a metal filing cabinet in November, 2009. For that, she filed for Workman's Compensation. She said her case was still pending, but Schwartz could find nothing further on it. Pam's proffered attorney, Michael Goldberg, stonewalled when asked if he had been retained to represent Pam.

"You have a head injury?" Schwartz continued.

"Yes," Pam answered shortly.

"What is your head injury?"

"I have no idea."

"How do you know you have memory issues?" Joel asked.

"Well, because you're asking me questions and I don't remember."

That excuse would be pulled from Pam's bag of disclaimers in a later interrogation.

Chapter Eight
Lead-Up to a Trial

Joel Schwartz, Russ Faria's new criminal defense attorney, and his co-counsel, Nathan Swanson, continued to pour over paperwork, videos, and audio recordings from interviews. It just became stranger as they went. So many accounts and contradictions in Pam Hupp's stories! Yet, the prosecuting detectives never seemed to challenge her. In fact, they commiserated with her on certain topics.

During an interview with Detective McCarrick, shortly after Pam got the $150,000 insurance money as Betsy's beneficiary, Pam was looking for sympathy about the family turning against her. "It really hurts my feelings," Pam said. "I didn't put a gun to her head and make her fill out the form." Detective McCarrick assures her that her feelings are normal. The family is just striking out because of their grief.

According to Bobbi Wann, Betsy's friend who was staying with Janet Meyer and took Betsy to chemo the last day of her life, Pam "just stopped coming over" after the insurance thing came out.

Even though Pam's story changed about what happened after she and Betsy stopped at the Winghaven Library to have the form witnessed, her evolving details never seemed to raise a red flag to the investigators. First, she said she couldn't remember if they went to the Post Office to mail the change of beneficiary form to State Farm or not. Next, she said, she didn't remember if Betsy mailed it, but that they did stop by the Post Office so that Pam could "mail some stuff to my mother's house." She decided not to mail anything because she remembered she would be seeing her mother later on. The story changed again on January 17th, 2011, when Pam tells State Farm that she and Betsy had gone straight to the Post Office because Betsy was adamant that the form be postmarked that day [Friday, December 23, 2011, the Friday before Betsy was murdered].

At first, it appeared as if Pam filled out the form and suggested she and Betsy take the change of beneficiary document to the Winghaven Library to have it witnessed. That in itself seemed odd. Both Betsy and Pam had worked for State Farm Insurance. They knew their way around insurance forms. Why not have a licensed notary witness their signatures, or simply do it at the State Farm office? Why a librarian who had no legal credentials but was simply standing behind the library counter at the time? Yet, Pam later told detectives that she was simply sitting at the library when Betsy approached her with the form already filled out, so they just decided to have it witnessed while they were there. The Winghaven Library is only minutes from Pam's home at the time in O'Fallon.

Pam switched her story again when she amended her statement concerning the Silver Nissan she had seen parked in the driveway the night that Betsy was killed. Maybe, she said, it had been Russ' dark blue Ford Explorer SUV she had seen. This, after bringing up the Silver Nissan three times during her first police interview the morning after Betsy's death. Had she heard which car Russ had been driving? Had she found out that the Nissan was actually Betsy's daughter's car and it was being held at the house while some things got straightened out between Betsy and Leah. Whatever car Pam thought Russ was driving that night was the one she reported seeing in the driveway. Yet, the detectives never questioned her faulty memory.

During Pam Hupp's March 20, 2012, deposition by Joel Schwartz, she was questioned further about the life insurance. Schwartz was not prepared for what she told him. She informed the defense attorney that she didn't have health insurance because she couldn't afford the premiums. She then shockingly said she does not have life insurance either because, "I don't believe in it for myself." Odd thing for an insurance agent to say. But it was her next statement that practically turned Russ' attorney out of his chair.

Pam told Schwartz that her husband Mark Hupp *did* have life insurance with her as the beneficiary. "...and amazingly, he's still alive, because it's a lot."

"I'm sorry?" Schwartz asked incredulously.

"I said, amazingly he's still alive, because it's a lot. And I sold it to him."

"What do you mean by that?"

"I mean, I guess if I wanted a lot of money, I could kill him instead of her."

"Instead of who?" Schwartz asked, his mind whirring.

"Betsy."

"Who said you killed Betsy?"

"You did, or your private detectives told my friends that."

"And you didn't kill Betsy?"

"I did not kill Betsy."

"You still willing to take a polygraph?" Schwartz asked.

"No." And with that, Pam skated away from being hooked up to a lie detector, again...'faux' or not.

It was a strange and unsettling statement: "I guess if I wanted a lot of money, I could kill him instead of her." Pam would utter a similar statement about her mother, Shirley Neumann, to Detective McCarrick during an interview in June, 2012.

"In my world, 150,000 is not a lot," Pam told McCarrick. "If I really wanted money, and I hate to say it, my mom is worth half a million dollars I get when she dies. My mom has dementia and half the time doesn't know who we are. She's been living in a condo, and I know that sounds really morbid, but I'm a life insurance person. If I *really* wanted money, there's an easier way than trying to combat somebody that's physically stronger than I am [Betsy], I'm just sayin'." Words so similar to what she said to Schwartz concerning her husband, and they were words that would echo eerily only fourteen months later when Pam's mother mysteriously dies.

The only time it seems that Detective McCarrick chastised Pam was during this June 2012 interview when they talked about the life insurance money. Pam had agreed to share the money with Betsy's daughters. Pam told police that Betsy had said to her shortly before the beneficiary switch, "I'm going to make you the beneficiary. If you could, when my daughters are older, give them some money." Pam said, "Ok, how much is it?" Betsy said, "150,000." Keep in mind, this is Pam's account. No one in Betsy's family, not even Russ, knew anything about the switch from Russ to Pam as beneficiary until after Betsy's murder.

Detective McCarrick admonished Pam, "You now have this money and have not turned any of this money over to the family members." "That's correct," said Pam, head nodding continually as he speaks. "That's a *huge* problem," McCarrick says emphatically. "Betsy has told you that she wants you to hold onto this money to make sure the family, the girls are taken care of, yet they haven't seen a dime of that money and you still have it." Pam continues to nod in agreement. McCarrick tells Pam that with Russ' trial coming up, it will look suspicious that Pam, who was the last person to see Betsy alive, has kept all the insurance money that was assigned to her only four days before Betsy's murder. The detective encourages Pam to put the money in a trust for Betsy's two daughters, Leah and Mariah Day, before the trial so that it doesn't look bad. Pam creates the trust for the daughters in June, 2013. She created the trust, but she didn't put the money into it yet.

The astonishing thing is that the detective is actually advising Pam, (who should have been a suspect for the very reasons he just stated) what to do to remain beyond suspicion and keep the heat on Russ. Pam nods her head throughout the detective's mild lecture, seemingly agreeing with everything he is telling her. She does indeed set up a 'revokable' trust for Mariah and Leah Day, in June of 2013. She doesn't fund that trust until only a few days before Russ' trial. She puts $100,00 into the trust, and saves out $50,000, ostensibly to help another family whose wife and mother has been diagnosed with cancer (Nora Murphy). Pam later tells McCarrick in a September 2013 interview, when he asks if she has funded the trust yet, that she kept out $50k because her mother has Alzheimer's and she might need it for her medical bills. One month later, Pam's mother dies from a tragic fall from her third-story balcony. Pam inherits $100,000 from that fall, and suddenly there is $100,000 to put into the revokable trust five days before Russ's trial.

As usual, with Pam, she never knew when to stop talking. Hand gestures waving continually, she went on to convince police why it would make no sense for her to kill Betsy four days after they signed the change of beneficiary form.

"If it's mailed Friday," Pam said, "...we had Christmas. She had to be killed—how does that work? She has to be killed, or they have to receive it before she's killed; otherwise, he's [Russ] still the beneficiary. So, if I set it up in my own little mind, why didn't I just wait for Friday to make sure they got it?"

That is an interesting question. It was apparent to armchair sleuths that if someone other than Russ killed Betsy, their best chance was while he was away at Game Night...and he was *always* at Game Night every Tuesday. If Pam was the killer, why not give it a couple of weeks after the change of beneficiary switch, just to deflect the attention from her? For Betsy to be murdered only four days after Pam's name is put on a form granting her $150,000 seems like a huge red flag. Yet, Betsy is murdered on December 27th. Was there an urgency we are not aware of? Why not just wait a week after the beneficiary switch, while Russ is at Game Night again, and give the insurance switch some time to cool off? Was it because Pam knew that once the family found out about it, it would be hotly contested? Or, had Betsy changed her mind?

As it was, Pam just barely got the money. The form arrived at State Farm the morning after Betsy's death, and the detective gave the agency the green light to give Pam the money. Afterall, she was not a suspect. And with the bloody slippers and Pam's testimony against Russ, it was, in their mind, a slam dunk that he would be arrested.

Detective Ryan McCarrick went as far as to tell Joel Schwartz that "Based on training and experience of dealing with hundreds of interviews with suspects and with witnesses and victims," the detective said, "I did not see any signs of deception that would lead me to believe that she was indicating anything that was untrue to me."

"Did she ever disclose to you that she's been fired from not one but two life insurance jobs for forging signatures?" Schwartz asked him.

"No."

"Have you ever seen any evidence of a brain injury?"

"No. But I've also not gone through all her medical records," McCarrick said.

"Have you asked for the medical records?"

"No."

Schwartz quickly realized that Pam had the detectives wrapped around her little finger. With her ingratiating humor, confidence, and never faltering cadence, she could play the perfect part depending on what was needed at that moment. She could be the long-suffering friend, unjustly judged by Betsy's family, or the witty buddy, engaging and breezy. Hands in a constant flutter, one never got the impression she was making things up out of the ether. As she reminded people more than once, "I'm in sales. I can read people." And indeed, she could.

The year 2012 melted into 2013. Russ sat behind bars as his attorneys Joel Schwartz and Nathan Swanson continued to look over the evidence that would be provided at the trial. In the meantime, while Betsy's family regularly asked Pam for the money promised to the girls, Pam and her husband Mark purchased the house on Shelby Point. Pam declared the house was sold at auction "on the courthouse steps." The Hupps later sold the house for $250,000 in 2015.

Shirley Neumann's Death

Twenty days before Russ Faria's trial for murder was to begin, a tragic event happened at the retirement complex where Pam Hupp's mother Shirley Neumann was living on the third floor in apartment 336. Lakeview Park Retirement Village in Fenton, Missouri, was a nice complex just south of St. Louis. Its name has since been changed. Each apartment has a kitchen, bathroom, bedroom, living room, and balcony or patio. It was listed for "active senior retirement," intimating that the residents were in reasonable health. It was surrounded by the "spectacular wooded hillside of the course at Lakeview Golf Club." Catering to the 55+ age group, it was minutes from restaurants, medical facilities, and shopping. The amenities included three meals per day, housekeeping services, laundry services, transportation, and scheduled trips. The price tag was just under $5k a month. Each apartment, Lakeview advertised, "is equipped with an emergency call system." Yet on the evening of October 30, 2013, that call didn't come.

Pam Hupp had picked up her mother from the hospital after Shirley suffered an accident on October 29, 2013. A member of the staff at the complex had found Shirley laying across her bed, unresponsive. Pam and her brother stated that Shirley Neumann had fallen a couple of times and seemed disoriented. Pam took her mother to the hospital but they did not admit her. She took her home with her and Shirley spent the night. The next day, October 30, 2013, Pam drove

Shirley back to her apartment at Lakeview Park. It was 5:00 p.m. They went straight to Shirley's room. Not long after, Pam came down to the lobby and told them that Shirley would not be down for dinner, nor for breakfast the next morning. If they hadn't heard from her by lunchtime, would they please check on her? Pam left. The fact that Pam said her mother would not be down for dinner intimates it was before the dinner hour ended at 6:30 p.m.

At 2:30 p.m., the following day, a housekeeping staff member knocked on Shirley's door. She had not shown up for lunch. When no one answered, she entered the well-maintained apartment. She stopped. She could hear water running in the bathroom. Checking, she found the faucet running but no one was there. She then noticed that the balcony door was ajar. She went over to it and noticed a garden gnome and a water glass knocked over on the balcony. Worst yet, several aluminum spindles on the balcony railing were bent out and two were completely missing. The attendant looked over the railing and saw Shirley Neumann lying in the wet grass, three floors below.

The police found Shirley lying on her back. A bright maroon blanket was over her. It may have been placed there by the complex while awaiting the police to shield her from the rain and other residents. According to the autopsy report, Shirley was wearing a red cardinal short-sleeve shirt (x-large), black pants, floral panties, black shoes, gray socks, and a white bra. One of her soft walking shoes was lying near the body. "These clothes are wet and green stained as well as on the body," according to the autopsy report. "She was also wrapped in a wet maroon colored blanket... There were no injuries on the hair and the face appeared unremarkable...

"Reflecting the scalp revealed an area of subscapular hemorrhage present in the frontal scalp and this measured 5 x 4 cm. This extends from the forehead to the mid frontal region. Also noted was another area of small scapular hemorrhage present in the left occipital region which measures 2 cm in diameter. The cranium revealed no fractures...Rigor mortis was advanced and generalized." It had rained that morning and everything was wet. Shirley's fingers were somewhat pruned from the moisture. She was lying on her back. She was dead.

The coroner's report would show that there was eight times the amount of Ambien in her bloodstream that was normal for someone to have. According to medical experts, that amount of Ambien would make someone completely disoriented, if not flat-out drugged.

A police photo looking down from the third-floor balcony. One of the bent spindles is at the left, still protruding from the balcony. The Park bench is to the left with something white on its seat. Shirley's head is facing away from the balcony, her left-hand rests on the sidewalk. The maroon blanket covers her.

Crime Scene photo of broken balcony railing and Shirley Neumann's body (blurred) on the grass below. St. Louis Police Department.

Crime Scene photo. View from Shirley's balcony to where she fell. One of the spindles is still in the grass. St. Louis Police Department.

Shirley Neumann's apartment with open balcony door at the back.

There was no further evidence presented at the time. Nothing about whether there was a bottle of Ambien in Shirley's apartment, if it was prescribed for her, etc. Shirley Neumann's death was ruled an

111

accident.

In June of 2013, Pam told Detective McCarrick during a police interview that "Mom was in an accident two months ago." Shirley was 77-years-old and had supposedly been slipping lately; mentally and physically. Shirley died four months after that interview from an "accidental" fall. If Pam was responsible for her mother's death, was she already setting the stage in that June police interview for her mother's fall from the balcony in October?

When Chris Hayes with *Fox 2 News* interviewed Pam at her door on Shelby Point, January of 2014 [two months after Shirley's death], he asked Pam about her mother: "How did your mom die?" Pam, who kept herself partially hidden from the cameraman, said, "How did my mom die?" Pam is seemingly surprised at the question. "What do you mean?" Chris asks, "How did it happen?" Pam answers, "She died. Like, the people in the home say she committed suicide, so I'm not quite sure what's going on." Chris is sympathetic. "Really? I'm sorry to hear that. She just jumped?" Pam, "Well, I don't know, cuz...we don't know yet, what's going on, so..." Chris, "Was she suicidal?" Pam, "Ummm, I don't think so. I don't know. How do you know with Alzheimer's people?"

Pam describes the balcony at her mother's house to Chris Hayes, "The bars going up and down are hollow aluminum, decorative, they're not welded in, they're popped in, so, if you wanted to, I would suppose...it might take a little bit, but it's not like they're welded in, they're not hard, they're hollow, they're just only this big..." Pam indicates with her two fingers an object about an inch wide. What is interesting is that Pam stops herself after she says, "so, if you wanted to, I would suppose it might take a little bit..." If you wanted to what? Kick them out?

The bars were bent in the same area, making experts believe someone may have stood there and kicked at the bars until they popped out of their moorings. Several tests were done on similar railing sets to see if it was possible for an elderly woman, weighing 218 pounds, to crash through the spindles by falling and hitting them head-on. First, a rigged "body" on a pendulum was pulled back to the point that it would simulate Shirley's weight hitting the spindles full tilt. They didn't budge. Next, they doubled the force exerted on the spindles. Still nothing. The test went on, until finally, it was determined that a car or riding lawn mower would have to hit that railing in order for it to show the damage it did—basically almost 2,000 pounds of force. One of the people involved in the experiment then kicked the spindle, near the bottom, and it burst out, looking exactly like the bent spindles from Shirley's railing. Yet, the case remained classified as an accident. The medical examiner said Shirley's body showed she died from "blunt force trauma" in her chest. One linear abrasion was found on her face, and one small 2 cm circle by her occipital area. That was the only damage listed from a supposed head-long fall through 6 spindles, two of which were completely busted out. And if she did fall head-first through the balcony railings, how did she end up on her back?

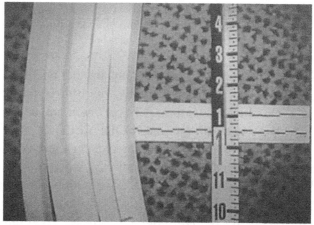

Police evidence photo of balcony railings, all bent at the same location.

Shirley's balcony showing missing spindles and the toppled gnome.

Crime scene photo of Shirley's balcony showing drinking glass and
overturned gnome near the railing.

The balcony railing was removed and another one put in place. Her
tiny apartment was gone over. Sadly, there were family photos on
the wall above the television in her apartment and a vinyl quote that
read, "FAMILY is a gift that lasts FOREVER." A stack of books
sat on the small table, with another one on the chair by the open
balcony door. Her late husband's photos were everywhere, along
with the folded American flag handed to widows at their husband's
military burial. The display case also had a collection of ceramics;
some appearing to be Hummel collectibles. A light sweater is
thrown over an out-turned chair at the dining table, as if Shirley just
walked in, took it off and draped it hastily over the back of the chair.
Why was the chair turned away from the table? Was she sitting
there, drugged, just before her fall?

This author called the apartment complex to find out about their
dining schedules. Dinner was always served from 5-6:30 p.m. It was
the night before Halloween. The apartment brochure advertised their
emphasis on holiday events. It was dark that night at 6:03 p.m. and,
according to the weather report for that day, "cloudy skies were
expected to bring showers and thunderstorms by the afternoon,
mostly after 3 p.m." Pam Hupp brought her mother home at 5 p.m.,
just when all the residents were headed to the dining hall. There may
have been a Halloween party planned as well. If the other residents
are at dinner, could someone have stood on the balcony and kicked

out the spindles without it being heard? If Shirley is drugged with Ambien, would it have been hard to walk her to the railing and push her over? The blunt trauma to her chest could have come from the fall. She may have even hit the park bench first that was directly beneath the balcony.

The coroner's report showed that her liver temperature was 91 degrees and that rigor had set in. There was a problem with what Shirley's body was telling them. She could not have lain outside, dead, beneath her balcony all night before the housekeeper found her at 2:30 p.m. the following day and still have a liver temperature of 91 degrees. That reading implied she had not been dead longer than a few hours. If Pam had pushed her over the railing the night before, it meant Shirley Neumann laid out in the dark and the rain, *alive*, throughout the night and into the afternoon of the next day, before she finally died.

In the photo on the previous page, we see a large drinking glass, or beer mug. The housekeeper reported the water running in the bathroom. Was the scenario supposed to look like Shirley had filled the glass, walked out to the balcony to water the flowers, fallen forwards, or backwards, and gone through the railing, hence, the water had not been turned off? Did there need to be a logical reason presented in a staged balcony scene to suggest a reason for an elderly woman to go out onto the balcony? Why else would she be out there on a cold October evening, or morning? The photos of the potted plants show only dirt, not living plants. Many outdoor plants are dead in October in states that see cold temperatures. The fog the morning of October 30, 2013 was so thick, you could barely see the top of the St. Louis arch. Several wrecks occurred on the bridge that morning due to it.

St. Louis Arch in October 30, 2013's morning fog

115

Shirley's shoe and hand in Crime Scene photos.
St. Louis Police Department.

The rules at the apartment complex are that no one is allowed out after dark without an escort or permission. And, it was raining that night. If a body is lying on the grass, in the dark, in the rain, would anyone even see it? Obviously, they didn't. Shirley wasn't found until 2:30 in the afternoon the following day.

Was it Deja Vu that the moon was in its Crescent phase, as it had been the night of Betsy Faria's murder? While October 30, 2013 was in the Waning Crescent, while Betsy's had been in the Waxing Crescent, the lunar light was only 18% the night Shirley died. Once again, so many things hidden in darkness.

Shirley Neumann's Obituary

Shirley Neumann
Nov. 16, 1935—Oct. 31, 2013

Neumann, Shirley, (nee Russell) on October 31, 2013. Beloved wife of the late Victor Joseph Neumann Jr. Loving mother of Michael (Alexis) Neumann, Sheri (Mark) Wasserman, Pam (Mark) Hupp, and Dan (Juliann) Neumann.

Shirley's grandchildren and siblings are also named in the obituary. She had 12 grandchildren, 3 great-grandchildren, and two sisters. It went on to tell of Shirley's career as a teacher to grade school children after graduating from Florissant Valley Community College and the University of Missouri St. Louis.

In all fairness, we do not know if Shirley Neumann died on the evening of October 30th, or the morning of October 31st. Her obituary reads October 31, 2013. As mentioned, the liver temperature and rigor timeline gave some clues. There may be more to learn from the full autopsy report.

On July 27, 2015, Pam was confiding again to Prosecuting Attorney Leah Askey, as they discussed Russ' upcoming second trial four months away in November. The subject of Pam's mother came up. Strangely, Pam now steers away from the Alzheimer's theory:

"Did she really have dementia?" Pam is saying to Askey. "I just found out last week she didn't really have dementia. Before she went into this home [Lakeview Park Apartments], we had to have her tested, so we'd know what home to put her in, so the doctor said...I don't know, my brother did it, to a neurologist to do the Alzheimer's dementia test... and the doctor said, 'Yeah, she's got a little bit of a problem, whatever, she's 77.' Did she have dementia? No! Do we say that in our family? Heck, yeah! The joke is 'Oh there goes Grandma again! She's got Alzheimer's, 'Oldsheimer's,' all those jokes. So, to me, it's like 'Yeah, she had dementia.' But to a neurologist, she did *not*. That's why she was placed in that home, and that's why it was no threat to be on the third floor.

"But to *everybody* else on this planet, I took a 210-pound woman and *threw* her through railings!" Pam's voice shows some emotion as she says, "How do you do that? How does a *man* do that?"

Leah Askey replies, "Yeah, well, I understand how stories get out of hand."

117

Pam also confided that her family had sold everything of Shirley's to be able to put her in the apartment. "We were getting ready to move her," Pam said, concerning the apartment. "She couldn't afford it anymore."

The death of Shirley Neumann remained an 'accident' until another tragedy occurred the following summer; suddenly putting fresh eyes on Pam Hupp's mother's fatal fall from the balcony.

Crime scene photo of Shirley Neumann lying atop one of the spindles.

Chapter Nine
Russ' Trial

November 18, 2013, Russ Faria sat in a Lincoln County courtroom, flanked by his attorneys, Joel Schwartz and Nathan Swanson. He had been in the Lincoln County jail for almost two years. Seated at the table for the prosecution was an athletic-looking woman with shoulder-length dark hair and a gaze of fierce determination. Leah Askey was new as a prosecuting attorney for a murder charge. It was the first murder case being overseen by Judge Christina C. Kunza Mennemeyer. She was a judge for the 45th Circuit Court in Missouri, elected on November 6, 2012, barely one year before Russ' trial. Lincoln County had only seen two murders in the three years leading up to Betsy's death. 2009 had not seen a single homicide.

PA Leah Askey   Judge Chris Mennemeyer

The prosecution was confident in their case. They felt they had ample nails for Russ' coffin, and the person holding the hammer was

Pam Hupp. All of her stories of Russ' abusive nature, his putting a pillow over Betsy's face, the tainted Gatorade only a week before her murder, his anger when he found out Pam was now the beneficiary of Betsy's life insurance money, his explosion when he found out Betsy wanted to move out of their new home, his drinking, smoking pot, and his degrading nature to his wife, all added up to a snapshot of a man who would fly into a rage and kill. Even Betsy's mother, Janet Meyer said, "Russ had told the husband of a friend of mine that if he was ever in a fight, he would fight to kill."

In a trial that was filled with contention, sidebars to debate items before the judge filled as many transcript pages as actual witness testimony. Paramount in these discussions was whether to allow in testimony about Betsy Farias' life insurance policy.

Then, there was the forensic evidence: Russ' bloody slippers in his master bedroom closet, blood on the light switch leading into the bedroom, and him finding the body—something law enforcement always looks at. The crime scene detectives said they found a bloody trail leading from the living room into the kitchen where Russ said he had gone, and a towel with a suspicious stain in the kitchen drawer. They also claimed to see a blood stain on Russ' yellow cap.

Crime scene photo of the kitchen counter with butcher block knife set, and two knives on the counter. The small black-handled knife to the left showed stains. Just beneath this knife is a drawer. In that drawer detectives found a green kitchen towel with what appeared to be a blood stain. In the far left of this photo is the refrigerator. This counter with the knives was mere steps from the couch where Betsy was lying. Her face was turned away from the kitchen.
Photo courtesy of PA Mike Wood.

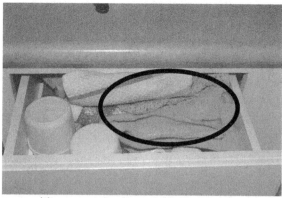

Kitchen drawer with green stained towel (r). You can see the tip of the black knife handle above it on the counter. Photo courtesy PA Mike Wood.

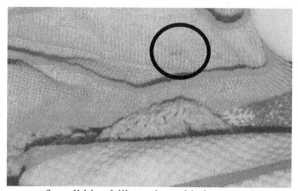

Close-up of small blood-like stain on kitchen towel in drawer. Photo courtesy of PA Mike Wood.

The detectives showed photos of their Bluestar test for blood. Cardboard is taped over windows with red tape to shut out the sunlight while they used Luminol to look for blood stains. Luminol reacts to the iron in the hemoglobin of blood. When the Luminol is sprayed evenly across an area, trace amounts of an activating oxidant make the Luminol emit a blue glow that can be seen in a darkened room. Oddly, the photos showing the bloody trail through the kitchen were not in evidence. The crime tech said the camera had malfunctioned and those photos had come out black. The jury would have to trust his description.

In the Bluestar test photo, you can see the basic layout of the rooms. To the far left (out of view) is the kitchen. The kitchen snack bar is where the chair is balancing atop it. To the right of that is the dining room table; the sliding glass door to the back yard next to it. In the right foreground, with a chair laying atop it, is the sofa where Betsy had been lying before her attack. The cushions now show white after being stripped of their covers. An ottoman has been moved closer to it. It was originally farther to the right of the fireplace. This shows how close the kitchen and the knives were to where Betsy's head was lying on the sofa that night. It was literally a few steps from the kitchen, past the dining room table, to the sofa.

Bluestar test with windows covered.
Furniture is piled up to allow for testing.

Photo of couch (r) after fabric has been removed. Kitchen is to the left.

Leah Askey brought up other evidence pointing to Russ. It was the semen found in Betsy. It proved, Askey told the jury, that Russ had "violated Betsy one last time" the night she was murdered. It was her theory that the reason no blood was found on Russ' clothes was that he butchered his wife while naked. He had made love to Betsy while she was lying there on the sofa in the family room, and then killed her, stabbing her many times with the knife. He had then showered, and after drying off, had put on his slippers. He went about the crime scene, getting rid of evidence, staging things, and then called 911.

According to Askey, you can hear Russ moving around during the 911 call. She posits that he realizes he has on slippers that have gotten blood on them and he hurries to the bedroom closet where he tosses them, getting blood on the room's light switch in his hurry. He is dressed and wailing in an "over the top" performance when the police arrive.

Attorney Leah Askey tells the jury that "In December of 2011, December 24th, the Faria family Christmas kind of took off without a hitch, initially. And the family, Betsy, the defendant [Russ], and Betsy's two daughters went and celebrated Christmas on the 24th with the part of his family. They all then came back to Troy so that they could spend Christmas morning together…You're going to hear that they left separately and they then went to Betsy's family [her father. Her parents had recently divorced] that afternoon for Christmas.

"On Christmas evening then, Betsy would return back to Troy with the defendant and on the 26th, the next day, they got up early went to his family and then right after that, went to her family [her sister Pam Welker's home.] Mariah gets sick with the flu and is in the hospital. Russ and Betsy leave his family and to go her. Betsy is not allowed in the hospital due to her low immune system, so she goes to her mom's and Russ stays with Mariah before delivering her to Betsy's mom's home. "Betsy didn't come home again after that…she didn't return until the evening when she was murdered," Askey states.

Members of Betsy's family are put on the stand. They have been inundated with information from the prosecution's team for years. In the beginning, they could not believe Russ capable of killing Betsy. But as the "evidence" against Russ is presented, they begin to doubt his innocence. Even one of his game buddies wonders if maybe he killed her before he left to come to Game Night, where he established an alibi. He would later learn that Betsy was still alive at 7:04 p.m. when Pam put her on the phone to Mark Hupp to say "Merry Christmas." By then, Russ was in the middle of watching *Conan* with his friends, thirty minutes away.

Mary Rodgers, Betsy's sister took the stand and stated she had often witnessed Russ angry and condescending to Betsy over the years. He had once exploded during an argument and said that someday "he would cut her up and bury her." Pam Hupp would later use those same words during an interview with detectives just before Russ' second trial. Had Pam heard them here and decided they would benefit her later?

As each relative on Betsy's side of the family denigrated Russ, Schwartz and Swanson repeatedly challenged them, asking "Isn't it true that after Betsy was diagnosed with cancer in 2010, that things were better between them?" They begrudgingly admitted they were better. One relative added the caveat "for a time."

Mariah Day, Betsy's youngest daughter, told this author how Askey and the detectives were treating the family leading up to the trial:

"Leah Askey would bring my entire family, all my aunts, their husbands, my grandma, me and my sister, into one of their rooms in Troy a week or so after everything happened," Mariah said, anger still apparent in her voice. "They told us their theory, all their conspiracy theories, and basically just feeding us what they thought happened. They manipulated us to the finest. We didn't have any idea how this process goes. I asked the detectives recently (2021) who brought us in if that's normal, and they said 'No.' They fed us their theory for five years. Before Russ' first trial, they brought me out to lunch, because my sister and I were constantly asking in the interview rooms where it was taped, 'Well, what about Pam? She was constantly hanging out with my mom, and her stories kept changing? Have you looked at her?' And they would always have an excuse. With the beneficiary thing, they would say, "No offense, but your mom is dying anyway so why would Pam do this? She was going to get it eventually." Mariah thought it was interesting that they took her to lunch to discuss Pam, away from the police station video cameras.

At Russ' trial, Leah Askey faced the jury as she played Russ' 911 call. She pointed out that it was "over the top," obviously theatrics trying to convince the dispatcher. The testimony from Betsy's family was damning as they each shared their recollections of the darker side of Russ. Mary Rodgers, Betsy's sister, told of a call from Betsy's daughters that she felt was alarming. "The girls called me crying at work that he was using foul language, so I went to their house and he was out of control. I actually called the police, took the girls and got them out of the house."

Leah, Betsy's daughter told of regular fights between her mother and her step-father. "It wasn't the *Brady Bunch*," she said, sardonically. As with most 20-20 lens, if you are focused on the negative aspects of a person, they are going to show up. Russ was now put under a microscope and innocuous things became sinister in the reprisal of events.

And then, it was time for the star witness. Pam Hupp took the stand and settled in. She appeared as someone holding court; doubtless disappointed that no television cameras were allowed in the courtroom. With her effortless stream of dialogue, she recounted all the horror stories she had told detectives; embellishing small details to improve the sensationalism. It was a role she was born to play. No one would suspect Pam's mother had died only three weeks before the trial. She was her usual confident self.

Pam maintained direct eye contact with the PA and jury, as effusive as ever as she told how Russ was degrading to his wife, calling her 'simple' and even showing displeasure over the side effects that come from chemo. Pam said that Betsy's friends stopped coming over if they thought Russ was going to be there.

Pam told the court how she was on disability. She stated it concerned "an accident. I lost some discs. I have a plate in my neck and I use a TENS unit to stimulate nerves down my right side." She said the accident had happened four years prior. Askey moved on. "Prior to that, you said you were working in the insurance business. Did you know Betsy Faria?" "I met her when I moved up here. As soon as I moved up here, I was transferred from an office down there to an office up here where she worked." It is not clear if Pam is referring to Florida when she says she "moved up here," or if she is referring to a different part of Missouri.

Leah Askey asked Pam, "Did you and Betsy have a Christmas Eve tradition that you guys shared?"

"Yes...every Christmas Eve, we would go out to lunch or spend most of the time together and after lunch, then would part ways for the Christmas holidays and then get back together."

"Ok," Askey said, "Christmas 2011 was a Sunday...That makes Christmas Eve Saturday...Did you spend that Christmas Eve, that Saturday, with her?"

"I did not," Pam said. "I spent Friday with her. All day Friday."

"How come Friday instead of Saturday?"

"Because as far as I can remember, she was going to her mom's for the weekend and she was going to, it was just going to be a long holiday. Her mom and dad had divorced, so she had more places to go to."

"Do you see Betsy on Christmas Eve or Christmas Day?"

"No."

"The day after Christmas, that Monday, did you see her?"

"I don't remember," Pam said. "I don't think so."

"Okay. So now that would take you to Tuesday, which I believe is the 27th? You hadn't seen her since this last Friday?"

"That's correct."

Pam then recounts her day on the Tuesday she is supposed to take Betsy to chemo. She leaves out that Betsy asked her not to come, only that Bobbi Wann was taking Betsy.

"Even in those situations in the past, had you gone ahead and shown up just to sit with her?" Askey asks in an effort to dilute Pam's showing up uninvited.

"Yes."

"Did you do that on this Tuesday?"

"I did."

"After that, do you recall where you went after sitting there with her?"

"I went home and had dinner with my husband and she went home and had dinner with her mother," Pam said.

Pam doesn't say Betsy took Bobbi out for dinner after the chemo treatment. She says Betsy went home to have dinner with her mother. Had Betsy told her that to keep her from butting into a restaurant dinner with Bobbi, or, was Pam diverting attention from the fact she was not invited to Lion's Choice restaurant after the medical procedure?

Hupp also says earlier that Betsy was "going to her mom's for the [Christmas] weekend." This is a statement Pam repeatedly harps on: that Betsy was away from her home all weekend. It's obvious Betsy was at home with Russ in-between their outings to family Christmas celebrations. Had Betsy told Pam she would be at her mom's all weekend to keep Pam away? Is that why Pam thought she was gone all weekend? It's another part of a mysterious five days. We do know the Friday Pam "spent all day" with Betsy was the day they went to the Winghaven Library to change the life insurance form. Had Betsy felt the need to distance herself from Pam after that, perhaps regretting what she had done, or feeling she had been coerced into it? She had not wanted Pam to show up at her chemo appointment that Tuesday and had not seen Pam since Friday. Rita Wolf stated Betsy was avoiding Pam lately. Pam had not gone to Branson or on the cruise.

Askey next asks Pam what time she arrived at Betsy's mother's house to pick Betsy up and take her home the night she was murdered. Pam responds that she picked her up at 6:00 p.m. and it was dark. Pam told detectives she arrived "at 5:15-5:30 p.m." Why is she changing the timeline by 30 minutes? This would not be the only inconsistency in her trial statements.

Pam goes on to say that she pulled into Betsy's driveway when they arrived at the Faria home and the two of them sat in the car "and gabbed" for a few minutes. She said Betsy was trying to convince her to spend the night but Pam didn't want to. Pam then puts Betsy on the phone at 7:04 p.m. to wish Mark a "Merry Christmas." Pam states the house is completely dark; no lights are showing, not even the porch light. Then amazingly, she states that she did not see another car in the driveway. This is after she harped on seeing the silver Nissan in the driveway that night to the detectives the morning after Betsy's murder. Now, years later, she testifies she didn't see any car there at all that night. This is problematic, as Pam testified to detectives that Betsy went out to the Nissan to get her chemo bag when they got to the house.

When Joel Schwartz rises to take on the woman he has been preparing to take down since 2011, he realizes he is in for a tough time. The judge had tied his hands on most of the testimony he wished to elicit from Pam, citing rules of "hearsay" and "impeaching the witness." Pam lets him know right out of the gate that she will not make it easy for him.

"Ms. Hupp," Schwartz begins, "you had known Betsy in 2011. You testified earlier or you've stated you knew her about ten years?"

"Correct," Pam says succinctly.

"You testified earlier that Russ was degrading and made her feel simple?"

"I can hardly hear you, I'm sorry," Pam says. This is the same tactic she will use later with the attorney for Betsy's daughters during their civil trial against Pam. It was to keep them off-balance and play by her rules.

Amid myriad objections by the prosecution, Schwartz tried to elicit information from a very hostile witness.

"How was Betsy positioned when you last saw her?" Schwartz asked Pam.

"She was going to get cuddled up to watch a movie on the couch with her blanket."

"You told that to the police. Did you say that she was sitting on the couch, she had a blanket on her and she was going to watch T.V.?"

Mr. Hicks, the co-counsel for the prosecution objected. "This is improper impeachment of the witness."

"This is not even impeachment. This is what she testified to," Schwartz countered. He pressed on.

"What did you tell the police two days later when you talked to Detective Kaiser when she came back to see you? She asked you, 'when was the last time you saw Betsy?' What did you tell her?"

"I don't remember," Pam said.

"Isn't it true that you told her the last time you saw Betsy was at the front door waving goodbye?"

"I don't remember."

"Would it refresh your recollection if I showed you a copy of her report?" Schwartz pressed.

"No."

"It would not?"

"No."

"So you don't remember telling Detective Kaiser that two days later?"

"No."

"Now, during the course of this interview," Schwartz said, "towards the very end, you had asked the Detective, you wanted to go see Janet [Betsy's mother]; is that correct?"

"Uh-huh."

"Yes?"

"Yes."

"And you asked if she even knew about it; is that correct?"

"I don't remember that," Pam said.

"Well, you wanted to ask if it was okay and the male Detective, Detective Perry, he just wanted to make sure that everything would be okay; is that right?"

"I don't know what you are talking about." Pam said stubbornly. This would also be a line she would later use in the civil trial between herself and Betsy's daughters.

"At that point, did you ask them, towards the end of your interview, 'what time did this happen? This morning?'"

"I don't remember that."

"Would it refresh your recollection if I showed you a copy of the transcript?" Schwartz demanded.

"No, it wouldn't." They argue for a moment about whether hearing a recording would help her remember, an objection is raised, and Schwartz finally presses on.

"So, you are saying you don't recall asking at the end of the interview 'what time did this happen? This morning?'"

"No....which day? I don't know which day you are talking about."

"The very next morning, at 6:40 a.m., when the police arrived. They were there for about three or four hours, correct?"

"Correct."

"Right at the end of that interview, you asked 'what time did this happen? This morning?' You don't recall that?"

"No."

Doubling down, Schwartz played his trump card as to this point of his questioning. "Okay. During the course of that interview, early on, maybe a half hour, hour into it, you got a call. You have a brother, Mike, right?"

"Correct."

"You were supposed to go deal with some financial stuff with Mike and your mother?" Schwartz asked.

"I did not get a call from him. I called him," Pam countered.

"Are you sure?"

"Yeah."

"Would it refresh your recollection to listen to it?"

"No."

"No, it wouldn't?"

"Objection," Mr. Hicks shouted. "Relevance. What is…what is the relevance?" After haggling back and forth with Hicks, Schwartz withdraws the question.

"When you got that phone call," he said, circling around again, "from your brother, you told your brother, early on in this interview, 'my friend, something happened to her last night and I have the police officers here asking me questions.' Do you recall telling that to your brother?"

"Yes, I do."

"That was early on, yes?"

"I guess, yes."

"So, why did you say later to the police, why did you ask them, did this happen this morning?"

"Objection," Hicks shouts. "Improper question. She already said she didn't recall making the statement. He's now asking her to comment on it."

Pam, without waiting for a ruling, states, "If I did—I just found out my good friend had been killed and I don't know. I--."

Schwartz pounced, "But you said it?"

"Obviously, I did just say it. I have a little bit of a memory problem. I'm 55 and going through menopause. It's been two years. I can't tell you every minute of what I have said about anything, honestly," Pam offered, hoping that blanket statement would absolve her of all her inconsistent statements.

"Is the memory problem the reason that you would have told the police that you didn't go inside?" Schwartz demanded.

"No."

"Is the memory problem the reason that you would have told Betsy, or that you would have told the police, you called her when you got home?"

"No."

"Okay. When you went inside, you went through the house and you said Betsy showed you what she got for Christmas; is that correct?"

"Correct."

"And there was a leg broken on that jewelry chest, correct?"

"Correct."

"And that was at seven something on the 27th when you saw this?"

"It would have been seven something, yes."

"Nothing further." Schwartz stated.

Joel Schwartz had scored some major points with his cross-examination of Pam Hupp. Besides pointing out her failed attempt to look innocent concerning whether Betsy died the prior evening or that morning, he annihilated the prosecution's attempt to imply a sinister meaning out of the broken leg on the jewelry stand. Their position was that it had been broken the night of the murder during a scuffle between Betsy and Russ in the master bedroom. Schwartz' question to Pam just showed it was already broken when Pam saw it that evening before Russ got home. Russ stated he had broken it trying to move it to the bedroom from the family room Christmas.

Another oddity came out during one of the copious sidebars occurring at the judge's bar. It seemed there was a statement made by Pam Hupp and Bobbie Wann that Betsy had stated during her chemo treatment that she had actually left some insurance documents out on a table at home that she not completed filling out—ones where she was removing Russ as the beneficiary. It was ruled inadmissible as it was "hearsay." Betsy was not here to either confirm or deny it. It smacked of something Pam Hupp would say, as one more reason for Russ to kill that night, but it was never allowed in. The police reported finding no insurance documents at the house.

Points scored by Schwartz or not, the question remained, how was the prosecutor going to explain away Russ' alibi? He had the backing of four different people, swearing he was there that night with them, from 6 until 9 p.m. There was video from three surveillance cameras at stores and the gas station. What about the receipt from Arby's showing he had been there at 9:09 p.m.?

Leah Askey was ready. She told the jury that all of Russ' alibi videos, receipts, and friend's testimony were part of an elaborate plot. It was proof of his guilt that he had gone to so much trouble to show where he was and kept receipts, etc. No one else would make so many unnecessary stops. Why didn't he get the dog food when he got the cigarettes? Why that gas station? Why did he cancel dinner with his mother when it was tradition that he ate with her on the way to his Tuesday Game Nights? And his friend's testimonies?

She pointed out that all their stories were suspiciously alike. They had rehearsed them, she opined. Besides, friends lie. They lie to the point that Askey submitted they covered for Russ. Russ must have left his cell phone with Brandon Sweeney so its coordinates would show him in O'Fallon when he was really home in Troy murdering Betsy. Then, Brandon went through Arby's, got the receipt, and brought the phone and paper trail to Russ, before disappearing just before the police arrived. It was tied up in a neat accusatory bow.

Russ' attorney came out swinging. How could anyone believe Russ would be stupid enough to call 911 and claim his wife had committed suicide, Joel Schwartz asked incredulously? There were stab wounds in her back. She had post-mortem wounds, including deep slashes to her wrists. That's hard to pull off if you're already dead. If he was going to stage this, wouldn't he have called to report a murder, not a suicide? Schwartz was convinced that the police had tunnel vision where Russ was concerned from the start. "Confirmation bias" became the rule of the day. They would make the evidence confirm their existing theory, rather than the other way around.

Joel went after the most-damning evidence—the slippers. He pointed out that there was very little, if any, blood on the top of the slippers. It was only on the bottom and sides. There were no bloody footprints leading from the crime scene to the bedroom, which there would have been based on the blood on the bottom of the shoes. There was no imprint in the blood on the carpet that would have showed a shoe stepped there. The slippers looked as if someone had "dipped" them in Betsy's blood and then tossed them in Russ's closet, after swiping them on the switch plate of the master bedroom. The pattern on the light switch showed a weave pattern rather than a fingerprint. And Russ' DNA had not been found in any blood evidence.

As for the multiple wounds, Schwartz said they looked carefully placed, as if someone had stood there and plunged the knife over and over into a target that was no longer moving. In other words, to make it look like overkill…a crime of passion. As for that passion? Betsy's mother said Betsy never told her that Russ had put a pillow over her face to scare her. She was sure Betsy would have told her something like that. He also stated that Russ missed "half the Tuesdays" he usually ate with his mother; making it about twice a month that he dined with her. It was no big deal. All Russ' mother asked was that he let her know if he wasn't going to make it.

Schwartz pointed out that when Russ walked into the house, Betsy was dead, her tongue protruding from her mouth. Crime scene techs said she had been dead probably a couple of hours. Rigor had set in. There was also the testimony from Betsy's daughter, Leah, that convinced Schwartz that Betsy had died close to 7:21 p.m.

Betsy had made an arrangement with Leah to call her concerning her new cell phone plan. Leah had called Betsy twenty minutes prior to say she would be calling her from US Cellular that night to upgrade her cell phone coverage, which Betsy would have to authorize. Betsy said she would have her phone ready for the call. Leah would call from the store to authorize the new charges over the phone as she was on Betsy's phone plan. Leah called her mother at 7:21 p.m. No answer. She called her again at 7:26 p.m. and 7:30 p.m. Betsy did not answer. This was not like her.

Chris Hayes with *Fox 2 News* interviewed Pam Hupp at the front door of her home on Shelby Point in January of 2014. He asked Pam if she heard Betsy's phone ringing while she was there, going off the information Leah Day provided.

Chris Hayes with *Fox 2 News* questioning Pam at her door.
Photo's courtesy of *Fox 2 News*.

"Betsy doesn't not pick up many calls," Pam said.

"Right," Chris agreed, "so I'm wondering why she didn't pick up those?"

"That I can't answer," Pam said, keeping just inside the door to avoid Chris' cameraman who was filming the conversation. "Maybe we were either in her bedroom then…I don't know…I don't know where her phone was…I never even heard any calls…I don't know if I left right before she got a call…I don't know. Like I told them, I wasn't' expecting police to come to my door that next morning. I wasn't taking notes."

"I wasn't taking notes," Pam said during her conversation with Chris Hayes of Fox 2 News.

If Pam had been given the time of Leah's first call—7:21 p.m.—she could have simply said she had left about then. But that would look strange that Betsy wasn't answering her daughter's call only moments after Pam said she left the Faria house to go home.

Askey wasn't going to let Russ off the hook just because Betsy's body was stiff when he supposedly got home. She asked Dr. Kamal Sabharwal about a little-known effect called *cadaveric spasm*. Dr. Sabharwal had performed the autopsy of Betsy Faria. He said the spasm was rare, but possible. It was a controversial condition that can cause rigor almost immediately if preceded by extreme physical exertion. Based on the almost pristine crime scene, where the only thing disturbed was a hearth rug, there didn't seem to be a lot of prior 'physical exertion.' The other problem was it didn't explain that several detectives and crime scene investigators arriving on the scene, immediately after Russ' 911 call, stated the blood pooled beneath Betsy's head looked "dry and coagulated." They opined she had been dead about two hours.

Medic Mike Quattrochi testified on the stand that he arrived at the Faria house that night at 9:51 p.m.; eleven minutes after Russ' 911 call. He said Betsy was "cold and stiff." He also commented on the deep cut to her right forearm had cut through muscle, tendons, and nerves and went clear to the bone. According to him, this deep cut "bled out when it was done to her." Meaning, she had lost all her blood and was dead when the wound occurred or there would have been blood coming from the gash.

Two detectives from the Major Case Squad were questioned. Detectives Patrick Harney and Mike Merkle were responsible for taking Russ in for questioning the night of the murder. These two detectives would later be responsible for questioning Pam Hupp in several recorded interviews leading up to Russ' second trial. Harney would actually be recorded providing Pam with a scenario that involved her seeing Russ in a car outside the Faria home the night of Betsy's death.

When cell phone evidence was discussed, it was stated that Leah and her boyfriend had both been cleared due to their cell phone location history.

During Lieutenant Schimweg's (Commander of the Major Case Squad) testimony, Schwartz questioned why Leah Day and her boyfriend Devan Rogers had been cleared as suspects after their whereabouts were confirmed, phones checked, etc., and yet Pam Hupp had not been cleared? Why hadn't the detectives done all the background checking they did on Leah and Devan regarding Pam? Schimweg countered that Pam had been interviewed, a buccal swab taken, and the clothes she was wearing handed over. However, they did not do a cell phone history on her whereabouts that day—the defense's expert did that—they did not process the clothes they collected or ask any of the several people who saw Pam that night what she was wearing. They did not process her car, nor was Pam's husband asked what she was wearing when she returned home that night, what T.V. show they watched together, when she took a shower, or myriad other questions that should have been asked of the last person to see the deceased alive.

And somehow, it had not looked suspicious that Pam volunteered the make, model, and the year of the car she had been driving that night to the detectives who interviewed her the morning after

Betsy's murder at the Hupp home. "A four-door 2004 Honda Accord." The car was right there at the house, if not in the driveway. Why offer so much information about the car she was driving? Was it possible she had been driving a different car? One that did show blood residue?

Schwartz also pointed out that Russ Faria had a rock-solid alibi and more and he had been sitting in jail for two years and was on trial for his life. He had receipts, video surveillance footage, proof of the items he purchased, and four confirming alibis from the people who were with him from 6-9 p.m. that night. Pam had provided none of that. The problem was, Schwartz was shut down with objections each time he came near Pam Hupp's movements or motive. The objections flew like confetti each time he crossed into that arena.

During the trial, Crime Scene Investigator Amy Pratt described the difference between a latent print and a patent print. Basically, she said, a latent print is invisible to the eye. "That is one that needs to be processed with fingerprint powder or with some type of chemical, some type of processing. A patent print is the ones you will see that your kids leave behind on your window glass, the ones you can actually see the sweat and the actual secretions behind." Amy stipulated she had been a CSI for eleven years and was not a member of the Major Case Squad, but that a member of the Squad calls her in. She arrived at the Faria home at 5:00 a.m. the following morning of the murder. Betsy's body was still on the scene. She took crime scene photos of the exterior and interior of the residence at 130 Sumac.

Pratt testified that during her photographing of the scene, she did not see any forced entry to the home. She stipulated that nothing is moved at this time. She testified the bloody light switch was about 8 feet from the master bedroom closet where the bloody slippers were found. It was the light switch to the bedroom.

A photo of the butcher block knife set in the kitchen was introduced. It was certified that the large Master Chef knife was missing from the other knives housed there.

Butcher block knife set in Faria's kitchen.
Photo courtesy of PA Mike Wood.

It was during Dr. Sabharwal's testimony that the brutality of the attack on Betsy Faria hit home. As the coroner who had performed her autopsy went over every wound, it was hard to fathom how anyone could do this to someone. Betsy Faria had literally been butchered.

Elizabeth "Betsy" Faria's autopsy was done on December 28, 2011, at 1:00 p.m. in the afternoon, the day after her murder. The knife had been left in her neck, her hands and feet had been bagged. Her clothing was removed and the gruesome work began to try and document all those stab wounds.

Dr. Sabharwal explained that many wounds consisted of both "sharp force" entries, and incised wounds. "A stab wound is a penetrating wound which penetrates deeper into the skin and tissue than the actual injury on the surface of the skin. An incised wound is basically a cut wound. It's another word for a cut, and the incised wound is longer on the surface of the skin than it is deeper into the skin and tissue."

The coroner then went over each wound, sometimes referencing the crime scene photos Askey put up. Many of Betsy's family exited the room or kept their head down during this portion of the trial. Without all the talk of centimeters and distance from the head, Betsy Faria's injuries came down to this:

It was believed the most egregious wound was to the left side of her neck as she laid on the couch on her right side. It was made clear over and over that all the wounds inflicted on her neck and head "track backward and to the right." This was highly significant. It would indicate the position of the killer when the stab wounds were delivered and probably to whether the killer was right-or-left-handed.

There were two "through-and-through' necks wounds, including the one with the knife still embedded. The wound running parallel to that one was the one considered to be the one that would have essentially killed her on its own. The large butcher knife had entered the left side of her neck below her ear and literally sliced through her trachea (windpipe) and come out the other side, slicing the jugular vein on the right side of the head. It was then pulled out and a frenzy of stab wounds followed. The wound with the knife still inserted was finally believed to be have been dealt post-mortem.

It was during the attack that Betsy reacted and tried to escape. As her feet kicked out as she lunges from the couch, the hearth carpet is flipped on its back and the cell phone flies from her hand. The phone may have been in her hand when the stab wounds were delivered to her head and left arm, as blood appeared on its surface.

The coroner said the cuts to Betsy's hands and arms could have been defensive wounds as she tried to fend off the attacks. An abrasion on the right side of her shoulder was discussed. It was classified as a possible "rug burn." If Betsy hit the floor immediately after the initial flurry of knife wounds, she may have pushed forward with her feet to avoid the attack and rubbed her shoulder against the carpet. She would have had to have her right side exposed at some point in order for the wounds to the right side of the stomach and arm to have been delivered. There were no "defects" found in the blanket that is still shown wrapped part-way around her in the photos.

Next followed all the gory details of the multiple wounds: She had been knifed in her left ear twice; one going all the way into her ear. There were stab wounds to her left lower eyelid, gashes to her left cheek, stab wounds to her scalp (one chipping the bone) and multiple ones to her neck area. Her left bicep had been penetrated twice, the force of the large knife going completely through the bicep, into the ribcage and finally puncturing a lung. Many incised wounds were found on her forearms and stab wounds to her upper and lower arm areas. Both wrists were slashed, with the most egregious one being the gaping wound on her right wrist that went to the bone. Several deep stab wounds were inflicted upon her stomach area, penetrating into the stomach and liver. Two back wounds penetrated the pancreas and spleen. Only one wound was found on her legs and that was at the top of her left thigh. None were found on the other areas of her feet or legs.

With the penetrating blow to the neck, not only would the shock to the body be horrific, but Betsy's air supply would be cut off. It was also found that blood was entering the body from the wound. She probably suffocated before she bled out, which would have only taken minutes. Finally, the knife was once again inserted into her neck, its tracking parallel to the first one that was through-and-through. There it remained, with a bloody imprint resembling fabric as part of a staged scene.

Fifty-five wounds were listed. A vial of Betsy's blood was collected for DNA purposes and toxicology analysis. It was obvious by the position of the body on the floor, the blanket still half-tucked around her mid-section, and a trail of its fabric behind her, that she had not gotten far once she pushed off from the couch. Her white blood cell count was already low, showing a compromised immune system. She was said to be tired and looking 'blah' by the end of the UPWARDS game that night. Basically, she didn't have a chance against a determined attacker wielding a large knife. As for that knife, Dr. Sabharwal testified it was his belief at the conclusion of the autopsy that all the wounds had been caused by the same knife. If red stains were found on the smaller knife on the kitchen counter, it did not seem to factor into the murder. It appeared the attack had occurred without much physical contact by Betsy against her murderer.

Speaking of physical contact, what of Askey's claim that Russ "violated Betsy one last time" while naked that night, and then killed her. His sperm was found in Betsy. Schwartz pointed out that there were only 8 sperm cells found. Only 8. His forensic specialist stated that there are typically over 100 sperm secreted during intercourse. Russ had admitted that he and Betsy had sex on Sunday, two nights before her murder. That would account for the low count still remaining. Sperm can last up to 72 hours, the expert stated. As for Russ washing up? Schwartz pointed out that there was no blood left in the pipes…anywhere in the house. They had been dismantled and taken away for testing.

As for the damning 911 call and Russ saying his wife had committed suicide, Schwartz pointed out that Betsy was wearing dark clothing which hid most of the wounds. The shock of seeing his wife lying there in a pool of blood with slit wrists and a knife protruding from her neck convinced Russ she must have killed herself, perhaps after hearing bad news during her chemo treatment that day. She had tried to end her life with a knife before. Russ had no idea that there were back wounds included in the over 50 other incisions throughout her torso. He was in shock and his grief was evident in the call to authorities.

Russ and Pam's cell phones were brought up. The Lincoln County investigators had never checked Russ' phone to track his whereabouts that night. Schwartz put his expert cyber technician on the stand, Greg Chatten, who testified that Russ' phone was still 10 miles from his home at 9:25 p.m. that night. It showed up in the cell tower quadrant where his home was at 9:27 p.m. Russ called 911 three minutes later. And Pam's phone?

As stated earlier, it was during Schwartz' cross of Pam Hupp that things fell apart. Question after question was blocked by the prosecution. When Schwartz asked if Pam Hupp's phone had been looked at for its location history, he was told he could not ask that question. He was thwarted again when he asked her about all the inconsistent statements she had made during her testimony with deputies. Askey argued, and was sustained, that he could not cross-examine Pam along those lines, stating it was "impeaching the witness." When the Judge sustained the objection, Schwartz lost it. "I don't know if I should strip naked, tear my hair out, or ram my head into the bench to get your attention!" he shouted.

It did no good. Every time he tried to illicit information from Pam, he was stopped. When he tried to ask about Pam's sudden windfall as Betsy's insurance beneficiary, Askey successfully shut it down before Pam could answer, objecting that Pam "had no direct connection to the case." No direct connection? She was the last person to see Betsy alive that night, and came into $150,000 of her late friend's estate after a last-minute name change on a form. He felt like he was throwing punches at shadows that evaporated before he could land a jab. He had never seen such a case. A defense attorney should be able to cross-examine a witness if their testimony can impact the client's defense. This judge would not open that door.

Judge Mennemeyer finally let Schwartz question Pam about the insurance money outside the hearing of the jury. It's called an "Offer of Proof" procedure. The jury was dismissed and Schwartz squared off against this formidable opponent. When asked why she had only funded the trust set-up for Betsy's daughters just five days before Russ' trial started, Pam answered "My mom just died of Alzheimer's on October 31, that I was taking care of." Pam also added, for the first time, that her son has cerebral palsy. This was never mentioned in a single interview with her. Her grown son, Travis Hupp, lived just down the street from Pam.

Schwartz asked why she had only put $100,000 into the trust instead of the entire $150,000? Pam said, "My other girlfriend died of breast cancer in August, and she has a 12-year-old daughter that I'm trying to help." That family never received any money, and knew nothing of Pam's plan to help them.

The only admission Schwartz got from Pam concerning all her conflicting stories was when she said, "I have a little bit of a memory problem. I'm 55 and going through menopause." During a video-taped deposition the following year on July 21, 2014, Pam was asked if she had memory problems, and she said, "No." Schwartz did make one salient point however. Pam, in defense of Betsy suddenly changing her beneficiary on her policy from Russ to herself, said, "Betsy changed it all the time, depending on who she was mad at." Schwartz countered with the fact that Russ had been on the policy for the ten years it was in effect. It had never been changed before.

Incredible. The jury heard none of this concerning Pam Hupp. Facts that could have given them a "reasonable doubt" as to Russ' guilt were never heard. As far as they were concerned, there was no other person who had a motive for killing Betsy. They never heard that there were 150,000 reasons for another person to be looked at.

Chris Hayes is an investigative journalist for *Fox 2 News*. He covered the Faria murder case more than any other reporter. His list of Emmy awards for outstanding journalism are myriad. He was there in the courtroom during Russ' trial. This author asked him his impression concerning Schwartz's cross-examination of Pam Hupp.

"During Russ' first trial, beyond the tension over Joel Schwartz' being thwarted over asking Pam's questions, it was the bewilderment and trying to understand and take this in, in real time, what was going on. There were two times when she was questioned: one in front of the jury, and one not in front of the jury. I had never experienced the second questioning he did of her called an 'Offer of Proof.' In the end, it did get Russ a second trial. We were just incredulous about this process.

"She was very comfortable and not thrown by anything," Chris said. "Even then, she would talk down to people. There were times that I was thinking Joel Schwartz could be perceived as really much too aggressive to her. Here's this woman that is wearing a TENS device for her hip. I think it's in the police report that she answered the door with a cane when the two officers came to question her the morning after Betsy's death. Pam stated while she was on the stand for Russ's trial that she is wearing a TENS device to stimulate her spinal cord because of some condition she's got. So, because she is sitting there with this device, it seemed at times as if Joel is bullying her on the stand. I mean, "Come on, her mom just died." I think the jury could have thought that at times," Chris Hayes surmised.

Pam Hupp, wearing a TENS device on her hip, leaves the courtroom after her testimony in Russ's first trial, Nov.18, 2013.

That Pam played up her "injuries" was no surprise to anyone. The detectives who interviewed her the morning after Betsy's murder had barely gotten seated before she told them of her back problems and that she used a cane. There is no record that she was ever seen with the cane. When Joel Schwartz talked to Pam's husband, Mark Hupp, in a deposition, Schwartz asked him:

"Are you aware of what her injuries are?"

"No. Not totally," Mark answered.

"At what point in time was she injured?"

"I don't have an answer for that one," Hupp replied.

That conversation is interesting in that Pam and Mark were married during 2009 when Pam said she had her fall into a metal filing cabinet while working at State Farm. She tried to collect monthly disability for that claim. Yet, her husband didn't know when it happened or what her injuries were?

At the end of the testimonies, Russ Faria was put on the stand to satisfy the prosecution that he wished to turn down his right to testify. They wanted to hear it from his own lips, not just from his attorney's. Joel Schwartz approached him and said, "You and I have had extensive discussions regarding your rights to testify?"

"Yes, sir," Russell answered.

"You understand that you have an absolute right to testify and an absolute right not to testify?"

"Yes, sir."

"And what is that decision?" Schwartz asked him as the court reporter typed away.

"Not to testify."

"With a full understanding that you do have the ultimate right if you choose or desire to testify?"

"Yes, sir."

"That's it." Schwartz said.

"State is satisfied," Mr. Hicks declared.

The judge then asked the usual question to the defense attorney at the end of a trial: "Do you want to file your motion?"

"Yes, judge," Schwartz replied. "I would file a Motion for Judgement of Acquittal at the close of the State's Evidence."

Leah Askey began her closing arguments. Joel Schwartz assumed it would be a summation of her case, but what came next shocked him to the core. After going over the damning evidence of the hysterical 911 call, bloody slippers, semen in Betsy, etc., Askey throws out her final theory. To an astonished courtroom, the prosecuting attorney claims that the murder of Betsy Faria was the result of the ultimate role play between Russ and his friends. They had taken the Game Night *Rolemaster* game to its zenith...they had murdered someone.

According to Askey, as soon as Russ heard Pam was bringing Betsy home that night, he decided it was the perfect set-up. Askey said the role players had been talking about it for months, maybe even years. This would be *"the* night," Askey said. And the friends provided Russ with his alibi, cell phone location, and even an Arby's receipt.

Joel Schwartz felt every nerve ending in his body go off. He had previously surmised that Askey was a bit naïve about her declarations during her first murder trial...the whole Russ naked while he's killing Betsy scenario... when there was not one thread of evidence pointing to it. But this? Joel jumped to his feet and told the jury that the prosecutor had just accused four innocent people of being accomplices to a murder!

Still agitated by this latest "Hail Mary" attempt by the prosecution to railroad his client, Schwartz offered his closing arguments to the jury. He attacked Askey's theory that Russ had "violated Betsy one last time" by having sex with her and then showering. "And then what?" he asked sarcastically. Russ redresses Betsy's dead body after he's killed her while they're naked? "There were no irregularities in those stab wounds," Schwartz pointed out. They were inflicted after Betsy was dead to look like rage.

Schwartz went over Russ' alibi again, the video surveillance (how did the prosecution explain those when they were date and time stamped)? According to Askey, Russ did all those on the way to Mike Corbin's house for Game Night, then left his phone with his buddies, went back home and killed Betsy. One problem with that scenario. Pam brought Betsy home at 7:00 and Betsy was on the phone to Pam's husband at 7:04. Pam even said Betsy was alive and well when she left her "at the front door" around 7:21 when Pam headed home. So, Russ shows up minutes after Pam leaves, and kills her, then leaves, and returns at 9:37 p.m. to "discover" his dead wife?

Even a Lincoln County detective would hand-feed Pam that

possibility during another video-taped interview after the trial.

Askey, as prosecuting attorney, was given the final say. She told the jury, whose heads must have been spinning, that "There is no evidence that points anywhere else." Schwartz was on his feet objecting. There *was* other evidence but the jury had not heard it when they were excused during his questions to Pam Hupp. His objection was sustained and the jury asked to disregard Askey's statement. It's hard to unhear something you just heard, simply because you're directed to. One juror even scribbled on his notepad, "They're trying to pin this on Pam Hupp."

Russ Faria (middle) flanked by Joel Schwartz (l) and Nathan Swanson (r). Judge Chris Mennemeyer is in the middle background.

The tension in the courtroom was palpable. This was the telling moment as the jury filed out to deliberate their verdict. Four-and-a-half-long grueling hours went by. Finally, they returned to their seats, eyes averted. Russ would later say that he simply held his breath and tried to keep his legs from giving out from underneath him. It seemed to take forever for the words that would determine the rest of his life.

The verdict was posted as Russ stood barely breathing. Then he heard the words that shattered the still courtroom like a ball breaking glass: "Guilty to First-Degree Murder." His family burst into sobs and Russ held it together for their sake. He was later sentenced to life in prison without the possibility of parole, plus 30 years. It took two beefy bailiffs, one on each side, with Bailiff Dodder holding Russ's arm, to keep Russ from collapsing as he was led out of the courtroom and across the parking lot to the Lincoln County Jail, where he had already spent two years of his life while awaiting his trial. He would be transferred to the Jefferson City Correctional Center to spend his days as a prison inmate.

Russ Faria being escorted from court to the Lincoln County Jail
after receiving a verdict of "Guilty" for murdering his wife.

How in the world did this happen, his mind demanded? He had an air-tight alibi. He loved Betsy. She loved him. He would never hurt her. All the lies Hupp told about him. Why? How could his friends and Betsy's family believe him to be guilty; even taking the stand and testifying against him?

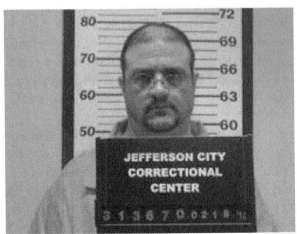

Russ Faria being booked into the Jefferson City Correctional Center
after being convicted of the First-Degree Murder of Betsy Faria.

146

Joel Schwartz assured his client he was not through fighting for him...not even close. This was wrong. There was someone else with a bigger motive and opportunity to kill Betsy Faria than Russ. The jury had not gotten to hear the conflicting evidence. They had been sent from the courtroom during testimony that could have given them 'reasonable doubt' to Russ' guilt. But even as Schwartz gave his client a look of assurance, Russ' world turned on its side, and Bailiff Dodder held him up.

Chapter Ten
"Money Makes People Do Crazy Things!"
--Pam Hupp

Perhaps, with rare exception, do we get a chance to pull back the curtain and see how the act is accomplished. There's an old detectives' adage that says, "Follow the money." Never, was that directive more applicable than with the story of Pam Hupp. When one puts the events surrounding the tragedies revolving around Pam, between 2010 and 2016, in chronological order, the timing is hard to ignore. And with the exception of the murder of Louis Gumpenberger in 2016, it all revolved around money. Yet, the note found in Louis' pocket was all about money. Pam's claims of why Louis was there to kidnap her was all about money. "I'm taking you to the bank to get Russ' money," Pam claimed Louis kept repeating, as he threatened her with a knife.

The murder of Louis Gumpenberger would be two years down the road. Right now, Pam was facing the question of the $150,000 life insurance she inherited when Betsy died. After years of trying to get the money from Pam, Betsy's daughters were finally taking her to court.

Right after Pam received the $150,000 insurance pay-out, she bought a new house in an upscale neighborhood on Shelby Point. From that home, Pam and Mark ran their house flipping business, H2 Partners LLC. The name was changed to H2 Partners Building Solutions in 2014. Pam is listed as President, and a new 2016 GMC Acadia is registered under the business name, as well as for herself and Mark Hupp.

Pam bragged to Lincoln County detectives before Russ' trial, saying, "I have no debt. Still don't have debt. I drive a 2004 car [she bought the Acadia shortly before Louis Gumpenberger's murder]. "I didn't have immediate need for money," she continued, assuaging their suspicion of any need to murder Betsy for money. "Is it great? Yeah. It's great." Pam shrugged off any motive for Betsy's death. "She was dying. If it worked out that way, great...$150,000 when you're not expecting it, that's pretty damn nice, yeah."

Pam elaborated on her monetary mind-set: "I had a life insurance on my son, it's almost like that. I know if our son gets in a car accident or dies, whatever, cuz he's young, I'm going to get that money... You don't think about it. You don't think, 'I'm going to get some *money*... get a boat!'" Interestingly, Pam says she '*had*' a life insurance policy on her son Travis... was it no longer in effect? And, she uses the word 'I'm' twice when referring to who will benefit from her son's policy. Mark Hupp is Travis' father. Is he not included as the beneficiary? Was it because Pam drew up the policy? Her State Farm license number ending in 303 had been activated April 09, 2002. It expired six years later on the same date in 2008.

Lawyers for Mariah and Leah Day weren't as easy on Pam as the Lincoln County investigative team had been. She was pressed to explain a deposit in her bank account. Pam answered that she did not know where it came from:

"Where else would you receive $134,000 from?" the investigator asked, incredulous at her answer.

"I could receive it from anywhere," Pam railed, losing the breezy "I'm your buddy" persona she reserved for the prosecution's detectives and attorney. She was in enemy camp now. "I could receive it from anywhere. I could receive it from my brother. I could receive it from my mother, I could receive it from—what do you think I am, poor? I don't know people? I don't know what you're insinuating."

During one interview, detectives brought up Pam's sale of the house on Shelby Point Drive, which she sold in 2015 after she and Mark purchased it with the proceeds from Betsy's insurance policy.

"You did pretty well," the detective told her. "Because not many people can sell a house for $250,000 these days"

"You haven't seen my house," Pam shot back.

It's true. The house on Shelby Point Drive was a beautiful home. Boasting 4 bedrooms and three bathrooms, it measured 2,065 sf. The house was purchased on March 27, 2012, four months after Betsy's murder. It was listed for sale on May 31, 2012, but the listing was pulled down less than two weeks later on June 12, 2012. It was listed for $184,900. It sold a month later on July 6, 2012 for an undisclosed sum. The property agent is MARIS (Mid America Regional Information Systems) in St. Louis. It was listed June 26, 2015 for $259k. Pam was living at this address when Chris Hayes with *Fox 2 News* interviewed her on January 2014, just after her mother's death, and Russ' conviction.

Pam and Mark Hupp's home on Shelby Point Dr in O'Fallon, MO, shortly after Russ' conviction and Pam's mother's death.

Interior of the home on Shelby Point Dr.

The confusing part is the house's sale history. It seems likely the Hupp's purchased it July 6, 2012 (roughly 7 months after Betsy's murder). Mark and Pam Hupp sold a home they own on Falcon Hill Drive in O'Fallon on July 20, 2012, where it appears they had been living since returning to Missouri from Florida in 2001.

House on Falcon Hill Drive in O'Fallon, Mo. Google Earth

Oddly, the Falcon Hill home follows the same sale history as the Shelby Point home. It is listed 'For Sale' April 5, 2012 for $254,00. Three months later on June 11, 2012, the listing is taken down. One month later, July 16, 2012, it sells for an undisclosed amount. Again, the agent is MARIS. The listings could have been pulled because the properties were under contract, and re-listed because the finances fell through. It could have something to do with auctions. Pam said she bought the Shelby Point house "off the courthouse steps."

The new prosecuting attorney for Lincoln County, MO, Mike Wood, told this author that he "thinks it was during the Civil Trial that Pam testified she had taken Betsy's insurance money, purchased a house, put the house in an LLC, was living in it, and then was renting the house to themselves in the name of the LLC. Those are pretty sophisticated measures that even lawyers use to make yourself judgement proof; to prevent creditors from garnishing your wages, and putting a lien on your house. I have to believe she had invested a lot of time and effort into avoiding creditors," Wood said.

Perhaps that accounted for the fluctuating sales' history on the Hupp's homes.

It is interesting that both the Falcon Hill home and the one on Shelby Point did not list the selling price. The Hupps were in the 'house-flipping business,' so it's hard to know all the details.

Detectives were asking Pam about the insurance money in September of 2013, when they asked if she had put the money in a trust for Betsy's daughters yet, and Pam replied, "No." To recap: She was advised by a detective to put the money in a trust for Mariah and Leah Day before Russ's trial on November 18, 2013. Pam was warned that if she didn't, she may be looked at as a suspect, as she was the last to see Betsy alive and due to "your sudden windfall." Five days before the trial started, Pam created a $100,000 'revokable trust' for the girls, and twenty days after Russ was convicted of Betsy's murder, in December of 2013, Pam drained the account of $99,700. Pam's reason for doing so? "I do this with all my accounts."

Pam's mother took a tragic fall from the balcony of her third-floor apartment on October 30/31, 2013, only a month-and-a-half before Russ' trial, fortuitously leaving Pam $100,000. $100,000 appears in a revokable trust for the girls a little over a month later, just in time before the trial begins. Interestingly, Pam had told the detective in June of 2012, that if her mother died, Pam would receive $500k. Reports show the money was split with her siblings and Pam received only $100k, plus $3,593 for her share of a $10,000 death benefit. Pam's mother died only one year after that interview in September of 2013. Did Pam Hupp murder her mother in order to have $100,000 to put in a revokable trust for Betsy's daughters just before Russ' trial to divert suspicion away from herself concerning Betsy's proceeds? It wouldn't be the last time Pam went to drastic measures to save her skin.

Pam Hupp's Deposition for the Day's Civil Trial

On July 21, 2014, at 9:13 a.m., Pam Hupp walked into a conference room and seated herself in a high-back leather chair. Russ' trial had ended badly for him, and Pam was feeling a surge of confidence. She was there for a video-taped deposition to answer questions in preparation for the civil lawsuit Betsy's daughters were bringing against her. Pam was wearing a pink shirt with a white sweater, nicely coordinating with the maroon wall behind her. She is patently aware of the video camera trained upon her, often facing it as she answers questions, as though it is a jury. At times her look is coquettish, as if she is trying to woo the lens, at other times, the face hardens into the condescending grin for which she is famous.

Across from Pam are the two attorneys representing Betsy Faria's daughters Mariah and Leah Day: David T. Butsch and Christopher E. Roberts. Their questions are heard but the camera stays trained on Pam who at times fidgets with the single gold bracelet on her left wrist. While still very much in control of the flow of her words, there is a slight hesitation at times, and one notices a few facial ticks indicating she may be slightly nervous about the questions coming at her concerning what she did with her dead friend's life insurance money. She also keeps her hands clasped firmly in front of her on the table; uncharacteristically different from the effusive hand gestures we see in her other videoed interviews.

The attorneys wasted no time in honing in on Pam's plans for the money.

"Today, I intend on doing nothing with that money," she stated. On the next question, when asked if she planned to spend the money, Hupp replied, "I do." She then ended the pretense and boldly announced that she had already invested the money in the "housing market."

Pam Hupp during the video-recorded July 21, 2014 deposition.

Hupp's deposition testimony and related exhibits revealed that Hupp established a trust for Faria's daughters in June 2013, primarily because I "felt pressured into it" by the police, the prosecutor, and Faria's family. Hupp funded the trust with $100,000 in November 2013, near the time of Russell Faria's first trial. Hupp stated that she did not place the full $150,000 in trust for the girls because her own mother was suffering from Alzheimer's, and she was trying to guess what some of her mother's medical expenses would be. [Gone is the story of helping a friend dealing with cancer and her own son's cerebral palsy.] Hupp acknowledged that she withdrew $99,700 from the trust in December 2013, stating that "I do that with all my accounts."

Then, if there was any doubt left as to whether Betsy's daughters might still have any chance of getting some of their mother's money, Pam said she revoked the trust entirely a few days before this July 2014 deposition because the Days (Mariah and Leah) had said hurtful things about her in their deposition.

Pam grimacing, looking more strained than in other interviews
where she is controlling the conversation.

The air in the room fills with tension. It's reflected in Pam's messing up on a few details, such as calling Joel Schwartz "Joe," saying '97 when she meant to say '77, and mispronouncing "Faria." She presses her lips and is slow to remove her glasses after reading statements put before her. Pam becomes particularly testy when asked how much she collected from her mother's recent death. At first, she refuses to tell the two attorneys. They remind her of her videoed statement to Detective McCarrick in June of 2012, when she bragged that "when my mom dies, I get half-a-million dollars..." She laughs at them in a condescending manner and then haughtily reminds them that that money had to be split between herself and her siblings.

The two lawyers representing Mariah and Leah got a glimpse of Pam's famous flip-flopping when David Butsch asked her if she was Betsy Faria's best friend. She is "*one* of my best friends," Pam states. And then, only moments later, Pam says, "She was my best friend...Betsy loved me. Whether she said to people I was her best friend, she loved me." This seemed to be something Pam needed to underscore. Butsch asks if she has anything to show that would prove that? Pam feebly says she has cards signed, "Love Betsy."

"She would want me to have whatever she had," Pam said. "In her view, I was rich...in her eyes. She would always tell me I was rich." Pam leans back in the chair amused, "She thought I was rich. She wished she was rich like me. I wasn't rich," she says, and looks uncomfortable. There is a short snort and she looks down at the table as if self-conscious. It seemed an incongruous thing to say. Why would someone give you $150,000 if they thought you were doing so well? Oddly, she had also confided during her upcoming civil trial that "Betsy had gone for food stamps, two weeks before..."

"Did she mention to you that she wanted the money to be used for her daughters?" the lawyers asked her.

"Absolutely not," was the short answer.

Pam had been videoed in June 2012, telling Detective McCarrick why Betsy would want her to have the money instead of Russ or her daughters. Pam told him that Betsy was afraid Russ would "piss away" the money, either on gambling, or in his grief, blow it all at once on the girls. Pam was going to set up milestones for the girls so that the money would be doled out when needed. She told McCarrick that "in honor of Betsy" I will hold them to certain "criteria," such as no spending it on wild parties, cars, etc. Now, she blatantly said she and Betsy had never had a conversation concerning the $150,000 as to it being set aside for her girls. Yet, it was all on video.

When Butsch asked Pam about using the trust money to buy the house on Shelby Point, once again she changes her story and says she didn't use the trust money to buy the house. Pam had just told them earlier in this same interview that she had already invested the $100,000 in the "housing market." She now claims she cashed in her IRAs from "MetLife with Little Snoopy." Always one to toss in a line that made the situation lighter, "Little Snoopy" was to defuse a tense moment. It didn't.

To wrap up things once and for all, in Pam's mind, she calmly said, "It's a revokable trust, so I revoked it."

While Pam's confidence in the matter seemed to indicate she felt she had won this round, the attorneys saw it as something else...something Russ' attorney, Joel Schwartz should know about. When the phone rang in the attorney's office, he felt the call was 'Manna from Heaven.' He leaned back in his chair, stared at the portrait of Marilyn Monroe hanging on his wall (a gift from an artist who could not pay his legal bill), and smiled. This could be what he and Nathan Swanson had been praying for.

The Mooney Motion

A Mooney Motion is a motion an attorney can file for his client based upon newly discovered evidence. After David Butsch called Joel Schwartz, following Pam Hupp's deposition for Mariah and Leah Day's civil case, Joel felt he had that new evidence he needed. Pam Hupp had closed out the trust that she had set up for Betsy's daughters. If the Court of Appeals would look at this new finding, along with the fact that Pam was the last to see Betsy alive, and had only been named beneficiary to her $150,000 life insurance policy only four days before Betsy's murder, Russ might get a new trial.

Joel was hopeful but cognizant of the fact that a Mooney Motion had been granted only three times previously in the State of Missouri. It was rare to have one approved. But he told Russ that he was going after it. The jury had not heard all the evidence in Russ' trial...not even close. They were out of the room when he cross-examined Pam. They never heard about the life insurance money, Pam's conflicting stories, driving Betsy home that night, etc. He crossed his fingers and waited.

To his surprise, his motion was granted! A judge would listen to his new evidence and decide if Russ would get a new trial. He was also delighted to get a new judge to hear him out. Steven Ohmer would sit the bench.

One week before the Mooney Motion hearing, on May 27, 2015, Pam Hupp and prosecutor Leah Askey entered Room 2—an interrogation room at the Lincoln County Sheriff's Office. What followed would baffle many who watched the video-taped conversation. Pam is wearing an electric blue short-sleeved shirt and her ubiquitous capri-length pants…this time denim. Pam appears to be carrying a large Dierberg's bag. Leah Askey sits across from her dressed in a black dress suit and heels.

Pam Hupp entering Room 2 with Leah Askey May 27, 2015.
This is possibly the Dierberg's bag with cash inside.

In this pre-trial meeting with Prosecuting Attorney Leah Askey, shortly before Russ Faria's second trial, Pam is seen within seconds of entering the room turning to look up at the police video camera she is all-too familiar with. What happens in the next few seconds (around the 12:51 marker) is telling. With her right hand, she grabs the top of the chair and moves it over further into the room, and then glances up at the camera again, making sure she is in the camera's viewpoint. Why? The discussion during this meeting will make it very clear.

Pam Hupp moving the chair and looking up at the camera
at the 12:52/53 marker on the video.

The two discuss the $150,000 life insurance proceeds that Pam got after Betsy's death. They talk about how Pam promised to give Betsy's daughters some money, and then refused, finally revoking the trust. In the video, Pam is leaning forward and becomes emotional. Her voice is strained, hands emphatic, as she says, "The more people kept telling me to do it, the more I didn't want to do it," she said, yet another explanation for why Mariah and Leah never saw a dime of the money. "I didn't!" she says. "It was really pissing me off!" Leah Askey commiserates with her and says, "You were getting bullied."

They then discuss what results they think the Mooney Motion will have. Pam asks Askey what she thinks the chances are of an outcome in "their" favor. It's as if she and Askey are a team now. Askey reassures her, and goes into a mud-slinging campaign against Schwartz, accusing him of asking for the hearing due to his "feelings being hurt" after he lost Russ' trial. The two agree with each other like two old chums as they denigrate the attorney. Incredulously, Pam says, "I believe in the system, but it's so tainted now." They also complain about the invasiveness of all the media coverage.

What's so odd about the entire meeting is that Askey was the prosecuting attorney against Russ. She wasn't representing Pam, yet they are sharing insights, gossip, and important information that a PA should not be stating aloud...in front of a running video camera!

Finally, the topic changes to Pam's mother's recent death seven months prior. This is where Pam's voice cracks as she tells of how they had to "sell everything" Shirley had to get her into the condo where she died. "But to everybody else on this planet," Pam says emotionally, "I took a 210-pound woman and *threw* her through railings! How do you do that? How does a *man* do that?" Once again, Askey soothes Hupp by saying, "I know how stories get started."

During an interview with Mike Wood, the residing Lincoln County Prosecutor, he told this author something very poignant about that Dierberg's bag Pam brought in to show Leah Askey:

"What I found curious, is that between Trial 1 and Trial 2, is that I can see a lot of communication between Prosecutor Askey and Pam where Askey is saying 'Look, I need to know where this money is, do you have this money, because we're coming up on Trial 2 and I need to know where the money is.' Leah's concern was, it would diminish Pam's credibility as a witness if that money was gone.

"At that point, Pam had liquidated the money from the trust," Wood continued, "she had dissolved the trust, and that's when, I'm sure you heard the scandal, about Pam showing up here at the Prosecutor's office with a bag of cash and saying, 'Look, it's right here, I didn't spend it, like I told you, I didn't need to murder for the money because I have it here..." She literally brought in a bag of cash to show Leah that she had the money. The question I always ask myself is, 'What does a $100k in a Dierberg's bag look like? Did they count it?' When you have cash, you don't know where the source of those funds came from. She could have borrowed against any account, taken it out of a credit card and put it back in; we don't know. The point is, that Pam brought in a bag of cash to show Leah to establish she still had the money and hadn't spent it, which was Joel Schwartz' argument, that if you're in financial distress, you would have spent the money."

What Schwartz, Swanson, and others who watched the footage found incredulous, was that this entire conversation was video-taped. Askey had to know it would be on the record. All the gossiping about the case, the injured ego of Schwartz, her need for Pam to tell her where the money is or it will hurt her case...all of it! Pam saw it as good PR. She got her story out, not only about why she hadn't given the girls any money, but that she had the money here in a large tote bag. Plus, she put on an emotional portrayal of how she couldn't have killed her mother. Her chair positioned perfectly for the camera, she may have been the smarter head in the room.

Or, the entire meeting between the two women was orchestrated. Askey knew it would be recorded. Pam made sure her chair was in perfect position for the camera. If you look at what was discussed before that voyeuristic lens, it served both women equally. Askey was desperate to keep Russ in prison and uphold the original verdict, vindicating her and her team for their work. The one thing that could give the judge reasonable doubt as to Russ' guilt was Pam. Let's head it off and have Pam actually show up at the interview with cold, hard cash to prove she still had it. It's hard to hold a bank statement up and have the camera zero in on it...but cash? That's hard to ignore.

Leah Askey also got in her licks against Schwartz, delighting in the denigration as she and Pam slammed his ego. Finally, Pam got in her denial of hurting her mother, using emotion rarely seen. Had the meeting been planned, just before the Mooney Motion hearing?

May, 2015, was a busy month. Mark Hupp was brought in for a deposition and testified about his and Pam's finances. He stated that Pam never told him why Faria had named Hupp as beneficiary, that he was not aware whether she ever told him she intended to use the money for her mother's medical bills, and that he could not recall whether she ever told him that she used the $50,000 of the insurance proceeds to help the family of a friend with breast cancer.

Mark further testified that he and Pam had been married for 32 years, that she had back problems, that he was not aware she was ever diagnosed with memory issues, and that she did not suffer from dementia or any condition of that nature. During the civil case trial, Mark testified about his and Pam's finances and their various house purchases since receiving the life insurance proceeds.

It was finally time for Russ Faria's hearing. Judge Steven Ohmer listened for almost two hours as Joel presented what he had during the Mooney Motion hearing. The judge listened, and left the room at 11:00 a.m. to take it under consideration. He said he would be back with his ruling at 1:30 p.m. Joel waited anxiously while Russ paced in his jail cell. The hours dragged. He was almost afraid to envision himself a free man: hoisting a beer again with friends, hugging his family, and feeling the wind in his face as he rode his Harley down streets he had almost forgotten.

Judge Steven Ohmer

1:30 p.m. arrived and Judge Omer did not return from chambers. At 1:45, Joel was feeling nervous. Finally, at 2:00, he asked one of the Sheriffs if there was a problem. To approve an appeal does not take long. To deny it requires more paperwork and Joel was fearful that the delay was not a good sign. All he could think of was having to face Russ with the bad news if they were denied a new trial. The Sheriff looked into the anxious face of the attorney and simply said the judge was late because there was a "printer problem." Judge Omer returned to the courtroom minutes later and took his seat. Joel waited, heart hammering. After a few moments of silence, Ohmer looked at Joel and said the words he had been hoping for. The judge agreed there was enough here for an appeal. Russ' second trail was granted. It will be held soon—five months later, in November.

The walk to the jail cell where Russ Faria was waiting was one that felt lighter than air for attorney Joel Schwartz. Finally, good news for Russ. Russ grabbed him, hugged him, and lifted him off his feet. It was one of those moments you never forget. "It was fulfilling at that point," Joel Schwartz said, in a huge understatement. Russ was released on bond until his second trial could take place. He walked into the waiting arms of his mother, relatives, and friends. Someone plopped a St. Louis Cardinals baseball cap on his head, and cheers were heard from the waiting crowd.

Russ Faria hugs his family as he's released on bond pending his second trial. Photo courtesy of *St. Louis Post-Dispatch*.

Now Joel and his co-counsel Nathan Swanson had to roll up their sleeves and put together a case that was as air-tight as they could make it. The prosecution and investigative team from Russ' first trial were compelled to hand over everything they had in the form of "discovery." It was here that the darkness veiling this case since the night of December 27, 2011, beneath that sliver of moon, began to recede, illuminating new truths. Yet, the truths coming to light were, in Joel Schwartz's words, "very troubling."

Leah Askey and her investigators also began preparing for trial number two. They would reinvestigate the case and that meant questioning witnesses again. And their star witness? Pam Hupp.

162

Chapter Eleven
"Oh, What a Wicked Web We Weave..."

The events leading up to Russell Faria's second trial for the murder of Betsy Faria was akin to a Shakespearean play. In a saga that many had thought could not get any stranger, prosecuting investigators and Pam Hupp scripted scenarios that would defy reason.

On June 17, 2015, detectives for the prosecution, Patrick Harney and Mike Merkle, brought Pam in for an interview. Russ's trial loomed only four months ahead and Askey and the Lincoln County Sheriff's Office needed to nail this case. Were they so desperate to find new evidence, that they would ask investigators to lead a key witness by offering them a murder theory? Evidently so:

Detective Sergeant Patrick Harney is speaking to Pam Hupp: "Here's what I'm going to offer you. Like Detective Merkel and I have said, we were the first detectives at the house and we have spoken in *theory* before about what we believe may have happened. Russ knew that you were there, whether by phone call or just the sheer presence of your car. So, now I'm going to hand that to you and ask, is any part of that correct, and is in fact, did you see Russ that night?"

Pam answers a short, "No."

Pam returns in October, four months after this interview, after thinking it over, and has a new recollection of the night Betsy died. Over three-and-one-half-years after the murder, Pam suddenly remembers something important and goes back to the two detectives. She suddenly remembers seeing a car parked along the side street next to the Faria home on that dark evening. She picks up the thread. Once again, it is recorded:

"Two men sitting in there. Two. Two men," Pam says, excitement in her voice, as she describes seeing a car.

Detective Harney: "And you think you recognized one of those men?"

Pam: "I do. Yes."

Harney: "And who do you think you believe...who do you believe that person was?"

Pam: "I believe it was Russ! ...I saw someone duck," Pam says, stating that one of the men ducked inside the car so she would not see them.

Pam had 13 interviews with the police. Inside those investigations, her stories changed frequently, sometimes within minutes. In the same June, 2015, interview with Harney and Merkle, Pam elaborated on where she went when she left Betsy's house that night, now aware that her cell phone location data had belied her original statement. In Pam's first interview she said that she called Betsy the night of the murder at 7:27 p.m. to tell her she was home safely. The cell phone data proved that was impossible. Pam had to have a reason why she was still within the cell tower quadrant *at* or near Betsy's house at that time. For Pam Hupp, coming up with a new story was child's play:

"She was very angry 'cuz she wanted me to stay and I left anyway, and I got partway down there where it starts to fork off, and I stopped and I called her 'cuz I was pissed. [Laughing] I didn't want her to be mad."

"Right," Harney agrees.

And so, rather than go back and confront Betsy or wait until she got home to see if Betsy was still "mad," Pam says she waited at that fork in the road not far from Betsy's home "maybe ten or fifteen minutes. Then I left and still had a...get the hell out of Troy." [Laughing]

It is Pam's light-hearted banter...the occasional laugh...the verbiage, that seems to cast a spell on all who talk to her. The detectives got what they were hoping for. They succeeded in leading Pam to give them the information about seeing two men the night of the murder, parked by the Faria home...and according to Pam, one of them was Russ.

The newly found "eye-witness" statement from Pam, about seeing Russ that night as she left Betsy's house, was just one of the things coming to light that troubled Joel Schwartz as he prepared for the second trial. It was about to get sinister.

Strange Evidence

As Schwartz and Swanson poured over the new photographs that were handed over by the prosecution—132 in all—they found something that made their hackles stand up. It was now that they realized the officer's statement on the stand during Russ' first trial had been false. He testified that a Bluestar Luminol Test had been conducted at the crime scene and that it showed a trail of blood leading to the kitchen, where Russ had said he went after finding Betsy's body. During that same testimony from the stand, this officer said there had been a camera malfunction and those photos had not developed...they were "black." The jury would have to take his word for it.

Mike Wood, current Lincoln County prosecutor.
Photo courtesy of PA Mike Wood.

Mike Wood, the current prosecuting attorney for Lincoln County, has been painstakingly going over the same evidence that Schwartz and Swanson saw, plus a lot of new leads as he prepares for a new case…this time without Russ as the accused murderer. He told this author in a phone conversation more information about what occurred with the Luminol test:

"Initially the case came over and the prosecutor said, 'We don't have enough to charge this man. I'm going to need more evidence.' So, what they do is, they get a search warrant for the house…what I think is important to point out is that the house had already been *released* back to Russ, so it was not a secure crime scene. What they did at that point…they do the Bluestar, and they come back and they say, 'Bluestar hit, it glowed really well, which is an indicator that there was a clean-up.'

"The problem that we had was that they took photographs of it," Mike continues, "which was appropriate, but then 15 months later, they draft a report that says they had conducted this Luminol search. Then they said there was an error with the camera and the camera malfunctioned and they couldn't turn over the photographs of the Luminol. Mind you, I will also point out that there was a report that indicated that the Luminol test came back 'not blood.'

"When the Luminol hits, it's presumptive," Wood stated, "but it's not conclusive until a lab says 'Yes, that's blood, or 'No, it's not blood.' All you can say at that point is, is that it's bodily fluid. So then, the prosecution never turns over to the defense the report regarding the search. The photographs were never turned over as well. It wasn't until Russ' Trial Two that the photographs were then turned over to the defense, and the shocking point was that when you look at the photographs, there is nothing there! And by nothing there, I don't mean that they didn't develop, I mean that the Luminol they tested to didn't exist showing a massive clean-up. They used that to bolster the case to show there was probable cause to move forward with the prosecution.

"The quality and substance of that evidence was manufactured to lead the prosecution to believe it was a lot stronger than what it actually was," Wood said. "That's what got the case moving. Yet, that never materialized. That's part of the problem I have because I think, in my mind, that they knew the photographs didn't show what they wanted them to show, so they just lied and said, 'Oh, well, there's a camera malfunction and that's why you don't have the photos.'

"The testimony of one of the crime scene investigators in St. Charles was that there wasn't any clean-up because it was obvious to investigators on the scene at the time of the murder that the house was grimy and dirty," Wood continued. "After the house is released back to Russ, now they go in and say, 'Look, there's all this evidence of clean-up.' Once the strength of that evidence is questioned, when the crime scene isn't secure anymore, and you've got a witness testimony of a technician who was on the scene at the time saying there was no clean-up, you've got a problem," Mike Wood stated, clearly upset at the lengths the former prosecution team went to.

"I think the Search Warrant was served on January 3rd or 4th, and the murder occurred on the 27th. It was like a two-day span before they turned the house back to Russ. I don't know if that information came from the State that Russ's cousin, Mary, had told his attorneys that 'Yeah, it was a fresh murder scene, of course we were trying to clean the house up as much as we could, because law enforcement had been in there for days.' That didn't seem unreasonable to me at all. It wasn't indicative, because the lab reports came back and said, it wasn't blood. So, what are we even talking about?"

The house had been searched, furniture stacked, a Luminol test done, and the house returned to Russ. He was at Betsy's funeral January 3rd and arrested on the 4th. His family began the heart-wrenching task of cleaning up the mess. But the prosecution used their cleaning to say the scene had been tampered with and a clean-up of evidence had been undertaken. To all who went over just this one piece of the "troubling" data coming in, it was hard to wrap their minds around.

"I especially don't want to go to sleep at night feeling like I've sent somebody to prison who didn't deserve to go to prison," Mike Wood said, "and I think that's also part of the reason that they pushed so hard on Trial Two, is they thought, no one wanted to reconcile the fact that this man was really innocent."

Russ had been in prison for over three years on the charges that he killed Betsy. Had an officer testifying for the prosecution perjured himself on the stand? It's a strong allegation. But if Schwartz thought the Luminol test results were the high note, Pam was about to hit an octave a soprano would covet.

"Betsy Loved Me!"

Inside the new evidence sent over to Joel Schwartz' office was a tape recording of Pam speaking to Detective Mike Merkle. The second trial was coming up fast and the defense attorneys were working overtime to understand all the moving parts. But when Russ Defense Attorney Nathan Swanson heard the newly released recording, he was in shock. The voice was Pam Hupp's and she had saved the best for last:

"So, our relationship started pretty soon...fast...I was a huge confidant of hers. So, she knew that she could talk to me about *any*-thing. So, we had a special bond that way. We spent a whole lot of time together, you know. I did...I replaced what a husband would be."

Nathan Swanson sat in his chair, jaw hanging. She did not just say what he thought she was saying! Surely not! Did he just hear that Pam and Betsy had an affair?

"It's honestly a relationship with two women who really aren't attracted to women," Pam said, in her usual breezy, chatty style. No hint was given in her dialogue that she was dropping a bombshell.

"It's not...I'm attracted to men. Love everything about them. Can't wait for *Magic Mike XL* to come out...but she's the same way. It's not like she was a lesbian or anything like that. It wasn't such an evolution of emotional trauma for her."

Pam underscored Betsy's love for her. "She had a mad crush on me. She really, really, really loved me at that time, and it just kept growing from that. She started indicating that she wanted more from me than just, you know, a friend. And I was, it's just not gonna happen. I loved Betsy. I'm not *in* love with her. Never was *in* love with her. She was in love with me. She was *in* love, and at that point, when I knew what was happening with her and my friend, I just let that go because it was a small, small thing to give her."

Pam goes on in almost a monotone voice, as if this is of no consequence: "We were drinking wine and stuff like that. She'd start crying or whatever. You try to console and whatever. It wasn't that many times. It's just something I sacrificed...for her...because it's no big deal to me."

The last part of that statement was said almost in a whisper, but to

Schwartz and Swanson, it may as well have been a sonic boom. Pam was not finished, not by a long shot.

After Pam's sudden admission to being Betsy's lover, she finally exploded the bomb with the follow-up conversation with Detectives Merkel and Harney. It was *now* that Pam's reason for this sudden revelation would come to light. As the audio recorder ran, Pam embellished her story, and this time, it was about Russ, and his supposed jealousy at finding Pam and Betsy together *in flagrante delicto*.

"He pushed me against the wall," Pam said. "He was all red-faced..."

"Kind of like gritted teeth?" the detective chimes in, eagerly adding filler statements as Pam goes on.

"Oh, he's about this far away from my face...Yeah! He was right there. I could feel his spit. Nasty! And he said, 'You two muff-thumpers, something to that effect, if I ever catch you together again, I'll bury you out in the back yard.'"

"Just a few weeks prior to her being killed?"

"Yes."

So now, three-and-a-half-years later, Pam has not only remembered seeing Russ with another man parked just down the street from the Faria home the night of the murder, she now decides to expose her "affair" with Betsy, *and* Russ' rage over finding out about it. Why? It gives the ultimate reason why Betsy would change her life insurance proceeds to Pam instead of Russ. Afterall, Pam had "replaced what a husband would be." And Russ' rage? Pushing her up against the wall and threatening to kill them if he caught them together again? It was all right there. Pam saw him in a car, "ducking down" when she looked his way; he had seen her leave his house where she had been alone with Betsy, doing *Heaven knows what* with his wife; and all the insurance money was going to Pam. Everything Pam could think of to set this man up as the killer was handed to the detectives in this last interview, only months before Russ' second, and only, shot at freedom. For the prosecution team, Santa had just come early.

Pam was desperate. Everyone knew Schwartz was going to name her as the real murderer. This time, the judge was going to let in all the evidence Schwartz had against Pam that had been hidden from the jury in the first trial. And this time, Joel was going for a bench trial. There would be no jury. Only a judge would hear the case. And that judge, Steven Ohmer, was the same judge who had just granted Schwartz an appeal in the form of a Mooney Motion hearing. He had heard the new evidence...and let Russ out of prison on bail.

Russ' defense attorneys may have been thrown by Pam's new recordings about she and Betsy's affair and Russ' rage. They didn't think anyone would believe it, and indeed, everyone they interviewed laughed at the notion. Betsy liked men. There had been a few brief affairs during her marriage to Russ, and he had engaged in one as well, but there was never anything that showed Betsy with another woman. With as many times as Pam's stories changed—and they changed with every one of her 13 police interviews—they hoped the judge would see this as a desperate attempt to keep Russ behind bars, and for Pam to keep the insurance money as well.

If Schwartz and Swanson thought this whole "affair" was nonsense, the next discovery was a lot more threatening to their defense. Their cyber expert had found the email on Betsy's laptop that Pam had been telling them about since the first police interview the morning after Betsy died. The email Pam said Betsy wrote her telling her of Russ putting a pillow over her face, the insurance beneficiary change...all of it. When the two attorneys read the letter, it was as if a black cloud had just scudded across the sky outside their office window. It is only two weeks until the start of Russ' second trial.

That Letter

Greg Chatten is a Forensic IT Specialist who worked with Joel Schwartz and Nathan Swanson on the Betsy Faria murder case. He's a cyber expert.

"I've been involved in IT in one way or another since 1976," Greg Chatten told this author. "I figured out a way to go back and recover as much data as the customer needed by doing forensics on the crashed hard drive. I did a Galaxy Note 20 phone...a brand new one. I intentionally did a factory reset which they say is supposed to clear everything out. Now you are thinking, 'Ok, now my phone is safe to sell or throw away, or whatever.' I did forensics on it and almost all of my text messages were recovered, my call log, my contacts. I couldn't see them on the phone, but through forensics I found them. I just found out that when you do a factory reset it doesn't erase all that stuff permanently. This happens a lot more in civil trials. I'm working on one right now where someone deleted a bunch of data, and said, 'Oh, I didn't copy it from the company,' and I just laugh. When they got sued, they had to send in their thumb drives and any removable drives and I get them and I'm like 'Yeah, you deleted the stuff, and I just recovered it.' And we won that case, and it involved 21 computers!

"I did not know about the letter meta data until the second trial," Chatten continues, "about the letter that Pam Hupp put on Betsy's computer. "The Club" was the Wi-Fi that was connected to the laptop at the time with a date and time stamp, and it matches perfectly, because Betsy would have been on the tennis court. That was the one at the second trial that I went "Oh, my God! We've got her!" Betsy did not have a lot of Word documents, but she had enough where you can get a feel for her style of writing and her sentences. Betsy was quite refined in her writing. I came across that document, and I'm like 'Betsy didn't write this.' That's where my curiosity was sparked because it was not the way she wrote.

"I dug into what they call the meta data, which is data that Microsoft hides in the file," Chatten said. "You can see it in Word when you go to look for it, and then there are some items that don't show up on the computer, but I can get them, and that's when I found out the 'Author' doesn't match any of the documents on Betsy's computer. Plus, the machine name was not correct. Then, when I checked the Wi-Fi and I checked the date and time of that particular Word document, everything just matched up. Betsy was not in possession of the laptop at that time. She was either playing tennis or on the court at that time.

"I believe Pam had already constructed the letter and downloaded it to a thumb drive. There are a couple of ways that she could have gotten it on there," Chatten said. "The easiest way is to throw it on a thumb drive, because that's fast, and then you just stick it in the laptop and copy it over. There was a thumb drive inserted into that laptop during that time range, as well. I can tell the date a thumb drive was first inserted and the date they were last inserted. It gives me a serial number. Could Pam have created the letter at the tennis court? I don't know. I think it would be stupid. [She would need her laptop, as well as Betsy's and sit there and type out a letter, download it, and then put it on Betsy's laptop. It was easier to just bring the thumb drive containing the fake letter along with her.]

"I asked for Pam Hupp's computer," Chatten continued. "They said, 'She doesn't have it.'" She never turned it over. She told the cops 'I don't have anything,' or she said it broke or something else that was total BS. Everyone had a computer then. I was going to go looking for the letter if I had Pam Hupp's computer, whether or not it was still there or whether it had been deleted. Since we can recover deleted files, that was primarily what I wanted off Pam Hupp's computer and anything else that might be incriminating. We never got a Pam Hupp computer of any type. We just got her phone."

West James Tennis Courts, St. Charles, MO.

The data retrieved from the letter on Betsy's laptop pointed to someone other than Betsy writing that document. It was the only document in the computer that said 'Author Unknown.' The letter was also written on Word 97; a software not installed on Betsy's laptop. Pam admitted to going with Betsy that day to watch her play tennis at the West James Tennis Club. These are indoor courts, and the Wi-Fi that shows up as the one used to upload that document is 'The Club.' Pam asked the detectives several times shortly after Betsy's murder to look for that letter. She even knew what was in the letter, and that it was on Betsy's laptop. If Pam had hoped the letter would be the final nail in Russ' coffin when it was found, it backfired. Technology and a cyber expert by the name of Greg Chatten turned the tables on her.

The letter read:

> Pam,
>
> I know we talked about this yesterday, but I feel I really need you to believe me. I really do feel that Russ is going to do something to me. Last night (Wednesday), he asked me why I came home instead of staying at my mom's. I told him I had things to do. He was very angry with me for being in the house. I couldn't figure out why. Then I caught him with my lap top. He was reading my emails. When I asked him about it, he said he could do what he wants. He said I won't be around much longer, so what do I care. He continued to tell me how much money he would make after I die. He has been talking like this for months. He wants me to stay at my mom's, he likes the house to himself. He tells me it's his house and I'm just a guest. Right now, I stay at my mom's, linda's or a friends for most of the week. I was home last night and have to go back on Friday for the weekend. My mom has a friend staying with her from out of town so Idon't have a bed to sleep in. Last night was the worst. I fell a sleep on the couch while watching tv. I woke up to Russ holding a pillow over my face. I didn't know what was going on. I broke loose and started to scream at him asking him what he was doing. He said that he wanted me to know what dying feels like. I need to change my life insurance policy out of his name, but can't let him know that I have taken him off as beneficiary. I need your help with this. I can't give it to my girls because they will blow it. Do you think I could put it in your name and you could help my daughter's when they need it? I really need to talk to you about this. I am so tired from cancer. I am so afraid of staying out in Troy alone with Russ. If anything happens to me would you please show this to the police.

The text in the letter is as it was found, with misspellings and grammar. There are important points to this letter that are poignant to this case:

1-Pam is very fond of the word "really." Her interviews are peppered with it. She even uses it three times in a row when describing her affair with Betsy: "She really, really, really loved me." She is heard saying repeatedly during taped interviews: "If you *really* check your information…if you *really* listen to my phone messages…if you *really* read those texts…" The word "really" shows up three times in this letter—twice in the first two sentences.

2-Interesting as well is the sentence in the letter about Russ looking at her laptop. It was important to put when this happened…Wednesday. It's typed in parenthesis. Why was it necessary to point out which night Betsy caught Russ reading her emails? Because if Russ is looking at Betsy's emails on Wednesday, would he also be looking at them on Thursday? Thursday was the day the fake letter was uploaded to Betsy's laptop at the tennis court accusing Russ of horrible things. Seeing that letter would make Russ very angry.

3-Again, it's mentioned that Betsy will begin staying at her mother's house on Friday for the weekend. Friday was the day Betsy and Pam went to the library in Winghaven to have the change of beneficiary form witnessed. Betsy did not spend the weekend with her mother. It was Christmas weekend. She spent it with Russ. She only spent Monday night—the night before her murder—at her mother's house. Yet, Pam harped on the fact that Betsy was gone all weekend from her house, and that her purse had been left at home *all* weekend. Why? Pam mentions to detectives the morning after Betsy's death that Betsy was gone all weekend. She brings it up three times. Now we see it again in this letter—that she was leaving Friday to go back to her mom's for the weekend. She also stayed Monday night and had chemo on Tuesday. That would mean, Betsy left for her mom's right after the trip to the library on Friday to sign the policy proceeds over to Pam. Was Pam adamant about saying Betsy was gone all weekend because it meant the first time Russ could confront her about the change of beneficiary would be Tuesday night? The night she died?

4-The letter states that Betsy "fell asleep on the couch while watching tv." Where was Betsy murdered? On the couch while watching TV. If the letter is to be believed, Russ put a pillow over Betsy's face while she was lying on that couch, the same night Russ was looking at her emails. Had he gone from the pillow threat to using a knife less than a week later? Is that why a knife is found under the couch pillows where Betsy was murdered? Was it supposed to appear as if Betsy kept a knife there because she was afraid of Russ, or that Russ put it there to have it handy?

5-Finally, the reason for why Pam is named the beneficiary on Friday (one day after the email is created) is listed.

The letter was a neatly laid out blueprint for murder. Years went by before Greg Chatten recovered it from Betsy's laptop. If Pam wrote it, one has to wonder if she was disappointed it had not turned up yet. In the long run, Russ was convicted and went to prison. It was a moot point then. Or was it?

The laptop letter/document was uploaded to Betsy's laptop only one day before the visit to the Winghaven library to have the life insurance put into Pam's name. It was uploaded only five days before Betsy was murdered. Pam had pointed it out repeatedly to the detectives the morning after Betsy's death, begging them to look at Betsy's laptop and find it. It never surfaced…then years go by. Pam must have assumed it would never be found. Here's the rub: Pam has just revoked Betsy's daughters' trust, emptied the account, and made it abundantly clear she was keeping the money and that Betsy never told her to give it to the girls. Yet now, if this letter is to be believed, Betsy, in own words, is telling Pam in the letter to take care of her girls with the money!

The irony is that if the letter had not been found out to be a fake, and it was written by Betsy, Pam's case for keeping the money for herself would have crumbled. As it was, the letter was immediately proven by Greg Chatten to be put there by someone else at a time when Pam was at the tennis club watching Betsy play tennis. It was also proven to be impossible to have been created on Betsy's laptop. By it being proved a fake, Pam had dodged a bullet where the money was concerned, but the letter helped fashion a noose for herself for Betsy's murder as the probable creator of the document. As they say, 'timing is everything.'

Russ is portrayed in the letter as a monster. Pam had recently told detectives that Russ caught she and Betsy in a compromising situation and pushed her up against the wall, threatening to "bury them in the backyard," words Betsy's sister Mary had quoted on the stand at Russ' first trial. Had Pam borrowed them? Yet, less than a week after this letter was composed, Betsy is murdered and Pam is interviewed by detectives the following morning. Pam told the detectives most of what was in the letter...including the pillow incident. But when the detectives ask Pam about Russ the morning after the murder, she says, "He seems nice enough. I just don't know him that well." Nice enough? The man who pushed her up against the wall and threatened to kill them both? To keep track of Pam's changing stories was akin to keeping plates spinning atop poles before one crashed to the floor.

In the June 2015, interview with Detective Merkel, just after the confession that she and Betsy had been lovers, Pam plays the sympathy card. Ironically, she is accusing others of "inconsis—flat-out lies..." She stops short of finishing the word "inconsistencies." "When people say a lie about me," Pam said, "I make it a point to prove them wrong, if I can. I'm not a perfect person, not even really a nice person..." In a voice filled with emotion, she laments how she has been treated, including accusations of fraud, and claiming she has been "drug through the mud."

As Merkel listens, seemingly empathetic, she finishes with a bold statement: "If you *really* want the truth, you're going to get it...Might as well go all the way with it."

Merkel asked Pam in a hesitant voice, "As far as 'going all the way with it,' how far—how close are we to that?" Pam avoided answering.

Joel and Nathan looked over all the evidence and felt they had a strong case. It was not only all the information they had about Pam Hupp, but more insidious still, was all the data coming in about possible subterfuge going on behind the scenes through the prosecution of Russ' first trial.

A print-out of an email was sent anonymously to Schwartz, just before the second trial. The email appeared to be sent to Prosecutor Leah Askey from Mike Lang, who was the acting captain of investigations for Lincoln County at the time. It was a love letter.

"This is not a puppy dog crush on the hot girl in high school kind of love, this is an epic, shit stories are written about kind of love. I will do my best to be everything you need," it read. If what Schwartz was beginning to believe was true, that the two had been complicit in manufacturing "evidence" and framing Russ, then it would appear that Lang had indeed been "everything you need" to the prosecutor.

Askey denied the affair and said the email had been "doctored." Neither she nor Lang would answer questions concerning it. Schwartz looked over his notes and saw that it was Lang who had not requested Russ' cell phone data the night of the murder. It was Greg Chatten, Schwartz' IT expert, who had located those records, and they backed up Russ' alibi.

The defense team may have been holding their breath, wondering what else Pam or the prosecution would come up with next. Russ' second trial was making headlines and people were lining up for gallery seats. The question on everyone's lips was "Would Pam Hupp take the stand?"

Chapter Twelve
Russ Faria's Second Chance

As Pam continued to fill the prosecution team's coffers with more and more "remembered" information, oddly, she also began to offer herself a way out of all the lies she had told. When asked if she had memory problems during her deposition for the upcoming civil trial, filed by Betsy's daughters, Pam simply said, "No," pressed her lips together and shook her head. Yet, in the two final interviews with Merkel and Harney leading up to Russ' second trial, Pam begins to offer a way out of all her changing stories.

"My brain has been almost like a boxer's brain," she suddenly admits. "Severe head injuries, three accidents in a row...plus the Ambien all those years, 'cause you can't sleep with a head injury."

Pam goes on to say how Ambien does some pretty weird stuff to your memory. She jokes about the many things she had done while taking the medication... "you just don't even remember. That's that stuff...you can get up and do something...and not remember doing it the next morning... I'm a lot better than I was," she says. "Part of it was the Ambien." Once again, the detectives back her up.

"So you have a little bit of a foothold here," the detective says to her. He tells Pam he has a son who can eat an entire pie while taking Ambien and not remember it the next morning.

Bolstered by the validation, Pam states, "The more I talk about it, the clearer it gets." Pam's mother, Shirley Neumann, was found with eight times the amount of Ambien in her body normally prescribed the day she died.

The memory issue will also be an excuse she uses during the civil trial the following year during the lawsuit brought on by Betsy's daughters as they try to recover the life insurance money Pam received from their mother. How does one pin down a testimony given by a witness who one minute is describing in great detail events that could return a man to prison for life, and the next minute claim faulty recollection? Schwartz had a solution for that.

Trial Number Two

November 2, 2015 dawned, and Russell Faria found himself once more seated between his defense attorneys Joel Schwartz and Nathan Swanson in a courtroom, his fate in the hands of justice. This time, it would be only Judge Steven Ohmer hearing the testimonies. A jury had let Russ down the first time. He hoped a bench trial this time around would change his luck.

Steven Ohmer was a no-nonsense judge but one who came across as a good ol' boy, with a dry wit and easy cadence. His remarks were sometimes surprising as he folded a witty comeback into his stream of directives. When he was told the sketch artist was only "getting the back of heads" from his position in the courtroom, Judge Ohmer told him to come up front where he could see better. The Judge welcomed the media but warned them there would be no recording devices of any kind.

Where the first trial had been replete with long-winded sidebars, Ohmer kept them to a minimum and resolved them quickly. The five-days of testimony went by smoothly and one gets the sense of a well-oiled machine. The biggest difference in this second go-around was the massive information allowed in against Pam Hupp.

Leah Askey and her team were ready. Her hair was shorter and there was a look of defiance about her. She and her team had been accused of misconduct, mishandling evidence, and even perjury. While it had not been filed officially, the claims of the prosecutions' questionable handling of the Faria murder case was no secret. The email letter sent to Askey from Mike Lang, swearing his undying devotion, was already fodder for water cooler gossip in judicial offices. There was a lot at risk here, and this time, it wasn't just Russ' head in the noose.

Chris Hayes with *Fox 2 News* covered the Faria murder and other crimes associated with Pam Hupp. He was the only reporter who ever interviewed her in person. Chris attended Russ's second trial, as he had the first. With the admission of all the evidence against Pam, "it was like two different trials," he said.

The Opening Statements

The courtroom and judge soon learned what tactics the two tables would take. Leah Askey, as the prosecuting attorney, was up first to present her opening statement and outline what she intended to prove through witness testimony.

Leah Askey, Prosecuting Attorney

"'My name is Russell Faria,'" Askey begins, mimicking Russ's 911 call. "I just got home from a friend's house and my wife killed herself. I left at 5:00. She was at her mom's house and a friend was going to bring her home. I want you to call my mom. Her name is Lucy Faria. Her phone number is _____.' Three times the defendant is crystal clear on his 911 call. Three times. And the evidence, Judge, that you're going to hear is that 911 call, which is going to be very telling. Those three times were the only time that the defendant is crystal clear. 'I want someone to come and help me. What am I going to do? Why did she do this to me? She's dead. Her arms are slashed and the knife is buried in her neck.' These are all statements that the defendant makes on the 911 call.

"The evidence will be that during that call he doesn't start crying until the 911 operator asked him what's the emergency. The line comes live. The recording starts. '911, what's your emergency?' And then he starts crying. The evidence will be that he's inaudible unless he's telling about my name is Russell Faria, I just got home from a friend's house, and my wife has killed herself. It's almost a minute into the call before he ever gives an address. He never once asked for help for his wife. Only help for himself. He will tell the 911 operator that he just arrived in the house, yet he knows that no one else is there and he knows that the dog is out on the chain.

"He will later tell a detective that he didn't touch her because he was worried that he might disturb an investigation or a crime scene, but he had already told the 911 operator that no one else was in the house and he wasn't worried for his own safety. We believe that the evidence will show that based on his own statements there's no possible way that he could have come into the house the way that he did, the way that he describes, fallen onto the floor in the manner in which he demonstrates on video for the detective, specifically lay down by his dead wife, without having any blood on his clothing or his person. The evidence will be that he first tells the officer that he couldn't stand to look at her, so he had to go in another room and there he collapsed on the kitchen floor where he called 911. But later to a second officer, he's able to describe with specificity the slashes to both of her arms, specifically her left one. He's able to describe a knife being buried deeply within her neck and describe it as being one that came from the butcher block of their kitchen. He'll describe her tongue hanging out of her mouth. And you'll see photos where you, yourself, will not be able to artic- -- to determine that. These are statements from the defendant.

"The evidence will be that he said that he came into the front door with dog food on his shoulder and his keys in his hand, and he walked in and he set the dog food down and then he began taking off his coat. And it was in an area in a room smaller than this. And as he lay his coat down across the chair with his wife halfway between you and I, he wasn't able to see her there. He called for her. And then when he saw her lying on the floor with the lights on fully illuminated, he thought maybe she doesn't feel too well. But when he approached her, he noticed a knife protruding from her neck and then decided she must have committed suicide. These are statements from the defendant.

"We believe that the evidence will be that when law enforcement arrives on the scene, the deputy meets him inside the house, he's not eager to meet the detectives. And you'll hear him on the 911 call. He's not at the door waiting for them. The detective comes in -- the law enforcement comes in, the patrolman walks into the room, immediately notices Mrs. Faria's body on the floor, immediately notices it's not a suicide, and says, "Sir, come with me." He then goes out and gets in the vehicle and for somewhere around an hour smokes cigarettes, laughs, and talks about his childhood, where he grew up, with no emotion other than just idle prattle. Another officer comes to the scene to do a protective sweep of the house because it's become apparent that it's not a suicide. He checks the closets, he checks the bathrooms, places where a person can hide, and notes there are water droplets in the shower of the master bedroom, yet the defendant when talking to detectives states that he had not showered that day. And the victim, based on what the evidence will show, was wearing the same clothes that she had on when she left her mother's house earlier that evening.

"You will hear from at least six individuals who will talk about the controlling and abusive relationship that Betsy Faria was in. You will hear how the defendant attempted to alienate her from her family and from her friends and from the areas in which she was most accustomed to. You'll hear how she was diagnosed with cancer, and on the actual day that she got her mastectomy he closed on a house in Troy to move her away from her doctors, from her cancer center, from her parents, from her sisters, from her daughters who had gone to school in the Wentzville School District their entire lives, and from all of her friends to move her out here. You'll hear how her kids didn't want to move, how she didn't want to move, but that was his doing to further alienate her.

"We believe the evidence will show that within a week before her murder, he held a pillow over her face when she was sleeping and she woke up in a gasp and was told by the defendant that this is what dying feels like. We believe the evidence will show Betsy Faria was fearful of the defendant, and that she was desperate to get her insurance policies changed and things in order immediately because she was terminally ill with cancer. She was worried that he had been hacking into her computer, and the evidence will show that the computer she used on a daily basis is the one that didn't have a hard drive in it of 13 computers left in the house. The evidence will further show that the older computer that she had had for years is one in which a letter was found where she wrote a letter in which it articulates these items about the pillow over the face, it articulates the items about changing her beneficiary and having to get them out of the defendant's name, it articulates finally if something should happen to me, please show this to the police.

"You will hear that that letter was written just a day before she changed her life insurance policy and that she had told a friend, 'I tried to send you a letter and I couldn't get it to send.' We believe that the evidence will show, Judge, that she hadn't been home for several nights. This was Christmas week. And that the defendant had a routine Game Night every Tuesday and had been doing that for some 15 years. And on that Tuesday night, he would religiously have dinner with his mother before he would go to Game Night.

"That particular night, Betsy Faria had at the direction of her husband, left her purse at home on the 26th when they went to a Christmas gathering. She wasn't feeling well. She left her purse at home. They drove to the Christmas gathering. Her daughter was sick and she stayed down at her mother's residence. You will hear that the game had been canceled, the original game that normally was played on Tuesday night was canceled and the defendant knew that it was canceled. Betsy reached out to the defendant and said, "Do you have a game tonight?" Instead of answering no, the evidence will be that he began immediately reaching out to his friends and saying, "I know there's no game tonight, but how about we get together and play a game of Talisman?" Before he responds to his wife and he gets everybody else to agree that that's what they are going to do, he finally responds back, "Yeah, I have got a game tonight." She later then says she has a ride home with a friend who is going to bring her back to Troy. And he says, "Home, Troy?" She says, "Yes."

"She asks him to pick up dog food. He calls his mother. He cancels dinner plans because now he has too many errands to run because he has to pick up dog food. As soon as he cancels his dinner plans with his mom and leaves his house in Troy, his errands consist of going to the Conoco Station in Troy, Missouri, and getting three gallons of gas. He then drives from the Conoco Station in Troy about 12 miles to Wentzville to a U Gas and he buys cigarettes. From there he leaves and he goes just down the road a bit further to a -- to Greene's Country Store and he buys dog food. From there he goes just a little bit further to the QuikTrip on the same road, another gas station, and buys two teas to take to his friend, Michael Corbin's, for his Game Night where he's going to play Talisman. His bank records will indicate that at the QuikTrip he also withdrew $200, though he never -- he never tells the detectives about the $200 nor was there any money on his person that was checked into the jail when he was booked in. He later goes to Arby's at 9:00 that evening and buys two sandwiches. The previous transactions all except Arby's were done on his bank card. The Arby's transaction is done with cash.

Askey continued: "The evidence will further show that Mr. Faria has had a mistress and has had since his wife was diagnosed with cancer, and has had throughout his dying wife's illness, and that that relationship continued up and including the day she was killed, and that she presumably was pregnant with his child at the time of Betsy Faria's death. The evidence will suggest that the defendant had knowledge that Betsy's cancer diagnosis was terminal and that she intended to change her insurance policies out of his name.

"As for our forensics, Judge, the evidence will be that Betsy Faria's blood is on the defendant's slippers and that those slippers are located in his closet, that her blood is on the light switch in the master bedroom, that his semen is still inside of her body and that his seminal fluid is still on the exterior of her body. We believe that the evidence will be that there is a paw print on her hip of her pants in her blood, yet the defendant's statement is that the dog is outside on the chain.

"The evidence will be through our medical examiner that Betsy Faria was brutally stabbed in excess of 55 times, many of which were likely after she was already dead. Her right arm was nearly severed off. And she had a stab wound that went through her tricep, through her bicep, through her rib, and into her lung which punctured it. An amount of force necessary to make that happen is quite significant. She had several stab wounds to her head, one of which was through the ear that fractured her skull, and three stab wounds through her neck that were through and through and where the knife was ultimately left.

"We believe, Judge, that the evidence will show that it was clearly a crime of passion and one of rage. The State believes that after you hear all of the evidence, all of the witnesses, you'll be able to determine that the defendant, Russell Faria, committed the crime of murder in the first degree and armed criminal action for these brutal acts taken upon his wife on December 27th, 2011, here in Lincoln County, Missouri, and you will find him guilty on all of those charges. Thank you."

Defense Attorney Joel Schwartz

Russ' attorney Joel Schwartz opened with a quick review of the facts he would be underscoring during the trial. He wanted to make it clear that Russ had provided ample evidence of where he was the night Betsy died:

"He stops at Conoco. He gets out of the car, pumps the gas, gets back in the car. You'll see the video from Conoco shows exactly what he's wearing. He stops at U Gas. The bank records will show that's where he always stops and gets his cigarettes, a couple cartons, because they are cheaper. He stops at Greene's Country Store. He buys the dog food. They give him a receipt. And then he stops at QuikTrip right before he gets to Michael Corbin's. He gets there right around 6:00 o'clock. Two of the other individuals, Brandon Sweeney and Marshall Bach, show up moments after him. He walks in and they put the movie on. The movie had just been put on. They watched the movie *Conan the Barbarian* which was new apparently in 2011. They sit around and they talk a little bit about a motorcycle that he wanted to buy from an uncle, that he talked to Betsy about. They watched the movies. They put on a new movie called *The Road.* They will tell you they never told police that they were playing a game that night. They said that's what they usually do, but they all consistently couldn't play the games because Richard May, one of the witnesses, wasn't there, one of the people who normally played. Not one, not two, not three, but four people will tell this Court that Russ arrived at 6:00 and that Russell left at 9:00."

Schwartz continued: "Russell leaves the house, Michael Corbin's house, at about 9:00. He stops at the Arby's there right on the corner. He goes through the drive-thru and pays for a couple of sandwiches, which by the way the trash from the sandwiches along with the order form when he pays -- when he orders them are sitting wrapped up, trashed in his car with an empty box of cigarettes in there and, I believe, an empty iced tea from the QuikTrip. That receipt shows 9:09. And it is wrapped -- it is in the trash, but sitting in his car all trashed up. He arrives home. Google maps will show you it takes about 30 minutes. He shows up at 9:39. He tells the detectives, as is such, he had a bag of dog food over his shoulders. And you will see pictures of the bag of dog food sitting there right by the front door. He walks inside, lays the bag of dog food down, throws his coat on the chair, and he sees Betsy lying on the floor. He immediately calls 911. And, Judge, I would ask you to listen to the 911 tape. You'll make your own interpretation of what went on in that call. He does call in and say, "I think my wife committed suicide." Now, you will hear evidence that Betsy had attempted suicide before, that that was a reaction of some of Betsy's sisters. And her daughter had given Russ a note just recently showing how Betsy had left a suicide note. Was it suicide? Absolutely not. And it was clear upon looking at it, if you're clear-headed, that that wasn't suicide."

As Judge Ohmer listened, Schwartz wrapped up his opening statement: "What you will see, Judge, is Russ was -- was detained that evening. He talked to the police. They asked him where he was. He replayed and replayed his actions throughout the night. He told them about 'I stopped at Conoco, I stopped at U Gas' -- and he may have gotten the order backwards at one point in time between two of them, but they then go and fortunately they are able to secure those tapes. They go to Greene's Country Store. Fortunately, they are able to get the receipt. They take all of those to confirm where he said he was and what he did.

"They went and talked to the alibi witnesses while he's in custody. The alibi witnesses all confirm from 6:00 o'clock to 9:00 o'clock he was here. They found that receipt in his car crumbled up showing that he stopped at Arby's on the way home. You'll also hear from a guy named Captain Robert Shramek along with the EMS supervisor Mike Quattarocchi, and they will tell you that when they showed up at approximately eight minutes after the call, they went in and it was clear she was gone just like Russ had said. They felt the body. They touched the body. Both of them independently. And they will both tell you she was cold, she was stiff, and that blood was setting up. And the blood had been there for some time.

"Judge, in listening to the evidence you will learn that the police went and talked to the alibi witnesses immediately. This is Major Case Squad. They went and talked to the individual who wasn't at game night. They looked in Russ's phone and may have talked to 100 of his friends and 100 of Betsy's friends. What you will also hear is they went to talk to Pam Hupp the next morning. Pam Hupp told them she dropped Betsy off. Originally, she said she didn't go in the house. She originally said she called her to tell her she was home. But of all those hundreds of witnesses they looked to about

Russ Faria, they didn't even talk to Pam Hupp's husband to confirm what time she got home. They didn't image her cell phone to compare records. They didn't talk to her neighbors to see what she was doing and when she got home. They didn't talk to a soul to confirm anything whatsoever that she said, and frankly, neither has the State. Judge, after you hear the evidence, we will ask you to base your verdict on what the Court hears and not theory and innuendo. And after the Court hears all the evidence, we feel confident that the Court will find Mr. Faria not guilty. Thank you, Judge."

The Witnesses

Leah Askey first called Betsy's daughter Mariah Day to set the tone for the dynamics of the Faria household. It became clear that the marriage had been rocky and Russ had a temper. While all the witnesses from Betsy's side of the family claimed to have knowledge of his condescending nature to his wife, and his screaming at her and the two girls, none of them stated he had ever physically hurt Betsy, other than when he pushed her once.

Mariah went over the details of that Christmas weekend. She said it was out of the ordinary that she and Leah each received a $100 bill from Russ in their Christmas stocking. She said it was usually around $20. She also stated that Russ's insistence on a Christmas family photo was unusual. The photos were presented as evidence and Mariah confirmed they were taken Christmas morning. They show her, her sister Leah, Betsy, Russ and the dog, Sicily.

Leah also asks Mariah about Betsy's computers and tries to pin down which one she would typically use. A great deal was made of the laptop with the jewels glued all over it. Mariah stated it was Leah who had "bedazzled" it with fake pink gems.

During Schwartz's cross of both Mariah and Leah Day, he defused the innuendo put forth by the prosecutor that the $100 bill in each of the girl's stockings or the sudden urge to have a family portrait taken had any insidious undertones. He delicately had them admit that Betsy had just been told a month or two earlier that she had terminal cancer. There was no telling if this would be her last Christmas, even though she had been given a 3-5-year prognosis. Could it be Russ wanted this family gathering to be extra special and memorialize it?

Schwartz also had the girls admit they too yelled at Betsy. There

187

was a lot going on with the kind of problems that teenagers get into and the Faria household was not a harmonious one. He also talked to them about Betsy's suicide note that Mariah had found on her pillow once. Mariah admitted the note was found after a bad argument she had with her mother and that it was probably left to make her feel badly.

Schwartz zeroed in on Pam's relationship with Betsy. He asked Mariah the following questions:

Q. "She was close with her mother, Janet? A. Yeah. Q. And she was very close with all her sisters -- A. Yeah. Q. -- correct? Yes? A. Yeah. Q. She was closer with all of those people I just mentioned than she was with Pam Hupp, right? A. Yes. Yes. Q. And Pam Hupp really didn't start hanging around her until the cancer diagnosis; would you agree with that? A. I can see it. Q. Okay. Do you agree with that? A. Yeah."

During Leah Day's testimony, Leah Askey had her testify to how Russ would treat the dog. Leah agreed he had been mean to the pet, punching him, picking him up by his neck and tossing him out the back door, etc.

Askey also went over Leah's last phone conversation with Betsy the night she was murdered:

Q. "You spoke to her on the phone on the 27th? A. Yes. Q. And do you remember approximately what time you spoke to her on the phone? A. No. I don't know the times. Q. Okay. Do you remember what that conversation was about? A. Yeah. I wanted her -- I needed her to answer because I was going to get a new phone. I'm on her phone plan, so I needed her permission. And she said yes, I will answer. Q. Okay. So, you called her ahead of time to let her know you were headed to -- A. Correct. Q. -- change the phone plan? A. Correct. Yes. Q. And she would need to verify that with the company? A. Yes. Q. Okay. And so, when you got to the phone store, did you try to call her again? A. Yes. About three -- three times. Q. Okay. Did she answer on those times? A. No. Q. Do you remember when you spoke with her if she indicated whether she was at home or where she was? A. Whenever I spoke with her, she said she was just going home to lay on the couch to lay -- she was going home to lay down. She'll answer. Q. Okay. A. I made sure she would promise me she would answer. Q. Okay. And you were going to the phone store with your aunt? A. Yes. Q. After that conversation, did you have any other conversations with your mom? A. No."

Schwartz cross-examined Leah to firm up the times she called her mother that night. It was evident Leah wasn't in the mood to be helpful. She and her sister Mariah stated they didn't want to be there and both made use of the tissue box.

Q. "Now, the night of December the 27th, you had called your mom, and you know it was right around 7:00 p.m., and you were headed to US Cellular? A. Yes. Q. And you called your mom -- do you remember your mom's number? A. _____. Q. And you would have called your mom three times, right? A. Correct. Q. Specifically you would have called her at 7:21:09 seconds. Does that sound correct? A. I guess. So long ago. Q. And what happened when you called her? A. The first time? Q. Yeah. A. She answered. Q. The first time. I'm talking when you called -- that's when you told her you were going to US Cellular? A. Yes. Q. At 7:21 there was no answer? A. No answer. Q. And then you called her again at 7:26? A. I don't know the time, but yes, I did call her a second time. Q. Okay. And there was no answer the second time? A. Correct. Q. And then you called her again at 7:30:06 seconds or about 7:30; would you agree with that? A. I don't know the time, but yes, I called her a third time. Q. Okay. And all of those calls, there was no answer? A. Correct. Q. And that was where approximately 20 minutes prior your mom promised you and knew how important it was and promised you she would answer that phone? A. Correct. Q. And she didn't answer any of those calls? A. Yes. No. She did not."

Schwartz moves on to his questions to Leah concerning Pam Hupp: Q. "Now, just briefly, do you remember me asking you questions way back in March of 2013? A. In my deposition? Q. In your deposition. A. Yes. Q. Do you remember being deposed? A. I mean, I remember being in the deposition, yes. Q. Do you remember I asked you about your mom's relationship with Pam? A. I don't remember. Q. Would it refresh your recollection if I showed you a copy of your deposition? A. Maybe. **MR. SCHWARTZ**: May I approach, Your Honor? **THE COURT**: You may. A. I was young. Q. (By Mr. Schwartz) I'm sorry. I didn't hear what you said. You were young? A. I was young and it was all shocking. Q. Well, so -- A. I was in shock. Q. What you're referring to is as far as your mom's relationship with Pam, you said she wasn't close, she was down on the list of friends. That's what you said in 2013, correct? A. I mean, compared to her other friends. Q. Right. She was much closer with many other people as well as her sisters, correct? A. I mean, I really wouldn't know. Q. But that's what you said at the time on March 18th of 2013, right? A. Okay. Q. Is that true? A. I guess I said it then. Q. All right. And you were under oath when you said it then, right? A. Okay. Q. Is that true? A. Correct. Q. And as far as her relationship, you said that she became -- Pam became close with your mom after your mom's cancer diagnosis. And that's what you said in March of 2013, correct? A. Correct."

Pam Welker, Betsy's youngest sister testified that Betsy was different on Christmas day, only two days before her murder:

Q. "The days leading up to your sister's murder, she was at your house for a family gathering; is that right? A. Yes. On Monday. I hosted Christmas. Q. And describe her disposition. A. I was worried about her. She was clearly tired, you know, maybe from the chemotherapy, but she -- she wasn't very dressed up. She sat in a chair very quiet. At dinner she went to my son's room and played with my great nephew, which was not normally at all what she would do. And when she left that night, my husband and I just -- we were worried about her and we talked a bit about was she tired, was she sick, was she upset? But definitely not in her usual disposition that night. Q. So when you say her usual disposition, she had been diagnosed with cancer for some time? A. Yes. Q. And so you had the opportunity to interact with her over the course of time -- A. Yes. Q. -- since her diagnosis? A. Uh-huh. Q. Was her disposition on Christmas similar or different to what it had been during her cancer battle? A. Very different because Betsy didn't like to lose and she was fighting for her life, so she -- she didn't even want to act like she had cancer. I mean, she was always happy, always positive. Always -- yeah. Just never letting on any internal conflict or anything. Q. But that wasn't her disposition that day? A. Correct."

Betsy's sister Pam also described to Joel Schwartz Betsy's mindset:

"Okay. Ms. Welker, when the police first spoke to you, your first impression was that Betsy must have committed suicide? A. Yes. Q. And that -- A. She had had a lifelong challenge with thinking about that, so it didn't have anything to do with the cancer. She had always struggled with a bit of depression and thinking about the loss of her own life. Q. And that was a lifelong situation? A. Yes. Q. Are you aware as to whether or not that was some of your other sisters' first impression? A. Oh, I have no idea. Q. You don't know, but that was yours."

Another of Betsy's sisters, Mary Rodgers, took the stand.

Q. (By Ms. Askey) "Mary, you were in the courtroom when your nieces testified and had the opportunity to listen to them testify about the hostility between the defendant and your sister; is that correct? A. Yes. Q. Is that something that you ever had the opportunity to witness? A. Yes. Q. And, specifically, I think Leah talked about an incident where they called you? A. Yes. Q. What happened in that incident? A. They called me crying and frantic that he was using a lot of foul language. I took an early lunch and then went there because that's just what I do with my nieces. And he was -- when I got there, he was calmer. He was laying on the bed and kicking his feet. I don't remember what happened, but at some point, he pushed Betsy and that's when I called the police. Q. You called the police? A. I called the police and then took the girls out of the house. Q. And when you say the girls, you're talking about the young girls? A. Yes. Leah, Mariah and my stepdaughter Ashley. Q. What, if anything, did the defendant say during that time? A. When I was leaving the house, I heard something about cutting her up into bits and pieces and burying her or some robust thing that I would never say."

Joel Schwartz cross-examined Mary Rodgers. He first got her to admit that she had told detectives the mornings after the murder that Russ and Betsy had a loving relationship and that Russ was taking care of her. She said she had been proud of Russ for getting his degree so that he could start an IT job. Schwartz then zeroed in on Pam Hupp:

Q. (By Mr. Schwartz) "How many times do you -- when did you first find out that Pam Hupp was the beneficiary? A. She told us one of the days when we were congregating at my mom's before the funeral. Q. Pam Hupp told you? A. Yes. Q. It was right around the funeral time? A. Right. Q. And once you found out, the entire family confronted her, right? A. I don't know. Q. You talked to her and said you'd given money to Leah and Mariah? A. All I can recall is that she made the statement that she was the beneficiary, and then we didn't talk anything more about it because we were planning a funeral. Q. And did you form an assumption she was giving the money to the girls? A. Yes. Q. Do you know where that assumption came from? A. She said. Q. She said. What did she say, that I'm giving the money to the girls? A. Yes. Q. Betsy wanted that? A. Right. Not just handing it over. I -- the way I understood it, is she would form a trust and as they did certain things, they would get it. Q. And you became aware that -- well, this case was tried in November of 2013, the first time, right? A. Yes. Q. And Ms. Hupp created and funded that trust, if you're aware, just a few days before that trial? A. Yes. Q. Put $100,000 into that? A. Yes. Q. Are you also aware that about a week to ten days after the trial she then took out $99,700 from that trust? A. I don't know what she did. Q. You don't know that? A. Huh-uh. Q. But you know the trust has since been revoked? A. Yes. Q. And you know the daughters have gotten nothing? A. Correct. Q. Now, you made a statement earlier in this proceeding, not today, that you came to find out that Betsy was planning on leaving Russ, right? A. Yes. Q. That came from Pam Hupp, didn't it? A. Pam Hupp never told me that. Q. Who did? A. I don't remember. Q. You made -- A. I thought Betsy was fighting with every part of her being to keep the marriage because she didn't want to have another divorce. Q. That's my question. You came to -- you made a statement that you found out at some point that Betsy was fighting with everything she could to keep that relationship together, correct? A. Right. Q. She -- so if you made a statement that she was planning on leaving Russ, that wasn't your statement, that came from somewhere else? A. Yes. Q. Would that have been Pam Hupp? A. I don't know. Q. You don't know where that came from? A. No. Q. You made a statement that you found out that Russ had put a pillow over Betsy's face? A. Yes. Q. That came from Pam Hupp, didn't it? A. No. It came from Bobbi Wann. Q. Came from Bobbi Wann after talking to Pam Hupp? A. No. Q. Pam Hupp was at the house the following morning, correct? A. After Betsy's death? Q. Yes. A. I think so. Q. And who else was there? A. Everyone. Everybody. All the family. Q. When did you find all that information out? A. I don't remember. Q. It would have been sometime after Pam Hupp left, right? A. I don't know."

Bobbi Wann was the family friend who took Betsy to chemo the day she died. The conversation about the pillow and Betsy wanting to leave Russ would come up again during the trial. Bobbi's testimony was highly anticipated. She had not appeared during

Russ' first trial, possibly due to health issues and travel distance. She had much to say.

BY MS. ASKEY: Q. "Bobbi, please introduce yourself to Judge Ohmer. A. I'm Bobbi Wann. I live in Windsor, California. Q. So you traveled quite a ways to be here today? A. Quite a ways. Q. I appreciate you coming. A. Thank you. Q. And how do you know Betsy Faria? A. We used to be neighbors with her family in 1969 to 1972. I babysat Betsy a lot. Q. You became friends with her mom? A. Yes. Very good friends. Q. And so you've obviously remained friends? A. Right. Q. Were you in town visiting Janet Meyer during the December month of 2011? A. Yes, I was. Q. And specifically on December 27th of 2011, did you take Betsy to chemotherapy treatment? A. Yes, I did. Q. And did you have an opportunity to have conversations with Betsy that day? A. Yes. Q. Did any of those conversations involve her abuse from the defendant? A. Well, Pam Hupp brought up the incident of the pillow over her face. And I asked Betsy if he was abusive to her. She said he was very verbally abusive. Q. And did she say to you that she was fearful of him? A. Not directly, I don't believe. Q. Did she talk to you about the incident with regard to the pillow over her face? A. A little bit, yes. Q. So she verified that was a true statement? A. Yes. Q. And did she verify how recent that had occurred? A. No. Pam is the one that brought it up. Q. About how recent it had occurred? A. Uh-huh.

Q. "Did she talk to you about wanting to change her life insurance policies? A. She had already changed it then. Q. Okay. And so, she verified with you that she had already changed a policy? A. Uh-huh. Q. Did she talk to you about wanting to change another one? A. Yes. She wanted to change another one. Q. And did she say anything about having changed that beneficiary? A. Yes, she did. Q. What did she say specifically? A. She said she had changed it, and she had left it on the counter at the house in Troy. Q. And did she -- did she say anything about what her intentions were with regard to mailing that policy? A. She had mailed one policy, but this one was just on the counter to be mailed.

"Q. Okay. And did she let -- talk to you about whether or not she was going back to Troy? A. Yes. She was going back to Troy that night. Q. And what was her intentions, or did she describe to you what her intentions were about going back to Troy that night? A. Well, she didn't have a car, so Pam Hupp was going to take her back.

Q. And had there been some discussions about what she had planned to discuss with Russ when she got there? A. Yes. Q. And what were those discussions about? A. She planned to discuss with him the fact that she wanted them to buy the house on Seasons Parkway and to rent the house out in Troy, and that it would be paid for in 20 years and then they would have enough money to move to Florida. Q. Were her intentions to stay living in the Troy house? A. No. Q. And what, if anything, did she tell you about that? A. She said that it was too far. She could not continue to drive in for her chemotherapy. She played tennis in St. Louis, and everything that she did and everyone that she loved was in St. Louis. Q. Did she make any statements with you about why she didn't have her purse with her? A. She said that Russ told her to leave her purse at home and that he would leave the door open. Q. And that was the day before? A. That was on the 27th. Q. She had come down on the 26th, though; is that correct? A. Yes. And spent the night. Q. And he had told her to leave her purse at home on the 26th? A. Uh-huh.

"Q. Did she make any statements to you with regard to why she was changing her beneficiaries? A. She wanted to be sure the girls got the money and Pam Hupp -- Pam Hupp said the money was definitely for the girls and they would get the money. Q. Did she make any statements as to why she wanted to take it out of her husband's name? A. So the girls would be sure and get the money. Q. At some point, did you express your concern for Betsy to go home to Troy that evening? A. Yes. Because she was going to talk to Russ about moving to Seasons Parkway, and she knew that he was not going to like it. And I suggested that they go in together, and before they went in that they would determine what they were going to say to Russ. Q. And when you say they went in together, who is they? A. Pam Hupp and Betsy. Q. You suggested that the two of them go? A. Yes. Q. Was Pam Hupp in a rush to get Betsy out of the house when you all were at the house? A. She didn't appear to be. Q. Whose suggestion was it that she leave Janet's house to go back to Troy at that time? A. I'm not sure. We had finished playing the game. She stayed while we finished playing the game, and then since Betsy wasn't feeling good after the chemotherapy they left."

During Schwartz' cross of Bobbi Wann, it was obvious he did not believe her more damning statements were of her own fabrication:

"Now, that particular day when you took her to chemo, do you know -- and you had a conversation and she told -- you know she told Pam Hupp not to come, correct? A. Yes. Q. And Pam Hupp just showed up? A. Correct. Q. Were you quite surprised? A. I wasn't as surprised as Betsy was. Q. She was very surprised, correct? A. I think so by the look on her face. Q. She didn't want Pam Hupp to be there, she wanted to just spend time, you and her? A. Correct. Q. You know she told that to Pam Hupp? A. Yeah. Q. Do you have any idea why Pam Hupp came up there? A. No. I have no idea. I don't know her thoughts. Q. She was uninvited, correct? A. She had been told not to come. Q. And she intruded on your and Betsy's time? A. Yes.

Q. "And then during chemo, Pam Hupp told Betsy she'll take her home, right? A. Yes. Q. And Betsy said that, well, Russ is coming to get me? A. I don't recall her saying that. Q. Do you recall Pam Hupp insisting on taking her home? A. I don't recall her insisting. She just said she would take her home. Q. She said she would take her home. And then afterwards you and Betsy left and Pam Hupp went wherever Pam Hupp went? A. Correct. Q. And you didn't see her again until she showed up at Janet's house later on when you guys were playing a game? A. Correct. Q. Is that correct? A. Correct.

Q. "And you spoke to the police the next morning and you had just -- we're talking what time do you think you left chemo, three o'clock maybe? A. What was the question? Q. What time do you think you left chemo on the 26th -- I'm sorry. On the 27th. My bad. Two or three o'clock in the afternoon? A. Probably around two. Q. All right. The next morning you spoke to two detectives, correct? A. I don't recall it, but I guess I did. Q. And you told the detectives about chemo. You told the detectives that Betsy was in a great mood and good spirits that day, right? A. Yes. Q. And you told them how Bobbi said that they had talked -- that Betsy had talked about an investment home in Lake St. Louis with Russell and Elizabeth and Janet -- A. Yes. Q. -- correct? However, when you spoke to the police that morning the next day on the 28th you said nothing about insurance? A. I told you I was in a state of shock.

Q. "Okay. A. It never occurred to me to say anything about insurance. Q. But as we're here today, don't you think the fact that Pam Hupp got that insurance is very important at least to discuss with the police and let them know? A. I don't know. Q. But you didn't tell it to them? A. No. I didn't tell it to them. Q. And you also didn't tell them about anything about a pillow over the face, did you? A. I don't recall. Q. Would it refresh your recollection if I showed you a copy of the report? A. I've read it. Q. And in that report, you don't say anything about it, do you? A. It wasn't brought up. Q. Well, the police couldn't have brought it up. They didn't know. Correct? You would have had to bring it up. A. That's right. Q. You talked about she was in good spirits, you thought it was important to talk about the investment home that Betsy had discussed, correct? A. Because that's what brought her death. Q. Well, we're -- how do you know that? How do you know Russ -- can you even say that Russ had any idea about what she was going to tell him that night when he got home? A. I don't know whether she told him or not. Q. Well, you were with her the entire time until she left, correct? A. (Nodding). Q. Yes? A. That was her intent when she left, to talk to Russ when he got home.

Q. "As far as you knew, Russ was at Game Night like he does every Tuesday night, right? A. Yes. Q. So she wasn't going to see Russ until after 9:00 that night as far as you knew -- A. Correct. Q. -- right? So, when you're talking to the police the next morning -- I don't mean to be callous, but Betsy was deceased at that point in time, right? A. Right. Q. Yet all you told them about the discussion the previous day, you told them how Pam arrived and you talked about that, and you talked about her being in a great mood, and you talked about an investment home between Russ and Betsy that they were going to -- do you know the story behind the home? Was that discussed? Was it discussed that the house that Janet or Betsy's sister was living in was going to be foreclosed and they could purchase that house for a lowball offer -- A. Yes, I knew that. Q. -- and then they could rent their home in Troy? A. Yes. Q. That was all discussed, right? A. Yes. Q. Yes? A. That was discussed at chemo. Q. At chemo, right. And you talked about that with the police? A. Yes.

Q. "And you knew -- everybody knew Russ wasn't going to like that they had just bought this house, right? A. I don't know when they bought it. Q. Well -- okay. But that required Russ to live with Betsy's sisters and Betsy's mother, right? Right? A. As far as I know. Q. What they were talking about. And Betsy surmised that Russ wasn't going to be happy about that, correct? A. Correct. Q. And you told that to the police? A. I don't recall. Q. You didn't tell that part to the police, but you talked about the investment home. Now, you met with the police again and made another statement, and you actually made a written statement. Between the time you made that initial statement and your second statement, you had seen Pam Hupp, she came to the house? A. Yes. Q. Now, is that when you learned about the insurance? A. What do you mean when I learned about the insurance? Q. Ms. Hupp (sic), I don't mean to pry. How old are you, ma'am? A. My name is not Ms. Hupp. Q. Believe me. I know that. And I'm so sorry if I just called you Ms. Hupp. A. And what does my age have to do with it?

Q. "Well, let's go back. You had made a written statement on December the 30th. Now we're three days after Betsy had been deceased, correct? A. If you say so. Q. Well, it was on the 27th, you made a statement on the 30th. Do you recall making that statement? A. Yes. Q. Have you read your statement? A. Yes. Q. And in that statement, you go into significant detail; is that correct? You talked about what time the appointment was and where the appointment was, agreed? A. Correct. Q. You talk about at that point you brought up Russ being abusive verbally, correct? A. Yes. Q. And you talk about the whole situation with the house and you talk about a lowball offer and renting out the house in Troy. You talk about all of that, correct? A. That was during chemotherapy, yes. Q. Right. But you talk about that in your written statement on the 30th? A. Yes. Q. And you felt that that was important? A. Yes.

Q. "While you're making this statement, are you still in shock? A. I'm still in shock. Q. Three days later. You're still in shock today? A. I'm still in shock today. Q. I mean, you even talked about who would have room in the house if they were going to buy in Lake St. Louis, correct? A. That's what Betsy said. Q. You tried to be as detail-oriented as you could for the police, right? A. Correct. Q. You told them that Russ would not like the idea of living with his mother-in-law, but she was going to talk to him anyway? A. That's what Betsy told me.

"Q. "You talked about where you went afterwards. You went to Lion's Choice, right? A. Correct. Q. Betsy didn't want to live in Troy, she wanted to move into Lake St. Louis? A. Correct. Q. With Russ? A. Correct. Q. And rent out the house in Troy so they could move to Florida eventually, right? A. But she was going to move regardless of whether Russ moved or not. I believe I said that. Q.

Well, I don't think so. She did say she hated living in Troy, though. She talked about what she did in St. Louis, chemo, and her friends and tennis. And you go on about other details. You talked about how you told Pam to stay in the house that night. A. No. I told Pam to go *in* the house. Q. To go in the house and discuss it with Troy (sic) because Pam actually brought it up, didn't she? It was Pam's idea that that's what they could do, right? A. What do you mean it was Pam's idea what they could do? Q. About moving to Lake St. Louis and renting out the house in Troy. That was Pam's creation, right? A. I don't know if it was her creation, but that was her statement.

Q. "Right. And then you got back and Betsy -- you played the game and Betsy wasn't feeling great so Pam took her home? A. Correct. Q. And they left about 6:30 or so? A. Correct. Q. Nowhere in your statement/statements do you mention the discussion about Pam being a beneficiary, do you? You have heard your statement, haven't you? A. Yes. Q. Nowhere in your statements do you mention anything about insurance in your statements, correct? A. I guess not. Q. Nowhere in your statements do you talk about another policy being changed, do you? A. No. Q. Nowhere in your statements do you talk about a policy being left on the counter, do you? A. No. I said it was left on the counter. Q. Are you sure? A. I'm positive. Q. Would you like to see a copy of your statement? A. I would. **MR. SCHWARTZ:** Judge, may I approach? **THE WITNESS**: The one that was taken -- **THE COURT**: You may. **THE WITNESS**: -- in San Francisco? Q. (By Mr. Schwartz) The one that was taken in San Francisco was by me, right, and that was years after this occurred? A. So -- Q. When was that? A. It was in 2013. Q. 2013, yeah. In 2013, you said at that time that it had been discussed. I'm talking your statements after this. December -- A. You have the statements? Q. Okay. In December, 2013 when I questioned you, you said about the insurance, right? I'm talking about what you said to the police in those statements. You didn't mention anything about a policy being left anywhere in the house or on a counter or any other policy at all, did you? "

MS. ASKEY: Judge, asked and answered. **THE COURT**: Well, overruled. She's not answered at this point. Q. (By Mr. Schwartz) Did you? A. No. Q. You said nothing in either of your statements to the police on the 28th and on the 30th about a pillow being put over Betsy's face, did you? A. No. Q. As we sit here today and you're testifying to those events, I assume you're recalling them because you think they are important? A. Yes. Q. You do think they are important, right? A. Yes, I do. Q. When you made these statements, Betsy was deceased, correct? A. Yes. Q. Yet you talked with actually four different police, two different sets, and in either of those statements do you say anything about insurance or anything about a pillow? A. Correct. Q. After you learned about the insurance and the pillow, why didn't you tell the family about that until after the next day after Betsy had been killed? Why did the family have to find out from Pam Hupp? A. I don't know. Q. You don't know, do you? **MR. SCHWARTZ**: Nothing further.

Schwartz's frustration spilled over when he questioned Bobbi Wann in a recross: "Q. And you felt it important to note that Betsy said he was verbally abusive, right? Right? A. Yeah. Q. You put that, right? A. Yes. Q. But you didn't think it was important to say he attempted to suffocate her? I guess not because it is not there, is it? A. I told you I was in a state of shock. Q. But you remember he was verbally abusive? A. That was in my statement. Q. So, you weren't in that much of a shock because you remembered a decent part of the conversation. You remembered every detail about the house and about moving and that Russ wasn't going to be happy about it. You remembered all that. So, you weren't in too much shock, were you? A. Yes, I was. Q. And finally the insurance proceeds. Pam Hupp who wasn't supposed to be there that day shows up at chemo, offers her a ride home, gets an insurance policy, and you didn't think to bring that up with the police? A. I didn't talk to the police after, I don't think. Q. I'm sorry? A. I don't remember talking to the police after that. Q. Well, other than the other two times, correct? The 28th and the 30th, you didn't bring it up? A. No, I didn't. **MR. SCHWARTZ**: Nothing further.

Chapter Thirteen
Trial Number Two Continues

The next sequence of testimonies concerned the 911 call, responding officers, and the crime scene investigators. It was here that Schwartz and Swanson rolled up their shirt sleeves and came out swinging. It was their premise that the evidence taken during the crime scene investigation had been misrepresented and that certain witnesses had been asked to lie on the stand. Those that fell under the umbrella of suspicion were associated with the prosecutions' case. The Crime Scene Investigators made it clear in the opening statements of their testimony that they were not part of the police department but were brought in as specialists.

Prosecuting Attorney Mike Wood, who would become the new PA in 2019, after Russ' trials were over, said, "Rumors of police and prosecutorial misconduct had begun circulating at the conclusion of Russ's first trial. Several witness' were believed to have received instructions on how to testify." In 2021, as this misconduct was being investigated, the number of tainted witness testimonies had climbed to seven individuals.

Chris Hollingsworth with the Lincoln County Sheriff's Office was the first to arrive on the scene after Russ' 911 call. His testimony in Trial 2 was primarily the same as that of Trial 1. He at first had Russ sit on the front porch. Due to the cold and Russ' near-panic condition, Hollingsworth asked a medic to give him a blanket. He finally moved him to the patrol car and sat with him, shared his cigarettes with Russ, and tried to calm him down by talking about safe topics such as where he grew up, etc. Medical units were there and other branches began arriving quickly. Sergeant Mike Pirtle arrived shortly after and went inside to view the situation.

Mike Pirtle's testimony would be one that would stand out as it was different from Trial 1. Now, after three years, the officer recalls seeing something suspicious at the Faria residence, as he does a protective sweep through the house:

Leah Askey is questioning. Q. "When you arrived on the scene, what were your duties as far as that scene is concerned? A. I responded inside and observed a female who appeared deceased, and from there it was apparent that it wasn't a suicide, so I secured the scene and I contacted my supervisor. Q. Okay. And when you say you secured the scene, what does that mean? A. I conducted a - - well, I advised anybody who was still inside the residence to exit such as medical personnel, and then I conducted a protective sweep of the residence. Q. What is a protective sweep? A. Verifying that there's no one else inside. Q. Okay. And incidentally, it was cold outside that night? A. Yes. It was very cold.

Q. "And when you got there then, medical personnel were already on scene? A. Yes. Q. The door was open? A. Yes. Q. How many people would you say were in the residence? A. I don't recall. Q. Any -- less than ten? A. Yes. Q. But Deputy Hollingsworth was already there? A. Yes. Deputy Hollingsworth was already there. Q. Do you recall whether or not the defendant was still inside the residence? A. I believe Deputy Hollingsworth had already brought him outside at that point. Q. So medical personnel were the only people inside the residence at that point? A. Yes. Q. When you do a protective sweep, what are you looking for specifically? A. I'm looking to see if there's anybody hiding inside the residence. Q. So you're looking in areas where a person could hide? A. Yes. Q. You're not looking inside drawers or things like that? A. That's correct.

Q. "Okay. So, what areas did you look in specifically? A. I checked the upstairs bedrooms. I looked through the rooms, looked through the closets, looked through the bathrooms. Q. Okay. When you look in the bathrooms, do you look in the showers? A. Yes, I do. Q. Do you look in the bathtubs? A. Yes. Q. What, if anything, were you able to observe in the closets? A. Clothes. The floor. Q. Nothing of any significance? A. Correct. Q. Did you look inside -- when you looked inside the showers -- and there is a shower going down the hallway, is that right, or a bathroom rather going down the hallway? A. Yes. Q. And did you look in that bathroom? A. Yes. Q. Did there appear to be any water standing in that bathroom shower? A. No. Q. Did you have the same opportunity to look in the bathroom shower in the master bed? A. Yes. Q. Did there appear to be any water in that shower? A. Yes. I observed some water drops.

Q. "And did you write a report to that effect? A. No, I did not. Q. Why not? A. I had briefed the -- I briefed the investigating officers of my observations. I was unaware that the information didn't make it into the initial report. Had I been aware, I would have completed my own supplement. Q. For clarification, you're not a member of the Major Case Squad; is that right? A. That's correct. Q. This is a case that was turned over to the Major Case Squad? A. Yes, it was. Q. And so once the Major Case Squad takes over, what happens to the patrolmen that are not members of the Major Case Squad? A. We go back to doing our normal duties. Q. So you don't have any interaction with the case? A. That's correct. Q. So if you -- did you give this information to someone in that department? A. I believe I gave it to one of our initial investigators that showed up. Q. And at what time did you learn that this information never made it to a report? A. It was sometime after the initial trial."

The implication was to show that someone had showered and water droplets were still visible. Yet, this was never mentioned in the first trial. All the evidence photos show dry drains and tubs. Askey's premise was that Russ showered and cleaned-up after he murdered Betsy.

CROSS-EXAMINATION BY MR. SCHWARTZ: Q. So just so we're clear, you noticing some water droplets is not in a report anywhere with all this documentation, correct? A. That's correct. Q. And you learned that in 2013 -- late in 2013 or sometime in 2014? A. It was sometime after the initial trial. Q. How did you learn that? A. I believe I was talking to one of the investigators. Q. And -- but you had a specific recollection after doing a search -- how many calls do you think you go on a year? A. I don't know. Q. Hundreds? A. Possibly. Q. So, since this has occurred you have been on 500 maybe? This was in '11. A. Possibly.

Q. "In 2013 or 2014, when you realized you noticed some water drops, did you complete a report at that time? A. I'm sorry. Q. Did you complete a report after you talked to somebody about this? A. No, I did not. Q. When did you meet with Ms. Askey and tell her about that? A. It was sometime over this summer. Q. This summer? A. Yes, sir. Q. And did you ever prepare a report for Ms. Askey? A. No, I did not. Q. But you told her about it? A. Yes, I did. Q. And the water droplets, you're not saying somebody took a shower, are you? A. I'm just saying I observed water droplets. Q. Droplets? A. Yes, sir. Q. Like beads of water? A. Yes, sir. Q. How many? A. I don't recall. Q. Two to three? A. More than two or three. Q. Five? A. I don't know. Q. Could have been two or three, could have been five, but you have -- correct? A. Correct. Q. Have you ever had a leaky faucet at home? A. Yes, sir. Q. Leaves water droplets, doesn't it? A. Yes, it does. Q. As far as you know, this could have been from that, correct? A. It's possible. Q. There was no evidence that you came across that anyone had taken a shower, no wet towels? A. Not that I recall. Q. No wet drain, no wet walls, no nothing. A few water droplets, right? A. Yes. I observed water droplets. Q. And that's it? A. That's it."

Judge Ohmer questioned Sergeant Pirtle about the droplets. He asked how big they were, where in the tub they were, if he could tell how long they had been there? Pirtle answered he remembered them being in the middle of the tub with no trail running to the drain. He did not know how long they had been there. He did not touch them…just noticed them. He did not call anyone's attention to them at the scene.

Amy Buettner (Pratt at Trial 1) was questioned next:

DIRECT EXAMINATION BY MS. ASKEY: Q. Please state your name for the record. A. My name is Amy Buettner. Q. And where are you employed? A. I'm employed with the St. Charles County Police Department. Q. What are your duties there, Amy? A. I'm a crime scene investigator. Q. What does that entail? A. That entails responding to crime scenes, taking photographs, processing evidence, seizing evidence and putting pieces of the puzzle together. Q. Okay. Are you a member of law enforcement? A. I am a civilian. Noncommissioned. Q. Okay. And so -- but you work with law enforcement? A. Yes, ma'am. Q. Were you working in that capacity in December of 2011? A. I was."

Attorney Joel Schwartz does the cross-examination: Q. "You also took pictures of every one of the dog's paws, correct? A. I believe so, yes. Q. Did you notice any blood whatsoever on any of the paws? A. Not visibly, no. Q. Did you notice any blood whatsoever on the dog? A. Not visibly, no. Q. Blood can be invisible, correct? A. Yes. Q. Did you do any testing to find invisible blood? A. No. Q. Why not? A. Because when I wanted to do that we were told not to. Q. I'm sorry. Who told you not to? A. We were told that by Detective Harney. Q. Okay. But you didn't notice any? A. No. Q. All right. Speaking of invisible blood, did you perform any Luminol testing or BlueStar testing of the house at all? A. No. Q. Do you typically do that? A. We would do that if we believed that a scene was cleaned up or that a body had been moved, and obviously the body did not move from its original location and the scene did not appear to be cleaned up. Q. All right. So, you had absolutely no indication there would be any hidden blood there anywhere? A. No. Q. Anyone ask you to do any Luminol? A. No. I refuse to do it. Q. I'm sorry. You said you refuse to do it? A. I refuse to do it. Q. Okay. So, somebody did ask and you said no? A. Someone asked -- it was either Detective Black or Detective Harney -- if we were going to do Luminol and I said no, that we are not doing it. Q. And that is because there was no evidence whatsoever of cleanup? A. Correct.

Q. "What about contamination? A. That scene was extremely contaminated when I got there. Q. Even though the officers should have maintained the integrity of the scene, it was already contaminated before you got there? A. I believe so, yes. Q. This was on the morning of the 28th? A. Yes. Q. It's only going to get more contaminated as time goes on, correct? A. Yes. Q. So by the 3rd it would have been really contaminated? A. Correct. Q. Okay. Did you also process the Explorer located at the driveway of the home? A. CSI Tiffany Fischer did. I had no part in that. Q. You had no part in that, okay. A. No.

Q. "Let me show you State's Exhibit 33. Showing you State's Exhibit 33, that's the light switch plate, correct? A. It is. Q. How many crime scenes do you think you have been to? A. Thousands. Q. How many bloodstains have you photographed and processed? A. A lot. Hundreds. Q. Hundreds. Bloodstains from hands? A. Yes. Q. Bloodstains from cloth? A. Yes. Q. How many bloodstains from cloth do you think? A. I would say it's below a hundred. I would say very few. Probably ten, 20. Q. Okay. Do the stains on the light switch plate resemble a bloodstain from cloth? A. Yes. Q. Based on what? A. There's an actual pattern to it and it gives a crisscross-like pattern. Q. In fact, there are two patterns to it, correct? A. Yes, there are. The other one is not distinguishable. Q. One is crisscross and the other one looks more wavy? A. Yes. Q. Did you locate any bloody fabric in the house whatsoever besides the shoes? A. And the victim? Q. And the victim. A. No. Q. So whatever blood made that stain you didn't find it? A. No. Q. All right. Which means somebody took it with them when they left? A. I don't know." An objection was made to the final statement.

Co-Counsel Nathan Swanson scored major points with CSI Buettner concerning the blood evidence at the scene, in particular, Russ' bloody slippers:

Q. "There is a dark spot right there, correct? A. Yes. Q. Two dark spots? A. Correct. Q. And they move laterally, they move along the seam of the shoe, correct? A. Yes, they do. Q. Is that consistent with stepping into blood? A. No. Q. Is that consistent with being swiped in blood? A. That is given a consistency of the blood -- the dark end of the blood at the bottom or towards -- if you're leaning it this way, this blood is pooling there. That means that blood got onto that shoe somehow in this direction. Q. So it went like this on outside? A. That's possible. Q. But not that someone stepped in blood? A. No. This blood is pooling.

Q. "Okay. I'm going to hand you State's Exhibit 42. Do you see those droplets of blood? A. Yes. Q. Are those consistent with someone stepping in blood? A. No. Q. State's 43 -- A. That's the up-close picture. Q. That's the up-close picture. The furthest stain to the left? A. This direction? Q. Up at the top. A. Up here? Q. Yes. A. Okay. Q. That appears to be moving downwards, correct? A. Yes. Q. Again, that would not be consistent with someone stepping in blood? A. No. Q. State's 40. On the bottom of the left-hand slipper, what do you see there? A. On this slipper, I see a red blood-like substance near the toe area of the slipper. Q. Are there gaps in that substance or gaps in that stain? A. There are. Q. Is that again consistent with someone stepping down into blood? A. If you stepped in a pool of blood, no. Q. If you stepped into some amount of blood or some droplets of blood, maybe that? A. I would believe that it would spread across the entire tip of that toe and fill in this gap.

Q. "So, again, your testimony would be that is not consistent with someone stepping in blood? A. I would say no. Q. Those stains, most of them are consistent with someone placing the shoes in blood, correct? A. I don't know. Q. Fair enough. This was a very bloody crime scene? A. Around the victim it was, yes. Q. The victim had quite a few wounds to her, correct? A. Yes, she did. Q. Resulting in quite a bit of bleeding? A. Very much so. Q. That blood would have gotten on the assailant, correct? A. Yes. Q. It would be almost impossible for someone to commit the crime and have no blood on them? A. It would be impossible.

Q. "Okay. I'm going to hand you what's been marked as Defendant's Exhibit D. Do you recognize what that is? A. This is the knife to -- or the handle of the knife that was protruding from the victim's neck. Q. Do you notice anything on that handle? A. Originally, we had thought that we may have -- there's a pattern. We thought that we may have a fingerprint or palm print on there. Q. All right. And what was the palm print in if that makes sense? A. I'm sorry? Q. I got a little ahead of myself. You said you noticed a palm print? A. We thought so, yes. Q. What substance, if any, was that palm print in? Is it just -- A. It's blood. There is a red blood-like substance. There is a pattern and blood. Q. Would it be possible for somebody to hold that knife and not get blood on their hand? A. No.

Q. "And just to back up one last time. You seized all the pipes and the drains from the house, correct? A. Swabs of them, yes. Q. You took swabs of them? A. Yes. Q. Okay. Let's talk about Luminol very briefly or BlueStar. What are those? A. Luminol and BlueStar are used as a presumptive to locate blood that is not visible. Q. And when you say they are presumptive, they are not conclusive, they react -- A. They react to numerous things, but blood is -- they are designed to react towards blood.

Q. "Okay. But they will also react with other things? A. Correct. Q. Such as? A. Cleaning agents. Q. Anything else? A. I believe rust minerals, that type of thing. Q. In fact, some of the formulations will react with beet juice, correct? A. Yes. Q. And they will react with the residue with any kind of animal protein, correct? A. Yes. Rats' blood especially. Q. Rats' blood, blood from meat? A. Yes. Q. Remnants of dog food? A. No. Q. If there are animal proteins in it? A. I don't know. I never tested that one. Q. Dog food? A. Possibly. Don't know. Q. Okay. But it will react to invisible blood, correct? A. Yes. Q. When you see a cleanup, you see large swoops in the BlueStar; is that correct? A. Swipes, yes. Q. So when you apply BlueStar and there is evidence of a blood cleanup or any kind of cleanup, there is big 'ole swipes showing where the person moved cleaning material back and forth? A. Yes. Q. Not little dots? A. No. **MR. SWANSON**: Nothing further, Your Honor."

It could not have been lost on all within earshot of this testimony that the statement about the assailant getting blood on them cut both ways. Whether the murderer was Russ, or Pam as Schwartz believed, how did they clean up after? No blood was found in the drains. There were no wet towels. Two small stains were found on a bath towel and a lime green kitchen washcloth…that was it. Russ was found wearing the same clothes he is wearing in the camera videos from the gas station and two stores he stopped at that night. There was no blood found on his clothing. Only *his* DNA showed up under his fingernail clippings. Nothing suspicious appeared on the swabs they did of his feet and hands at the police station.

So, how does one do such a brutal murder and show no signs of a clean-up at the scene? If it was Pam Hupp, had she taken her bloody clothing with her as she left? Had she perhaps brought a change of clothes, wet wipes, a hair net, latex gloves in one of her over-sized purses, and then bundled up all the incriminating evidence and taken it out the door? Had she then disposed of it somewhere before going home to watch T.V. with Mark? Her son Travis lived just down the street from her home. It was found he had an alibi and was not home that night. Had she gone inside and cleaned up, left, or disposed of, the clothes and retrieved them later? Police never processed her car for blood and never even asked Mark Hupp what time she arrived home. Three text messages between herself and Travis that night still remain a mystery at the writing of this book. They were short, under a minute each. 9:09 p.m.- 9:10 p.m.

Day Two of the Trial: Tuesday, November 3rd

It started with Leah Askey questioning another CSI agent, Tiffany Fischer:

DIRECT EXAMINATION BY MS. ASKEY: Q. "Ma'am, please state your name. A. Tiffany Fischer. Q. Where are you employed? A. St. Charles County Police Department. Q. And what are your duties there? A. I'm a crime scene investigator. Q. How long have you been employed as a crime scene investigator? A. Seventeen years. Q. And have you always been with St. Charles County? A. Yes. Q. And what do you do as a crime scene investigator? A. We respond to scenes, we photograph the scene, we document items of evidence, we collect the evidence, bring it back to the station and we process evidence. Q. And are you a commissioned law enforcement officer? A. I am not."

Tiffany arrived at the crime scene at 7 a.m. the morning of the 28th (morning after the murder) and stayed until 3 p.m. She went on to say how she processed the back sliding door for prints and found two belonging to Russ Faria. She looked for blood clean-up and found none. She mentions the receipts found in Russ' SUV from two stores and an Arby's verifying Russ' alibis for the previous night. Tiffany also went into the paw print found on the back of Betsy's pants as she lay on the floor. Nathan Swanson did the cross:

Q. "All right. And the other reason that you didn't conduct any BlueStar testing was you were unable to locate any evidence of clean-up, correct? A. Correct. Q. There was no odor of cleaning products, correct? A. Yes, sir. Q. There were no wet towels anywhere? A. No. Q. No paper towels anywhere? A. No. Q. No wet mops? A. No. Q. All right. And when you did the area canvas you looked at all the drainage? A. The manholes, yes. Q. Did you look in the trashcans? A. On the property, yes. Q. And, again, you didn't locate any evidence of cleanup? A. No. Q. You did not locate any clothes? A. No. Q. Towels, nothing? A. No. Q. All right. Did you assist in taking the paw impressions from the dog? A. I took photographs and I had treats. Q. And the dog didn't appear vicious at all, correct? A. No. Q. The dog wasn't barking at all? A. No. Q. Dog wasn't jumping at all? A. No. Q. All right. Did you look very closely at the dog's paws? A. I did not. Q. All right. Did you notice any blood on the dog at all? A. No. Q. Did you notice any paw prints of the dog inside the house whatsoever? A. No. Other than the potential pattern on the back of the pants." CSI Fischer was also one of the CSI's that commented on the dirty kitchen floor and that there were dog treats scattered there. It was evident no clean-up of that floor had been made. It was still gritty, as were the counters.

Joel Schwartz questions CSI Don Smallwood concerning the prints found on the knife:

Q. "Okay. Is that photo as it was when you compared it? Is that a knife from the crime scene as far as your understanding, a picture of a knife from the crime scene? A. That's my understanding. I don't know exactly, but yes, this is the photo I was asked to look for -- look at possible palm prints is what I was told on it; however, I did not find one and reported that finding. Q. But you do see some sort of -- there is blood on it and there seems to be some sort of ridges or something on there, correct? A. There is some kind of strikes in pattern there. I would agree with that is. Q. What would you think that is from, some sort of cloth or something? MS. ASKEY: I would object. Calls for speculation. MR. SCHWARTZ: He's an expert. THE COURT: Overruled. You may answer if you know. A. Honestly, I have no idea. I would have to do a further analysis and determine what could possibly make those marks. They are not -- I'm not seeing anything unique enough to identify it to an object. Q. But you would say it's not a palm? A. I would say, in my opinion, it is not ridge consistent with ridge detail from a palm. Q. So it is different from somebody's bare hand, but you just don't know what? A. Correct."

During re-direct, Leah Askey asks something that would come back to haunt this case:

BY MS. ASKEY: Q. "Just briefly, Mr. Smallwood. That ridge detail or whatever it is on that knife, which is Defendant's Exhibit - - I don't know -- L. A. L. Q. Could be made by a sock, right? A. I do not know. Q. But could be? A. I do not know what made those impressions. Q. Mr. Schwartz asked you it was something other than a palm? A. A palm -- I can say, in my opinion based on looking at it, I do not see friction ridged detail consistent with a palm. Other than that, I'm not prepared to say what could or could not have made that mark. Q. And you didn't compare it, correct? A. No. MS. ASKEY: Nothing further."

It is with the next witness that the meat of the defense's claim of misconduct gets the full spotlight. Mike Merkel with the Lincoln County Sheriff's Department in Troy, Missouri, would play a key role in the case against Russ Faria. Merkel was commander of the Internal Investigations Unit. He and his partner, Detective Patrick Harney, interviewed Russ the morning he was brought in, and Pam Hupp on several occasions leading up to Trial 2. He was now on the hot seat.

Askey showed Merkel photographs of Betsy's body and the surrounding clutter. There were several upright packages containing presents, including the Kohl's bag showing blood spatter that one detective described as "cast-off" being flung from the bloody murder weapon as it made strikes to the victim. The prosecutor then asked Merkel if he could any way, tell from the photos, that Russ could have laid down next to Betsy on the floor without getting any blood on him? Russ had stated he laid down by her when he arrived and found her. Merkel stated he could see no way there was room for him to do so without getting blood on him or disturbing the clutter around Betsy. Askey also went over the Luminol test in the kitchen area:

Q. "Specifically, were you present during a search warrant that was executed on January 3rd? A. I believe that was the date, yes, ma'am. Q. Was that a search warrant wherein BlueStar was applied to certain areas of the house? A. Yes, ma'am. Q. Do you recall if there were any positive reactions as a result of that BlueStar application? A. After reviewing my reports and what were photographs that were taken, yes, ma'am. Q. Now, in fairness this was during the daylight that you -- that the BlueStar was applied; is that correct? A. Yes, ma'am. Q. So how, if at all, did that affect the ability to photograph the evidence of the luminescence? A. Beings though it was daylight, you have to fashion some sort of window covering to limit the light. There's some ambient light that can be present, but the darker is the better. So, we did the best job we could really.

Q. "And what did you do specifically? A. We fashioned some window coverings. I want to say they were cardboard boxes. And then I think we used evidence tape. I can't remember if it was evidence tape or packing tape, but we used the tape to secure up the windows. Q. To cover the windows? A. To the best we could, yes, ma'am. Q. But sunlight was still coming through? A. Yes, ma'am.

Q. "As far as the camera that the Lincoln County Sheriff's had in 20- -- well, it would have been early 2012? A. Yes, ma'am. Q. That was a previous administration; is that right? A. Yes, ma'am. Q. Different equipment? A. Different equipment than we have now? Q. Yeah. A. It was -- it was not in working order. Not in good working order that it could have been then. It's since been repaired. Q. Okay. And what was wrong with it, if you know? A. I have the maintenance records here and it's in Nikon language so I can read it to you, but there was some issues with our aperture and our flash, so various programming issues.

Q. "Did that affect the way those photographs were able to be developed? A. I believe it could have, yes, ma'am. Q. And did -- so when you came into the residence, where did you apply BlueStar? A. If I remember correctly, we prepared it in the foyer and then we applied it to the -- I'll call it the kitchen and dining room area. Kitchenette maybe is what it is called. Q. So the linoleum area? A. Yes, ma'am. Q. Did you also apply it to any cabinet facings? A. Yes, ma'am. That would have been in the kitchen, yes, ma'am. Q. So not just the floor? A. Correct. Q. Did you apply it to the living room area where the victim's body was found? A. I believe we did just as a standard to make sure -- I mean, we -- obviously we knew blood was there, so -- Q. To make sure that it reacted? A. Yes. That's typically -- Q. And then you applied it in the kitchen? A. Yes, ma'am. Q. And were there any luminescence? A. Yes. Q. And where were those luminescence? A. If I can refer to my report? Q. Would that refresh your recollection? A. Yes, ma'am. Q. That would be great. A. It says here it was present in several areas of the kitchen and dining room and then areas where the present -- areas where the luminescence was present was photographed and then seized -- physically seized for further examination.

Q. "And when you say physically seized, those tiles or whatever would have been seized from the floor? A. Yeah. I believe from reviewing some of the photographs, we took sections of the linoleum and then maybe a couple cabinet facings. I would have to look at the evidence log for that. Q. Okay. But you don't remember as you sit here today which ones -- what luminesced or any specific pattern? A. If I remember correctly, it would have been -- the luminesce would have been in the -- in the dining room area in the kitchenette on the floor, as I call it an egress to the back patio. And then, again if I remember correctly, it was on a cabinet face. Just don't remember which cabinet face it would have been. Q. It was a cabinet or a drawer? A. Well, it was the face of the -- I'm just going to say kitchen cabinets as a whole. I don't recall if it was a drawer or one of those false ones.

Q. "I gotcha. A. So I will say the front of the cabinets. Q. One of those? A. Yes, ma'am. Q. And then an egress, which the path -- A. To go out, yes, ma'am. Q. -- to the back door? A. Yes, ma'am. And if I remember correctly, that was a -- was a bay window. I believe so. Q. Sliding door? A. I believe so, yes, ma'am. MS. ASKEY: I don't have anything further, Judge."

Joel Schwartz approached the judge at the conclusion of Merkel's testimony with a grievance he had been reiterating:

(A lunch recess was taken.) THE COURT: "Be seated, folks. Good afternoon. (Counsel approached the bench and the following proceedings were held:) MR. SCHWARTZ: There are some items that this detective seized from my client in his interview, all of his clothing specifically. I've asked the State to provide it. The State said to call the custodian and talk to the sheriff. I spoke to the sheriff as we began the break and the sheriff said, "Well, you have to talk to Merkel." And the State so far apparently has refused to call and get that stuff over here. I don't have it, and I don't have the capability to get it here. I have made the State aware at least twice this morning." MS. ASKEY: "Well, before lunch." MR. SCHWARTZ: "I was told she doesn't have to put on my evidence or my case." MS. ASKEY: "He asked me this morning if I had the defendant's clothes. I said I don't. I didn't bring them over. I wasn't going to put his clothes on." MR. SCHWARTZ: "I said to get it. I need it." MS. ASKEY: "I called over at lunch and they were at lunch. And then I kept working with my people." THE COURT: "Okay. So, can we call them and get it here now?" MS. ASKEY:" I mean, I can. I left the message over there, but I –" THE COURT: "Let's get it here. We'll take a short recess while we get some evidence."

Schwartz had mentioned earlier in court proceedings that he was concerned the prosecution had been withholding evidence from him. This time, a judge would listen and act upon it. It was now time to attack the accusation that there had been a blood trail coverup leading from the living room to the kitchen the night of the murder which only showed up with a Luminol test.

"Absolutely Nothing!"

Schwartz to Merkel: Q. "As far as you know or whether or not you know, Russ and his family had gone back there? A. I don't know. Q. You don't know. You don't know what cleanup occurred -- you don't know what had occurred at that residence between December the 27th and January 3rd? A. I'm not sure when the residence was released. But from the moment of release to January 3rd, yes, sir, that's fair to say. Q. Now, you went in there and what was your purpose of going there? A. I believe a search warrant had been secured for identification or retrieval of any blood evidence. Q. And when you went in there, there was some talk in your direct testimony about a camera? A. Yes, sir. Q. And you took photographs? A. Yes, sir. Attempted to. Q. You attempted to take photographs? A. Yes, sir. Q. And I asked you about those when you testified back in November of 2013? A. Okay. Yes, sir. Q. Is that correct? A. Okay.

Q. "And I asked you what they showed. Do you remember your answer? A. No, I don't. Q. Your answer would have been, "Absolutely nothing." Correct? A. That's fair to say. Q. And I asked you again, "They showed absolutely nothing?" And your answer was, "Correct." Is that accurate? A. That's fair to say, yes, sir. Q. Well, I don't want it to be fair to say. I want -- would it refresh your recollection if I showed you a copy of the transcript? A. Yes. Yes, sir. Q. Does that refresh your recollection? A. Yes, sir.

Q. "Just so we're clear, I asked you before I said that, I said, "Did you review the photographs?" And you said, "What? I did," answer. A. Yes, sir. Q. And I said, "What did they show?" And your answer was -- A. I think you have already given it to me. "Absolutely nothing." Q. "Absolutely nothing"? A. Yes, sir. Q. And then I reiterated they showed absolutely nothing, and your answer was what? A. Again, I believe I said, "Absolutely nothing." Q. Correct. And then I asked, "Why?" And you said, "Because of a malfunction in our camera that has since been repaired." Is that correct? A. Yes, sir.

Q. "So there were no pictures that were developed that day? A. I don't believe so, no, sir. Q. I'm going to show you what I've marked as Defendant's Exhibit -- it is a bad O, but it is an O. What's that? Take your time. A. It would be photographs from that day. Q. It would be what? A. Photographs from that day. Q. Did it show absolutely nothing? A. As far as the chemical luminescence, no, sir, it does not. Q. Well, that's not what I asked you back in November of 2013, was it? A. It is open for interpretation, but yes, sir. Q. That's open for interpretation. Your answer was, "Absolutely nothing." There's how many -- do you know how many pictures there are there? A. There's a lot. Q. There's about 130 of them, aren't there? Actually, about 132 if my count was correct? A. I believe that's what it says here, yes, sir. Q. And there is not any of those that show absolutely nothing, is there? A. No, sir. Q. Not one. Why don't we pull one of those out? Pull any one out. What's that a picture of? A. This would be the returned-in-inventory from -- well, it's not being returned inventory. It's a photograph of the returned-in-inventory. Q. All right. So that shows something, it is not absolutely nothing, is it? A. No, sir, it is not.

Q. "What's the next one? A. Looks like it is blurry, so it is probably the same thing. Just an overall. Q. All right. Here. Why don't we -- let me have that for one second. A. (Complying). Q. I will just grab pictures as we go. Let me show you what I've marked O1. What's that a picture of? A. Looks like a sink drain. Q. And that was a picture that was taken on January 3rd during the course of your search? A. I believe so, yes, sir. Q. When you testified under oath in trial that there was absolutely nothing that developed from those pictures, is that absolutely nothing? A. No, sir, it is not. MS. ASKEY: "Judge, I'm going to object. It mischaracterizes the testimony of the November trial." MR. SCHWARTZ: "How?" THE COURT: "Overruled. It is cross-examination. Proceed."

Q. (By Mr. Schwartz) "Why did you take that picture? A. I don't recall. Q. You guys actually looked and seized the drains because you were looking for blood evidence, correct? A. I believe. Q. And none was found and you looked through all these drains? A. I don't have those results or anything, so I can't speak to that. Q. Let me show you what I've marked O2. Does that depict how that appeared when that picture was taken on January the 3rd? A. I would assume it does. Q. Let me show you what I have marked O2. What is that a picture of? A. Looks like it is more of a broad range of the same photograph. Q. That actually looks like there is some cabinets removed, doesn't it, some drawers? A. I would assume so if they were there beforehand. Q. Okay. That is not a picture of absolutely nothing, is it? A. No, sir, it is not. Q. And does that picture depict how that area looked on January 3rd when that was taken? A. At some point during the day, yes, sir.

Q. "Let me show you what's been marked O3. Don't worry. I'm not going to go through all 132 of them. A. Oh, you're fine. Okay. Q. What's that a picture of? A. Again, it looks like just another -- I don't want to call it a close-up, but another -- Q. That's actually a picture of a pipe taken off, correct, under the sink? It looks like the pipe had been dismantled? A. No. It actually looks like the bag in this picture by the trap is in front of the pipe. I can't say it's been dismantled. Everything looks to be intact. Q. Does that picture depict what that area looked like when that photo was taken on January 3, 2012? A. I would have to assume so, yes, sir. Q. Let me show you what's been marked O4. What is that a picture of? A. It would be the part of the living room area and a dining area kitchenette. Q. So it is the linoleum tile where you laid some placards down because you found what you were calling drips of luminescence, correct, or drops? A. There was an indication for chemical luminescence. Q. That's not absolutely nothing, is it? A. No, sir, it's not.

Q. "Let's go to -- that was 4. A. Are you talking about O4? Q. Yeah. Does that reasonably depict the condition of that area when that photograph was taken on January 3, 2012? A. I believe so, yes, sir. Q. Let me show you what I've marked O5. What is that a picture of? A. It looks like a tile portion that's been removed. I can't say tile because it's linoleum but a section of linoleum that's been removed, but I can't tell where, though. Q. Does that show absolutely nothing? A. No, sir, it does not. Q. Does that depict the way that area looked on that particular day? A. I would believe so, yes, sir. Q. Let's go with O6. Can you tell me what that's a picture of? A. I will call it not really an overall, but maybe a medium view of the kitchen area. Q. Does that depict the way that particular area looked that day? A. I believe so, yes, sir. Q. I'm going to show you what's been marked as O7. A. Okay.

Q. "Can you tell the Judge what that is? A. It appears to be another area where we removed a sample of linoleum. Q. And does that reasonably depict the way that room looked on that day when that photograph was taken? A. I believe so, yes, sir. Q. And just so we're clear, there were nine particular tiles seized where you felt there was luminescence? A. I would have to look at my evidence. Q. Well, let me show you the return you just looked at. A. Oh, okay. Q. Nine final tiles seized? A. That's what it says here, yes, sir. Q. And how many cabinet faces seized? A. I can't tell if that is a two or seven, so do you have my evidence log by chance or an evidence log? Q. I don't. I'm sorry.

A. "Okay. I don't know if it's a two or a seven. Q. We agree there were cabinet faces seized and tiles seized? A. Yes, sir. Q. What were they seized for? A. I believe they were seized for further examination because they indicated they had a chemical luminescence, so -- Q. And all of those were seized and turned over to the lab, correct? A. They were seized. I -- if they were turned over to the lab, somebody else would have handled that portion of it. Q. Are you aware of the results of those lab tests? A. Not particularly, no, sir. Q. So you have never been told that none of those created --

contained any blood? A. I can't tell you that I have never been told. I just recall the results of them. Q. You have been told that? A. Okay.

Q. "But you would agree with me today what you testified to in 2013 was not accurate? MS. ASKEY: "I would object as to argumentative." THE COURT: "Sustained." Q. (By Mr. Schwartz) "What you testified in 2013, if the picture showed absolutely nothing, you just saw approximately 130 pictures of something? A. Yes, sir. Q. And this is not absolutely nothing? A. Correct. MR. SCHWARTZ: I don't have any further questions, Your Honor."

Raymond Floyd next took the stand. He was with the Major Case Squad in December, 2011, when Betsy was murdered. He relieved Merkle and Harney during the interview process with Russ at the police station during his initial time there. Russ had been undergoing hours and hours of questions when round two of the interrogation began. Interestingly, Russ had yet to be read his Miranda rights.

Attorney Leah Askey:

Q. "The first lead that you were assigned to, was that the one that was related to interviewing Russ Faria? A. The reinterview of Russ Faria, yes, ma'am. Q. And how did you begin that interview? A. I made contact with Mr. Faria, myself and Detective Keith Rider with the Chesterfield Police Department, introduced myself and I started getting basic information as far as who he was, where he lived, who else lived there, things such of that. Q. And was he willing to speak with you? A. Yes, ma'am. Q. Did you read him his Miranda rights when you entered the room? A. Not at that time, no, ma'am. Q. At some time during the interview did you read him his Miranda rights? A. Yes, ma'am. Q. Did he continue to talk to you? A. Yes, ma'am. Q. Did he initial the Miranda paper? A. He did.

Q. "How long would you say your interview lasted? A. I arrived at the Lincoln County Sheriff's Office prior to 4:00 o'clock [A.M.]. I believe our interview started a little bit before 4:00. We talked on and off until after 4:00 o'clock in the afternoon. Q. So on and off for 12 hours? A. Yes, ma'am. Q. During that time was Mr. Faria able to leave the interview room, go to the bathroom, get a drink, get food, that sort of thing? A. He used the restroom -- any time he asked to use the restroom he was allowed to use the restroom. We supplied soda, water, asked him several times if he wanted food. At some point, we did wind up getting McDonald's food and he ate some McDonald's.

Q. "And was he aware of whether or not his wife had any life insurance policies? A. He indicated that she did. Q. And did he indicate to you how much he thought she had in life insurance? A. Between three and $400,000. Q. And did he indicate how many policies he thought she had? A. He believed it to be three. He knew that he had one through his work. He thought there was one through where Betsy used to work being, I believe, State Farm. And the last one he thought may have been through MetLife. He wasn't one hundred percent sure on the MetLife, but he did say he thought the total amount was between three and $400,000. Q. Did he indicate to you who he believed to be the sole beneficiary of those policies? A. He indicated he was. Q. Did he tell you anything about increasing the face value of those policies in the recent months? A. Yes. Q. What did he say? A. He said when he had open enrollment at his work, which I believe was in October or November, that he increased it to the maximum amount. That him and Betsy had discussed it and he increased his life insurance on her to the maximum amount."

[Schwartz' cross of Floyd:]

Q. "And when you started talking to Russ based upon the information you had and in the conversation with him, he had been up at that point in time for about 24 hours when you began talking to him? A. When I began talking to him, I think he said he got up at 6:30 on Monday and it was probably about 4:00 o'clock on Tuesday. So, a little under 24 hours. Q. And your interview lasted 12 full hours? A. I was with Russ 12 hours, yes. Q. Would you leave? Did you leave the room? A. Several times, yes. Q. Why did you leave the room? A. A lot of times to verify some of the information and pass the information on to the commander so they can follow up leads. The initial part of the interview the majority of the leads that the Major Case Squad was getting was information that was provided by Russ. Q. And the information provided by Russ was where he went and what he did? A. That was some of the information, yes. Q. And the first place he told you he went -- we'll get to that in a minute. When you talked to Russ you -- so when you finished your interview, he had been up approximately 36 hours, maybe 34 hours? A. Somewhere in there, yes. Q. And he had found his wife -- his wife was deceased, regardless of what your theory is? A. Correct. Q. And he smoked a little marijuana, according to him?

A. Correct. A. He was with me from 4:00 o'clock in the morning until he was taken to the Lincoln County Sheriff's Office about 5:00 in the evening. Q. And then he was held on a 24-hour hold, correct? A. That's correct."

Day Three of Trial: Wednesday, Nov. 4th

The part of the trial that everyone dreaded began day three. It was the autopsy findings for Betsy Faria. Dr. Kamal Sabharwal once again went over his findings. He testified there had been two through-and-through knife wounds through Betsy's throat. Major organs such as the stomach, liver, spleen and pancreas had all been punctured leading to internal bleeding. Fifty-five stab wounds had butchered Betsy's upper torso and head. Nine cuts to her left arm and ten to her right were gone over. Her legs had sustained only one wound and that was to the top of her left thigh.

The question by Schwartz was put to the coroner that was meant to underscore that most of the wounds inflicted were postmortem.

Q. "Again, and if somebody's rolling or moving with that depth you would expect to see some sort of irregularity with a knife, correct? A. You could. Q. But you don't, do you? A. Correct."

Schwartz: "Q. Now, you actually pulled the knife out of Elizabeth Faria's neck, correct? A. Yes, I did. Q. And that knife was soaked in blood? A. Yes. Q. Including the handle? A. Yes. Q. It would be hard to imagine someone committing this offense with these 55, I believe, stab wounds it was and not having some form of blood on them. Would you agree with that? A. Yes."

Leah Askey asked Sabharwal: Q. "Doctor, the stab wounds that produced all the blood in the cavity of Elizabeth Faria, you're pretty confident that she was still alive when those stab wounds happened? A. I think that her heart was still beating. Whether it was beating at a normal pace or irregular at the time, for there to be blood both in the chest and abdominal cavity I believe there was some beating of the heart still. Q. And those -- those stab wounds, there weren't irregularities; is that correct? A. Correct. Q. You don't know which stab wound got her to the ground? A. Correct.

Q. "If she's on the ground and she's being restrained, she's not going to be moving a lot; is that fair to say? A. Yes. Q. And would those stab wounds if she's being restrained while she's being stabbed

55 times, would they be also consistent with that scenario? A. Yes. Could be. Q. So as long as she's able to be restrained and not move around, there's not going to be some irregularity in those stab wounds? A. It's possible, yes. Q. So it's fair to say that these stab wounds, I know you can't say for certain, but they could also be consistent with having been restrained on the ground? A. Yes. Q. As far as the way the blade tracks, they all track the same direction, they all come in the same way and go out the same way essentially is the way that you've documented it? A. With the different areas of the body where the collection of injuries are, for the most part, yes. Q. You're not able to say which ones, if any, happened after her heart stopped beating; is that fair to say? A. Yes."

To satisfy the prosecution's premise that Russ violated Betsy one more time before he killed her, Schwartz asked the coroner about only 8 sperm being found in Betsy during her autopsy. Russ had said they had sex Sunday, three days before murder.

BY MR. SCHWARTZ: Q. "Just so we're clear, there's nothing inconsistent with eight sperm cells on Tuesday evening or Wednesday morning when you found it with somebody being intimate on Sunday evening, correct? A. Correct."

Detective Ryan McCarrick was next up. He was most noted for taking over after the Major Case Squad folded camp December 31, 2011, four days after Betsy was murdered. He interviewed Pam Hupp multiple times and was the one who suggested she set up a trust for the girls before Russ' first trial to avoid suspicion. This is a detective Pam was able to give multiple versions of story to and he seemed to not only buy it all, but commiserated with her. Yet, during Askey's first go at him, he tells her his specialty is linguistics. Q. "Forensic statement analysis, specifically what does that mean? A. It is the analysis of which words are used, how those sentences are structured, what words are not used. It is the scientific study of linguistics in the written form developed with the Federal Bureau of Investigation and several psychologists and people in think tanks that have developed information about how people choose their words and how they choose to put them on paper."

Detective McCarrick also chimed in with his opinion on why the Luminol test did not show up in the photographs. A. "Yes. Apparently, there was a mechanical malfunction with the camera that I believe had to be corrected by the distributor that did not allow the luminescence of the BlueStar chemical to show on the film. Q. So you were able to capture the photographs in the light? A. Correct. Q. And you were able to capture photographs in the dark? A. Correct. Q. But the lens that allows for that luminescence to come through wasn't working? A. Correct. Q. As you're testifying today, you witnessed the luminescence yourself? A. I did. Q. Detective Merkel was there and he witnessed the luminescence? MR. SCHWARTZ: "Objection. Calls for speculation."

McCarrick was asked about what he found on Russ when he arrested him on January 4th, the day after Betsy's funeral: Q. (By Ms. Askey) "You actually placed him under arrest; is that right? A. I did. Q. Now, when you placed him under arrest, I'm going to show you what's been marked as State's Exhibit 54. Do you recognize that? A. I do. Q. And what is it? A. It is a piece of paper or a couple pieces of paper that were in his possession when he was arrested. Q. And what do they denote? A. One of them is a piece of paper that has my name and my phone number on it, my personal cell phone number. One of them is the name of a Ryan Lance that has another phone number on it. And one of them has the name Mike at the top with a phone number underneath that; Elizabeth, a policy and a policy number. Russell F. Faria and Mary Rodgers and Deb Shoskey {ph} with $150,000 written underneath that.

Q. "Were you able to verify that that was, in fact, a life insurance policy that Elizabeth Faria had in her name? A. I was. Q. And did you call the particular company that that policy was associated with? A. I did. I actually called that name Mike and the phone number that's on there. Q. And what did you learn about the specific -- this specific policy? A. That specific policy had those three as the original beneficiaries to that policy. I was also told that it was a policy that had been filed with State Farm and eventually lead to information from State Farm about a change of beneficiary. Q. So this policy that he had the note written on was the State Farm policy that eventually -- that Betsy Faria had already mailed her change of beneficiary form to? A. Yes, ma'am. MR. SWANSON: "Objection. Assumes facts not in evidence. It's not clear as to when this form was mailed." THE COURT: "Sustained as to the form. Rephrase." Q. (By Ms. Askey) "This policy dealt with the policy that Pam Hupp is a beneficiary of? A. Yes."

During questioning by Leah Askey to McCarrick, another issue of discovery arose:

Askey: Q. "Did he have any information on his person or around him regarding the insurance policy that he owned on his wife? A. No. Q. Did he have anything in or on his person or around him dealing with the change of beneficiary form that Bobbi Wann had talked about for Mutual of Omaha that Betsy had left on the counter at home? MR. SCHWARTZ: "Objection." MR. SWANSON: "Assume facts not in evidence. Bobbi Wann didn't know where the form was from, so –" THE COURT: "Sustained as to the form". Q. (By Ms. Askey) "Detective, did you have an opportunity to interview Bobbi Wann? A. I did. Q. Was that on February 15, 2012? A. Yes. MR. SWANSON: "Your Honor, can we approach? Can we approach?" THE COURT: "Certainly." (Counsel approached the bench and the following proceedings were held:) MR. SWANSON: "This is another report I have never heard of, seen. You should have produced that sometime in 2012."

MS. ASKEY: "All these things have been. MR. SCHWARTZ: "I have never seen that." MR. SWANSON: "This hasn't been produced. That's why we put up such a big fight over it Monday morning." MS. ASKEY: "You came into my office and went through my entire –" MR. SWANSON: "You didn't even have the stuff you'd already given us." MS. ASKEY: "Oh, my gosh. That is the most ridiculous thing I've ever heard." MR. SCHWARTZ: "I have never heard or seen this report, Judge." MS. ASKEY: "Okay. I'm sure."

MR. SCHWARTZ: "It continues." [Meaning the withholding of evidence] MS. ASKEY: "I'm sure not. You had complete access to my office to look through all of my files." MR. SWANSON: "You recall having interviews with Bobbi Wann that were never disclosed to us; you recall that, right?" MS. ASKEY: "I recall you always arguing about Bobbi Wann. You came to us arguing –" MR. SWANSON: "No, I wasn't. I wasn't –" MS. ASKEY: "No. I believe he –" MR. SCHWARTZ: "No, I didn't. No, I didn't. And neither did he. We have a memory issue." MR. SWANSON: "We were here."

MS. ASKEY: "And she told you about having this interview." MR. SWANSON: "No, she didn't." MR. SCHWARTZ: "No, she didn't. I have never heard of this. Ever." THE COURT: "Okay". MR. SCHWARTZ: "I mean, it just keeps continuing." MS. ASKEY: "All right." THE COURT: "All right. What –" MS.

ASKEY: "I don't know what to say, Judge. That's -- they continually say that. That's why we are here. They continually put out things like I haven't given them things. I have told them, "Come in my office and get whatever you want." THE COURT: "It is one thing to say, "Come into my office." MS. ASKEY: "And he did." THE COURT: "There is another obligation for you to turn over everything –" MS. ASKEY: "Absolutely." THE COURT: "-- to them. Not to say, "Here, take what you want." MS. ASKEY: "I understand. And I have done that over and over and over."

THE COURT: "That's not what you just told me. MS. ASKEY: "No –" THE COURT: "You said, "I opened my office to them." MS. ASKEY: "No. I'm saying that I –" THE COURT: "Have you turned this document over to them?" MS. ASKEY: "Absolutely." MR. SWANSON: "Absolutely not." THE COURT: "Let's proceed. Don't ask him -- the form of that question is improper. So, rephrase your question." MS. ASKEY: "I don't remember what the question was." THE COURT: "You were talking about what a witness said. He can't talk about that. That's hearsay." MS. ASKEY: "I was asking – "- THE COURT: "Ask him a question about what you want to ask him, but not what some other witness said."

MS. ASKEY: "Am I allowed to ask him about his interview with Bobbi Wann? THE COURT: "Yeah. But I'm not -- I don't want to hear out of his mouth what Bobbi Wann said." MS. ASKEY: "She testified already." THE COURT: "I don't care. I don't know what you're asking. Ask your question. I said rephrase it. And we'll talk about this at another time, about discovery issues. And provide a copy of whatever to them at this time with one of your assistants."

(The proceedings returned to open court.) Q. (By Ms. Askey) "Detective, was there any reference to any other insurance policy on Mr. Faria when he was arrested? A. That was the only thing that he had on him was the piece of paper we just discussed."

Testimony turned to Pam Hupp: "Q. Do you know Pam Hupp? A. I do. Q. Have you had a conversation with her? A. I have. Q. That conversation was video recorded, was it not? A. It was. Q. We saw a snip-it of that on the news? A. Yes. Multiple times. Q. You have had the opportunity to watch the hour and 22 minutes of that interview? A. Yes. Q. Was your statement that was produced accurate in the context in which it was given? A. No. Q. What did you discuss during the entirety of that interview?

A. "We discussed several things about the upcoming trial. We discussed the insurance forms, the beneficiary, why Betsy told her she wanted it changed. We discussed what she intended on doing with that ultimately. We discussed the events that transpired that night involving her and Betsy. We discussed pretty much everything that had been discussed with her before just rehashed. Q. What specifically did you talk to her about with regard to insurance money? A. She said that -- MR. SWANSON: "Objection. Calls for hearsay." THE COURT: "Sustained." Q. (By Ms. Askey) "What did you tell her to do? A. I told her I didn't care what she did with it as long as she made a decision so that everybody knew what her intentions were. I told her that the family was obviously upset because they had no idea what she was going to do with it. Q. Was she the first one -- strike that. You were the report writer in this case from the beginning? A. Yes, ma'am. Q. So all of the leads that were followed up on were approved by you eventually? A. Yes. Q. They were all put in the Major Case binders? A. Yes. Q. And then any supplements would have been approved by you as well? A. Correct. Q. You have had your deposition taken by Mr. Schwartz; is that right? A. I have. MS. ASKEY: I don't have anything further."

CROSS-EXAMINATION BY MR. SCHWARTZ: Q. "This report that was just furnished to us today, that was never approved, correct? A. I'm sorry? Q. That report was never signed off on and approved by anybody, correct? A. I wrote it. Q. So if you wrote it, it doesn't need approval; is that correct? A. No. If I wrote it and I'm the approving officer on those reports, then it is kind of redundant."

Q. "Now, let's talk about initially that search you went back to conduct in January. The scene had been released, correct? A. Yes, sir. Q. And the scene, as far as you know, had even been cleaned? You don't know? A. Correct. I don't know. Q. And you went and you took pictures, but they didn't turn out to what you had hoped that they would show? A. Correct. Q. But the luminescence that you saw, every spot where there was luminescence, you cut up those tiles? I think there was nine tiles seized; is that correct? A. I believe there was nine, yes. Q. And I don't remember the number, but anywhere you saw luminescence on the cupboard or on a drawer, you seized that as well? A. Yes, sir. Q. And those were all turned in to the lab, correct? A. Yes. Q. And you're aware the lab didn't find any blood on any of those? A. No. Not exactly. Q. You're not aware of that? A. No. That's not exactly what was said. Q. All right. We'll talk to the lab then."

Schwartz is now going after McCarrick like a prize fighter in a rink who is finished with the showy footwork. It was time to throw punches.

Q. "You had all those courses and, you know, one of the first rules in this country when someone is represented [has an attorney], you don't talk to them, do you? A. Don't ask them any guilt-seeking question. Q. Do you talk to them when they are represented? A. Again, you don't ask them any guilt-seeking questions. Q. Let's talk about the interview you did with Russ Faria after you met me and after you knew I was representing him. A. Okay. Q. He got a letter from State Farm, correct? A. Correct. Q. And you opened that letter? A. Sure. Q. And you pulled him out of his cell? A. Yes. Q. And you knew he was represented? A. Yes. Q. And you videotaped this, correct? A. Yes. Q. And you read the letter to him that he was no longer the beneficiary on that policy, correct? A. Yes. Q. And this is all on video? A. Yes. Q. And you asked him if he had anything to tell you after he found that information out, correct? A. I believe I asked him if he had anything to tell me.

Q. "What did you ask? A. I don't remember asking him anything. Q. Why did you put that on videotape? A. So it would show I didn't ask him any guilt-seeking questions. Q. So what was your purpose of reading him the letter? You just wanted to see him? A. I wanted to make sure he knew about it. Q. Why? You're just a caring guy? A. It is my job as a policeman to make sure everybody is aware of what is going on. Q. It is your job as a policeman to pull my client out of his cell on videotape and talk to him about news he is no longer the beneficiary of his wife's insurance policy? That's your job? A. It is my job to make sure everybody is apprised of what is going on. Again, I didn't ask your client any guilt-seeking questions; therefore, I didn't do anything illegal."

A lengthy discussion ensued concerning Detective McCarrick's interviews with Pam Hupp. During this discourse between the detective and Schwartz, some interesting details come out that were not previously discussed in the first trial. Schwartz has just asked McCarrick about the timeline of interviews with Pam beginning with the first one the morning after the murder:

A. "There was the original call or the original lead where we went and interviewed her, and I believe there was two follow-ups. Q. Right. And one of those leads was to -- there was nobody who ever confirmed her whereabouts other than potentially her phone, correct? A. Other than her statement. Q. Other than her statement? A. And her husband. Q. Well, someone went to go talk to her husband, didn't they? A. They did. Q. But they didn't talk to her husband, did they? A. They talked to her husband. Q. You reviewed that lead? A. I did." MR. SCHWARTZ: "May I approach, Judge? THE COURT: "You may." Q. (By Mr. Schwartz) "Would it refresh your recollection if I showed you a copy of that? A. Sure. Q. Do you remember it now? A. I -- I remember the lead, yes. Q. Okay. So, these detectives that were dispatched to talk to Pam Hupp's husband were Donald Farmer and Mike Reider {ph}, correct? A. Yes. Q. And they sat Mr. Hupp down in the same room with Mrs. Hupp? A. They did. Q. And they started to talk to Mr. Hupp, and as they were talking to him, he said he got a call from her, and they listened to the voicemail with Betsy's voice on it, correct? A. Yes. Q. And you've not heard that, have you? A. No. Q. That was not recorded? A. No. I have never heard the voicemail.

Q. "Now, they went and talked to him on December 29, 2011, right? A. Yes. Q. Any idea why he saved that voicemail? A. No idea. I have got voicemails from six months ago on my phone. I don't have any idea why he would save it. Q. But that is the last known recording of Betsy's voice, correct? A. To my knowledge, yes. Q. And that occurred I believe it was -- according to his phone, was 70 -- 19:04, 7:04? A. Yeah. It was around 7:00. Q. And that was when Pam and Betsy allegedly arrived at Betsy's house, correct? A. Yes. Q. And that recording wasn't saved; is that right? A. What recording? Q. The recording that Betsy made that particular night. A. It was on his phone. Q. It was on his phone, but nobody recorded that for us to have? A. No. They listened to the audio at the scene. Q. They didn't seize his phone, did they? A. I don't believe so.

Q. "Nobody ever tried to confirm where Mark Hupp was that night, did they? There was never a lead assigned? A. There was never a reason to. Q. Well, didn't you just say that Betsy -- I mean, that Pam was the beneficiary of the insurance? A. Yes. Q. And you were also aware that Pam and Mark Hupp share an account, right? A. Yes. Q. So he's also the beneficiary of that insurance? A. Okay. Q. Let's say Pam dies. Who does that money go to? A. Goes to her husband. Q.

Right. Nobody ever checked him out? A. There was no reason to. Q. Well, you said there were differences in Pam's statement. Is another word for differences lies? A. No. Q. That's not another word? A. No.

Q. "So when she said she called him to tell her -- when she said she called Betsy to tell her she was home, that wasn't a lie? A. Again, it was a difference in her statement, but because somebody says something different doesn't mean it is a lie. Q. Let's get back to Mark Hupp. A. Okay. Q. After you told him about the phone call, next it says that Pam continued to engage us in conversation while we were trying to talk to Mark, right? A. Yes. Q. And then it's a three-page interview, right? A. Yes. Q. It is not recorded, right? A. No. Q. After they talk about the phone call, Mark doesn't open his mouth again, does he? A. No. Q. Not one word? A. Not that's documented, no. Q. Not one word that's documented. Did you see the report? Did you see their lead? A. I did. Q. Did you say, hey, somebody go back and talk to Mark Hupp and confirm where he was or confirm where Pam was? You never did that, did you? A. He confirmed where he was. He stated where he was. He said I was at home and my phone was in the truck, so I didn't get the message.

Q. "Right. And you talked to Pam as to why she called her husband when she got to Betsy's, right? A. I did. Q. What was the reason? A. She said that she's not very good with directions, she's not very good at driving at night, and she gets lost easily, so she usually calls her husband to let him know whenever she's getting somewhere or leaving so that he doesn't worry if she doesn't show up. Q. Right. But he wouldn't know that because his phone was in the truck, right? A. Correct. Q. Now, when did you leave Lincoln County to go to Florissant? A. October of 2014.

Q. "So were you aware of the continuing interviews of Ms. Hupp or no? A. After I left? Q. Yeah. A. No. Q. Were you aware up to December, 2014? A. No. October of 2014 is when I left. Q. Okay. A. And I wasn't aware that there was continued interviews after I left, no. Q. Now, Ms. Hupp actually said the $150,000 is not a big deal to her, it is not that much money in her world, right? A. I believe that's the way she characterized it, yes. Q. Were you aware that Ms. Hupp couldn't even afford health insurance before she got this money?" MS. ASKEY: "I'm going to object. Assumes fact not in evidence." THE COURT: "Overruled. You may answer if you know". Q. (By Mr. Schwartz) "Were you aware of that? A. No, I was not. Q. Did you discuss that with her specifically? A. Her insurance? Q. Yeah. A. No. Q. She couldn't afford Cobra, she didn't tell you that? A. Not to my recollection.

Q. "She couldn't afford to see the doctor because she couldn't afford health insurance and had to pay out-of-pocket, she didn't tell you that? A. I don't believe so. Q. But what she did tell you is she was going to give the money to the kids? A. Yes. Q. And you repeatedly asked her in that interview, could you please do it before trial, it just doesn't look good, correct? A. Yes. Q. You wanted it to look good for trial? A. Wanted it to look good for whatever was going to be the purpose of it. We needed to know what's going to happen so that my prosecutor knew how to prepare for trial, and it needed to look better for the family so that they had some piece of mind. I mean, there's several reasons why it needs to look better. Q. You also asked the family not to sue Pam Hupp until after the trial, right? A. I don't recall ever telling the family that.

Q. "Did you call Rita Wolf and ask her to lay off the family and quit telling them to sue Pam Hupp? A. No. Q. You're sure? A. Yeah. I'm pretty sure I didn't call Rita Wolf other than to talk to her during the interview when I interviewed her. Q. Did you ask her not to tell the family to sue Pam Hupp until after the trial? A. No. Q. How many times do you think you asked Ms. Hupp to please set up that trust before trial? A. It was about a five-minute conversation during that interview, so I don't know. Q. And she promised she would set it up before trial, didn't she? A. She did. Q. And, in fact, she did set it up before trial, right? A. Yes. Q. And she revoked it after trial, didn't she? A. That's what I hear, yes. Q. As a matter of fact, she took $99,700 of the $100,000 out within about ten days after trial; were you aware of that? A. No.

Q. "You told Pam that the family -- that you talked to the family and the family was saying that Betsy wanted to stay that night on the 27th at her mom's house as part of your interview, correct? A. Yeah. She said that the family was upset with her about the money situation and that they were -- I think the way she characterized it was pissed about the money. Q. But that's not what I'm talking about right now. In your interview you said to her that the family -- talking about the evening of the 27th -- why is the family saying to you that they wanted her to stay at her mom's house that night? A. I don't know why the family was telling me that. Q. And you also said -- you said it a couple times -- that they were kind of put off -- I think that was your word -- about Pam taking her home and wanting to take her home that night, correct? A. Yeah. That was the way the family characterized it to me. Q. That is what the family said to you. They were put off by Pam wanting to take her home? A. Correct.

Q. "And you knew that Pam wasn't supposed to go to chemo that day, that she was going with Bobbi Wann, right? A. Pam said that Bobbi Wann took her and that Pam went up there and met with them. Q. But you looked at the phones and you knew that Pam got a text saying she wants -- Betsy to Pam, that she wants to spend one-on-one time with Bobbi, right? You read that text? A. I don't remember. Q. Oh, you're right. It is in -- it is actually in Pam's initial interview. You reviewed that, right? A. I did. Q. And they reviewed Pam's text and it said, "I want to spend one-on-one time with Bobbi," right? A. Yeah. I believe she told Detective Kaiser and Detective Perry that. Q. Yet she went anyway? A. Yes. Q. After she was told to don't come, she intruded on their one-on-one time, right? A. Yes. Q. And then the family was put off by her wanting to take Betsy home that night, right? A. That's what they said, yes. Q. That's what they said to you? A. Yes. Q. And Pam told you she called her husband because she was uncomfortable going into unfamiliar areas at night, right? A. Yes.

Q. "And this distance she was traveling was from her house, which approximately is about a 25-minute drive to Pam's house? A. Sure. Q. So it is a 50-minute round trip on a cold, wet night in late December, right? A. Yes. Q. And Betsy already had a ride home from Russ, right? A. That's what she said, yes. Q. That's what she said and that's what is in Betsy's and Russ's text, right? You reviewed those? A. Russ said that he -- or Russ sent a text asking if she needed a ride and Pam said no, that Betsy was going to take her. Q. She actually said that Pam wants to take me home in the text, correct? A. I believe so, yeah. Q. And Pam had differences in her story? A. She did. Q. Pam actually initially said she didn't even go in that house, right? A. I believe she started to say that and then immediately changed her answer and said she did when she talked to me right -- Q. So, the answer is yes. She initially said I didn't go in that house. They asked her if she went in and she said no and then she said she did. A. Correct. Q. And then she said she only went in the kitchen and the living room, right? A. I think originally, yes. Q. And then it ultimately changed into, I went back to the bedroom and I saw this jewelry chest, right? A. Right. Q. So those are some of the differences you're talking about. You don't call those lies, though, they're differences? A. Correct. Q. Yet we're talking about the person who was the last one with her and you've never reviewed the cell towers to see where she was when she made that call, have you? A. No. Q. But you know she made that call at 7:27? A. I believe that was the time, yes. Q. And you wouldn't argue with me if I said she still could have been at or in the house based on the cell towers? A. I can't argue on cell tower activation records because I don't understand how to read them."

Another mystery to Betsy's insurance policy is the wrong city listed under her name. Schwartz asked McCarrick about it:

"Officer, let me show you what's been marked as Defendant's Exhibit Q. A. Okay. Q. Have you seen that form before? A. Yes. Q. A copy of it? A. Yes. Q. And is that form substantially similar to the form that you saw? A. Yes. Q. And is that the form changing the beneficiary from or making it Pam Hupp? A. Yes. Q. And Pam Hupp lived in O'Fallon, right? A. Yes. Q. Where did Betsy Faria live at the time? A. Troy, Missouri. Q. What's the address that Betsy Faria put on that form that's on that form? Under Betsy Faria's name, it says O'Fallon, Missouri, doesn't it? A. Yes. It doesn't give an exact address. It just gives the city of O'Fallon, Missouri. Q. It says the O'Fallon ZIP code, right? A. Yes. Q. Yet Betsy Faria didn't live in O'Fallon? A. No. Q. Now, on January 13th of 2013, you spoke with a representative at State Farm, right? A. I did. Q. And you talked to them about Pam Hupp being the beneficiary? A. I did. Q. And by the way, you also knew -- well, and you told them go ahead and release the funds, Pam Hupp's not a suspect; is that correct? A. Yes. MR. SCHWARTZ: Nothing further."

Chapter Fourteen
The Verdict

As the trial continued, the tension ran high in the courtroom. Both sides had a lot at risk. The prosecution needed to defend their earlier case that sent Russ Faria to prison, and the defense needed to free him. It was an "all or nothing" proposition. The verdict would be decided by one person, not twelve, and it was obvious Judge Ohmer was taking it all in.

Next to the stand was the librarian who had been the unfortunate person to be standing behind the counter that day when Betsy Faria and Pam Hupp approached her with an insurance form. Lauren Manganelli's typical routine was helping customers with research needs and checking books in and out. She admitted she was not a notary and this was her first, and last, time being asked to witness a document.

Leah Askey is questioning Manganelli: Q. "Did you at some point serve as a witness on a document? A. Yes. Q. I'm sure you're thrilled that you did that at this point. So, on December 23rd, 2011, do you recall two women coming with a change of insurance beneficiary form? A. Yes. (State's Exhibit 77 was marked for identification.) Q. (By Ms. Askey) Ma'am, I'm going to show you what's been marked State's Exhibit 77. Do you recognize this person? A. Yes. Q. And was she the woman who was changing her insurance? A. Yes. Q. And did she ask you to be the witness on that form? A. Yes. Q. I'm going to show you what's been marked as State's Exhibit 76. Do you recognize that? A. Yes. Q. And what is that document? A. It's a change of beneficiary form. Q. Okay. And is this your signature at the bottom? A. Yes. Q. And so you witnessed her signing it and then you signed and -- A. Well, what happened was they filled out the paperwork in the front of the library, and then when they brought it up to me it was already signed and then they asked me to sign it. Q. You say they. She was with a friend? A. Yes. Q. Did she appear to be in distress in any way? A. No. Q. Did she appear in any way to be upset or crying or anything like that? A. No. Q. Did she have any conversations while she was talking to you and asking you to sign it? A. Yes. Very briefly. Q. And what specifically was she talking to you about? A. She said that she was just changing her beneficiary form because she was getting a divorce and she wanted to make sure her children could be on the form someday. Q. Okay. And so, she said she was getting a divorce and changing her beneficiaries? A. Uh-huh. Yes. Q. Did she also check out a book that day? A. Yes. Q. And you confirmed that she checked it out under the name of Elizabeth Faria? A. I believe she checked it out under her card or her account. Q. I'm going to show you this document. I didn't mark it. Does that document look familiar to you? A. Yes. Q. What is it? A. It's a record of what a patron has checked out on their library account. Q. Can you see who this is a record for? A. Yes. Q. And who is it for? A. For Elizabeth Faria. Q. Can you see that she also checked out a book on December 23rd, 2011? A. Yes. Q. And so, the day that she was there getting her insurance changed and having you witness it, she also checked out a book with her library card? A. Yes."

Joel Schwartz did a brief cross-examination of Manganelli: Q. "So, when you testified that the person you identified from the screen told you she was getting a divorce, that's what she told you to convince you to sign the form, correct? A. Yes. Q. You have no idea if that's true? A. I did not. I just took it as what she was saying. Q. And she seemed very happy that day? A. Yes. Q. I think -- and have you ever seen that woman before? A. No. Q. Have you ever seen her since? A. No. Q. The other woman who was with her? A. No."

In earlier testimony by Pam Hupp, she states that she was at the library seated at one of the tables when Betsy came in with the change of beneficiary form filled out. Pam said it was Betsy's idea that as long as they were there, they could just get the librarian to witness their signatures. We have seen that for some reason, the area under the signatures where you list your city was incorrect for Betsy. She lived in Troy, not O'Fallon. Pam lived in O'Fallon. It also seemed like Betsy had been trying to avoid Pam ever since this incident with the form on Friday, December 23rd. It was only through Pam literally stalking her on the day she died that Betsy was in her company.

The heady topic of DNA and crime work came next. This is typically an area that goes over a lot of people's heads, as witnessed in the O.J. Simpson case. Here, however, it was kept in layman's terms and was pretty straight forward. Daniel Fahnestock with the St. Charles Police Department Crime Lab hit on some of the key points from the murder scene.

Leah Askey questions Fahnestock about an area on the pants Betsy was wearing when she was found murdered: A. "As the result of my examination, that did indicate the presence of human blood. And we could qualify that a little bit because we could also say it could be another primate. But luckily old-world monkeys are not running around in the area, so -- but to be fair, we do qualify that. It is consistent with human or primate blood. Q. Okay. And you generated a report to that effect; is that right? A. Correct. Q. And specifically the area in which you tested on the back of those pants was the area that had resembled a paw print?"

Schwartz objected as to it being determined to be a paw print. Fahnestock next went over Russ' slippers. He said the blood on the slippers was Betsy's DNA. He also said the inside of the slippers showed hers and Russ' DNA (not blood), intimating she at times might wear the slippers.

Fahnestock was asked by Leah Askey about the DNA findings on the bloody light switch inside the master bedroom door: Q. "Did -- and what DNA profile were you able to get? A. The profile was a mixture of at least two individuals, at least one of which is male. And the major contributor is consistent with the DNA of Elizabeth Faria. Q. So on the switch plate there are two profiles, a male and a female, but the major contributor is Elizabeth Faria? A. Correct. And in this case, even though there is an indication of a second person and there is an indication that person is male, that would be the only -- only conclusion I could reach. There was not enough material present from that minor contributor to do a comparison. So, we would say that is of no comparative value. There is DNA there, but it is not useful for doing a comparison."

Leah Askey elicits from Fahnestock that he did find one area on the nine kitchen tiles sent to him that "glowed" from the Luminol test he performed. He also agreed he found human blood on a brown bath towel from the master bathroom and a small amount under Russ Faria's nail clippings. He stated the DNA from the nail clippings belonged to Russ. Next was a rather long discussion on sperm and seminal fluid as Askey continued to put forth her hypothesis that Russ had sex with Betsy the night she died and then showered after he killed her.

Schwartz stepped up for his cross-examination of the DNA specialist and diluted the prosecution's accusation of bloodstains and a possible clean-up of blood evidence in the kitchen: Q. "And you were unable to locate any of Betsy Faria's DNA on Mr. Faria's hand and feet swabs, correct? A. Yes. Q. All you were able to locate was his DNA? A. Correct. Q. And then let's talk about the tiles you got from the Major Case Squad or from Lincoln County. A. Correct. Q. You got nine tiles, correct? A. Yes. Q. And your information was that there had been a positive BlueStar reaction to those, correct? A. Yes. Q. And I think you testified a second ago BlueStar is pretty nonspecific, correct? A. There are many things that will give false positives, yes.

Q. "Can you give some examples of what those are? A. Plant material, cleaning products like bleach, grease. Often grease has animal product in it which will give a false positive as well. Those are just a few examples. Q. And what about other animal proteins, meat? A. Yeah. Because often meat has blood from the animal as well. So very often with, you know, like I have seen a frying pan full of grease, for example, a lot of animal byproduct in there and that will give a positive result.

Q. "And when you say blood, to clarify, you don't mean human blood? A. I mean animal blood. Q. We're not talking about -- A. Right. This would not be specific for any species. Q. Okay. So, Ms. Askey asked you about the tiles? A. Yes. Q. And she asked you if the presumptive test that you ran was positive for human blood? A. Yes. Q. That's what she asked. But actually, they were positive for blood; isn't that correct? A. The -- Q. The test that you ran. A. The test that I ran, yes. Q. Was positive for blood? A. Was positive for blood. It is a presumptive test. Q. It is not specific to human blood? A. No, it is not. Q. In fact, the only tile that had a positive result was Q37, correct? A. Correct. Q. When you looked for human blood on

Q37 you were unable to locate any, correct? A. Correct. Q. The only reaction was some kind of blood, but it wasn't human? A. It -- yeah. Possibly could have been blood or possibly could have not been blood at all. Q. But it wasn't human blood? A. No. I -- I was not able to locate anything that was consistent with human blood. Q. On any of the tiles? A. No. Q. No human blood? A. No.

Q. "You were given cabinet faces? A. Yes. Q. No human blood on any of those, correct? A. I did not detect any, no. Q. No blood at all on any of those, correct? A. Not that I detected, no. Q. You were given a J pipe? A. Yes. Q. That's the pipe that goes under the drain, correct? A. Correct. Q. No human blood in there? A. I was not able to detect any, no. Q. No blood at all in there? A. Not that was detected. Q. You were given swabs from various drains and faucets in the house, correct? A. Yes. Q. No blood whatsoever? A. Was not able to detect any blood. Q. Not human, not animal, not plant -- plants don't have blood but -- A. Correct. Q. No results whatsoever? A. Yes."

Daniel Fahnestock continued his DNA report, item by item. No blood found on any of Russ' clothing he was wearing that night, including his shoes and socks. No human blood on the towels, lime green washcloth in the kitchen drawer (though a stain was pointed out by CSI), nothing at all at the crime scene, including the murder weapon, showed Russ' DNA except to show he had worn his slippers at some point. Betsy's DNA also showed up inside the slippers indicating she too had worn them at some point. The brown bath towel showed only Russ' DNA on the suspicious brown stain. Finally, the sperm cell count was made moot: sperm can remain in the body for 72-hours, which would satisfy the time frame that Russ and Betsy had sex two nights prior to her death, on Sunday.

Betsy's mother, Janet Meyer took the stand. She answered the questions put to her by both the prosecution and defense succinctly. She was more combative with Joel Schwartz: Q. "You told that to the detectives when they came to talk to you the next morning, correct? A. I don't remember. Q. She had -- she had a bit of a rocky relationship with her daughters? A. Somewhat, yes, uh-huh. Q. They were teenagers and there were some problems, but you have no reason to believe she didn't love her daughters? A. No. Q. You have no reason to believe she wouldn't cut them out of her inheritance? A. No. No. She wanted the money for them. Q. As a matter of fact, you would think the opposite, right? Correct? A. She wanted the money for them. Q. Right. As a matter of fact, a month or so before her death, Betsy had been talking to you about telling you specifically that you, Russ and the girls would be well taken care of with her insurance, correct? A. That's what she said, yes.

Q. "And you talked about it at least three times that you recounted to me? A. Okay. Q. You agree with that? A. Uh-huh. Yes. Q. Yes? A. Yes. Q. You, Russ and the girls will be well taken care of. And you responded, "You don't need to worry about me." A. Correct. Q. A lot of times when she had things in St. Louis she would stay with you, correct? A. Yes. Q. She would stay with you before chemo frequently? A. Yes. Q. And she would stay with you before tennis frequently? A. Yes. Q. That was simply because of the distance? A. Yes. Q. And Russ worked at home so she needed drivers because he had to work, right? A. Yes. Q. Now, she had no fear of Russ at all and no problems with Russ that you were aware of, correct? A. Yes and no. Q. Do you remember me asking you that back in March 18, 2013, I asked you if she had any fear? And do you remember responding -- I said, "Did she voice any fear of ever going home or being with Russ or any problem whatsoever with Russ like that?" And you responded: "No, she didn't." A. Okay. No, she didn't then. Q. Is that accurate? A. That's just what I was observing, I guess."

Schwartz made a point of bringing up the cruise that happened five weeks before Betsy's death and who the friends were on that special occasion. Pam Hupp was not one of them. Schwartz to Janet Meyer:

Q. "And Betsy was very close with all those people? A. Yes, she was. Q. And she was very close with her sisters? A. Yes. Q. What about Pam Hupp? A. Well, she had been. I can't tell you how many years. I know you have been asking that question, but I do not recall how long it's been. It might be before she had the cancer that she was friends with her. Q. I have been asking people. Do you remember me asking you about that back in 2013? A. No, I don't. I really don't. Q. Do you remember you said maybe she's her tenth or 20th best friend? A. Okay. Yeah. Q. Yeah. A. I do. Q. And do you remember telling me that she also started to see her more after Betsy was diagnosed with the cancer? Do you have a recollection of telling me that? A. I'm not sure about that. Q. At that point in time, you had an opinion as to why Pam started seeing Betsy. Do you remember what your opinion was? A. Refresh me. Q. Well, do you think she would use the term for her as a money grubbing not a nice word. Do you remember that? A. Yeah. But I didn't make the connection with how long she had been seeing her. I just used that term with her. Q. And we're talking about Ms. Hupp? A. I said she was not a murderess, but she was a money hungry -- Q. But you don't know if she is a murderess, do you? A. I believe she is not. That's my opinion. Q. You believe? A. Yes. That's my opinion."

Betsy's friend Rita Wolf was next. Askey is questioning her about the night Betsy died: Q. "And, in fact, on the 27th, you guys were planning a trip or something like that? A. We were. I talked to her around 5:00 that afternoon. We had been planning on going on vacation together. Q. And what initiated that phone conversation? A. I recall -- I don't know if it was the day before or that morning, I don't remember when, but we had talked off and on throughout that week about planning a vacation. And I think I had left her a message earlier that day, if I recall correctly, and she was calling me back. Our conversation was very short because I was on my way to a birthday dinner. And so, we talked maybe five minutes. And we were going to get back together the next day to discuss. She had some timeshare somewhere in Hawaii and I had been many times, so we had talked about going to Hawaii.

"And then I reminded her I had a national sales meeting there in, I believe, January. So, she was going to maybe tag along with me so it could be just her and I. Q. And so, during that phone conversation did she say anything to you that -- did she say anything to you about having forgotten her keys? A. Yes. She told me on the phone that -- it's kind of interesting, but when we were talking, she says, "Oh, crap." I said, "What?" She said, "I left my keys at home. I'm going to need Russ to leave the door open for me." Q. And that was something that stuck out in your mind? A. That's the only reason I remember it because she was kind of funny about the way she said it. Q. Did it strike you as odd that she didn't have her purse? A. Not me. It didn't really -- I didn't even think about it to be honest with you."

Askey asked Wolf about Betsy asking her to be the beneficiary on her life insurance policy and Wolf telling her she had four loving sisters that would be a better choice.

"Q. And her goal was to get the money away from Russ? A. Her goal was to make sure that the money was not mismanaged and went towards the girls. She wanted to make sure -- her biggest concern is that they were well taken care of in her absence. Q. Would you disagree with the statement that she wanted Russ off the policy because he would piss all the money away? A. That is kind of word for word what she said to me. She was worried he would piss it away. Q. And so she was taking steps to remove him from those policies? A. She only talked to me about the one policy."

It is also pointed out that when Rita was going over how to form a trust with Betsy, the cost of doing that was brought up. To create a trust for the girls would have cost around $1400 which was a hardship for Betsy at the time. She elected instead to go with the insurance policy as it was, but to change the beneficiary.

Rita Wolf then goes over with Askey Detective Ryan McCarrick's former testimony at this trial that he did not ask her to influence Betsy's family to wait until after the trial to file a civil suit against Pam Hupp for the insurance proceeds they deemed should go to Betsy's daughters.

Q. "Have you ever met Ryan McCarrick? A. In person I believe only at the last trial I saw him, but I don't recall ever like physically meeting him. Q. Okay. A. And I saw him here today. Q. Okay. So, he wouldn't know you? A. I don't recall. I don't think he would. I don't recall meeting him in person. Q. But you have had a conversation with him? A. Yes. Q. And that conversation was about you trying to help the family file a civil suit against Pam Hupp? A. Yes. Mary and I -- I don't think I talked to Julie or Pam about it. But I know Mary and I talked several times about getting an attorney now, don't wait. I think Pam will spend that money so fast and then the girls will never see it. And I was very adamant about it because I knew what Betsy's wishes were. And so, I can't remember if he called me and I returned his call. I don't remember who initiated the call, but I did have a lengthy discussion with him on the phone when I was on my way home from Jeff City from a work trip. And he -- he was wanting me to quit forcing the issue of them suing at that time. He wanted them to wait until after the trial. Q. He was concerned? A. Yes. Q. It is possible that he forgot having a conversation with you? A. I would venture a guess based on his answer earlier, yes, because I don't think that he'd intentionally lie about it. I just think he forgot talking to me, but we had quite a lengthy discussion. Q. But that's the only time you have ever talked to him? A. I believe so. Q. And never met him in person? A. Correct."

Nathan Swanson next questioned Rita Wolf:

BY MR. SWANSON: Q. "Ms. Wolf. A. Hello. Q. You were in here when Detective McCarrick said he'd never spoke with you, correct? A. Yes. Q. That's not true? A. That is correct. It is a lie. Q. It's a lie? A. Yes. Q. Not just a difference. It's a lie? A. Yes, it is incorrect. Q. He had an extensive conversation with you, correct? A. Correct. Q. During that conversation he told you -- and I think we have spoken about this before. A. Yes. Q. That this isn't his first rodeo? A. Word for word that is what he told me. Q. And he wanted you to lay off the family about suing Pam Hupp? A. That is accurate. Q. It would be better for the trial if you did. A. That is accurate. Q. He had that conversation with you? A. Yes. Q. And when he denied it, he lied? A. Correct. Q. Okay. You said you -- sounds like you had very extensive conversations with Betsy about at least one insurance policy? A. Yes.

Q. "Were you aware of the other policy? A. I was aware she had a couple. I didn't know how many. When I -- when we were talking about it, I asked her if this is your only life insurance, and she said, no, she had a few policies. But we never really -- we didn't talk about the other ones because she was mainly concerned about the daughters getting this particular one. Q. Your impression was that she was fine with the beneficiaries on the other policies, correct? A. Yes. Q. And that would have been Mr. Faria, correct? A. I would assume. I mean, I didn't know. She never really talked about that at all. It was just mainly about how is she going to take care of her daughters when she was gone. She did not think she was going to live much longer. She wanted to make sure that they were well taken care of. Q. All right. And I think you said "piss it away?" A. Yes. That's the verbiage that she used.

Q. "Did she give any idea why she was worried about that? A. Well, a couple times she talked to me about a motorcycle that he wanted to buy. And just to be honest, she told me that Russ never thought money was all that important, but she was worried that if she died, he would piss it away and that would be it. Q. When she said "piss it away" did she mean out of, you know, making it rain, free spending, or he would be so depressed he would spend it all? A. Well, the impression that I got was out of grief he would spend it

238

all. Q. That would be grief over her death? A. Yes. Q. And, again, extensive conversations? A. Quite a few. Q. And she asked you to be the beneficiary? A. Right. At least twice. Q. And you made her aware that just making someone a beneficiary, there is no control over that, correct? A. We did talk -- we did talk about that there would have to be more of a trust or an executor of the will rather than a beneficiary. We talked about a transfer on death, but I didn't think that worked with life insurance policies, that you had to have a physical beneficiary. So that's why we talked about one of her sisters being the primary person with something notarized stating the items -- when the dollars would go to the girls. Q. So she knew that she wanted the money to go to the girls. It wasn't enough to just give it to somebody, correct? Something more needed to happen? A. I would hope she knew that. I did try to explain it. I gave her all my notes from the attorney that I met with so I would hope that she knew that."

Rita recalled one incident when Russ had been cruel to his dog:

Q. (By Ms. Askey) Did you have an opportunity to witness the temper of Russ Faria? A. On one specific occasion, yes. Q. And what was that occasion? A. She was having a Beauty Control party at her house and Sicily, their dog, had jumped up on me and Russ did grab the dog by the throat and slam her to the ground. And I don't remember what verbiage he used, but he was pretty angry at the dog. Q. And did you and he have an altercation because of that? A. Not really. Q. You didn't argue with him? A. Well, I said a couple things to him. I'm an avid dog lover. So, I might have said a few things, but I don't remember specifically."

Robert O'Neal with the St. Charles City Police Department cyber unit testified about the letter found on Betsy's laptop. He was the prosecution's answer to the defense's cyber expert Greg Chatten. His findings were to show whoever typed that letter found on Betsy's laptop, talking about the pillow incident, insurance, etc., did so at her computer, not by inserting a thumb drive. During Swanson's re-direct, it was ascertained only that someone at 2:10 p.m. the Thursday before Betsy's murder, and while she was at the tennis club, tried to access her Outlook email account on her laptop to upload an email, but it wouldn't send because Betsy used WebMail and didn't have Outlook set up. Someone also tried three times to access her signature block and to even type "Love Betsy" but it didn't work. In essence, O'Neal did not refute Chatten's findings, but he did still maintain the document could have been created on the laptop, not transferred onto it.

It is pointed out during this testimony that the letter document found on Betsy's laptop had no signature. If someone were sitting there typing it real time, wouldn't it be a simple thing to add the signature of "Love Betsy"? But, if the document had already been created elsewhere, uploaded into an Outlook email account (that wasn't set-up) there was a problem. The document was already created without the signature. Someone tried three times to access that signature block and couldn't. The document remained unsigned and unsent.

Lee Lester with State Farm Insurance was called to the stand. He was the agent for Betsy's life insurance policy that had been transferred to him. He stated Russ Faria called him on New Year's Eve, December 31, 2011, to inquire about getting money from the insurance to pay for Betsy's funeral. Russ said the funeral home suggested he call the insurance agency. While the defense tried to make the request look nefarious, it was brought out during cross and during the testimony of the funeral director Eric Pittman, that the funeral home had suggested it, and it was common practice. Many policies include death benefits. Was that why Russ was found with Betsy's insurance papers on him the day he was arrested?

An odd piece of testimony was brought in by State Farm agent Kathy Kilo Peterson. She testified she received a threatening phone call on January 5, 2011, the day after Russ was arrested for the murder of his wife. The caller said they were a sister of Russ Faria and they were threatening to come to the agent's office to get the insurance money due him. The caller said her name was "Sue." Schwartz pointed out the name was fictious, that Russ didn't have a sister named "Sue." Leah Askey questions Peterson about the call and her calling the police due to it:

BY MS. ASKEY: Q. "Ms. Peterson, as a result of you filing the police report, calling the police that day, they actually brought Pam and Mark Hupp with them to respond based on the other call that you received; is that right? A. Correct. Q. So that call had nothing to do with them? A. The call that I received. Q. They weren't the callers? A. No. MS. ASKEY: "Thank you. Nothing further.

RECROSS-EXAMINATION BY MR. SCHWARTZ: Q. "Just so

we're clear, Ms. Peterson. I was not insinuating to the Court that Pam Hupp made that phone call. But you do know Pam Hupp and you do know she was fired for allegedly forging documents, correct? A. That's my understanding, yes."

Day Four of the Trial: November 5, 2015.

Harry Belcher with the Lincoln County Prosecutor's Office was questioned about several areas of the case, including his testimony concerning being present during two of Pam Hupp's interviews with detectives, including with Ryan McCarrick. The topic of choice was the letter on Betsy's laptop. Schwartz is questioning Belcher:

Q. "So you don't know what she told to these previous detectives numerous times about a document, nor what its contents might be? A. That's correct. I did not review them. I don't know what she said to anybody else except what she said when I was present. Q. Okay. When you were present, did she tell you that the document was going to say that Russ put a pillow over her face? A. Yes. Q. When you were present, did she tell you that this document saved was going to say that Betsy wanted her to be the beneficiary? A. Yes. Q. Did she say in this document that she talked to you about that he was reading her emails? A. Yes. Q. Did she say in this document that she talked to you about that she's afraid of staying out in Troy alone with Russ? She didn't go back to Troy with Russ? A. I believe that was in there, yeah. Q. Did she say that it would say in this document that he was going to have all this money after she died?

A. "I'm sorry. I didn't understand your question. Q. Did Ms. Hupp tell you that this document that Betsy saved on her laptop was going to read that Russ was bragging about all this money he would have when he died? When she died, I'm sorry. A. Yes. Uh-huh. Q. And when did you have this conversation with Pam Hupp? A. That would have been -- that would have been on the 30th. Q. Of September, 2015? A. Whatever -- whatever that date was that you referred to. Q. That's the date I have an interview where you're present. A. Okay. Yes. Q. So, September 30th, 2015, Pam Hupp told you all those things would be in the document, right?

A. "She told us all those things. I don't remember if she said they would be in a document. But she told us about the incident with the pillow and all of those other things that you mentioned. Q. And all

241

of those things, every single one of them, are in that document you found, right? A. Correct. Q. And, again, it wasn't in an email, was it? It was in a document just like Pam Hupp said it would be? A. Yes. Q. And as far as when and where it was created, you don't know? Did Pam Hupp tell you in your -- when you talked about this that she was with Betsy when it was created? A. No. She wasn't. Q. What did she tell you? A. She said that Betsy had tried to send her a letter or send her an email and couldn't get it to print and couldn't get it to send out through email. Q. She also indicated she had never seen this document, correct? A. That's correct."

Carisa Barton was questioned about her statements that she had an affair with Russ Faria and was pregnant with his child. She admitted to lying about being pregnant and that she only told him that while Russ was in prison in 2014. Nathan Swanson questioned her about the affair that the prosecution was underscoring as a motive for Russ to get rid of his wife, besides getting money from Betsy's policies:

BY MR. SWANSON: Q. "Ms. Barton. A. Yes. Q. You and Russell Faria had a relationship in 2010, correct? A. Correct. Q. That relationship ended in September of 2010, correct? A. Yes. Q. It ended because you saw pictures of Mr. Faria and his wife Betsy on Facebook having a good time, correct? A. Yes. Q. And you told Mr. Faria you're having a good time with your wife, we need to end this? A. Yes. Q. Did you talk to him at all after that before -- before December of '11? A. I think there was a hi-bye in like maybe January or February of 2011, but that was it. Q. Between September 2010 and December 2011, you never told him you were pregnant? A. No, sir. Q. You never told him you had a baby? A. No, sir. Q. You never told him that you were giving the baby up for adoption? A. No, sir. Q. All that came -- A. In 2014. Q. Correct."

Patrick Harney was someone Schwartz was eager to get at. Harney was with the Lincoln County Sheriff's Office and had participated not only in Russ Faria's interrogation but in helping Pam Hupp out with some scenarios she could use to cast suspicion on Russ. It was Pam Hupp's interviews Schwartz went after:

Q. "And you have reviewed and participated in many Pam Hupp interviews, correct? A. Several, yes. Q. Several. And in those initial interviews, you reviewed those from December 28th that Detectives Perry and -- Perry Smith and Stefanie Kaiser did, right? A. I read their reports, yes. Q. And Pam Hupp said in that entire decade she knew Betsy, she's maybe only met Russ three times, right? A. I believe that's correct, yes. Q. And she also went on to say -- they asked her what she thought of him and she said I don't really know him, he's always been nice to me, right? A. I don't recall that part of that report. Q. We'll deal with Mr. Smith. You recall him saying -- her saying: "I don't know him that well. I have only met him three times. I mean, he seems nice enough." You don't remember that? A. If that's in Detective Kaiser's report, then I would agree with it. Q. All right. He was also asked if he's ever been physically mean to you, meaning Pam Hupp, and then she corrected it to her, that you know of, and Pam's response was, "I don't know. I never really got into conversation with her about the guy." Do you recall that? A. Not from Detective Kaiser's report, no, sir, I don't. Q. You don't recall that. You then reviewed several other reports, correct? A. Yes.

Q. "And you also interviewed Ms. Hupp several times, correct? A. Yes, sir. Q. And Pam Hupp, you knew about the insurance, you knew about the trust, you knew about all those things when you interviewed her, correct? A. I had some understanding of them, yes. Q. In fairness, Ms. Hupp has been interviewed, I believe, 13 times? A. I don't know if that's a correct number. Q. All right. You wouldn't argue with that, would you? A. I have only interviewed her several times, so I -- Q. You, yourself, has interviewed her several times? A. Yes. Q. Before we get to those, let's talk about some of the other things you reviewed prior to those interviews. A. Okay. Q. She was asked initially by Detective Smith and Kaiser if she knew whether or not that insurance beneficiary change form had been mailed and her response was, "I don't know, I don't know." Do you recall that? A. Not off the top, no, sir.

Q. "Okay. I will save that. Now when you talked to -- prior to talking with Pam Hupp on June the 17th, you had reviewed everything to prepare for that interview, correct, reports, interviews, things like that? A. No. I had not reviewed the entire report. Q. Prior to June 17th of 2015, Ms. Hupp had never stated anything about a sexual relationship with Betsy, had she? A. Not that I'm aware of, no. Q. On June the 17th when you talked to her, she told you they had a sexual relationship, correct? A. Yes, sir. Q. She said that it began in 2006? A. I believe that's correct, yes. Q. And that Betsy really, really, really loved her, correct? A. I believe that's correct. Q. And it just kept growing, correct? A. I believe so, yes. Q. She said,

"She was in love with me," right? A. I believe that's correct. Q. And she said that early on Russ found out about it and accused them of having a sexual relationship, correct? A. Again, I believe that's correct. Q. And Ms. Askey was actually in that interview, too, and specifically said, "Did you have a sexual relationship with Betsy?" And Ms. Hupp's response was, "Yes." Correct? A. Correct. Q. And that had never been said -- now we're talking three-and-a-half years after Betsy died? A. After she was killed, yes, sir.

Q. "Right. Now, just so we're clear, you reviewed the phone calls because you talked to Ms. Hupp, when she pulled into that driveway is when she told you she called her husband and that was 7:06 p.m. [7:04], December 27, 2011, right? A. I don't recall the exact time, but I would agree with that. Q. Okay. And did she acknowledge to you she first told the detectives she didn't go into the house? A. I don't recall asking her that question. Q. But you talked to her about money, right? A. I believe we did. Q. She said, "Look, I don't have any immediate need for money. I don't gamble. I don't drink. I don't have a boyfriend on the side." Correct? A. Correct. I believe she went on to say that she didn't have any outstanding debts or large outstanding debts. Q. That was in 2015, right, when you talked to her? A. Yes, sir. Q. Were you aware in 2011 she didn't even have health insurance? A. No, I was not.

Q. "But she also said, "Money, it doesn't matter, people want it, you got it, they are going to try to do what they have to do to get it." Remember her saying that to you? A. Not specifically, no, sir. Q. Would it refresh -- and she also said, "And money, while it makes people do crazy, crazy things." She told you that, too, didn't she? A. Again, I don't recall that specifically, no, sir. Q. Would it refresh your recollection if I showed you a copy of the transcript from that? A. Yes.

MR. SCHWARTZ: "May I, Judge?" THE COURT: "You may." THE WITNESS: "This doesn't have anything to do with money. Q. (By Mr. Schwartz) Top -- not the highlighted. I'm sorry. Top two sentences. A. Okay. Yes, sir. Q. She's talking to you about money makes people do crazy, crazy things, doesn't she? A. Yes, sir. Q. She also told you $150,000 is not a lot of money to her? A. I believe I recall that, yes. Q. Yeah. She also told you, "People say I'm bossy. Always sticking my nose in other people's business when it shouldn't be. I'm very resourceful." Right? A. I don't recall that specifically, no, sir. Q. Would it refresh your recollection if I showed you a copy? A. Yes, sir. Her brothers say she's bossy. Only sticking her nose in other people's business when it shouldn't. And then further down after some other questions, "I'm very resourceful." Q. Pam Hupp told you she's always -- her brothers have accused her of sticking her nose in other people's business where it shouldn't -- where it doesn't belong? A. Yes, sir. Q. And that she's very resourceful? A. Yes, sir.

Q. "She found a way to pay her health insurance, didn't she? A. I don't know. Q. Now, she talked with you about this beneficiary form; is that correct? A. Yes. I believe that's correct. Q. And did she tell you that she went to the post office with Betsy after they signed it? A. I don't recall where she said she went. I thought that they went to the library. Q. Well, they went to the library. Did she tell you that they went to the post office after they mailed it -- I mean, after they signed it? A. I don't recall that, sir.

Q. "You don't recall it. Now, she told you that Russ hated her for sure and she was afraid of Russ? A. I recall her saying that she believed Russ didn't like her, yes. Q. Now, you reviewed those reports where she said she met him maybe three times in a decade, right? A. I -- Q. Would it refresh your recollection? A. If you would, please. Where is the part -- you said meeting? Q. I will find that as well. Okay. A. The last time was their 40th birthday party. Q. And she said -- that's what she said was the last time she saw him? A. Apparently to Detective Kaiser, yes. Q. And he says -- she says, "I mean, he seems nice enough." Correct? A. "I mean, he seems nice enough. I just don't know him that well."

Q. "Okay. And on that other section I showed you, she said, "And, though, he's always been very nice to me." Right? A. Is that the section that we were just looking at? MR. SCHWARTZ: I'm sorry, Judge. Q. (By Mr. Schwartz) Yeah. Where you just looked. "I really don't know him that much. Just Betsy." A. "Though he's always been very nice to me, I don't know the hardcore stuff he's said to her. He's verbally nasty, especially -- Q. But he's always been nice to her, to Pam, right? A. Yes, sir. Here.

Q. "Thank you. Now, that's not what she said to you. This was on December the 29th -- 28, 2011, this interview that we're referring to right now, correct? A. As I understand it, yes, with Detective Kaiser. Q. The morning after Betsy was murdered? A. Yes. Q. Now, in

2015, June of 2015, you talked to Pam about a relationship with Betsy, correct? A. Yes. Q. And you talked to her about her relationship with Russ? A. With Pam's relationship with Russ? Q. Right. A. I didn't take it that there was a relationship there. Q. No. As a matter of fact, what did she tell you about the last time she saw him maybe a week or two prior? A. I believe that was when she said she was in the basement and Betsy was upstairs and Russ came home. Q. And what did Russ do to Pam? A. There was a verbal confrontation. I don't remember what Ms. Hupp said he specifically said. Q. Did Ms. Hupp say specifically that he pushed her up against the wall, put his arm around her neck, and said if you ever come over here again it will be the last time, so she kind of broke his arm and went upstairs. Did she tell you that? A. If that's what's in the transcript, yes, sir. Q. And he also called them effing muff bumpers? A. Yes. If that's what's in the transcript, yes, sir. Q. And she said this happened in November when he said this to her just before she died, right, November, 2011, right? A. Yes, sir. Q. And he said to her in 2011 that if he catches them -- if he catches her again, he's going to stab her and bury her in the backyard, correct? A. If that's what's in the transcript, yes, sir. [It's interesting that this says Pam "was in the basement and Betsy was upstairs and Russ came home." Why was Pam in the basement alone where Russ' computers are kept? He works from the basement for his IT business.]

Q. "You recall that, right? A. Not specifically until you reread it, yes. Q. Okay. And she was so close to him and he was so mad she could feel the spit from his lips coming on her face, right? A. I believe she said that, yes. Q. Did you ever say, "Why haven't you ever told this to anybody before?" A. I don't believe I said that. Q. You never questioned her on that, did you? A. I don't believe I did, no. Q. And you know she never said anything like that before. She also said, "Russ is a nice guy. have only met him a few times." Agree with that? A. Well, if there's 13 interviews with her, I have not read every interview, so I don't know if she said that. Q. You had no information she's ever said anything like that before, do you? A. I don't recall having any information of that sort, no.

Q. "She never said anything before about a sexual relationship with her and Betsy until June of 2015, correct? A. No, sir. Not that I was aware of. Q. Did you -- did you review the interview with Stefanie Kaiser and Perry Smith when they went back to return her phone, and again the following day, the 29th, they asked how -- they asked Pam Hupp how the family viewed Russ and she said the family liked him, and that Hupp said Russ was also nice to her. Did you review that? A. I don't recall that report, no, sir. Q. Would it refresh your recollection? A. Sure. Hupp said she thought the family liked him very much. Q. What else? A. Hupp said Russ was also nice to her.

Q. "Now, in fairness, she did say that he could be a smart ass, right? A. In this report? Q. Yeah. A. I didn't read that. Q. Well, she talked about seeing him last week, meaning I guess early in December or something, where she went downstairs to say hi and he said, well, what took you so long to get here, why are you late, or something along those lines? A. Russell asked Hupp why she was so late. She said the directions were difficult and he commented to her that every normal person knows about the highway signs. Q. Now, that information that you're reading in the reports and that you read in those transcripts in the interview, that would fly 180 degrees in the face of what Ms. Hupp told you in June of 2015, correct? One of those is a lie. A. I don't know that. Q. They can't both be true, can they? A. I –

Q. "Let's talk about it. She says a month earlier he was in my face because he caught us together and he threatened to kill me, right? A. Yes. Q. She told that to you? A. Yes. Q. And that's in 2015? A. Yes. Q. 2011, at least more than once she says, "I have only met him a couple of times. He's always been nice to me." Correct? A. To Detective Kaiser, yes. Q. Right. And those aren't two opposites? A. They are. Q. One of those is not true, right? A. Presumably. Q. They can't both be true, can they? A. I wouldn't think so.

Q. "Did you review the trial testimony before your interview with Ms. Hupp? A. No. Not that I recall. Q. You're not aware as to whether or not she originally told detectives she didn't go in the house? A. No. Not -- Q. You talked to her extensively about the car that was outside, correct, the car that was outside the house? A. Yes. Q. Right? A. We talked to her. Q. When she -- A. We talked to her about where she parked. Q. What's that? A. We talked to her about where she parked. Q. Well, you knew she had said in many, many interviews she was certain that it was a silver Maxima in the driveway when she got there, right? A. Again, I have not read the -- you said there were 13. I have not read every interview, so –

Q. "Okay. But to you she said it was the blue Explorer in the driveway when she got there? A. I believe that's correct. Q. Now, there's been an issue about a call that Ms. Hupp made. You were aware that she originally told the detectives she called Betsy to tell her she was home safe and then she changed it to almost home? A. No. Not specifically aware of that. Q. Okay. Then you're -- are you aware that she then said, "Well, I called her to let her know I was "home free"? A. I believe that's correct. Q. Now, when you interviewed her in June of 2017 (sic) [2015], she told you when she made that call she stopped at a fork in the road just down from the house, correct? A. Yes. Q. And she sat there and she called Betsy, correct? A. My recollection, yes. Q. And it was completely dark out and she sat there ten to 15 minutes? A. I don't recall if she identified how long she sat there. Maybe ten 15 minutes maybe, yes, sir. Q. So she said maybe she sat there ten to 15 minutes? A. Yes, sir. Q. Now, the area we're talking about is just a couple of miles from the house, not even that far, is it? A. It's several miles, but I don't know how many. Q. Instead of sitting there in the dark ten or 15 minutes, she could have just come back, couldn't she, it'd been a lot quicker, right?

A. "I'm sorry. Can you repeat the question? Q. She said, "I sat there. It was really dark. It was pitch black." Correct? Did you see that on that transcript, or do you recall that? A. I don't recall that part of it, the 10-to-15-minute part. Q. All right. So, she sat there and she called Betsy? A. Yes. Q. Right? A. Yes. Q. She didn't make any other calls, you have seen her records, right? MS. ASKEY: "Judge, I would like to object to hearsay over and over." THE COURT: "Sustained." MS. ASKEY: "Thank you." THE COURT: "Argumentative. Let's move forward somewhere."

Q. (By Mr. Schwartz) "Betsy never called her back and she went home. She told you that, right? A. I believe that's correct, yes, sir. Q. And then -- well, we'll move on. You talked to her about whether or not she saw Russ that night? MS. ASKEY: "Same objection." THE COURT: "Sustained. Counsel, let's move forward. We have been over and over and over -- let's get to the point." MR. SCHWARTZ: "This is a different area, Judge." THE COURT: "I'm not hearing it so far. We're beating it to death. Let's get to where we're going." Q. (By Mr. Schwartz) "Okay. Detective Harney, what is your job as a detective? A. I investigate crimes that are reported to the sheriff's office and forward them to the Detective Bureau. Q.

And you take witness statements, correct? A. Yes, sir. Q. Your job is not to suggest what occurred, is it? A. No. Q. That would be very, very wrong, right? You don't put ideas in witnesses' minds, do you? A. No.

Q. "Why did you say to Ms. Hupp in that interview, "What we believe, Merkel and I, is that you were present, that Russ was not there when you and Betsy got there, and that prior to you leaving somehow or another Russ knew that you were there either by a phone call or just the sure presence of your car or that he walked in and saw that you were there, and it was that particular moment, motivating factor for you to leave, him coming into the house, that is what we discussed amongst ourselves. Is any part of that correct and is it, in fact, did you see Russ in the house that night?" Did you suggest that to her? A. I have not read that transcript. I don't know if I said that to her or not.

MR. SCHWARTZ: "Judge, can we get permission?" THE COURT: "You may." Q. (By Mr. Schwartz) "You are not denying you said that to her? A. I am without having seen the transcript. There were two of us talking to her. Q. Right there. A. Yes. I did say that and I said we had spoken in theory before about what we believed. Q. Right. And you suggested that she saw Russ that night, right? A. I told her what I believed. Q. She responded, no, that she didn't see Russ in the house at all, she saw nothing, correct? A. She said no. Q. Yeah. And later in the interview you also asked her, did you see Russ around there or Russ's vehicle there at that point? And she said, 'No, I did not see anybody driving around the subdivision. I wish I saw someone but I didn't.' A. If that's in the transcript, then I will agree with that. Q. Did she say, no, I did not see anyone driving in the subdivision, I wish I saw somebody, but I didn't? MS. ASKEY: "Same objection, Judge."

MR. SCHWARTZ: "Your Honor, this door has been opened regarding Ms. Hupp. THE COURT: "You know, sustained." Q. (By Mr. Schwartz) "Now, that was June 15th, right? A. Excuse me. Yes, sir. Q. You participated in an interview with Pam Hupp on September the 30th, correct? A. I know -- Q. I'm sorry. October the 6th -- about a month ago, three or four weeks ago, right? A. I believe that's correct. Q. And in that interview, she said, you know what, I saw Russ and somebody else sitting in a car outside that night. MS. ASKEY: "Same objection, Judge." THE COURT: "Sustained."

MR. SCHWARTZ: "I'm impeaching the earlier statement." THE COURT: "Impeaching who? Sustained." Q. (By Mr. Schwartz) "All right. You suggested that she saw Russ that night, correct? A. Are we talking about on October 6th? Q. No. I'm talking about in June? A. I told her what I believed. Q. And she disagreed with that, she said that's not true? A. Yes. Q. But in October she no longer -- October of 2015 she no longer disagreed with that? MS. ASKEY: "Same objection."

THE COURT: "Sustained". Q. (By Mr. Schwartz) "Have you reviewed this document that was retrieved from the computer? A. I can't see it from here without my glasses on. I sure can't see it there. Yes, I have seen this before. Q. Now, you discussed that document with Ms. Hupp, correct? A. I have never discussed that document with Ms. Hupp. Q. Well, that -- not that particular one, but she told you Betsy had not an email but a document that she had saved, correct? MS. ASKEY: "Same objection, Judge." THE COURT: "Sustained." MR. SCHWARTZ: "Your Honor, I would proffer to the Court that this instrument is hearsay and I would say that the door has been opened regarding that as well as the Court has ruled the direct interaction rule applies." THE COURT: "Sustained." MR. SCHWARTZ: "Nothing further then at this time, Judge. I would ask this witness be subject to recall."

During a re-direct session with Detective Ryan McCarrick, Schwartz is able to nail down one very important question:

BY MR. SCHWARTZ: Q. "Detective McCarrick, you -- it's been a long week, I think it was yesterday -- that you talked with Ms. Hupp at length on June 25th, 2012? A. Yes. Q. Specifically one question. You talked to her about a document that had been attempted to be emailed to her, correct? A. Yes. Q. She told you where that document was created? MS. ASKEY: "I would object as to hearsay." THE COURT: "I'm going to allow. You may answer." Q. (By Mr. Schwartz) Did she tell you where Betsy had allegedly created that document? A. She told me where they discussed the document. Q. Did she say to you she was at tennis, too, and that's when she had written me an email telling me -- and then she talked about it being a document? MS. ASKEY: "Same objection." THE COURT: "Overruled. I will allow that." Q. (By Mr. Schwartz) "Were those her words? A. Taken out of context, yes, but I think that's the way she worded it. Q. Okay. MR. SCHWARTZ:" Nothing further. Thank you."

Here, in this testimony, we hear that Pam stated Betsy actually wrote the email to her while at tennis that day. It was not sent. Askey picked up the gauntlet tossed down by Schwartz:

BY MS. ASKEY: Q. "Detective, was that relationship to conversation that they had had at tennis? A. Yes. Q. Not actually where the document was typed? A. Correct. MS. ASKEY: Nothing further." THE COURT: "Very good. Anything further?" MR. SCHWARTZ: "No."

REDIRECT EXAMINATION BY MR. SCHWARTZ: Q. "Those were her words, that it was written at tennis, too, but you believe that was out of context? A. The reason I say it's out of context is because of the conversation she had with the original investigators where she said she talked about the email during the tennis. She talked about the email that she wrote, but it was during the tennis that she discussed the email, not that she wrote it there. Q. Okay. But I'm -- I understand what she told the original investigators. But as far as you, she said she was at tennis, too, and that's when she wrote an email? A. I think that's what the exact words in the transcript were, yes. MR. SCHWARTZ: "Perfect. Thank you. Nothing further."

Linda Hartman, Betsy's "cousin" and friend went to Branson, Missouri, the weekend before Christmas. Her testimony elicited a piece of important information regarding Pam Hupp. She also talks about shopping for Russ while in Branson:

A. "We went to -- shopping that day, one of the days that we were there. We went to the Jelly Bean store and she was on the phone talking to him and she was buying all his favorite Jelly Beans. I remember that, on the phone. It was really important that she had to get those Jelly Beans for Russ. Q. She wanted to make sure he had something that he liked? A. Yes.

Q. "Do you recall -- if I told you that trip occurred between the 17th and the 19th, does that sound like the right dates? A. Say that again. Q. The 17th and 19th, does that sound like when that trip occurred? A. Yes. MR. SCHWARTZ: Of what? Q. (By Mr. Swanson) "Of December." A. Yes. Q. Do you remember what day of the week you came home? A. I get the feeling that we could have stayed until the Tuesday or Wednesday, but we came home on the Monday, meaning that the timeshare, she had the timeshare up until the Tuesday or the Wednesday. But we came back on the Monday and we were saying, "Oh, Betsy, why do we have to come home? Why don't we just stay? We are having so much fun here." She said, "I have to go back. I have to meet Pam." I said, "Call and cancel with her. Just tell her you are going to stay another day." She said, "No, I really do. I have to meet Pam, and I don't want to meet Pam." She was very tense about that. Q. All right. And when she said Pam, do you know what Pam's last name was? A. No, I did not at the time. Q. Do you know which Pam she was referring to? A. Yes, yes. Q. The person she was talking about, that was Pam Hupp? A. Yes. Q. It was not her sister? A. No. Q. Or Russ's Aunt Pam? A. No. It was definitely Pam Hupp."

Toward the end of the day, an interesting sidebar was called by the defense. Schwartz and Swanson informed the judge that Swanson had just received a message on his phone concerning the death of Pam Hupp's mother, Shirley Neumann. He is speaking to the judge and the prosecutors:

MR. SWANSON: "Look at my phone because they literally just emailed this to me in the last 15, 20 minutes. Apparently, when the police investigated, they spoke with employees of the nursing home who stated that earlier in the evening Ms. Hupp's mother had been found laying across her bed. Ms. Hupp was called. Ms. Hupp took her out of the home, supposedly took her to the hospital. She wasn't admitted. Ms. Hupp returned with her mother, took her mother up to her mother's room and came down and told people at the front desk that her mother wasn't going to be eating dinner, would not be eating breakfast. The next thing they knew when they went to check on her, her mother had fallen off the balcony. He said we might want to cross examine Ms. Hupp on this and find the witnesses who were involved in that.

"It is kind of interesting Ms. Hupp would now be the last person to be with two people right before they died and got money for it. **MR. SCHWARTZ:** "Apparently, she got money and apparently some part of the balcony was tampered with. The reason I bring it up is I would like to continue through today, but I would ask for a continuance until Monday to try to investigate this and see if I can find these employees." MR. GUNDY: "Judge, I think I'm supposed to argue this." THE COURT: "You are. Okay." MR. GUNDY: "I guess my first feeling is nobody has even called Ms. Hupp to testify.

She's here if they want to call her. They are scared to death to call her. She can testify as to any of this stuff. I think one murder case at a time is probably plenty."

THE COURT: "We have got a bunch going on here. You know, this has no connection here whatsoever. Of course, I have got a lot of stuff here that I'm not sure what the connection is. But -- no. I -- you know, we're not going to try a second murder case, which is really what you are wanting to do, to show that she has this propensity to kill somebody for their money, her close relatives. Glad I'm not closely related somehow. But, no, I'm not -- I just don't see that it's relevant. It is a fishing expedition. I -- you know, this is starting to remind me of a California trial where we just go on and on and on and on and we just add more and more and more. And, I mean, I can't see any -- any reason to allow that. There's another ground for the Court of Appeals to come in and say I didn't let evidence in that I should have let it in, but we're not going there, so -- interesting. It is very interesting. Okay."

The judge's jibe about being "Glad I'm not closely related to her [Pam Hupp] somehow," was the type of mild levity he brought to the court throughout the trial, while firmly holding the reins of the proceedings. He reminds this author of the judge who sentenced Ted Bundy to death row while maintaining a calm demeanor and peppering his statements with "Bless your heart."

Greg Chatten, the defense's cyber expert was the last witness called in this rather speedy trial. He testified in more detail about the document [p.doc] found on Betsy's laptop:

Q. (By Mr. Swanson) "And now going back to the P.doc. Were you able to locate the author or what was described as the author in the metadata of the P.doc? A. Yes. Q. What was that? A. It was the written word unknown as in U-N-K-N-O-W-N. Q. So, it was the word "unknown" not you didn't know. It was the word "unknown"? A. Correct. Q. But that's not what would automatically be the author if the document was created using the computer? A. That's correct. Q. What does that indicate to you? A. It indicates to me –

MR. GUNDY: "I'm going to object, Your Honor. I think it is insufficient foundation at this point.: THE COURT: "Rephrase the question. Sustained." Q. (By Mr. Swanson) "You were able to determine what this computer would automatically make the author as, correct? A. Correct. Q. And that was Betsy Faria? A. Correct. Q.

The P.doc's author was not the word Betsy Faria? A. Correct. Q. It was in fact the word unknown? A. Correct. Q. Can you describe how that could happen?" MR. GUNDY: "Well, I object, Your Honor, based on speculation, unless he knows."

THE COURT: "Do you know?" THE WITNESS: "I know two ways it could happen, Your Honor." THE COURT: "You may answer." A. The document was created on a different computer where the user name happened to be unknown, or the document was created on a computer and then someone changed -- changed the author to unknown. Q. (By Mr. Swanson) "Okay. And were you able to create a printout of the metadata for the P.doc? A. I was. Q. And I'm going to show you what's been marked as Defendant's Exhibit T. Do you recognize that? A. I do. Q. And what is it? A. It's the metadata report I created from the metadata I found in the P.doc file. Q. And aside from highlighting two columns, is it exactly as you located it? A. It is. Q. It shows the author of the P.doc is the word unknown? A. Correct."

In regards to the wireless network used for the laptop that day at the tennis club:

A. "Or 12-22. And right around the time that that Word document was saved that computer was connected to a network called 'the club.'"

Final Day of the Trial: Friday, November 7, 2015.

The last day of the trial called primarily the Game Night friends of Russ Faria's to the stand to go over their testimony as alibis for Russ the night of the murder. Two more experts were called to go over cell mapping to collaborate both Russ' and Pam Hupp's cell phone locations the night of the murder. Then it was over. Five days of testimony with both sides stating their interpretation of the evidence in the case. Which would the judge believe?

Leah Askey was first to go with her Opening Argument on Behalf of the State. There were no new smoking guns. New from the first trial was the testimony that Russ had a yellow belt in martial arts. She used that to underscore the fact that he could have easily subdued Betsy during the murder. However, it could not have been lost on Judge Ohmer that almost her entire case as she summed it up had been proven false by the Defense. Expert after expert had been forced to testify to the blood evidence, the problems with the document on Betsy's laptop, Hupp's changing stories, issues with how the prosecution's detectives handled interviews, and on-and-on. Yet, even though that evidence had been shot down, Askey still used it as her offer of proof during her Opening Argument.

She was followed by Joel Swartz in his Opening Argument for the Defendant. It was a summation of all the evidence he had provided as proof of Russ Faria's innocence and that Pam Hupp should be investigated.

Pam Hupp had been waiting for her turn on the stand. She was sequestered outside the courtroom, as was customary with a witness, so that other testimony could not taint their own. Schwartz felt her hateful stare each time there was a court break and he walked past her to his office. As the trial wore on, and neither Askey nor Schwartz called her, she began sending nasty texts to Nathan Swanson, heckling him to put her on the stand. She texted Russ' defense attorney that she had talked with Channels 4 and 5 News and bragged to them "that Schwartz based the whole retrial on me. They were confused why Schwartz wouldn't call me and I told them he was afraid of the truth!!! Sounds about right, don't you think?"

When Swanson refused to reply, and it was evident the trial was winding down, Pam ramped up the vitriol: "Did Schwartz forget his set of balls today? I would love for him to grill me for 8 hours!" Pam spat out in text.

Pam Hupp realized she was not going to be called to the stand. Whether it was to avoid reporters, or possibly fearing handcuffs after all the evidence just presented against her, she took off before Judge Ohmer gave his verdict. Hurrying across the parking lot in the darkness, Pam drove off into the night.

Joel Schwartz continued with his summation. It was all the proof the Defense had provided. He went over the disturbing actions of the detectives who lead Pam Hupp in her testimony. He covered the Game Night alibis, receipts, video and cell mapping proof that Russ was where he said he was that night. And that $200 Russ took from an ATM that was supposed to have nefarious reasons as it was not found on his person the night of the murder? It was the money he used to put $100 each in his step-daughter's Christmas stockings, not to pay an accomplice or anything else the prosecution was hinting about.

Schwartz talked about the blood evidence; both the seen and unseen. He highlighted two CSI experts stated the blood on Russ' slippers looked as if they had been dipped in blood. The only evidence that the blood had been stepped in was by one of their own, a Lincoln County officer. Schwartz came right out and said Mike Merkel perjured himself.

Joel Schwartz brought up a very salient point in his Opening Argument:

"Judge, isn't it interesting that the beneficiary and the last one with the decedent was not called to testify? She said Ms. Hupp said initially to those officers she didn't go in the house. Then she changed it to well, she only went in the front rooms. Then she said she went into the whole house and went into the bathrooms. That's because we know that's where evidence was found in all these, so she had to place herself there just in case. She called to tell Betsy she was home. Changed that to almost home. Never talked about a fork in the road where she stopped for 15 minutes. She had to change it because she knew I could show that she was still at or near the house at 7:27 when she made that call. She wanted to clear up where Betsy was when she left because she said, the last time I saw my friend she was standing there waiting at the door. She also said she was sitting on the sofa wrapped up in a comforter.

"He wanted to clear those things up. He wanted to clear up with her why the family was insisting that she was so pushy to get Betsy home. More importantly than anything he wanted to make sure she created that trust before trial because in his words "it simply wouldn't look good." Well, as we know, and we gave this Court, she did. About a week before trial that trust was funded with $100,000. About two weeks after trial $99,700 was taken out of that trust. And to this day those girls haven't seen a penny. McCarrick said to Pam Hupp don't -- we just needed to confirm the whereabouts. Actually, he said to me, no one confirmed the whereabouts of Pam Hupp with anyone ever. Her clothing, where she was, the condition she was in when she got home. Who knows? Nobody talked to her. And that conversation with Mark Hupp, her husband, was a joke."

It was an excellent point. Why didn't the prosecution call Pam Hupp to the stand?

Betsy's friends were mentioned as to her state of mind toward Russ those few weeks before her murder. It was that Celebration of Life cruise:

"Linda Hartmann, the cruise seems like they were honeymooning. They were on -- she was with her in Branson the weekend before when she had to come back to meet Pam and she didn't want to. Rhonda Graham, the same thing. These are all Betsy's closest friends. On her survival cruise Betsy wanted to spend as much time as possible with Russ."

The two Closing Arguments were final attempts to discredit each other's strongest points and reiterate their best shots. There was a court recess as the judge went into chambers to deliberate. When he returned to the bench, the tension in the room was palpable. Many were still amazed Pam Hupp had not made an appearance. Judge Ohmer looked out over the anxious faces and began:

The Verdict

THE COURT: "Good afternoon, folks. Be seated. Now, ladies and gentlemen, we've had no real incidents and I have been very appreciative of that, and I don't expect any from here on out. So, the deputies have been instructed if there is any sort of -- any sort of disruption of any sort, you'll be escorted out. So please, we're in session, and I don't -- I won't tolerate any sort of outburst one way or the other. So would the defendant please rise. There's no question that this was a brutal murder, and I'm sorry the family or any of us have to witness such horror. It's important to remember that under our law a defendant is presumed to be innocent and this presumption places upon the State the burden of proving beyond a reasonable doubt that the defendant is guilty. The charge here of murder in the first degree and armed criminal action are totally appropriate for the facts and circumstances of this case.

"There are two separate theories submitted to this Court by the parties. First, the State surmises that the defendant killed Betsy in a fit of passion and rage. Next, the defendant surmises that Pam Hupp conspired to kill Betsy and set up the defendant to take the fall. The investigation into the facts and theories of this case by law enforcement is rather disturbing and, frankly, raised more questions than answers. Inconsistencies and/or lies do not equate to murder where the hard facts do not support the conclusion, but rather support speculation, innuendo and supposition only.

257

"Unfortunately, the hard facts alone are insufficient to give a clear resolution to this messy case. A reasonable doubt is a doubt based upon reason and common sense after careful and impartial consideration of all of the evidence in this case. Proof beyond a reasonable doubt is proof that leaves you firmly convinced of the defendant's guilt. The law does not require proof that overcomes every possible doubt. If the fact finder is not firmly convinced of the defendant's guilt, the Court must give him the benefit of the doubt. Consequently, as to Count I, Murder in the First Degree, the Court finds the defendant, Russell Scott Faria, not guilty. As to Count II, Armed Criminal Action, the Court finds the defendant, Russell Scott Faria, not guilty. The Court further orders the defendant discharged in this cause. The Court stands adjourned and you may be seated." (Proceedings concluded.)

The disappointment of not witnessing the showdown between Schwartz and Hupp was replaced by heart-pounding joy as the Judge looked at Russ and his attorneys and said, "On the count of Murder in the First-Degree, I find you…Not Guilty."

It was not Bailiff Dodder who held Russ up this time as his knees gave out. He turned and melted into a heartfelt hug by Nathan Swanson, his co-counsel. He then hugged Joel Schwartz. Without preamble Russell Faria was a free man.

Joel Schwartz leads a tearful Russ Faria out of the Lincoln County Courthouse to the cheers of his loved ones. Photo courtesy of the *St. Louis Post-Dispatch.*

Judge Ohmer's statement that "The investigation into the facts and theories of this case by law enforcement is rather disturbing and frankly raised more questions than answers," sent a grave message to the prosecution team. Their previous actions that had sent a man to prison for almost four years was not out in the open with all the sinister implications documented. There might be ramifications in the future.

It was Russell Faria who walked out of the courthouse to the cheers and hugs of all those who had maintained his innocence. His eyes filled with tears as he kissed his mother and said, "I love you, too." The same jubilation was not seen in the prosecutor's camp. Nerves were humming as Leah Askey later released her statement to the press:

"While I believe in our justice system, I disagree with this verdict...My condolences go out to Betsy Faria's family," Askey said succinctly.

Joel Schwartz and Nathan Swanson were celebrating. Not with the braggadocio one might expect from the two men who refused to give up on Russ Faria. It was a deeper feeling. The kind one feels when they've done the right thing, fought the good fight, and seen it through to its joyful conclusion. Schwartz used the word "satisfying" when describing his feelings, but it went much deeper than that. He had changed a man's life. Russ would never again be tried for the murder of his wife. He would sleep well tonight, hoist a beer with his friends, and finally, mourn the loss of his beloved Betsy.

On that note, Schwartz vowed he wasn't finished. There was still no justice for Betsy, and there had been an insidious investigation that resulted in Russ Faria sitting in a prison cell for something he did not do.

Leah Askey refused to reopen the case. In her mind, Russ was the only person who killed Betsy. Schwartz wanted the entire case reviewed. There was someone else to look at as the murder suspect. He called the US Attorney's Office for the Eastern District of Missouri and laid out his request and his reasons for it. Pam Hupp was a danger. He felt it in his bones. If he was right, this woman had plunged a knife into the carotid artery of her best friend to disable her, and then went about stabbing her another 55 times. She then set-up that friend's husband by staging the scene and planting evidence, along with a maelstrom of false testimony,

until he was found guilty of killing his own wife. How could you get eviler than that? Mariah and Leah Day had been deprived of their mother, their step-father, and their inheritance.

If suppositions proved correct, it was also possible Pam killed her own mother, again for money. What else was this woman capable of doing? The answer would come in only nine short months. In the meantime, Pam would be back in court, and this time, she would get her chance on the witness stand.

Chapter Fifteen
Anonymous Letters

During a phone conversation with *Fox 2 News* investigator Chris Hayes, he told this author that he had received several anonymous letters, all insulting and threatening. Many people in Pam Hupp's circle received these "anonymous" letters, from neighbors to family.

"I was getting anonymous letters to the same effect…like 'You're an idiot!' I got three or four letters. And they are crazy. There is one that says that she (a supposed friend of Pam's) knows that I knocked on Pam's sister's door and that I talked to her sister, and called her sister a slut, and just awful, awful things that she says about people. The letter said that I'm in bed with Joel Schwartz, and that I'm Joel's pawn, all kinds of scary stuff. Recently, I sent Mariah [Betsy's daughter] a letter that I got, to see if it looked like the one she got. I told her 'I think I got one that looks like the one you described getting at the restaurant.' I sent it to her, and she said it was different. It was not quite the same thing. But the way Mariah described it, I thought it sounded very similar. Mariah's anonymous letter was ugly; describing how bad the girls are and that they are addicted to drugs, and they can't handle their money… really sad things to say about somebody. It's a shame they are typewritten. I went through the letters and looked for misspellings between the letters that I got and the letter that was found on Betsy's laptop. I thought, 'Oh, my gosh! That could be the smoking gun if I find a similar misspelling on the letter that was planted on Betsy's laptop…I did not find it.'

261

Chris Hayes' Anonymous Letters:

The following is the first anonymous letter Chris Hayes received at his office at *Fox 2 News*. Chris has covered the Faria case more than any other reporter and was constantly on the News covering Pam's every move. The email to this author from Chris Hayes containing this letter and envelope pointed out that the address was cut and pasted onto the envelope.

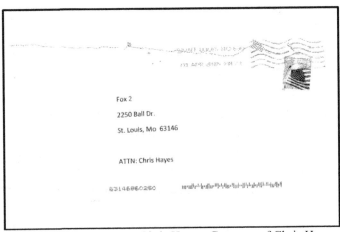

Envelope sent to *Fox 2* to Chris Hayes. Courtesy of Chris Hayes.

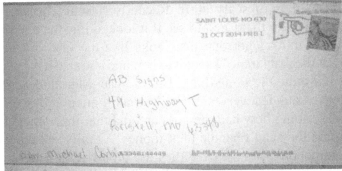

Envelope to the letter sent to Mike Corbin, Russ' Game Night alibi exactly one year after Shirley Neumann was found dead at her nursing home. Photo courtesy of Chris Hayes *Fox 2 News* Investigator.

Dear Sirs:

I think its getting a little silly that you keep accusing someone of killing their parent, when its not true. I have known Pam Hupp through her sister Sheri Wasserman, since Sheri and I have gone to nursing school.

Chris, Sheri told me how you went to her house and spoke with her regarding her sister killing her mother. Sheri, said you were nuts and trying to get a story for the Defense Lawyer, Mr. Schwartz. Anyone who watches the news knows that you are working for Mr. Schwartz, and know one really cares. The stories are so silly and fake, like most stories from Fox News. Anyway, if you really did your research you would find that Sheri and Mark Wasserman are the ones you should be looking at for a story. Here are a few reasons why and please try to practice telling the whole story, so the public can make up their minds with the facts, not what you want us to believe.. Here you go.

1. Late 90's Sheri Wasserman was arrested for writing scripts from Dr. Mark Wasserman's office. This was a big deal and the Attorney General was involved with the case against Sheri and Mark. Sheri lost her nursing licenses and Mark could not longer practice in Missouri. Mark worked on a reservation in Oklahoma (i'm guessing for his slap on the wrist). Mark now practices in Granite City clinic run by the Government. At one time he had a huge practice at St. Lukes Hospital, now he can't practice here.

2. They had an affair at this time, Mark left his wife and 5 kids and Sheri left her husband and 4 kids.

3. At a time when Sheri had her children, Mark and Sheri ran off to Vegas and left the kids in the care of the oldest daughter. The oldest daughter was only in middle school and the other three in grade school. Chris, you should know this information after you talked to her husband Kent.

1

Page 1 of anonymous letter to Chris Hayes. Courtesy of Chris Hayes.

4. Sheri and Mark are now married and neither side of their families talk to them. Mark Wasserman paid his wife a lump sum in November of about 2006 - 2007, and signed his children over. He has never seen his children since.

5. Sheri and Mark adopted a crack baby from one of Mark's clients a month after Mark wrote his kids off. They adopted another crack baby the same year in March.

6. Funny thing is Mark would talk his crack whores into giving up their babies. They were not allowed to adopt another baby so soon, so they had their oldest daughter adopt the last one and they kept it. Chris, check out that paper trail.

7. These 2 lost their last house in about 2009 for lack of payment and have never been able to own since, they move every couple of years from rental to rental. Chris, how do you be a doctor and not have any money??? And you have never paid child support.

8. I guess the best one is when Sheri tried to get her mom to move in with her and pay her. The mother was so afraid that she told her oldest son that she was afraid of Sheri and please don't let her take her away. At this time Sheri never even talked to her parents for years. Very odd don't you think?

9. The oldest brother placed the mother in a home and we all know what happened after that. I'm not saying that anyone did this, but Sheri did tell me she was very dissapointed that her mother did not have life insurance.

10. I guess the kicker is that Sheri or Mark Wasserman did not go to her mothers funeral. Don't you find that strange from someone just a year before wanted to take her in.

11. Sheri doesn't talk to anyone in her family, even though they have bailed her out for writing bad checks, etc. Anything you can think of this woman has done. The best part is that long ago before Sheri met Mark

2

Wasserman, she dated Joel Schwartz............. it's true, I was working with Sheri when she dated Joel schwartz.... isn't it a small, small world. Chris, Please do your homework and stop being Joel Schwartz's messanger. Fool!!

Pages 2 and 3

As with everything of which Pam Hupp is suspected, this letter in no way implies veracity and should not be seen as proof against the people mentioned. It's shocking to know that this vitriol was against Pam's own sister. It seems to insinuate that her sister Sheri had nefarious reasons for wanting their mother to live with her. Was Pam setting her own sister up for their mother's death with this letter? If Pam did indeed write this letter, it is more evidence that she would stop at nothing to throw someone else under the bus. Not even her family was safe. And notice in the second paragraph of the letter, the use of Pam's pet phrase "if you *really*..."

Chris Hayes,

i was at a friends house the other day talking about her church friend Russ Faria. She told me a crazy story about his two step daughters that are money hungry party girls. I'm not going to bore you with stories about these girls, as I don't know them.

What I did find interesting was the story she told about the girls doing a fund raiser for their financial needs. This caught my interest, as I remember you doing a story on a lady in the case, illegally raising money with their mom. My friend and I talked about this and at first my friend believed the story you had on tv. As we talked, my friend said that she thought you were just trying to make this woman look bad. She said there was never anyone that actually had this woman come to their door to collect. She said the husband of the woman that they supposedly collected for said 'none of his neighbors ever approched him about the collection' and to this day his neighbors don't know anything about it.

Enclosed is a copy that my friend gave to me about a scam the daughters of Betsy Faria came up with. The girls got together a fundraiser to help them 'build a financially secure future'. Her are some interesting facts that you seem to keep ignoring in order to get ratings.

1. Flyer of Fundraiser

2. Deposition statements made by Mariah that they raised over $5,000

3. The girls aunt Julie had told friends that they made a little over $10,000 at event

4. Deposition statements by Mariah that the event was 'Promoted as to help me and my sister'

5. Deposition statements by Mariah that the truth was 'that we were raising money to get a lawver'

6. Email from friend and Mariah that complain that people thought that the girls were lying to people about the fundraiser. (see attached email)

7. Email from friend and Mariah that people are upset that girls are spending this money on vacations, partying, new vehicles. (see attached email)

8. Leah bought a new BMW SUV, she makes $10.50 and hour, thought the law suit was going to make her rich. Now she can't pay for her vehicle.

9. Friend said the money has been used for new cars, and lawyer fees. Isn't this fraud???

This sounds like the story you made on the other lady, only this is the deceased daughters.

1

Interesting, that the old Christmas card found on the mothers computer was used as a flyer to raise money. Interesting. that the girls had access to this information and no one else did. Interesting, the daughters had been accused and kicked out of the house from stealing credit cards and money from their parents and grandmother. Odd these girls have stolen from just about everyone in their family to party and have a good time.

Seems to us that the old flyer to raise money for the unfortunate seems common practice in the girls life. How is it possible that the same scam is played twice in the same family, but somone else gets blamed for it? We don't think you dug far enough Chris Hayes.

Sad that the girls are fighting like heck to get their hands on money that they were never named on. You would think they might fight to get the money for their step dad, as it was his in the beginning.

Just something to think about. Not everyone believes that these girls are totally innocent.

cc: Leah Wommack

Page 1 (previous page) of Anonymous letter denigrating Betsy's daughters.
Page 2 (above) against the daughters.
Courtesy of Chris Hayes.

The first anonymous letter came just before Russ' second trial, slamming him for being Schwartz's "fool!" Both letters posted on the previous pages have 'tv' in lower case letters. Pam Hupp's neighbors reported getting ugly anonymous letters during her time in their neighborhood. Mariah and Leah Day received the one Hayes mentioned at their work place. Pam's former boss, Mike Boschert, hinted that he believed things had been done behind his back that resulted in him leaving State Farm. Ugly letters, forgeries, and other things seemed to be Pam's modus operandi. There were repeat patterns of insidious behavior that always surrounded her.

Michael,

I saw your post regarding Leah Askey. Thought you might want to know that when Pam Hupp lived in Troy (2007-2008) she was best friends with Leah Askey. She used to baby sit Leah's kids. I should know, I was Pam's neighbor when she rented a house at 470 Creekwood in Troy. Pam rented this house when she [the seller?] left her husband from Thomas Young who had been in a bar shooting. Pam's company bought the house when the owner let it go into foreclosure and then sold it.

It was rumored that Leah and Pam were having an affair. All the neighbors knew about it and they didn't really try to hide there [ms] feelings for one another.

Thomas Young died October 13, 2014. I went to the ceramoney [ms] for him and talked to some of my old neighbor's about everything that is going on with Leah Askey. Lots of skeletons in her closet. Leah will do anything and anyone to get what she wants.

Just thought you would want to another piece of the puzzle. Good luck!

Anonymous letter to Mike Corbin, Russ' Game Night host the night Betsy Faria was murdered. Incredulously, the letter says Pam was having an affair with Leah Askey, the prosecuting attorney who had tried to help her. The date on the envelope is October 31, 2014, exactly one year after Shirley Neumann fell from her balcony. Letter courtesy of Chris Hayes.

I have been following the Faria murder case, since Channel 2 Fox has been saying it's a slam dunk that someone else was responsible for the death of Elizabeth Faria. I have attended all the court dates for the murder trial and the trial dates for Pam Hupp.

It was obvious that Chris Hayes and Joel Schwartz are doing everything they can to cause doubt in the case for the appeal. I think everyone gets that. I have seen the recent reports on this woman and can't help but notice the sloppy 'story telling'.

If I was a writer this would make a great book it could be called Social Media - Judge and Jury. Both this case and the Michael Brown case are so blown up by social media and Fox 2 New (Chris Hayes), it's a really sad to watch 'rag' journalism at it's best, but now on prime time 'real news'.

Here are facts that go against everything the Chris Hayes is reporting. Some of these have been sent to him and he chooses to ignore, because of his partnership with Joel Schwartz and Michael Corbin.

1. Talked to family members of Pam Hupp. Yes, she did say her mother was worth a half million dollars. The sibling in charge of the mothers estate gave us copies of the Life Insurance Policy. Pam's mother had a Final Expense Policy (which covers funeral expenses). The policy was worth $10,660 dollars, divided out to three siblings to take care of the funeral. **Attached** copy of the policy and Pam's payout of $3553.58. **Attached** copy of the funeral bill from Hoffmeister South County of $8,242.87, which all three children paid for out of the above insurance policy.

2. **Attached** copies of a flyer that Mariah Day made to raise money for lawyer fees to sue Pam Hupp. They lied to people about what the fund raiser was for. **Attached** copy where a friend of Russ Faria called the girls out in a Facebook conversation (evidence in a deposition). Funny how this is exactly like the flyer Chris Hayes said Pam Hupp was using to collect money fraudulently. The flyer to collect money by Elizabeth and Pam was an old Christmas card that was on Elizabeths computer, had nothing to do with Pam Hupp. The daughters had access to that computer and again has raised money with lies. Chris Hayes again made up a story. There has never been anyone that said Elizabeth and Pam ever came to their door collecting anything.

3. **Attached** copies of Michael Corbin helping Chris Hayes with this smear campaign posted to the Tropix - Troy Forum, a story about Leah Askey and Detective Lang having an affair. This is also lies and Chris Hayes chose not to broadcast because it's not true. Now this would be news and a real story. Michael Corbin chose to put it on a Troy blog in order to contaminate Troy for the appeal.

Attached copies of court documents showing that Eliabeth's girls received all the Personal Property from the estate. All items have been sold off and Mariah drives the Ford Explorer today. The oldest daughter drives a newly purchased BMW, because she thought the law suit

1

Page 1 of Anonymous Letter sent to the St. Charles Court House, listing all the "lies" told by news reporter Chris Hayes. Courtesy of Chris Hayes.

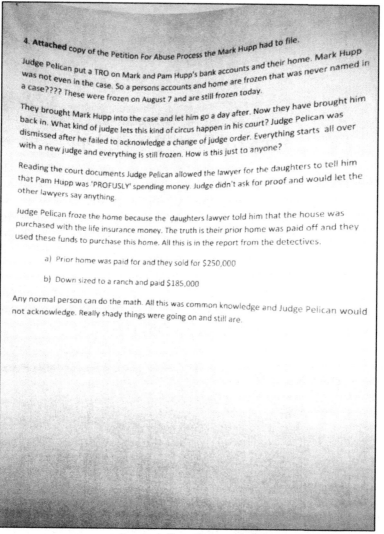

4. Attached copy of the Petition For Abuse Process the Mark Hupp had to file.

Judge Pelican put a TRO on Mark and Pam Hupp's bank accounts and their home. Mark Hupp was not even in the case. So a persons accounts and home are frozen that was never named in a case???? These were frozen on August 7 and are still frozen today.

They brought Mark Hupp into the case and let him go a day after. Now they have brought him back in. What kind of judge lets this kind of circus happen in his court? Judge Pelican was dismissed after he failed to acknowledge a change of judge order. Everything starts all over with a new judge and everything is still frozen. How is this just to anyone?

Reading the court documents Judge Pelican allowed the lawyer for the daughters to tell him that Pam Hupp was 'PROFUSLY' spending money. Judge didn't ask for proof and would let the other lawyers say anything.

Judge Pelican froze the home because the daughters lawyer told him that the house was purchased with the life insurance money. The truth is their prior home was paid off and they used these funds to purchase this home. All this is in the report from the detectives.

    a) Prior home was paid for and they sold for $250,000

    b) Down sized to a ranch and paid $185,000

Any normal person can do the math. All this was common knowledge and Judge Pelican would not acknowledge. Really shady things were going on and still are.

Page 2.

Page 3 had only one sentence and the scribbled word 'Next' with an arrow.
The sentence read:
"against Pam Hupp was going to happen fast..."like on TV" (her words)."

One thing is clear: whoever wrote all these letters seemed to know a lot about Pam Hupp and components of the case. They also smacked of desperation to paint Pam as a misrepresented victim.

Chapter Sixteen
The Civil Case: Day vs Hupp

Pam Hupp must have been spending some restless nights after Russ Faria's vindication. She was now in the crosshairs of an investigation. She was also due to take on the lawsuit filed by Mariah and Leah Day in an effort to get their mother's life insurance money. The charges against Pam were "constructive fraud and unjust enrichment." The Days asserted that Betsy changed the beneficiary on her life-insurance policy to Pamela Hupp in reliance on Hupps' promise and resulting agreement with Faria to use the insurance proceeds for the benefit of the Days.

Pam and Mark Hupp arrive for the Civil Trial.

Only two months after the conclusion of Russ' second trial, Pam Hupp arrived at the Lincoln County Courthouse all smiles. A light breeze lifted her short blond hair and she appeared as if she was enjoying the attention. She even shot a peace sign to the press cameras. Clutching Mark Hupp's arm, the two entered into the building. While Pam exuded her usual confidence, Mark kept his head down. This was serious business. His name was on the lawsuit as well, and Betsy's daughters wanted their mother's $150,000 life insurance money returned to them. This time, Pam would have her day on the stand, and it would be filmed.

The rest of the world would now have a chance to see Pam's personality on full display. Russ' first trial had allowed no media coverage inside, and Pam was not asked to testify in his second trial. If one wondered how this strange woman would perform on the stand and under oath, they were about to get ringside seats to the Pam Hupp show. She even did a giddy little step up to the lectern.

"State your full name, ma'am, and spell your last name," the clerk said as Pam stood before the judge.

"Pamela Marie Hupp...H-U-P-P," Pam answered.

Pam Hupp being sworn in at the Civil Trial. It lasted two days.

The attorneys about to go to battle with Ms. Hupp, as representatives for Mariah and Leah Day (appellants), were David T. Butsch and Christopher E. Roberts. Michael Kruse represented Pam Hupp (respondent). From the moment the questioning began, Pam let it be known she was in charge of this trial. She would not make it easy for Butsch as he began his interrogation. In a somewhat soft, almost apologetic voice, he began.

"You're the defendant in this lawsuit, is that correct?" he asked her.

"I'm sorry?" Pam asked.

"You're the defendant...the party being sued...in the instant lawsuit?"

"Uh huh. I can hardly hear you," Pam said calmly. It was the same ploy she had used with Schwartz in Russ' first trial.

"Is that correct?" he asked, non-plussed. "Did you hear the question, okay?"

"I did," Pam says in a hushed voice.

Realizing he was in for a confrontational exchange, Butsch stopped and turned to the judge, saying, "Judge, I would like permission to examine the witness as a hostile witness at this time."

A hostile witness means the witness you call to testify is not on your side, i.e., is "hostile" to your client's position. Nevertheless, you want to call that witness to testify in your case to satisfy your burden of proof. If the judge approves your request, you are then permitted to "lead" the witness with questions like "isn't it true that the light was red when you first observed the blue car?" If the witness is not deemed a "hostile" witness, the lawyer would not be allowed to lead them with their questions. The judge granted Butsch's request.

Attorney Butsch continues, "You recall talking to Detective McCarrick on June 25th, 2012, correct?"

"Yes."

They play a segment of the police video where McCarrick is saying to Pam, "However, you now have this money, and have not turned any of this money over to the family or the kids."

"That's correct," Pam replies in the video, nodding her head.

"You were nodding your head in that video, is that correct?" Attorney Butsch asks Pam.

"I'm sorry," Pam counters.

"You were nodding your head affirmatively in that video, is that correct?" he pressed.

"I don't know what you're sayin'," Pam answered, a harder edge to her voice.

"Were you nodding your head affirmatively...you know what that means, correct?"

"No. I'm nodding my head affirmatively...no," Pam stated firmly.

"Okay. Can you play the video again, Ed?" Butsch asks.

As the video clip is replayed, Pam interjects, "Oh! I'm nodding my head...I'm sorry...I thought you said something else...I can't understand what you're sayin'." Pam continued to try and keep the attorney off-kilter with her interruptions and derailing the stream of questions.

"If you don't hear me, or you misunderstand a question…"

Pam cuts him off, "I know what you're saying because I'm acknowledging. But I'm not saying 'Yes, yes, you're right,' I'm acknowledging him as a person speaking to me. I'm in sales."

In another question, Butsch asks, "Leading up to the first criminal case for Russell Faria, do you ever mention to those investigators that you were having intimate relationships with Betsy Faria?"

"No," Pam says flatly.

"Ma'am, when I say intimate relationship, I'm talking about a sexual relationship. Did you have a sexual relationship with Betsy Faria?" Butsch asks, his voice firmer and more challenging.

"Sexual on what basis? What's sexual to you?" Pam asks, leaning into the microphone. Her mouth is pressed into a firm line. It is clear she still feels she is running the show.

Pam Hupp on the stand, under fire.

A question that Pam may not have been expecting was one that hit at the heart of the matter concerning Betsy's wish for her daughters to have the insurance money:

"Have you ever made a phone call to Leah Day about the insurance proceeds?" Butsch asks.

"No."

"Have you ever made a phone call to Mariah Day about the insurance proceeds?"

"No."

"And you have no present intention about giving them any of those proceeds, do you?"

"That's not true," Pam says quickly.

"So, you do have an intention of giving them some money?"

"It's a possibility," Pam answers, perhaps seeing a loophole she can step through.

It wasn't' until Attorney Butsch asks Pam about the specific details of why Betsy would make Pam the beneficiary that Pam finally explodes.

"So, this was an easy way for her to keep the money from going to the defendant," Butsch said. "Her purpose was to assure that it got to her girls…"

"Whoa, whoa, whoa, whoa!" Pam shouts, circling her left hand in front of her face as if to cut him off. He tried again to ask the question, and she yelled out, "Whoa, whoa, whoa!"

Pam Hupp, "Whoa, whoa, whoa, whoa!"

Butsch turned to the judge and said, "I direct the court…"

Pam cut him off, "I don't know what you're talkin' about," she said, looking up at Judge Ted House to see what he's going to say. She keeps going before a motion can be granted.

"This has nothin' to do with me drawing up a trust," she states, glancing at the judge once more.

"Is it true that you lied to Julie Swaney [Betsy's sister] about what you were going to do with those life insurance proceeds?"

"Yes."

"Did you lie to anybody else that you've spoken to, Ms. Hupp about what you were going to do with these insurance proceeds?" he asked, sounding a bit weary from the battle.

"Possibly," Pam says simply.

"Okay. Who else might you have lied to?"

"Anybody that would bug me, and bug me, and bug me," she said, scrunching up her face as if she has smelled something odious. Cocking her head to one side, she wrinkles her nose again, as he asks, "Did the detectives bug you and bug you?"

"Yeah," she says, twisting her mouth to the side, and scrunching up her nose again.

"Do you think you might have lied to them?"

"No. They didn't bug me about the proceeds. They never...that wasn't their focus."

Pam Hupp, showing the contempt she feels for the attorney.

While on the stand, Pam states that she once had the insurance money in cash and showed it to Prosecutor Leah Askey. This was the video where Pam is seen moving the chair into view beneath the police security camera and carrying a Dierberg's tote bag. When Attorney Butsch tries to pin her down about having the money at that time and showing it to Askey, Pam, once again, becomes defiant.

"What did I just say?" she taunts him, raising her left hand in a dismissive gesture. "I had a sack of cash. Am I not clear?"

Pam is playing with her necklace; a double strand of black beads that she fiddles with throughout the trial.

Pam Hupp playing with her beaded necklace.

"So, you brought a sack of cash and showed it to Ms. Askey that you had $150,000? That's your testimony here?"

Raising her hand again, she says defiantly, "How many times do you want me to say it?" She does not directly affirm that Askey actually saw the money in the bag.

"Do you still have the proceeds of that life insurance policy?"

"Today?" Pam answers.

"Yes."

"No." She shakes her head, lips pressed.

"Okay. Where are they?"

"Uhhh...I bought...in *November*...I used that money to buy a house on the Troy courthouse steps. It was my money...my personal money in my checking account," she says, head bobbing, and looking up to Judge House to affirm what she's saying. Both hands are enmeshed in her beaded necklace as she pulls on it. There is a new nervousness to her demeanor. "I still had $150,000."

Pam's emphasis on the word "November" is interesting. Her mother had died the October before this civil trial, and Pam did receive $100,000. But the purchase of the Shelby Point Drive house was back in 2012, shortly after receiving Betsy's money. They had bought another house since then, but it was long after Pam spent the insurance money.

All this testimony flew in the face of Pam's original testimony to detectives when she was trying to convince them why Betsy left her life insurance money to her. She told police back in 2012, "She [Betsy] goes, 'Would you be my beneficiary on my life policies and make sure my kids get it when they need it?"

Anticipating this reversal of Pam's current story that Betsy wanted *her* to have the money, Pam's attorney, Michael Kruse played his only trump card as he addressed the judge in closing remarks.

"This was a criminal investigation going on and the murder charge against Russ Faria. The prosecution's concern was that Pam Hupp just received $150,000 on this life insurance policy…that's 150,000 reasons why she should have been named in that jury trial as a suspect," he said. It was a shocking statement to make about his own client. The premise he was going for was if she had done anything wrong, or the transfer of money to her had been suspicious, why wasn't she a suspect in Betsy's murder back then.

"The trust was nothing to do with Ms. Hupp," he continues, pointing toward her in the gallery. "It wasn't her idea. She was spoon-fed that idea by law enforcement in Lincoln County in order to create the conviction."

The Lincoln County Detective Patrick Harney, who had been the one in the video feeding Pam their theory of what happened the night of Betsy's murder, fought back with a statement in the *St. Louis Post-Dispatch*: "We've done everything we can to know every fact and detail of this case."

Important information concerning the actual life insurance transaction at the Winghaven Library was laid out during the civil trial. On December 23, 2011, Betsy and Pam entered the library and approached librarian Lauren Manganelli, who was behind the counter. She witnessed Betsy's execution of the change-of-beneficiary form. Manganelli testified at Russ' trial that she spoke with both Betsy and Pam. During her testimony then, she said it was Betsy who said she was divorcing her husband. Now, during her civil case testimony, she stated she believed it was Hupp who said that Betsy was divorcing and changing the beneficiary on her life insurance policy so that Betsy's children could be included.

The librarian was asked to read from her 2014 deposition in which she stated that she did not remember Pam or Betsy specifically speaking about spending the money. In her deposition, Manganelli stated she believed it was Betsy who mentioned the divorce and changing her insurance to her children. In a portion of her deposition, now read to the court two years later, she further stated that the implication for her was that the life insurance proceeds were to take care of Faria's children.

Bobbi Wann was the family friend who accompanied Betsy to her chemo treatment the day of her murder. Wann testified in her deposition that Betsy had told her no one else planned to attend Betsy's chemotherapy treatment that day. Wann said that Faria seemed surprised when Hupp arrived. Wann testified that Betsy stated in Hupp's presence that she—Betsy—had removed her husband from her insurance policy because she wanted the girls— Leah and Mariah Day—to receive the insurance proceeds. Wann stated that Hupp then stated she would make sure the girls received the money.

Wann went on to say that they had no discussion, nor did she overhear any discussion, about why Betsy named Hupp the beneficiary if Betsy wanted her daughters to have the life insurance proceeds. Wann stated that she did not hear Betsy say that she wanted the girls to have the money *immediately*. Wann did not ask Betsy why she wanted Hupp and not a family member to be the beneficiary.

Betsy Faria's sisters, Pam Welker and Julie Swaney, and their mother, Janet Meyer, all recounted how Pam had told them the money would go to the girls. This was shortly after the family found out about the insurance switch. Julie Swaney also testified that Betsy died intestate, and as far as she knew, Betsy had never established a trust or guardianship for her daughters. When Swaney telephoned Hupp in March, 2012, three months after Betsy's murder, she asked Pam what her plans were for the insurance money she had received. Pam told her that she gave it away to charity.

Julie telephoned Pam again, two weeks later, and Hupp told her at that time she had planned on establishing a trust for Betsy's daughters. Swaney testified that Betsy had trouble with her girls' behavior, including possible drug use, stealing, and irresponsibility. Leah's Nissan had been taken away after one such incident. But Swaney stated that despite these issues, Leah and Mariah "were always Betsy's top concern."

Betsy's best friend, Rita Wolf, was called to the stand. Rita talked to this author about how Betsy came to her for help in decisions about how to set up something for the girls after her death. Her cancer was now terminal, and these things had to be addressed. It was then that Betsy came to Wolf's home and they sat down with a legal pad and itemized the things the two girls might need as they grew up.

Rita Wolf testified at the civil trial that she had seen Pam Hupp at Russ' first trial. She confronted Pam and told her that Betsy really wanted her daughters taken care of. Rita said Pam told her they would be taken care of because she had just set up a trust, which indeed she had, only five days before. It was a revocable trust, and Pam emptied it shortly after Russ went to prison."

At Russ Faria's first trial in November, 2013, where Pam did take the stand, Hupp explained that Betsy changed her life insurance policies multiple times, depending on whom she was angry with at the time. Hupp stated that Betsy did not have a lot of discretionary money, and had applied for food stamps shortly before her death. She conceded that the change of beneficiary was an easy way for Faria to guarantee that the insurance proceeds went to her daughters instead of her husband. In that first trial against Russ, Hupp said she placed $100,000 in trust for Betsy's daughters (she would later claim Detective McCarrick had coerced her to do so), and the other $50,000 went to help the child of another friend who had recently died of breast cancer.

In Pam Hupp's video-taped deposition, she repeatedly denied telling Betsy's family that she would use the money for Faria's daughters. She admitted she lied to Swaney about donating the money to charity in an effort to make Swaney stop calling her. She denied telling the librarian that witnessed the insurance change form that the money was for Betsy's daughters. And, Pam denied having the conversation with Bobbi Wann at Betsy's chemo treatment that day about the insurance policy. When asked in that 2014 deposition what Pam did intend to do with the money, she answered, "Today, I intend on doing nothing with that money." She also said she had revoked the trust entirely.

During the civil trial, Pam admitted that she did tell detectives four times that Betsy told her to make sure the girls received some money. Hupp said she told the police that "Betsy would have liked her daughters to have some money." She said her initial intention was "to give them some money. Could be for a boat, could be for this... Could be for all kinds of things." Pam's point was that nothing was said about when or how much she would give the girls.

In Attorney Kruse's final statement to the judge, he admits his client has some issues. "I'm not going to argue about her credibility. She's not a credible witness, but that's not the issue."

Perhaps, it should have been.

As Mariah and Leah Day waited nervously in their seats, Judge House looked out over the court room. Pam was leaning against her right hand, elbow propped on the bench arm, seemingly nonchalant about the outcome. Her husband Mark nibbled on his lower lip, half-hidden by his short beard and moustache.

Pam Hupp, looking confident. Mark Hupp is to the right.

And then the words were uttered by the judge. The court entered a judgement in favor of Pamela and Mark Hupp on both counts. The published verdict in summary was that the Day's did not meet their burden of proof for the elements of either "constructive fraud or unjust enrichment." The evidence was insufficient to establish that Betsy Faria intended the life insurance proceeds to be used exclusively for her daughters. It found that Hupp made no forceable promise to Betsy, relying heavily on Pam's first statement to detectives where she says "I could" when Betsy asks her to give her daughters some money when they got older. It underscored Betsy's own words: "Would you be my beneficiary on my life policies and make sure my kids get it when they need it?" And Pam answers, "Well, I could...Okay."

The judge also stated that Betsy had been a life insurance agent and knew her way around a form. If she had wanted the proceeds to go to her daughters, she would have worded the form accordingly.

Judge House completed the trial by saying:

"The way to honor Betsy Faria's memory and the proper course of action for the court under the law and the evidence is not to speculate about what she might have intended. It is rather to give effect to what she actually did, which is to allow her close friend Pamela Hupp to use the money at Pamela's discretion."

As the judge's words penetrated Pam Hupp's alternating consciousness, she beamed, oblivious to the pain she was causing her "best friend's" daughters sitting only inches away.

Pam upon hearing the judge's ruling that she would keep the money. Mark Hupp is to the right.

Leah and Mariah Day listening to testimony.

Once again, Pamela Marie Hupp had woven her spell around the judicial system. Not only did she get to keep the $150,000 of Betsy Faria's life insurance money, Leah and Mariah Day had to pay Pam's attorney fees for her appearance in court.

Pam Hupp and Elizabeth "Betsy" Faria.

A jubilant Pam Hupp left the Lincoln County Courthouse. She held her husband's hand as she walked confidently down the sloping sidewalk to the street. There is no limp, no difficulty from her "back, leg, and hip" issues. No visible TENS device to stimulate her spine. No cane. Mark Hupp's face is, as usual, impassive. He looks away as he notices a cameraman filming them. Pam beams at the lens, recognizing to whom the crew belongs. As she passes the *Dateline* cameraman (camera rolling) and Christine Filmore, one of the show's producers, she glibly shouts out, "Say Hi to Cathy!" Cathy? Cathy Singer, the producer at *Dateline NBC* who had texted Pam from time to time requesting interviews and a photo that Pam declined to provide? *Dateline NBC* had already done several episodes covering the Faria case, which included questions about Pam. Was Pam's cheery greeting to the absent producer just being her usual narcissist self? As if to say, "You never did get that interview or photo you wanted, did you?" or, "Look! I just beat the system and I'm keeping the cash!"

In a long line of Pam Hupp ambiguities, this was just another example of the audaciousness of a woman who marched by the beat of her own drum. She never heard the dissonant sounds when the harmony of other people's lives is shattered. All she heard was the fractured composition of lies that played through her mind relentlessly. Others might have broken beneath the weight of remembering all the falsehoods, contrivances, and trying to stay one step ahead of an arrest. But Pam? Pam sailed along, plotting into the night, head filled with messages she would pour out in anonymous hate mail. Her days were filled with violent images of crimes committed and perhaps more to come.

And now this cheerful greeting to a cameraman only minutes after betraying the wishes of her dying friend that her daughters would be financially looked after. "Say Hi to Cathy!" Was it Pam being Pam, or, did it mean something more?

Pam Hupp beaming at NBC's cameras as she leaves the Lincoln County Courthouse after winning the Civil Trial between herself and Betsy's daughters. She shouted out "Say Hi to Cathy!" as they headed down the slope to their car. Her husband Mark Hupp is holding her hand.

Louis Gumpenberger

February 17, 1983-August 16, 2016

Chapter Seventeen
Lambs to the Slaughter

Pam Hupp had walked away from the Lincoln County Courthouse victorious after winning the judgement for Betsy Faria's life insurance money. At this point, she may have begun to feel invincible. She had fooled so many detectives and triumphed over a prosecuting attorney during the murder investigation that resulted in Russ Faria going to prison. The prosecution against Russ had bought every word she said. She and Leah Askey had appeared to be buddies in the recorded police videos from Interrogation Room 2. She had somehow convinced Betsy to sign over her life insurance policy to her, sidestepping more logical candidates such as Betsy's own sisters. She bought a house with the insurance money, got to keep the house, planted a phony document on her friend's laptop as she played tennis, and basically cooked Russ' goose. She had gotten away with it all.

There was, however, a thorn in Pam Hupp's side, and it came in the form of a tenacious reporter for the local *Fox 2 News*. Chris Hayes would not go away. He was everywhere. He reported on her police interviews, he pointed out her cell phone records, her changing stories, and even had the temerity to show up at her door two months after Russ was sent off to prison. Yet, Pam stood there that day and talked with this reporter for over 30 minutes.

Chris talked to this author in a phone interview and shared his thoughts about Pam's feelings toward him:

"I will tell you something that is really interesting with my relationship with Pam Hupp over the years," Chris Hayes said. "Not only was she obsessed with me, as you can tell from interviews when she brings me up—like the O'Fallon police interview. It's crazy. She's looking at the camera when she says my name, "Chris Hayes." I think she had this sick fantasy that I was going to get in trouble for making it look like I was the bad guy and it's just poor old Pam and that all these crazies were going to come after her because of my irresponsible reporting. I think that's what she hoped."

Chris Hayes with *Fox 2 News*.
Photo courtesy of Tauna L. Price

Chris covered the Faria case, Shirley Neumann's controversial death, trials, and every move Pam made for over 10 years. He is still covering this on-going investigation and has been instrumental in providing leads to the prosecution against Hupp. The time Pam mentions his name during an O'Fallon police interview will be clarified shortly. What he told this author next, was so shocking that it took a few minutes to process:

"I will tell you a story," Chris said. "As I'm getting these anonymous letters, six or seven months before the Gumpenberger murder, I'd have to go back and look…I believe it's the Spring of 2016, I get a call from the news room. I'm in kind of a side office, and the news' group yells at me, 'Chris, get out here! I think you should head to Lake St. Louis!' He has a Post-It and a name on the Post-It, and the name is Leslie Stanton. And he says, 'This woman says Russ [Faria] is threatening somebody with a gun at Image Makers Salon in Lake St. Louis. She was really cagey. She wouldn't give me a phone number. I got it off the Caller ID. When I asked for her name, she wasn't going to give me her name, and finally she says, 'Leslie Stanton,' but it was weird how she gave it to me.'

Image Makers Salon is two doors down from TJ Maxx in this photo of the Shops at Hawk Ridge in Lake St. Louis.

"I yell for my photog and say we're going to Lake St. Louis," Chris continues, using an abbreviation for photographer, "and as I'm heading out the door, I dial the phone number he gave me for this Leslie Stanton on my phone and I hit SEND, and the name Pam Hupp comes up! I had her programmed in my phone already because I talked to her. So, I hung up and I said, 'Oh, my God! Pam Hupp is trying to get me to go out to *frickin* Lake St. Louis, which is a remote area with this little strip mall. What the hell?' I thought, 'I'm not going to go out there. What does she have in mind?' So, I called this

Image Makers Salon. I said, 'Is there somebody threatening somebody with a gun out there?' The lady says, 'Oh, my God...NO!' I said, 'Hang on, I need to understand why I got this call. I'm with *Fox News*. I'm Chris Hayes.' 'Oh yeah! I know who you are.' I ask her, 'Do you know the name Russ Faria by chance?' She says, 'Yeah, yeah.' I said, 'I was just told he is there and threatening somebody with a gun.' She said, 'No...uh...there was a tense argument. He came in with his cousin Mary and told a hairdresser here that she better stop posting lies that he's a killer. But there was no gun; no threat of violence or anything.'

"So, I've always wondered," Hayes said during our phone call, "did Pam want me to go out there.... I mean...what did she have in mind? Was there something she had in mind for me?'

"Pam gets her hair done at this salon," Chris explains, "and she befriended a woman who does her hair. I reached out to this woman on FB Messenger to try and find out what had happened between her and Russ. She was very nasty to me and she said, 'I want nothing to do with you and don't contact me again.' When Louis Gumpenberger was murdered, I reached out to her again, and I didn't get an answer. I tried once more after Pam was convicted of Louis' murder and told her that I thought she seemed to be defending Pam Hupp at the time, and I was just curious what her thoughts are. She did reply to that, and said, "I do have a unique position, and I will think about talking to you.' But she never did. Somehow, Pam convinced this woman with some sick stories that she was the innocent one."

This author had two thoughts after this conversation with Chris Hayes pertaining to the Salon situation:

1- Had Pam used her hairstylist to embellish a story around Russ showing up and having an argument with a stylist there? Was the stylist Russ yelled at Pam's stylist? Seems reasonable that Pam would get this lady to put lies out about Russ and continue to call him a killer now that he's free. Were the taunts on social media calling Russ a 'killer' done to get Russ to come to the Salon? He knew where to find this lady. Did they make it easy for him to find her? Then, was the plan for this stylist to say 'I saw a gun. I'm not sure if anyone else did, but I saw a gun tucked in Russ' jacket, etc.?" Which brings me to Point 2.

2- Was the plan all along to incite Russ, get him to the salon, and plan to tell police he was carrying a gun (probably out of sight of other witnesses)? Then, Chris Hayes' TV station is called and Chris is called out to the salon. Was Chris, whom Pam hates, supposed to somehow get shot? Now, this friend/stylist of Pam's can say she saw Russ with a gun and he was angry. Chris got in the way. Chris is killed. Russ goes back to prison. Two birds with one bullet. Based on what would happen a few months later, when Pam trolled for Louis Gumpenburger and others, it is not that far-fetched. What Pam didn't count on was Hayes calling the phone number and seeing her name, or that Hayes would call the salon and talk to a woman who was not Pam's friend, who told Hayes there was no one waving a gun.

3-Russ has been living with his mother since his acquittal. His mother lives just down the street from this hair salon.

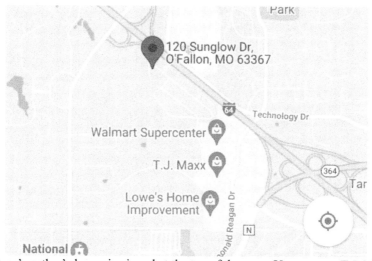

Russ' mother's house is pinned at the top of the page. You can see T.J. Maxx in the center. Image Makers Salon is two doors down from T. J. Maxx.
Map courtesy of Google maps.

Is the near proximity of where Russ is living and the salon a coincidence? Chris Hayes knows where Russ is staying. He interviewed him multiple times during the two trials. If, when Chris arrives at the salon to check out the story of Russ waving a gun, Russ has already gone home, would Chris then have gone to Russ' house to ask him about it? Probably so. Chris has nothing to fear from

Russ. They know each other well. Was the plan then, to get Chris to Russ' mother's house, only minutes away, and while Chris is there, somehow secretly shoot him and make it look like Russ shot him? Farfetched? It's the exact plan Pam will use on a stranger in only a few short months.

One more nagging question: Had Pam picked that salon due its proximity to where Russ was living? How long had she been a customer there? Was this one more thing she planned in the dark hours of night as she plotted and schemed? It would be interesting to know how long she had been attending this salon. Her home was ten minutes away.

The distance from Pam's house at Little Brave to where Russ was living on Sunglow Circle. Map courtesy of Google maps.

It's something Chris Hayes still thinks about today. Pam knew Chris covered all the stories to do with her and the Faria case. She called the TV station where Chris worked, not the police to report a man waving a gun around, and she did it anonymously. She knew Chris would be out the door and headed to the salon in record time, and indeed, he almost did. Why mention a gun if there wasn't one?

The fact that a gun was used only months later, this time with fatal results, is chilling. And even more chilling to contemplate—did Pam's foiled plan to get Chris Hayes out to the strip mall and somehow frame Russ for shooting him, become the impetus to form a new plan to frame Russ and take the heat off herself when Chris didn't show up? Joel Schwartz was coming for her. She knew that with certainty. What would be Pam Hupp's next move?

Louis Gumpenberger, Pam's next victim.

In August of 2016, eight months after Russ Faria was freed from prison, Pamela Hupp began a series of strange car rides throughout sections of O'Fallon, Missouri, not too far from her home at the time. She had moved from the Shelby Point house that she had purchased with Betsy's insurance money, and was now living on Little Brave Drive. She was painfully aware that Joel Schwartz had not been satisfied with just having his client vindicated and acquitted of his wife's murder, but that the tenacious attorney wanted justice for Betsy Faria. He was also convinced Pam Hupp had murdered her.

And so, on August 10, 2016, with that knowledge breathing down her neck, Pam got her favorite soda, placed her sunglasses upon her nose, and headed toward a trailer park north of her home. The shiny new GMC Acadia looked somewhat incongruous as it drove up, down and through the streets of trailers. What was she doing there?

Pam rounded a bend and saw a young blond woman leaning against the railing of her steps outside her trailer door. She was wearing a lime green hoodie and lounging pants. She was barefoot and appeared be to watching her small dog as it roamed the front lawn. The woman, Carol Alford, said a car went by slowly and the driver waived at her. A few minutes later, the car returned, and pulled up at the end of Alford's driveway.

Tim Lohmar, St. Charles County Prosecuting Attorney.
Photo courtesy of PA Tim Lohmar.

Tim Lohmar is the Prosecuting Attorney for St. Charles County and was paramount in discovering circumstances surrounding the events in early August of 2016. A handsome, articulate, and compassionate man, Mr. Lohmar is always impeccably dressed, treats reporters with respect, and, at times, with a sense of wit and a twinkle in his eye. This author deeply appreciates his generous time and insight into this tragic chapter of the Pam Hupp saga. Traci Johnson, the Litigation Assistant to Mr. Lohmar, spent copious amounts of time supplying this author with crime scene photos, the 911 call recording, and other pertinent information.

During an hour-long phone conversation, Mr. Lohmar related the events of what happened the day Carol Alford was confronted by a strange woman driving through her trailer park:

"As the investigation ensued, a female subject was later identified and interviewed," Mr. Lohmar said. "This female subject, on August 10th, 2016, six days prior to the death of Louis Gumpenberger, called 911 to report a suspicious circumstance to another St. Charles Law

Enforcement Agency. Just a few days after the murder [of Louis Gumpenberger], a detective with the O'Fallon police department who was not directly investigating this case, contacted the O'Fallon Detective Bureau to tell them of a 911 call they had received approximately one week prior to the murder. This was the call by the female suspect who reported being approached by a white female claiming to be affiliated with *Dateline's* television show.

"We were able to identify all 6 digits of the license plate," Lohmar said. "The car is registered to Pam and Mark Hupp. The witness (who got in the car with Hupp) is a firecracker. She immediately started to question the whole situation. She asked, "Where are your credentials?" Hupp skirted around the questions. The witness began to get a little freaked out and said, "Please take me back home, I need to get my shoes [she had gotten in the car bare-footed]. Pam takes her back home. Carol Alford goes in to get her shoes. A few minutes later, she comes out and let's Pam know she is no longer willing to participate. At the time, and again, this was brilliant on the part of the witness, she knew if she could get Pam to pull into the driveway, that there was a video camera there and that video would capture not only the license plate, but certainly an image of the driver herself; in fact, it did. It's Pam Hupp, clear as can be."

The video surveillance camera attached to Carol Alford's home, pointed toward the driveway.

Carol Alford approaching Pam Hupp in her car at the bottom of Alford's driveway. Video from surveillance camera attached to trailer.

"She was told that she would be given a script and she was promised $1,000 in cash, both up front and at the completion of the sound bite," PA Tim Lohmar continued. "The female subject later picked Hupp out of a photo array line-up and positively identified her as the person posing as the *Dateline* producer who lured her into the vehicle."

Carol Alford getting into Pam Hupp's car. The video clip is date and time-stamped: 10:58:46 AM, October 8, 2016. The license plate is in full view.

Carol Alford also stated that when Pam first called to her from her car at the bottom of the driveway, she asked Carol if she "babysat." Alford started walking up to the car but thought it odd that someone would drive around and ask a total stranger to babysit for her. When Carol said, "No," Pam quickly switched to the *Dateline NBC* 911 call reenactment offer. She told Carol to come with her for the *Dateline* reenactment, and that Carol was not to bring her cell phone, keys, cigarettes, or wallet because "the *Dateline NBC* producer does not like clutter."

Carol took her beagle inside as Pam waited for her. What Pam did not know, was that Carol was secreting two knives inside her hoodie for protection. There was something off with this whole thing, but Carol was curious to see where it led. She put a folding knife up one sleeve of the hoodie, and placed a large kitchen knife inside the front pouch of the sweatshirt. She was still barefooted when she entered Pam's car. As they drove through the trailer park, she became more nervous. The woman had this perpetual grin on her face. The driver then told her where they were going to record the segment. With a sense of Deja Vu Chris Hayes could relate to, the location was to be a house that *Dateline NBC* purportedly rented for the segment, and it was...behind the Shops in Lake St. Louis. The same strip mall where Pam tried to lure Hayes only months before.

Alford became concerned and asked Hupp to take her back home so she could get some shoes on. Pam pulls into the driveway, facing the trailer's front door. Alford states that Pam started to get out of the car with her, leaned forward and looked up through the windshield and said, "You have cameras." Alford confirmed she did have a security camera, and it was clear it was facing Pam's car. She went into the house, but moments later came out and told Hupp she had changed her mind.

Tim Lohmar later told Carol Alford what Pam Hupp was planning when she was going to take Alford to a "house *Dateline NBC* rented behind the Shops in Lake St. Louis." Lohmar told her that the house was 120 Sunglow Drive. It was actually the home of Russ Faria's mother, where he had been staying. Lohmar told Carol the plan was that Hupp was going to drive Carol to the house, have Carol make a false 911 call to the cops and implicate Russ in her death, and leave Carol dead in the front yard where Russ was currently living with his parents.

A neighbor's security camera attached to their house on Sunglow captured Pam's black SUV driving past Russ' parent's house the same day she approached Carol Alford. That address would factor later in the death of Louis Gumpenberger.

Distance from Pam's house to the trailer park where Carol Alford lived on Thoroughbred Drive. You can see Lake St. Louis where the salon and Russ' mother's house are located just up Hwy 64 at the top left (circled). Courtesy of Google maps.

Carol Alford had slipped the noose. Pam must have felt frustrated as she drove away from Alford's home. She had the victim in the car... she had been so close. But we are speaking of Pam Hupp. Undaunted, she continued through the complex looking for another "patsy." She finally spotted a robust man mowing the complex's lawns. Pam pulled up to the curb in front of him so as to intercept him when he got to her.

Brent Charleton was a busy landscaper for the area. He had all the lots to mow at the trailer park. A woman in a black SUV had pulled up in front of him, rolled down her passenger side window, and was beckoning him over. He left the mower running, put it in idle, and stepped closer to the car. Hupp gave him the same story as she had told Carol. Hoping $1,000 of easy money would tempt anyone living in a lower income neighborhood, she lowered her dark sunglasses, flashed her grin and put forth her offer to Charleton. He declined. He had too much work to do. She persisted, leaning forward eagerly. Showing some irritation at her insistence, he said he had to get back to work. Once again, Pam left with an empty bag.

If Pam approached others that day, or in the next several days, we do not have any reports to that effect. She may have become worried about Carol Alford's security camera and decided to lay low and see if police came to her door. After six days passed and nothing happened, she went out again, avoiding the trailer park and heading to the Cedarbrook Apartments in St. Charles, about 17 miles from her home. She would go into the next county rather than fishing in her own back yard this time around. The red brick apartment complex was tidy, with various chairs lining the front sidewalk, just outside the main entrance door.

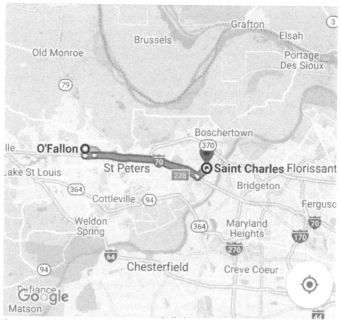

Distance from Pam's house in O'Fallon to Saint Charles where the Cedarwood Apartments were; about 17 minutes. Courtesy of Google maps.

It was here, on August 16, 2016, that a young 33-year-old man was sitting, having a cigarette. He often sat there, his mother reported. When a shiny black Arcadia SUV pulled up to the curb, he may not have thought too much about it. A chatty woman with short blond hair, wearing a black chiffon shirt and white gaucho pants called out to him. She had an offer for him. She said her name was Cathy and she was a producer for *Dateline NBC*. How would he like to make $1,000 for just a few minutes work recording a fake 911 call for an upcoming *Dateline NBC* episode?

Cedarbrook Apartments in St. Charles, MO, where
Louis Gumpenberger lived with his mother.

Where Louis Gumpenberger would sit at the end of the porch and have a cigarette or watch his son get on the school bus. It was here Pam found him.

The young man, wearing a gray tank top, black running shorts with a double white stripe, a black Nike ball cap with the name 'Louis' stitched upon it, gray running shoes, a silver chain necklace, and glasses must have asked some questions. Cell phone data pulled later from Pam's phone showed she stayed at Cedarbrook Apartments for approximately four minutes. We do know the young man finally acquiesced and got into her car. His name was Louis Gumpenberger.

911 Call

"911, what is your emergency?"

"Hey! Help! There's someone broken in my house. Help! Help!"

The voice calling for help tries to convey urgency.

"What is the address you're at?" the dispatcher asks, over the woman's calling out for "Help!"

A man's garbled voice is heard saying, "You want me to do to you what you did to your wife?"

"No! I'm not getting in the car with you…no!" the woman shouts.

"What is your address?" the dispatcher asks over the commotion, her voice sounding slightly agitated that she can't get any information from the woman.

"Help!"

The sound of pounding is heard. *Bam, bam, bam!*

"Help!"

"Ma'am, what's the address you're at?"

There are some unintelligible noises, like scuffling sounds.

"Ohhh…help, help!" the woman moans.

There are more scuffle sounds and some banging as the dispatcher tells someone "I have somebody breaking into a house." The banging is heard again.

Then, in a quieter voice, without the same urgency, you hear the woman say, "No, no. Go, go," as if giving stage directions.

This is followed by shouts of "Help!" with some silence in between the cries.

"Ma'am, can you hear me?" the dispatcher calls out.

"Help!"

"What's the address you're at?"

That question is followed by the sound of five gunshots in rapid succession.

"Help! Help!" the woman cries, sounding more distressed. "Help!"

The shrill beeping of the smoke alarm sounds, set off presumably by the loud report of the gunshots.

"Hello?" the dispatcher calls.

"Hellllpppp!" The shrill smoke alarm continues to sound.

There is some space before the woman suddenly shouts into the phone, "Hello? Hello? Who is this?"

"Are you there?" the dispatcher asks.

"Yes I am...

"Where are you at?"

"...I have an intruder in my house!" the woman shouts.

"Where are you at?"

"1260 Little Brave!"

"1260 Little Brave?"

"Yes!"

You can still hear the alarm beeping. It seems louder now as if the woman has moved closer to it.

"Who broke into your home?" the dispatcher asks.

"I don't know. A maaannnnn!!! OHHHH, Help!"

"Where's he at right now?"

"I'm going outside! I'm going outside." It then sounds like the woman is calling to something, possibly a dog. It sounds like

"C'mon _____."

The dispatcher reports to someone, possibly the unit on the way to the house, that "the fire alarms are going off, too."

"Hello?!"

"Is he inside?" the dispatcher asks.

"Yes!"

"Is he a white male, a black male?"

"He's white! Hurry, hurry, hurry!" she wails. "Hurry, hurry, hurry, he tried to get me in my car and I ran into the house."

"He tried to take you into his car?"

"He tried to take me in my carrrr," she wails, getting more emotional. "Help, help...hurry, hurry. Please send somebody."

"We have officers on the way, Ma'am. Where are you at right now in the home?"

"I'm in the garage. I'm in the garage...near my car. He's still in the house."

"Ok. Can you run to a neighbor's house?"

"I don't think there's anybody home. I have my dog. I have my puppy."

"You have your puppy with you?"

"Yessss."

"You have no idea who this subject is?" the dispatcher asks.

"No," the woman whines.

"Are there any weapons in the home?"

"Yes, I have a gun on my bed. I shot him."

"There's a gun on your bed, you shot him?"

"Yes, I shot him. He tried to get in my bedroom after me and I shot him."

The dispatcher sounds like she has turned to someone nearby. You hear a man's voice. "She says she has a gun on her bed and she shot him," the female dispatcher says. Returning to the woman on the phone, she asks, "As far as you know, is he still in the room?"

"No, he's in the hallway," the woman says.

"He's in the hallway? Is he moving?"

"He's in the hallway. No, he's not moving. Hurry! Hurry!"

"Ma'am, we already have help on the way. Just stay on the line with me. Is the garage door open?"

"Yes! Everything's open. I was leaving out of my car."

There are a few seconds of silence.

"Where are they? Where are they?" the woman pleads.

"They're on the way, Ma'am. Are you injured?"

"No! No! He didn't get me. He didn't get to me."

"He did *not* get you?"

"No. He did not get me."

Some radio static is heard from the dispatcher's end of the line.

"They're not here yet, they're not here yet," the woman whines.

"I'll let you know when they're close."

"Ok," sniffing.

"Ok, but you were not injured though?"

"No."

"What's your name?"

"My name is Pam."

"Pam?"

"Yes...where are they?" she wails, interrupting.

"Is anyone in the home with you besides the subject who broke in?"

"No. Just my dog."

"Just you and your dog?"

"I have my dog with me."

A few moments of silence pass. Then the woman says again, "Help. Please. Where are they?"

"We have help on the way. Let me know when you hear them."

"Ok!" she says breathlessly.

More silence, then a male voice announcing a code.

"I should have an officer pulling up…do you see him?"

"It's a white car…I don't know. It's just a white car."

"It's going to be one of our command staff. Is he in a uniform?"

"He's here! He's here!" she shouts.

"Ok, I'm going to let you go. Talk to the officer."

You hear the woman's wailing.

"Are you there?" the dispatcher asks.

"Yes!" emotional again.

"Talk to the officer…" The call is terminated.

Chief John Neske was the acting Chief of Police of the O'Fallon Police Department in Missouri during the time this author interviewed him about the Louis Gumpenberger case. He was the first officer to arrive on the scene after Pam's 911 call. His insight and training give us a rare glimpse into Pam Hupp's actions that August afternoon. Chief Neske has an easy-going, affable manner that belies his 35-years of dealing with the seedier side of humanity. He is gracious and caring, and quick to give credit to the detectives and PA Tim Lohmar who put together "a great case" against Pamela M. Hupp.

"At the time of the murder, I was Captain and I was over the patrol," Chief Neske said during a phone interview. "I almost always went home for lunch. I live here in town. We were building a new police facility on Bryan Road which is just around the corner from where Pam lives. I would take the long way back from lunch and I would purposely drive down Bryan Road to see the new facility going up. I was only a short distance from her house when this crazy call started coming out from the dispatcher who was dispatching the information as it was ongoing, and was on the phone with Pam.

"Normally, I don't respond to the scene," Neske continues, "unless it's a true emergency or just something crazy going on, but I had to go to this call, just the way it was setting up. She's saying 'someone has broken in, and someone is threatening me, and trying to burglarize me, and I shot him.' This is happening in O'Fallon. This is a bedroom community. We have very little crime per capita. We don't have 'stranger-on-stranger' crimes during the day to housewives. This is something that just doesn't happen in our community.

Chief John Neske of the O'Fallon Police Department.
Photo courtesy of Chief John Neske.

"I drive up and I park a house away and she's standing in the driveway with a dog. There's a car in the driveway. The driver's side is open, the garage door is open. I called to her and she's yelling, 'I shot him, I shot him, he's inside.' I said 'Is he moving?' She said, 'No.' I said, 'Is there anybody with him?' she said, 'No.' I asked 'Where is he?' She said, 'He's just in the hallway, right there...' She points inside the garage toward the door into the house. I went into the garage and I could see the man inside the house. I stepped into the hallway and saw who I later found out was Louis on the ground on the floor right there in the hallway. It was obvious that he had multiple gunshot wounds to the chest. He was an adult white male; obviously deceased. I went back out, and chatted with her just for a minute.

Pam Hupp's home on Little Brave with her SUV still parked in the driveway where Louis Gumpenberger reportedly attacked her.

"Another officer responded and we cleared the house. [Looked for anyone else there.] We walk into her master bedroom, where she said she was when she shot him. She told me she had left the gun in there. I see the revolver on the bed. We clear the bedroom and we clear the first floor. We couldn't clear the basement because Louis was crumpled up in the hallway and his head was up against the door to the basement. We didn't want to move the body yet and we couldn't open the door. We asked Pam, "Is there any other way in or out of the basement other than the hallway door?" She said, 'No.' We felt fairly comfortable that the house was secure, just in case there was somebody else.

Chief Neske continued: "She's pretty excited and she kept repeating, 'I don't know this guy, I don't know this guy! He got in my car and he threatened me with a knife, and he says, 'We're going to go get Russ's money!' So, I asked her, 'Who is Russ?' She said, 'I don't know...I don't know any Russ.' It was almost a mantra with her. She kept saying, 'I don't know this guy. He got into my car and said 'We're going to go get Russ' money.'" She repeated this two-or-three times. Each time she said it, I would ask her again, 'Who's Russ?' I don't know this lady. She seems like just a normal housewife. She told me, 'I was running errands all morning long. I came home for a little break. I got in my car, and I backed out and I was going to run some more errands again, when he jumped in my car with a knife. And he says, 'We're going to get Russ's money...we're going to get the money that you owe him.' I struck the knife out of his hand and I got out of the car and I ran into the house.'

"At that point," Chief Neske said, "and I had been doing this job for 30 years at the time of this occurrence, I've never known anybody to knock a knife out of somebody's hand. Not with a karate chop or a one-handed maneuver. We've had bigger guys wrestle a weapon away, but not like this. That one hit me like a ton of bricks. I'm thinking, 'You just disarmed a full-grown man with one fell swoop like Bruce Lee would do or something.' That one took me by surprise. She went on, and I had no reason to think she's lying, but it was strange. And a 'stranger-on-stranger' in this city is very uncommon," he repeated. "This whole thing just had weird written all over it from the beginning.

"We got additional police officers there and we start the log, and they pretty much are taking over the scene. My job there was pretty well done. I'm still on the scene, and Pam goes into the ambulance with one of the police officers and now we have a little space and time and we're looking around. We're calling our drug detectives and our undercover people. We're getting the beat cops and police officers that work that area and we're trying to find out if maybe this is a drug deal gone bad or maybe they got the wrong house. We're having our dispatchers check the area. Is there anybody by the name of 'Russ'? Has there been any drug activity nearby? We're needing to identify who this 'Russ' is because this has to be a case of wrongful identification—this guy must have hit the wrong house.

"Then, the police officer came out of the ambulance where they had been checking Pam to make sure she had no injuries, and he had taken a more formal, written statement from her. He came out and said, 'Do you guys know who this is?' We said, 'No, we don't.' He said, 'It's Pam Hupp!' A couple of the guys kinda groaned. When he said the name, I had a little spark of recognition, but I wasn't really clear. The guys are telling me, 'Pam Hupp...Russ Faria...the whole incident that happened up in Lincoln County! He went to prison, then he got out, they think she lied.' I then said, 'OH!

Ok…time out!' We had to re-set the clock and start looking at this thing from a whole new perspective. How does she not know who 'Russ' is? At that point, everything that happened with the Faria case came back. She got the insurance money from that murder…so in hind-sight, we figured, that's the money this guy is supposedly getting back. From there it went to the investigators and they put together just a really great case."

When asked what his thoughts were that Louis was found lying on a swatch of carpet, as though it had been decided beforehand where he would fall to prevent blood from getting on the good carpet, Chief Neske answered this:

"I never really picked up when I saw Louis the first time that he was lying on a carpet swatch. It was very close to the entrance from the hallway. It wouldn't be uncommon for someone to have a rug sitting there for a person to wipe their feet on. I never moved the body, and never saw what was underneath him, so it never dawned on me at that time. He was more on his back and a little bit on his side. The gunshot wounds to his chest were clear. The shots were in a very close grouping in his chest.

"I felt sorry for this guy," Neske said. "Growing up, it seems he was little bit of a pest. He never really hurt anybody, but he drank too much. He had incidents that we were aware of associated with that. It wasn't anything really bad. And then he was in a terrible car crash. He was both physically and mentally disabled. You talk about being really innocent. For her to do this to a guy like that was just doubly bad. Pam thought she had the perfect patsy.

"After she shot Louis, I got the impression she just corralled the dog, that I assumed was in the house," Neske said. "The dog was between medium and large. He was a puppy, maybe a little over a year old, and was very rambunctious, pulling on the lease she had him on. It was never addressed where the dog was during the actual shooting. [There are no sounds of a dog barking on the 911 recorded call, not even after five-gun shots and a smoke alarm are going off. Pam was still talking to the dispatcher when she said, "I'm going outside." She may have opened a garage door to the back yard and grabbed the dog. We hear her say what sounds like "Come on," moments after saying "I'm going outside."]

"I wasn't involved in the investigation," Neske said. "I was the first one on the scene but I did not direct it. I don't know if any of the neighbors reported hearing gun shots. I turned it over to the detective bureau as soon as they turned up.

"The initial call itself was unusual. We listened to the 911 tape while we were sitting there and her voice sounded rehearsed, it sounded planned, it didn't sound right. It sounded practiced. The dispatcher was relaying the information over the radio as it was happening so you may have heard the dispatcher's voice telling the responding officers what she was hearing.

"I'll never forget it. It was one of those calls that you never forget," Chief John Neske said, as our phone interview ended.

Chapter Eighteen
"The Worst of the Worst!"

Tim Lohmar, the Prosecuting Attorney during the Louis Gumpenberger case in August of 2016, told this author the following details concerning what happened that day at Pam Hupp's home at 1260 Little Brave Drive in O'Fallon, Missouri.

Pam Hupp's home with car still standing in the driveway with the driver's side door open. Photo courtesy of the O'Fallon Police Department.

"The investigation quickly began to reveal the following," Lohmar said:

"Hupp indicated that a silver 4-door sedan quickly pulled up onto her street and stopped directly behind her driveway. At that time, a male subject got out of the passenger-side of the vehicle, ran up to her vehicle and entered the cabin through the passenger front door. The silver 4-door vehicle then quickly left the area. Meanwhile, the male subject put a knife to Hupp's throat and kept telling her that she was going to take him to the bank to "get Russ's money." She said the subject kept looking back over his shoulder while yelling at her and at some point, as he is looking over his shoulder, Hupp struck his arm with her arm, knocking the knife out of his hand.

"She exited her vehicle and ran into her residence through the garage door," Lohmar continued. "The subject pursued her into the garage while yelling, among other things, that he was going to kill her. While trying to keep him from entering her home, she began to call 911 numerous times. The first two calls failed to go through. But the third call connected. It was at this point that she realized she wasn't going to be able to keep the subject out of the house. She ran into the master bedroom to get a revolver from behind the night stand and she shot the subject while he was advancing through her bedroom door. The subject was not armed with a weapon when he was shot by Hupp. She indicated that she shot him multiple times, until the gun stopped firing.

Entrance from garage door into the house (l); splintered door frame from one of the bullets. Photos O'Fallon Police Department.

"A search warrant was later obtained for Hupp's residence and her vehicle. Members of the St. Charles Crime Scene Investigation Unit, along with detectives from the O'Fallon Police Department, examined and processed the scene upon execution of the search warrant, in conjunction with her written consent to search. The deceased male subject was positively identified by his fingerprints as Louis R. Gumpenberger. He did not have a wallet or a cell phone, or any other identifying information on his person at the time he was found by the first responders.

Louis Gumpenberger is lying with his head against the door to the basement, just inside the open garage door. Photo O'Fallon Police Department.

Pam Hupp's bed where the gun was found. O'Fallon Police Dept.

In the photo of the master bedroom on the preceding page, you can see the nightstand to the left of the bed from where Pam said she grabbed the gun. Inside that drawer was found a bank envelope of money, two pairs of rolled-up socks, and an owner's manual. Interestingly, the title of one of the books on her bed is "Hunting Evil."

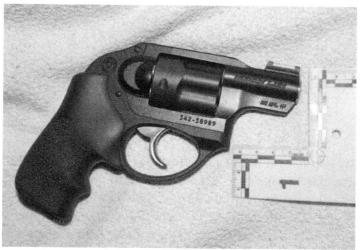

The murder weapon found on Pam's bed. Photo courtesy of the O'Fallon Police Department.

PA Tim Lohmar goes on to describe what they found on the victim's body:

"However, investigation revealed that a handwritten note and $900 in United States currency that was double-bagged in Ziplock bags was located in each of Gumpenberger's pockets. Further research into Gumpenberger revealed that he suffered a traumatic brain injury after a vehicle accident in 2005 [eleven years before his murder]. As a result of his traumatic brain injury, Gumpenberger had slurred speech and other physical and mental limitations. Gumpenberger did not drive or have a known income. He would sometimes limp or walk hunched over. His mother described him as operating on the level of a 12-year-old. She said he is extremely gullible and people have been known to take advantage of him.

Nine $100 bills found in Louis' pocket. O'Fallon Police.

"The money that was found in Mr. Gumpenberger's pocket in the plastic bag is of interest," Lohmar said. "The nine $100 bills were all sequential in number as far as the serial numbers go. The crime scene investigator, Tiffany Fisher, was able to look through the crime scene photos and she brought it to our attention that some of the other bills that were found in the bedside table at Pam's bedroom at her house matched up sequentially with the $100 bills that were found in Mr. Gumpenberger's pocket.

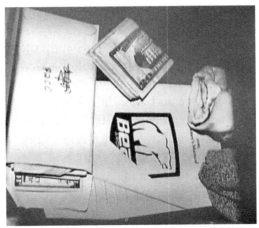

Packet of money found in Pam Hupp's bedside table. $900 has been scribbled out, and $200 has been written beneath it. A Bear 2015 Owner's Manual, and two pair of rolled-up socks. O'Fallon Police Department photo.

Finding the packet of money in Hupp's drawer was a huge piece of the puzzle surrounding Louis' death. The $100 bill found there matched the sequential numbers exactly that were found in a plastic bag in Louis' pocket. As one detective said, "It's extremely uncommon for two people who reportedly not to know each other, to individually possess $100 denominations...which contain the same identifiers (and) serial numbers...in order."

Also in the drawer, beneath the packet of money, was a Bear 2015 Owner's Manual. Bear sells guns, ammunition, and archery equipment. If the gun Pam used was bought in 2015, when the Owner's Manual was supplied to her, it would mean she bought a gun very close to the time Chris Hayes followed up on an anonymous call to his station that Russ was waving a gun around at a strip mall. It was later determined Russ was not there with a gun. The call was meant to set-up Russ again and to probably entice Chris Hayes to the scene. Was this the purpose for purchasing the gun so close to this incident? Months later, Louis Gumpenberger would be fatally shot to death.

As detectives and police officers arrived that afternoon to find a hysterical Pam Hupp standing in her driveway, they were repeatedly told by her that she "did not know" the man she just shot. That he would have matching serial numbers on the money in his pocket to that she had in her bedroom table was, as Tim Lohmar put it, "a billion to one chance."

Mr. Lohmar continued, "The handwritten note located in Gumpenberger's pocket appeared to be instructions for Gumpenberger to kidnap Hupp, get Russ' money from Hupp at her bank, and then kill Hupp, in order for him to collect the rest of the $10,000," Lohmar said. "The note also mentioned the last name Faria. After first telling first responding officers that she did not know a Russ, Hupp did acknowledge in a subsequent discussion that she did indeed know Russ Faria. Hupp surmised that the note was referencing a life insurance payout related to the Russ Faria murder trials that were held in Lincoln County. Extensive canvassing and interviews failed to produce any known links whatsoever between Gumpenberger and Hupp, or Gumpenberger and Faria."

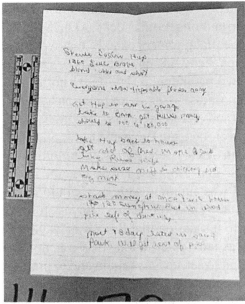

The folded note found in Louis' other pocket in a plastic Ziplock bag.
It references Russ twice. O'Fallon Police photo.

The note, written in clumsy handwriting says:

Stevie follow Hupp
1260 Little Brave
Blond. Older and short.

Everyone throw disposable phones (?) away.

Get Hupp in car in garage
take to Bank get Russ's money
Should be 100 to 150,000

take Hupp back to house
get rid of her. Make it look like Russ wife
Make sure nife (ms) is sticking out of <u>neck</u>

stash money at Mom Farias house
120 Sunglow. Put in woodpile left of driveway

Meet 18 [or 8] days later in same park. Will get rest of
$10,000.

The note was hard to read in places. There are scribbled out words. It is either "18 days later," or "8." No one knows who "Stevie" is. It was probably a generic name that could fit any one of the people she was canvassing for the murder. There was indeed a woodpile near the driveway of Russ' mother's house. What is interesting is that during Pam's interview with Detectives Mountain and Meyers, just after the shooting, it is obvious she is describing Russ Faria as the person who drove the "silver 4-door" that Louis jumped from (once again pointing to the silver Nissan that belonged to the Faria's). Yet, the letter says, "Follow Hupp..." It's one or the other. Either Russ wrote the note and hired someone to *follow* Pam, kidnap her, get the money, and then kill her, or, Russ *drove* Louis straight to Pam's house and let him out of the car. We now know neither scenario occurred.

Pam's 911 call set alarm bells ringing from the moment police officials heard it. What a lot of people don't know, is that a 911 call is being recorded for several seconds before the dispatcher says, "911, what is your emergency?" A lot can be discovered by listening to those few moments before the caller believes they are being recorded. Tim Lohmar said, "It sounded scripted. Almost like the minute the dispatcher came on, it was 'Action!'" Lohmar told this author that in the silence preceding the dispatcher coming on, there was nothing. No noise. No panic. No pounding or sounds of a scuffle. No screaming. Yet, the minute Pam heard "911, what is your emergency?" she started yelling. And who starts a 911 call with "Hey!"?

It was also interesting that Pam called 911 twice shortly before completing the call. This author asked Tim Lohmar what he thought Hupp was doing on those two abandoned calls?

"My sense is that she was feverishly trying to set the stage for the 'role play' scene with Louis, so it's very possible that she wasn't satisfied that the scene was properly set as she made those first 2 calls. Just my assumption."

It's chilling to think that she got Louis in place, reminded him of what to say, and as she dialed 911 to create her alibi recording, Louis may have asked a question, come too far into the room, etc., and Pam had to start over again. As Lohmar said, once that call went through, it was 'Action!'

While the O'Fallon police were puzzling over what had happened to the young man lying prone on Pam Hupp's floor, Pam had voluntarily gone to the Police Department to make a statement. She was no stranger to sitting in a small room with two male detectives, although the others were the obliging Lincoln County detectives. She was in O'Fallon's district now with this one. She may have felt some sense of security that she had the routine down cold. Yet, there appeared to be doubt and a sense of wariness in her demeanor this time around. Would she be believed this time, just as she had been during the Betsy Faria case? Pam is seen sitting in a chair in a black shirt, short gray pants, and white anklet socks. Pam is also seen wearing tennis shoes with neon green laces in the interview, but sitting in socks later, so it's possible she entered wearing shoes, and they asked her for them, along with her phone during the interrogation. Detectives Matt Meyers and Kevin Mountain are the two men seated across a round table from Hupp.

Pam Hupp's Interrogation After the Murder

August 16, 2016, Pam is turned sideways to a small round table. She has her head resting on her left hand, playing with her hair.

"I just want to know what's going on with all these people coming… at me," she says, turning to look at the detective across from her. She is in socks, and it may be this sentence occurred right after they took her shoes from her.

Pam Hupp being interviewed shortly after shooting Louis Gumpenberger. O'Fallon Police Department video.

"Is this going to be filmed because I always appear on the news with Chris Hayes?" Pam asked, looking annoyed. Chris Hayes is the *Fox 2 News'* reporter that covered Pam's stories more than any other reporter. He was the only reporter to interview Hupp that chilly January morning in 2014, shortly after Russ went to prison and her own mother fell to her death from her third-floor balcony. Chris is also the reporter that almost responded to an anonymous call that Russ Faria was "waving a gun around" at a hair salon in Lake St. Louis.

Pam impersonating Louis' speech. O'Fallon Police video.

Tim Lohmar commented that he believed Pam questioned the two detectives about the possible news coverage because it would link her to Betsy Faria's murder that occurred five years earlier in December, 2011. Pam had just told the police at the scene of Louis' murder that she did not know any "Russ." If she pops up on the News, it won't be long before the note in Louis' pocket, which read "Get Russ's money," and "Make it look like Russ' wife," would come back to her full circle. She is unaware they are already on to her.

Pam went into her death-defying story for Detectives' Mountain and Meyers, using wild gestures to underscore her story:

317

"I hit his arm with the knife and then shot out of my car and ran inside," Pam said dramatically.

It was her impersonation of Louis' speech impediment that gave the detectives a sick feeling. With slurred words and a droopy-face, Pam impersonated Louis' supposed words to her:

"He goes, 'Bitch, we're going to the bank, we're getting' Russ' money.' He started getting agitated and excited!" Pam said.

Pam described to the detectives that Louis was dropped off at her driveway by a squealing car. Louis then jumped out and jumped into Pam's passenger-side door, wielding a knife. Pam described who she saw in the car that brought Louis to the scene:

"When he started to whip around, all I saw was like a dark *dome*...sorry... [she references the detective across from her with his buzz cut hair] ...short hair like you," she says, pushing her own short blond hair up with both hands. "Maybe not quite as short, but it was dark."

Detective Mountain was not fooled. It was obvious Pam was trying to describe Russ Faria. What Pam did not know was that the police knew who she was from the time they interviewed her in the ambulance and got her name. The Faria murder case was very famous in Missouri. Seeing Russ in a car near a murder scene had worked for her before. Why not try it again?

Pam demonstrating the short hair of the man she saw in the car that day. O'Fallon Police Department video.

It was Pam's final description of Louis Gumpenberger that is hard to watch in the police interview surveillance video. With both hands waving and hunched over, Pam makes a face and imitates Louis' behavior. Her words describing the man she just murdered in cold blood are chilling:

"He was getting all excited, and he was 'uhhhh, uhhhh, uhhhh,' (done in a voice mimicking someone with slurred speech). Pam leans forward like she's confiding in two buddies, and says with a smirk, "I thought he was drunk, or on drugs or something, I guess."

Detective Mountain was upset by it. He said it indicated that she just didn't care at all for this stranger that she trolled through neighborhoods to find, and shot him five times. She had to know from the moment Louis stepped over to her car that he had some challenges. He limped, and his speech was impaired.

Pam continues with her story as she describes how she shot Louis. She places her two hands, palms together, in a pose to resemble a gun. Her forefingers are pointed like a barrel, thumb up like a hammer.

"...and I just started shooting him, walking towards him, cuz' I wanted to be sure I hit him, because everybody kept sayin' that's a little gun and blah, blah, blah, and you're not going to get very close..." She breaks off, as if she is getting too much into the embellishing of the shooting. She waves her hands furiously in front of her as if to wave away the memories.

"So, once that door opened and he was there," Pam continued, "I just started shooting him and walking towards him until I didn't have any more [bullets]."

In another telling of the story, Pam said she just kept firing until she heard "click, click, click." Detective Mountain said he never got the feeling Pam had been afraid of Louis Gumpenberger. She sat there before them, hair perfectly combed, clothes neat, and pale gray pants without a smudge on them. She wasn't hysterical, or shaking after just having a man jump into her car, press a knife to her neck, and chase her into her home, and cornering her in her room. Nor, did the act of firing five bullets into the chest of a man taller than she, and only a few inches away, leave any lasting trauma.

319

Pam demonstrating how she held the gun and shot Louis.
O'Fallon Police Department video.

Pam Hupp's Little Brave Drive sits inside the Great Warriors Subdivision. What she hadn't counted on was the warriors in the form of the O'Fallon Police Department and the office of the Prosecuting Attorney, Tim Lohmar, who would pick up the gauntlet she tossed down and bring home an arrest. The evidence they found in Louis Gumpenberger's pockets—the note from "Russ" and the $900 in sequential 100-dollar bills—was just the beginning of the treasure trove of information that would finally trap the woman who "thought she was smarter than everybody."

Prosecuting Attorney Tim Lohmar told this author the following information:

"Extensive interviews of people who knew Gumpenberger said that his mother drove him to his doctor's appointments and that he walked everywhere else. Investigation further revealed that Hupp described driving by her daughter's residence the morning of August 16, 2016, the day of Gumpenberger's death. Hupp's daughter lived approximately two miles from Gumpenberger's apartment. The investigation revealed that Hupp had her cell phone with her as she was driving around during the morning hours of

August 16, 2016. A search warrant was served on Google who provided historical location data related to her specific device. One latitude and longitude location provided by Google resolved to Gumpenberger's apartment complex. This occurred between 11:25 a.m. and 11:29 a.m. on August 16, 2016. The 911 calls were first placed at 12:04 p.m. on that same day.

"The other thing that was significant to us, when she was traveling…the morning of the shooting, she told us where she went. She traveled from her home in O'Fallon to St. Charles with various errands to run. Our detectives were able to use Google to pinpoint with precise precision where her car stopped in front of the Cedarbrook Apartments unit where Mr. Gumpenberger lived.

"The other significant thing about the Google Way Points was that it showed the video cameras along the route between Gumpenberger's apartment and Pam Hupp's home. It matched up nearly precisely with the timeline."

That video camera surveillance captured several images of Pam's car as it passed certain retail locations. Just outside a bakery, not far from her home, the camera clearly shows Pam's car with a male subject in the passenger seat. The baseball cap resembles the cap Louis was wearing when he was shot. Louis G is embroidered on the side of the cap. It is eerie to see it. Louis appears blurred as the car goes by, and we now know, he was on his way to his death.

Louis Gumpenberger lying on Hupp's floor, his hat next to him.
Close-up of Louis' cap (r) with his name embroidered on it. Photo's courtesy
of the O'Fallon Police Department.

"The final piece of evidence," Lohmar said, "was the search warrant the detectives served on the Dollar Tree Store in O'Fallon and they were able to find the exact same knife, the exact same Ziplock bags, notepad, pen [used to write the list from 'Russ' found in Louis' pocket]. There were several other household items purchased that are on that receipt. What was really interesting is that when they compared that list of items that were sold, they were able to look at photos taken at the crime scene of her pantry and closets, and see all of the items that she purchased that day at the Dollar Store. The evidence in this case was overwhelming from day one. By day three, we had pretty much all we needed. There were just a few more things to get done."

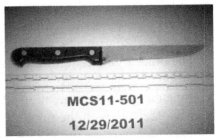

MCS11-501
12/29/2011

The knife from the Dollar Store Louis supposedly used (l) & murder weapon used in Betsy Faria's death (r). O'Fallon Police Department photo (l).

Tim Lohmar went on to impart other crucial evidence pertaining to Louis Gumpenberger's murder. While Pam was telling her story to detectives at the O'Fallon Police Department, she was asked if they could look at her phone.

"Larry McClaine did the Google search of Pam's cell phone," Lohmar said. "During her initial interview at the police station after just shooting Mr. Gumpenberger, she was asked if we could look at her cell phone. She handed it over. Larry took it to another room where he ran the Google search of her location history. He had the phone for about two hours and then handed it back to her." Pam's interview that day with the detectives lasted four hours. Detective Mountain said it was obvious she was hoping to convince them of her story if she just kept talking.

That cell phone location history would be invaluable to the case against Hupp. It may be why she made the comment in the interview room of wanting to know why "people keep coming...at me." No stranger to the collection of cell phone data—after her phone was searched during the Betsy Faria murder—Pam may have begun to feel as if her plot to frame Russ by killing Louis was about to unravel. The O'Fallon detectives during that interview not only wanted to look at her phone, but her shoes. Sitting there in white anklet socks, in unfamiliar territory, was Pam Hupp finally losing her confidence?

Mark and Pam Hupp carrying a white trash bag of articles to their car the morning after Louis' murder. Photo courtesy of the *St. Louis Post-Dispatch*/Polaris Images.

The day after Louis' murder, Robert Patrick with the area newspaper and his photographer were outside the Hupp residence. Robert Patrick is a journalist and reporter for the *St. Louis Post-Dispatch* where he has reported the news for seventeen years. On camera, he comes across as calm, articulate, and warm, with a ready smile and a grin his wife labels as his 'smirk.' Rarely at a loss for the correct interpretation of an event, his skill as a wordsmith is obvious. His integrity in what he reports is paramount to him, and you feel his empathy for many of the stories he covers. The sad story of the Faria and Gumpenberger cases are no exception.

"Chris Hayes from *Fox* was the one in the beginning who brought us in," Patrick said in a phone interview. "He attended the first trial and he said, "This thing stinks." If it was anything, the second trial, and I think it was, there just wasn't any real evidence. It was just slander and innuendo.

"The question all along for me was, you reinvestigate this case against a woman who is in prison for life without the possibility of parole—and I know the families want some resolution, and some of them thought in the beginning that Russ did it—but, it's one of those things that has been a stain on the judicial system for Lincoln County and it needs to be cleared up. The new PA Mike Wood feels strongly about that. They have more evidence now against Pam. You can make the argument that the evidence they had against Russell Faria was tainted, but the evidence we have against Pam Hupp is different. As that second trial for Russ approached, her story just changed and changed and changed. It evolved to make the case against Russ stronger. It's like now she says, "And, oh yeah, we were lesbian lovers." And Russ is like, "Where was this?"

"When she was released from the police department after Louis' killing," Patrick continued, "I happened to be at her house...I don't think I knew she was going to be out...but I was there to talk to the neighbors or something. She and Mark got home and I asked her if she wanted to talk about it. She and Mark were right there together...I was talking to them from my car with the window open and the engine running, because I'm like, 'I don't think they're going to come after me, but again, he's a tightly wound dude, so I didn't know.' This was the day after Louis was killed. I was out there with a photographer and that's when they were bringing a trash bag out to the car with some of Betsy's stuff and other things, and we got a shot of it."

Tim Lohmar, Prosecuting Attorney, said, "The white trash bag that is seen in the photo being carried out to the car at the Hupp home by Mark and Pam Hupp the day after the shooting was not confiscated immediately, as we did not have evidentiary proof at that time. It was apprehended and was found to contain a number of documents and clothing."

A partial list in the Search Warrant Return of items found in the trash bag was:

1-Death Certificate for Betsy Faria
2-Last Will and Testament for Shirley Neumann (Pam's Mom)
3-Manilla folder with numerous records of Shirley Neumann
4-Numerous bank statements for Pam and Mark Hupp
5-1099 form from 2005 with Betsy Faria as recipient
6-Transcripts from Pam Hupp's trial testimony during Russ

Faria's murder trial.

7-Documents on Mark Wasserman, Pam's brother-in-law

Also found in the bag were several striped shirts of different colors, two pairs of flip flops, a leopard print shirt, and a pink t-shirt.

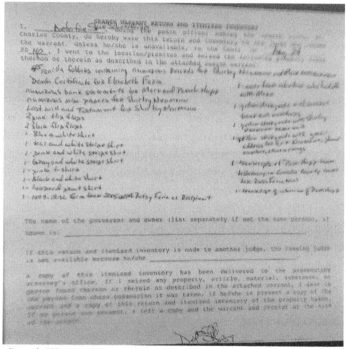

The Search Warrant Return listing the items found in the white trash bag.
Photo courtesy of the O'Fallon Police Department.

It's interesting to look at the contents of that trash bag. Why did Pam have Betsy's Faria's 1099-MISC form clear back from 2005? A 1099-R form would show life insurance. Other 1099 forms could show annuities and other cash reserves. Betsy and Pam were working together at State Farm in 2005.

Mark Hupp has obviously been looked into to see how much he knew about the murders in which his wife seemed to find herself involved, one way or another. Chief John Neske with the O'Fallon Police Department had this to say about Mark:

"Mark Hupp and I attended the same High School. He was a few years older than me and at the time our school had a very outstanding baseball team. I want to say Mark was a catcher. He had a very good personality, good reputation. He still plays golf with some guys that I know and trust and like. I never really knew Mark. These guys that know him say that he's a great guy. They have talked to him about it, and he said he just didn't know that he was married to a crazy woman until all this stuff broke. She was keeping secrets from her husband."

Many believe Mark was unaware of Pam's actions. Many don't see how he could not have known something was very wrong with her. Chaos swirled around Pam like a vortex of evil.

"One of the things I find so interesting about the Louis Gumpenberger case," Robert Patrick with the *St. Louis Post-Dispatch* said, "...we talked to a couple of people who she approached first. And you realize she is driving around St. Charles County approaching basically just random people and trying to find someone who is gullible enough to get into the car with her. Maybe I'm just not built that way, but I was thinking what if you messed up? What if the person you picked had just come back from overseas and couldn't have been involved with Russ, you know? There's a million ways you could get tripped up in that. From the very beginning, the friends and people who knew Louis were saying he was physically and mentally challenged. You could have run into somebody who made it impossible for this so-called plot. But she happened to pick somebody who it should have been obvious to her that he could not have physically done the things she was going to claim he did. It just didn't make sense to me.

"I told my wife after this happened," Patrick continued, "because we had talked about it before...it's an unusual profession where you have to confront people and say, "Did you kill Betsy Faria?" Pam hates Chris Hayes a lot more than she dislikes me. But I told my wife, "She's a lot more dangerous than I gave her credit for, because of that cold-bloodedness she displayed with Louis Gumpenberger.

"If you can get away with a 2011 murder [Betsy Faria], why turn around and do it again?" Patrick asked. "I mean, the Louis Gumpenberger case was so ham-fisted. It was so amateurish. It was clear that she bought the knife. I have the same knife in my garage, because I went to the same Dollar Store to buy it just so we could take pictures. It was so amateurish. I'm thinking 'How could she possibly get away with another one?"

Knife handle showing between seat and console where it had been placed. Pam's ubiquitous soda is in the cup holder. Photo O'Fallon Police Department.

While speaking with Chief Neske, the first official to arrive on the scene that day, he mentioned the knife that Louis had supposedly held to Pam's neck. Not only had he found it hard to believe that Pam knocked the knife out of her attacker's hand with one 'karate chop,' but even more interesting, was the location of the knife in Pam's car. Remember, she stated she 'knocked the knife out of his hand, jumped from the car and ran into her house.' And where is the knife found inside her car? On the floor mat? On the dashboard? On the seat? Prosecuting Attorney Tim Lohmar agrees with Chief Neske about the location of the knife:

"The other thing that was interesting was that at some point Hupp had mentioned that the suspect brandished a knife and threatened her with the knife and somehow she was able to knock that knife out of his hand. There was some kind of struggle. Officers were able to recover the knife almost immediately and it was tucked perfectly right between the seat and console of her car. Eventually, fingerprint analysis was done and the only fingerprints that were on that knife were Mr. Gumpenberger's fingerprints on the blade."

Photos of Pam's kitchen show she stored knives exactly the same way: blade down, between the stove and the kitchen counter.

Knives in Pam Hupp's kitchen, blade down between the stove and counter.

During the interview with Pam Hupp, shortly after Louis' murder, detectives asked Pam about her morning leading up to the murder.

"I took care of my dog, fed him, walked him. Got in the shower and headed out and I had to get gas." She then spent several moments describing her loyalty card that enabled her to get her daily soda. She has just shot a man and she's bragging about a rewards card and free soda.

If Pam thought her breezy account of her errands that morning would put the detectives at ease, she was mistaken. They soon zeroed in on her actual attack against Louis Gumpenberger.

"It's unusual, and here's what I'm saying," the detective told her, "without some form of tactical training, or military training, or law enforcement training, is to fire and then approach the target. When you and your husband go out, besides shooting, do you work on tactical movements?"

Pam laughs. "No! We just shoot at a target on a tree," she said amused. She had just shot a man to death, and she was laughing.

There is one moment of levity in this tragic story of a senseless murder. Tim Lohmar shared it with this author:

"I will share with you a side story that I haven't reported before. A search warrant was executed for the Hupp residence. While the detectives were carrying out that search, they came across a safe in the residence. The warrant didn't allow for the search of the safe and so another warrant specifically for that item had to be quickly executed. We took the safe back to the station. When it was opened, there was only one item in the safe. Care to take a guess what it was? A single tube of K-Y Jelly." Pam was basically telling the detectives to "Go f%#@ yourselves!"

It was discovered that important documents were inside the white trash bag Mark Hupp is photographed taking out of the house. Were they from the safe? Had Pam emptied the safe the morning after the murder, just in case the police obtained a search warrant for it? And then, gave them a little something to find once they opened it, with a not-so-subtle innuendo attached?

O'Fallon police officer carrying a safe from Pam Hupp's home.
Photo courtesy of *Fox2News*/Polaris Images.

Chris Hayes with *Fox 2 News* received phone calls from Pam Hupp's neighbors at 4:30 in the afternoon of September 1, 2016. It was 9 days after Pam was arrested and sitting in jail. Her neighbors reported hearing loud banging noises coming from her address. They were surprised to see at least ten officers from St. Charles County and the O'Fallon Police Department swarming the driveway. The banging sound came from the front door, which was being battered open. Shortly after the door was breached, the officer, seen in the above photo, came out of the house with the only item they confiscated that day: a silver safe. Prosecuting Attorney Tim

Lohmar said "At the time the search warrant for the safe was served, no one was home. The police had the right to break down the door, which they did. They also had to eventually pay to replace the door, which they did."

Plywood covering Pam Hupp's front door entrance after it was battered down by police on Sept. 1, 2016. Photo by *KSDK.com*.

Louis Gumpenberger's murder was so senseless. Pam Hupp literally went on a hunting expedition for the perfect prey to sacrifice for her freedom. If she could frame Russ and send him back to prison for a note found on a dead man (a note suggesting Russ hired him to kidnap her, and then kill her "with a knife in her neck"), the focus would go away from her for Betsy Faria's murder. Joel Schwartz was never far from her thoughts. In a sheer act of desperation, she decided another man's life was worth her dodging prison. Prosecuting Attorney Tim Lohmar summed it up when he was asked to describe Pam Hupp during a press interview:

"She's the worst of the worst," he said, without hesitation.

The two other victims that Pam tried to lure to their death, six days before Louis' murder, summed up Pam's murder plot in succinct shock:

"That could have been me," Brent Charleton said.

Carol Alford, upon hearing from Tim Lohmar what Pam Hupp had in store for her that day, said. "It was hard to breathe. She was going to *kill* me!"

Louis Gumpenberger's Obituary

Gumpenberger, Louis Royse, of St. Charles, MO, died on Tuesday, August 16, 2016, at the age of 33. Beloved son of Margaret Burch and Michael Kenneth Gumpenberger; devoted father of Desi Rae Wilmsmeyer and Trevelyan Lloyd Gumpenberger; dear brother of Michael Wayne Gumpenberger and Robert Jordan Deaton; cherished grandson of Carl Burch; dear step-brother of Adam J. Burch and James Burch; treasured nephew of David Burch and Gene Burch; loving step-son of Melba Burch. He is preceded in death by his step-father John Lloyd Burch.

The tributes left on Louis' funeral home's guest page talk of a kind man who loved his children. He is described as funny, gentle, and, above all, missed.

Sadly, the price Pam Hupp placed upon Louis Gumpenberger's life was a mere $900; the amount of money she had placed in his pocket to stage a kidnapping attempt. She knew the money would not be returned to her, as it was supposedly given to Louis from Russ as payment for kidnapping and killing her. Only $900.

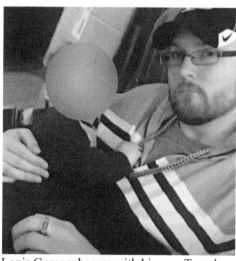

Louis Gumpenberger with his son, Trevelyan.

331

Chapter Nineteen
The Trap is Sprung

When Russ Faria heard Pam Hupp had shot someone, and that a note with his name on it was involved, he made a beeline to the O'Fallon Police Department to make sure he was not a suspect in this new twisted plot of Pam's. The detectives took his cell phone to look at his location history, and then handed him a sheet of paper and asked him to write down, line-for-line, the wording in the note found in Louis Gumpenberger's pocket. As a detective read the note, Russ scribbled away…not once, but six times, using both his right and left hands…just to make sure he wasn't disguising his handwriting. The detective began:

"Stevie. Follow Hupp…" Russ wrote the words down. "New line," the detective said, "Blond. Older. Short. Then skip two lines…" On and on it went, until Russ had written the entire note. And then they began again. Russ's hand was tired by the time he had completed writing the note six times. Russ told them he did not know anyone named "Stevie."

The notes Russ wrote were sent off to a handwriting expert. The expert came back with his results: Russ was not the author of the note found in Gumpenberger's pocket. The police were already looking at all the holes in Pam's claims. When you add the Google location history putting her at Louis' apartments, the video showing her car driving past the bakery with Louis in her passenger seat, and the *peace de la resistance*, the surveillance video from Carol Alford's home camera on August 10th, showing Pam posing as a

Dateline NBC producer to get Carole into her car, it looked pretty damning. Carol also identified a photo of Pam in a police layout of several women. The sequential order of the $100 bills, the Dollar Tree purchases, including the knife, pen and notepad used for the note in Louis' pocket…it was a gold mine of evidence. The fact that Pam actually used the name "Cathy" as the *Dateline NBC* producer for whom she was posing, shocked the NBC producer. Pam knew how many shows *Dateline NBC* had aired about her and the Faria case. Did she hope that media recognition would make her plot seem plausible to her victims?

It was when the detectives saw the footage from the video camera in front of the bakery near Pam's home, with who appeared to be Louis in her passenger seat, they put out the arrest warrant for Pamela Marie Hupp.

Two detectives drove to Pam's home on Little Brave and surprised her. She was dressed in a pale peach-colored shirt, capri jeans and flip flops. Her hair was pulled back on the top in a clip. The two officers led Hupp to their waiting car, handcuffed, and fully aware of the media cameras trained upon them. The female officer turned Pam toward the car, away from the cameras, to discreetly check her pockets. Pam is then loaded into the back seat of the vehicle where she sat stone-faced as cameras zoomed in on her profile. She was taken to the O'Fallon Police Station.

Police Officer checking Pam's pockets and waistband.

Pam Hupp being arrested outside her home for the murder
of Louis Gumpenberger. Photo's credit *St. Louis Post-Dispatch*.

The detective who rode with Hupp to the station stated her
demeanor as "cold and calm." As they drove through the familiar
streets Pam had driven a hundred times or more, the detective
explained to her that she was being arrested for the murder of Louis
Gumpenberger. He explained they had a plethora of evidence
against her. He told her basically, 'You're not getting away with
this.'

Pam sat without facial expression as the detective hammered home
his points. Finally, she made a statement…the only statement she
would make while seated in the car: "I'm a little cold. Could you
turn down the AC?" 'A little cold' was nowhere close to describing
the woman in handcuffs in the rear of the patrol car.

Pam was taken to an interview room at the O'Fallon Police
Department. Once again, she is seated at a round table, facing two
male detectives. The detective asks her if she would like something
to drink. "A little water," Pam says in a husky, subdued voice.

The interrogation began with reading Pam her Miranda rights.
They told her she was being arrested for the murder of Louis
Gumpenberger. It was all being recorded on a video camera in the
room. Detective Meyers looked at her for comment. She merely
nodded. When the other officer, Brian Hilky spoke with her, Pam
said she would talk to them, but she wanted to talk to her attorney.

She borrowed one of the detectives' eyeglasses in order to read the paperwork they were showing her, before she signed it with a pen.

The two detectives left the room to get hold of her lawyer. Pam is seen seated at the table, staring in front of her. On the table are both of the detective's eyeglasses they've left behind, a small yellow Post-It note, a writing pen, and Pam's bottle of water.

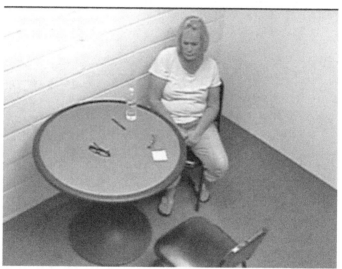

Pam Hupp seated at the table alone. O'Fallon Police Department Video still shots.

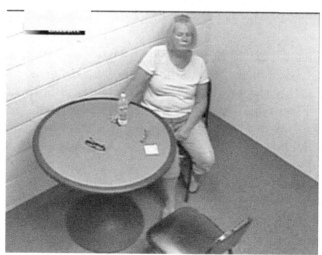

Pam, moving the pen with the water bottle toward her.

In the video, Pam is seen staring for a few moments at the table. And then slowly, she takes the bottle of water in her hand and in one swift movement slides it toward the pen, and then pulls the bottle and the pen back toward her. She palms the pen, like a magician would do, and then bends forward, slipping it into the back waistband of her pants.

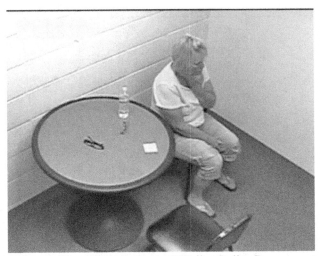

Pam touching her neck. Photo O'Fallon Police Department.

Pam twists away from the table and begins feeling the right side of her throat. After a few moments pass, the detectives enter the room and Pam asks if she can use the restroom.

[August 23, 2016] Prosecuting Attorney Tim Lohmar is holding a Press Conference: "As of this morning, Hupp is presently in custody and her bond is set for $2 million, cash only, no 10%, no surety." [The Chief of Police, Roy Joachimstahler, interrupts to make a statement.] "Let me interrupt to make a brief update: While in custody this morning, just before noon today, Pamela Hupp indicated that she needed to use the restroom. While inside the female restroom, Pamela Hupp began stabbing herself on her wrists and in her neck with a ballpoint pen she had secreted on her person before entering. An assigned female officer interrupted those actions and quickly rendered aid after summoning medical personnel. Pamela Hupp was conveyed to an area hospital where she is being treated at this time. She is in stable condition."

As the interrogation room video rolled, you see Pam exit the room to go to the restroom. A female police officer accompanied her. Suddenly, a man's shouts can be heard coming from the hallway: "Pam! Pam! Talk to me!" Tim Lohmar's press conference was only minutes away. The line-up of enforcement officers who would accompany Lohmar into the press area adjusted their ties and prepared to walk in with the PA. A detective admitted later that he did not want Mr. Lohmar to lead the interview in front of all those reporters with, "By the way, Pam Hupp just killed herself.... You never want someone to die while on your watch."

Pam had stabbed herself multiple times with the plastic Bic pen from the table. Crime scene photos show blood splatter and bloodied tissues strewn about the bathroom floor. Pam had entered the bathroom stall and when she didn't exit quickly, the female officer asked her if she was doing okay. Pam calmly calls out, "I'm good," as she is stabbing herself in the neck and wrists.

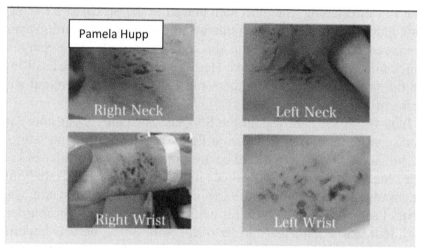

Crime scene photo of the wounds Pamela Hupp inflicted upon her neck and wrists with the pen. O'Fallon Police Department.

In the multiple podcasts that have aired covering Pam Hupp and her bizarre saga, it was perhaps her mug shot taken after her failed suicide attempt that drew the usual maudlin humor surrounding heinous events. The bandages on her neck were mentioned often, with one podcaster saying they looked like feminine napkins hastily applied by officials in the ladies' room.

Pam's police mug shot. The bandages cover the wounds to her neck. O'Fallon Police Department.

Pam was taken to a local hospital who reported her injuries were not life-threatening. She was then placed in the St. Charles County jail under suicide watch. She remained there as the prosecution team prepared for trial. By the time she surfaced again to face charges, three long years had transpired. Had she pictured Russ Faria sitting in the same place, watching the same 1,095 days pass without any hope of freedom?

June 19, 2019, Pam was in the St. Charles County Courthouse to face charges and offer her plea to First-Degree Murder and Armed Criminal Action. There would be no cameras allowed inside, and so the local media circus waited in the parking lot, satisfying themselves with footage of the arriving spectators, one of whom was Russ Faria. This time, it was his nemesis in the hot seat for murder. While it was not for the murder of his wife Betsy, he was hopeful that indictment was not too far down the road. Russ told reporters he was "Anxious, nervous…don't know what's going to happen. Hopefully, what everybody hopes is going to happen, happens…is that she is going to take a plea. But that's not a guarantee, so we'll see in a little bit."

Pam and Betsy's former State Farm Insurance boss, Mike Boschert, told this author an amusing story concerning Hupp's plea deal: "I went to Pam Hupp's court thing when she made the Alford plea in the Gumpenberger case. It was the first time I'd seen her

338

since 2003. I sat six feet behind her. I was on the front row. Some lady sitting behind me asked if she could sit next to me. I said, 'No problem.' I scooted over and she sat down. Turns out, it was the lady Pam had tried to pick up first and Pam had gotten her in the car but this woman changed her mind and got out. Found out later Pam would have killed her. This lady is sitting there right behind Pam flipping her off and whispering some bad words to her. A bailiff finally came over and told her she had to be quiet or move back. Pam could hear her. She never looked at us. She stayed faced forward, her back was to us. She may have peripherally seen me and this other lady. She never turned around. She had aged. Her hair was grayer. She didn't look nearly as professional. She looked like she had been in jail awhile."

It was three years since Louis Gumpenberger's murder. Pam Hupp had been in jail all that time. The detectives continued to work on the case. Due to Pam's current arrest for murder, the St. Louis County Coroner took another look at the death of Pam Hupp's mother, Shirley Neumann. She perused the reports, and due to Pam's current situation, changed the death certificate from "Accidental" to "Undetermined." The St. Louis County Police said Shirley's Neumann's case is still active, but also stated there was lack of evidence that a crime had been committed. They are accepting any new information, should it arise.

The medical examiner wasn't the only one to change her mind after Pam's arrest for murder. Pam's own brother, Michael Neumann, who was in the process of suing the manufacturer of the railing Shirley Neumann supposedly plowed through—falling to her death—called off the lawsuit. His sister's sudden notoriety had thrown a wrench in the works.

The Alford Plea

"Just a few minutes ago, Pamela Hupp pleaded guilty to the charges of First-Degree Murder and Armed Criminal Action, all of which arose out of the shooting death of Louis Gumpenberger," Tim Lohmar began, as he held a June 19, 2019 press conference to update what had happened inside the courthouse, away from cameras. "We previously asked for the death penalty. In exchange for her agreement to plead to the charges, we agreed to waive the death penalty in exchange for her receiving life in prison without the possibility of parole. This culminates a nearly three-year effort to finally bring some justice and closure to the victim's family. They have been extremely patient throughout this process. Death penalty cases just by their very nature tend to drag on a lot longer than they should. This case illustrates the outstanding—I cannot emphasize enough—the brilliance of the O'Fallon Detective Bureau. One of which was the initial 911 call.

"We don't ask for the death penalty unless we believe the person deserves it," Lohmar continues. "As I stand here today, I will tell you I believe she deserves to be put to death. There are a lot of factors that go into that. The victim's family is very supportive of us waiving the death penalty. Their preference was that she serve the rest of her life behind bars. From a practical standpoint, once a death penalty is imposed there are years and years of appellate rights attached to that. Most courts are looking for any excuse they can to overturn a death penalty case. We wanted to spare the family years and years of the back and forth.

"We also were happy to get a sure thing, and that sure thing is that she will be behind bars for the rest of her life. If we had insisted on a death penalty, that would have forced a trial that would have cost $300,000 of tax-payers money just for one trial, not to mention the years and years of taxpayer's money that would be used to fund her appeal process. We did ask her if she would like to offer any information about this case, or any other case—she didn't take our offer. The Alford plea basically acknowledges that the state's evidence is so overwhelming that should she go to trial, she would probably be convicted. Do you want my opinion [to a reporter]? I don't think she has the courage to say she did it. She has shown she's a coward and she's manipulative from day one.

"Her demeanor in court today looked like she was enjoying herself a little bit up there," Lohmar continued. "Maybe nervous energy. We may never hear her accept any responsibility for what she did. What you heard in court today is probably as close as we'll ever get to hearing her accept responsibility for what she did [Alford plea]. This was it…take the plea or go to trial. If she had plead 'Not Guilty' we were fine with that and ready to proceed to trial, but she took the plea. This was a last-ditch effort. She'll be housed in a maximum-security facility.

"I don't' know how she thought she was going to get away with it," Lohmar said, incredulous. "When you look at the evidence we have now, it's just overwhelming. It seems like such an elementary crime story. It was sloppy. Pam Hupp's name is now linked to three separate deaths. That was a motivator for us to say a person like this doesn't deserve to live anymore. But due to her rights to a fair trial, a significant amount of evidence that could have been heard about another case was going to be excluded from our case and the jury wouldn't hear anything about those other two situations.

PA Lohmar then mentioned Louis Gumpenberger's mother, who was in attendance. "As of this morning, the mother of the victim [Gumpenberger] has chosen not to make a victim's impact statement. She may someday change her mind, but I don't anticipate that."

When the judge asked Pam to state whether she was "Guilty" or "Not Guilty," she stood there, as immovable as a stone statue. The silence stretched out until it felt like the tension would break the room. A full six seconds went by…although it felt like an eternity to Louis' family and all those seated in the courtroom. Finally, knowing she was only admitting to guilt as far as the mandates of an Alford Plea dictate, she said the words… "Guilty." It was a hollow victory for those in attendance who had had their lives torn apart by this woman. She had had to do nothing but utter that one word. No apologies to the victim's family, no admission that she had killed Louis, no closure. Only the knowledge that she would spend her life behind bars.

The reporters swarmed around Russ Faria as he left the courthouse. He told them his thoughts: "Well, she took an Alford plea, which is not an actual admission of guilt," he said. "It's a bit of a disappointment, but again, still a relief that she's going to be locked up for the rest of her life."

There was a mixture of relief and regret in Pam's plea deal. The anticipation of seeing this woman actually face a trial and have her sins laid bare was not to be. Those not in the Gumpenberger family had looked forward to the sensationalism a murder trial brings. With the drooling appeal of tabloid fodder, this highly publicized event fizzled like a wet explosive. Pam would later say she took the plea to spare her husband and family the pain of a trial and the media frenzy.

Russ Faria outside the courthouse speaking to reporters
after Pam takes an Alford Plea deal.

Tim Lohmar faced the reporters as he exited the courthouse after Pam took the Alford plea. He was asked how he felt about the fact that moments before Pam Hupp was sentenced to life in prison, she was joking with her attorneys, and actually doubled over, laughing uncontrollably. Mr. Lohmar commented that it did not surprise him. Pam had to show she was in control of every situation. She was not going to give those in attendance the satisfaction of seeing her cry or show any signs of distress.

It was Pam's final assault on the emotions of Louis Gumpenberger's mother and ex-girlfriend, Shannon Zoll. Shannon was the mother of Louis' little boy. Not only had Pam shown no remorse for killing Louis, she laughed. With tearful memories of how Louis would always wave to his little boy as he boarded the school bus, Louis' mother had the look of one whose life had been destroyed. "He was an amazing father," she said, and Louis' ex-girlfriend echoed that sentiment. "Due to the plea deal, no one got to hear how wonderful Louis was as a father," Shannon Zoll said tearfully. "We were denied that when Pam took the Alford plea."

With a trail of broken people left behind, Pam entered a life foreign to her world of nice houses, cars, and her rewards card. Yet, she never let them see her sweat. Even her mug shot shows her ubiquitous grin—that, "you'll never see me break" look that was her trademark. Three years in jail had changed her. Her short blond bob now hung in gray strands to her shoulders. Her face had lost weight, giving it a more elongated, gaunt appearance. The eyes look dead and emotionless.

Pam Hupp's prison mug shot.
Photo courtesy of the Chillicothe Correction Center.

Pam Hupp was taken back to jail to await her transfer to prison. Her days of plotting and outmaneuvering the judicial system was at an end. She had been the last person seen with at least three people who died tragically. Not by natural causes, but vicious, insidious deaths. Did Pam's attempt on her own life go unnoticed by law enforcement? No…it did not. They commented on the similarities between Pam's wounds and Betsy Faria's—neck and wrist slashings. Coincidence? If Pam was willing to kill herself to avoid prison, and had been willing to take the life of an innocent man in order to frame Russ Faria and take the heat off of herself for Betsy's murder, what else might she be capable of? Murdering her own mother? Were there others out there that had yet to come under the radar? It was too horrible to contemplate. But with Pam Hupp, the possibilities for evil were endless. Afterall, she had murdered in three different counties, involving three different police departments. She was Missouri's biggest nightmare.

Chapter Twenty
Pam Behind Bars

As Pam Hupp sat in the St. Charles County Jail on suicide watch, the day she was arrested in August, 2016, news from the outside world trickled in. She found out that Larry McClaine had traced her movements the day of Louis Gumpenberger's murder when the detectives asked to see her cell phone the afternoon they first spoke to her in the interrogation room. Tracing her OnStar System in her car also showed them exactly where she had been. Pam told her husband in one of her daily phone calls from jail that she did not believe it. Hupp ridiculed law enforcement and officials from the prosecutor's office as she spoke from jail on a recorded line.

Kim Freter was acting as Pam Hupp's attorney at the time when there was still hope for a trial and a victory. Pam had not yet taken the Alford plea. The attorney told her client that the judge had decided to choose an out-of-town jury in April, 2017, which would obviously be more impartial than one in O'Fallon County. The problem was, all of Missouri knew the Pam Hupp saga.

After her June 8, 2018 hearing, Pam went after assistant prosecutor Phil Groenweghe because he stated, "This is a woman who went all over St. Charles County looking for someone she could set up and make a fake 911 call so she could execute the person while they were on the phone with 911." Pam accused him in a jail phone call to her husband of acting like Harry Hamlin in *LA Law*. "He's like this little old guy and he gets all red-faced like he's going to have a heart attack. He's real dramatic like he's on a movie or something."

The judge who presided over the hearing was also in her crosshairs. Pam told her husband from jail that the judge did not 'have a title to me...I didn't owe him respect.' Finally, realizing the wealth of evidence against her was too much to gamble with, Pam made the decision to take the Alford plea on June 19, 2019, rather than risk the death penalty. She would only acknowledge that the state had enough evidence to convict her, but she refused to admit she killed Louis Gumpenberger. Due to the terms and conditions of the plea, Pam cannot file an appeal for her sentence of life in prison. She was afforded a deadline to contest the plea, but that was all. Had she gone to trial, and been found Guilty, she could have appealed the verdict until she ran out of chances. She chose not to risk it, nor to give the gallery the pleasure of seeing her squirm. She may have also wished to spare her husband Mark, that many still believe was unaware of his wife's actions. On the day following the plea deal, she spoke with her husband Mark on the phone.

Phone Calls from the Edge

When Mark Hupp seemed confused concerning his wife's decision to take the Alford plea and not go to trial to prove her innocence, Pam spoke to him from the St. Charles County Jail phone. The conversations were recorded:

Pam: "I can present whatever I want and they can present it in a way that *they* want...and throw in all the other stuff and it looks like Holy S*** who is this person? That's what it looks like right now. It's *so* messed up and tainted, it looks like, you know, I'm Ted Bundy. I mean seriously." There is no emotion in Pam's voice. She could have been having a conversation at a local coffee shop.

"You don't understand what I'm dealing with," Pam continues, as she tries to convince her husband of her plight. "It's not the facts, it's, that's not what people are convicted on. It's what twelve people think you *did*. It has nothin' to do with...you know what I'm sayin'? 'If we didn't get her for this one, we'll get her for the other two' [Betsy Faria and Shirley Neumann]. But they had nothin' to do with each other and I didn't do anything, nor was I ever...you know...implicated in any of that...yet... Even everybody here...they go 'oh, you're up for three.' No, I'm not up for three of them, are you *kidding* me?

"You gotta remember, the judge and prosecutor are on the same team," Pam states.

In a weak voice, Mark says, "Oh yeah, I know."

Pam: "You know what I mean? So, I have been dealing with *that* for years."

The phone calls between Pam and Mark Hupp are very telling. If one were to go off these phone calls alone, one would assume Mark was not aware of the atrocities of which his wife was accused. When Pam brings up the two witnesses who claim she tried to lure them to their death in the same manner Louis Gumpenberger was killed, Pam had this to say to her husband:

Pam: "Ya got people comin' out of the woodwork sayin' 'we saw her do this and she tried to pick me up and all that.' I don't even know *who* these people were or the places that they're talkin' about! Everybody is just jumpin' on the bandwagon for their 15 minutes of fame and it's like 'who are these people?'"

Mark, who has done most of the listening, and is still processing that his wife is in jail on murder charges, presses Pam finally for why she took the Alford plea and did not go to trial:

Mark: "So then, how is it life in prison then I don't... I don't get that."

Pam: "Well, that's just...that was just the best offer they offered."

Mark even brought up why he wasn't present during Pam's hearings:

Mark: "I felt not good about not being there all these other times but I know you said not to come so..."

Pam: "Well, it's mostly protection of you because they're going to be all over you like, you know, like mosquitoes."

Mark: "Well, yeah, I know it's going to be a dog and pony show, I know that."

Pam: "And I don't want that. I don't want to give them that, you know?"

Pam stated they wanted to hear her say Guilty but they didn't get it from her:

Pam: "The judge said, 'she will not admit to anything...she's not admitting to anything.' You know, and they...and Kim [Pam's attorney] goes, 'I actually heard a gasp like (gasp) what?' Because that's what they were expectin'…gory details and me admitting that, and the judge said, 'No, she's not. That's not what it is.'

Mark: "Yeah."

Pam: "So, they were not happy."

Pam explains a few things she was told in the way of evidence against her, including how the detectives tracked her movements through her OnStar System in her car the day of Louis' murder. You can hear the hesitation in her voice when her husband backs up the detective's claim:

Pam: "And OnStar wasn't even on, so…"

Mark: "Well, it was still active. We weren't using it, but it was still active. I think it's always active."

Pam: "Oh, is it? (Quiet voice) Hmm…Ok. Whatever."

Mark: "Yep."

Pam: "Whatever. Ok." Pam feigns a nonchalant attitude but it is clear she is surprised by the revelation.

Pam and Mark spoke every day. One has to wonder at what point Mark saw the video footage taken by Carol Alford's surveillance camera the day Pam lured her into her car posing as a *Dateline NBC* producer. Here, in grainy black-and-white, were the images of his wife, their car, their license plate, and a woman Pam had accused of only wanting her "fifteen-minutes of fame" getting into her car. Pam had told Mark she had no idea who these people were who were claiming she approached them, nor had she been to the places they were talking about. With irrefutable proof like that, Mark Hupp's unwavering belief in his wife began to waver.

Mark Hupp Files for Divorce

Pam Hupp remained in the St. Charles County Jail until August 13, 2019, and was then transferred to the Chillicoathe Correctional Center; a women's prison with approximately 480 inmates. Mark continued to accept her collect calls until the evidence against her was overwhelming. On October 19, 2020, as the world dealt with an unyielding pandemic called COVID-19, Mark Hupp filed for divorce from his wife of 26 years.

Mark had walked by his wife's side throughout the civil trial between Betsy Faria's daughters and Pam. He had put his hand in front of a *Fox 2 News* camera to protect her from even more media coverage. He seemed devoted to her and caught like a deer in headlights with all the chaos surrounding the woman with whom he shared his life. But he had finally caved to the onslaught of evidence against her and that she was now spending the rest of her life in prison. The divorce papers sited that the "Marriage is irretrievably broken."

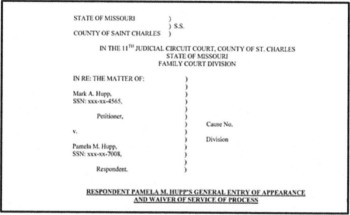

Mark Hupp's Petition for Divorce from Pam Hupp, Oct. 19, 2020.

At the time of the divorce, the new Lincoln County Prosecutor Mike Wood stated he was going after the murderer of Betsy Faria and he would be seeking the death penalty. If Mark Hupp decided to remain silent, using his rights under "spousal immunity," Wood could be losing a very strong witness. At the time of this writing, that caveat is still being looked over.

One thing that perhaps one could consider was whether Pam had told her husband to get a divorce, knowing she was depriving him of a life. She would never be free again. Could that conversation arise someday in a past recorded phone call, or a letter sent to him? It's hard to say. One thing is clear, however: There was no refuting that Pam Hupp shot a man to death in their home, and according to police video and witnesses, as well as the evidence from the Dollar Store and much more, his wife had murdered a man. The bullet holes had shattered portions of their bedroom door and his blood had stained their carpet swatch. That Mark Hupp remained in that same home long after his wife went to prison was a surprise to many.

Pamela Marie Hupp's new address is 3151 Litton Road, Chillicothe, MO 64601. After a litany of flipping lovely homes, and, as some believe, one purchased at Shelby Point with the insurance money from Betsy Faria's death, Pam was now a ward of the Chillicothe Correctional Center. Inmate DOC ID 1343848 is listed as White, Female, 5'6" tall, 132 pounds, Hair: Partially Gray, and Eyes Gray/Green. She is listed as Life W/O, 30 CC for Murder 1st Degree; Armed Criminal Action. Life without parole, plus 30 years was the same sentence Russ Faria received when wrongfully convicted of his wife's murder in 2011.

 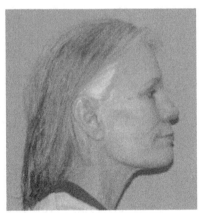

Pam Hupp's prison photo and profile. The date reads 8/13/2019.
The smirk never left her. Photo courtesy of the Chillicothe Correctional Center.

Pam's Next Moves

In the summer of 2020, Louis Gumpenberger's mother, Margaret Burch, won a 3-million-dollar wrongful death settlement against Pam Hupp for the murder of her son. Louis' own son, Margaret's grandson, now lives with her, adding to her financial burden. A *Go Fund Me* account was set up during Louis' funeral as the family asked for donations to cover his funeral expenses and the loss of his income that went toward providing for his son. Louis was about to start a new job when he was murdered.

Although Margaret won the large settlement, it is unlikely she will see any of the money. Unlike Margaret's lawsuit outcome, Russ Faria sued Lincoln County for his wrongful conviction and the biased case against him, and received his $2 million win. Lincoln County had the money to pay him; Pam Hupp does not have the $3 million awarded to Louis' mother.

In fact, when COVID-19 swept the world at the beginning of 2020, Pam applied for the $1200 stimulus check being awarded to US citizens. A ruling found in favor for inmates allowing them to be eligible for the government check. Congress is trying to protect inmates from having their stimulus checks become intercepted by creditors to satisfy debts, such as Margaret Burch's $3 million dollar judgement. Margaret's attorney is trying to overturn that ruling and allow access to Pam's prison account.

According to a form Pam filled out, called a Forma Pauperis Affidavit, she wrote, "I am currently in prison. The only money I receive is $800/month state pay and sometimes family will send money." Pam left out a decimal point. Inmates only receive $8.00 a month to use in the prison commissary, not $800.

Pam's handwritten appeal for stimulus money in 2020.

The stimulus check application was not the only paperwork Pam Hupp filed from prison. In a move that surprised many, she decided to file a form to overturn her Alford plea. In a lengthy handwritten series of complaints, Pam stated she had been coerced by her attorneys to take the plea against her better judgement. Pam claimed she filed the form late due to COVID lock-down, even though she filed it eight months after the February, 2020 deadline to file. A prosecutor at a hearing to negate her motion stated COVID did not cause a lock-down of the prison until April of 2020. That lock-down was ten weeks *after* Pam's deadline of February, 2020 to file a dispute to her plea deal. The Judge held firm, stating Pam had missed the deadline and she would remain in prison under the dictates of her Alford Plea deal.

Pam Hupp's form asking for her Alford Plea to be overturned.
It was filed September 21, 2020.

There's A New Prosecuting Attorney & Sheriff in Town

On July 12, 2021, Lincoln County Prosecuting Attorney Mike Wood held a press conference to alert the media and the world that he was here to find justice for Betsy Faria. In a move that may have caused a few panic attacks, he also announced he was going after the investigation conducted that sent Russ Faria to prison for a crime he did not commit.

Mike Wood at his press conference on July 12, 2021.
From left to right: Ray Juengst (St. Charles City Chief of Police), Randy Lamber (Chief Deputy-Undersheriff), Richard Harrell (Lincoln County Sheriff), Mike Wood (Lincoln County Prosecutor), Dulany Harms (Assistant Prosecuting Attorney), and Bill Wilcox (Investigator for the Lincoln County Prosecuting Attorney's Office).
Photo and identification of attendants, courtesy of PA Mike Wood.

Mike Wood took the podium in front of reporters and had this to say:

"As we came in in 2019 to work this case, City of St. Charles Chief Ray Juengst, was more than willing to work with us. He agreed to house our evidence, he gave us all of his facilities, he invited us to use every amount of resource to work this case. Sheriff Harrell, [Lincoln County] when he came in six months ago, he made this case a priority for him. He put all of his best detectives on this case…six months later, they were able to come to a resolution we are happy to present today.

"I am here to announce that we have filed murder charges in the first degree against Pamela Hupp in the stabbing death of Betsy

Faria. We will be seeking the death penalty in this case. I do not take lightly the decision to pursue the death penalty but this case stands alone in its heinousness and depravity, such that it shocks the conscience. For a decade, this case has loomed large as a dark cloud over Lincoln County. In late December of 2018, as I was sworn in as the prosecuting attorney, I knew we had to work diligently to do a thorough review of the facts surrounding Betsy's death. It's an obligation I owe to the family of Betsy Faria as well as to the citizens of this county. After a complete and comprehensive review and investigation, I came to the conclusion that beyond a reasonable doubt Pamela Hupp killed Betsy Faria, and I believe her motivation was simple…for greed.

"Just four days prior to Betsy's death, Pam Hupp became the sole beneficiary of Betsy Faria's $150,000 life insurance policy. The facts in this case are quite simply indisputable. Pamela Hupp was the last person to see Betsy Faria alive; cell phone records indicate that she was at or near the home at the time of the death; she knew that Betsy's husband would not be home that night; she lied about her whereabouts; she lied about the details; and lastly, she murdered an innocent man in cold blood to prevent herself from being considered a suspect.

"The probable cause statement attached to charging documents outline in great detail an extremely compelling circumstantial murder case, one that is very difficult to deny. Yet prosecutors and investigators denied it all the same. Sadly, all of these facts were available to prosecutors at the beginning, even while Betsy's husband was twice prosecuted for her death. This is one of the poorest examples of investigative work that I, as well as my team, have ever encountered. It was driven largely by ego, working toward an agenda rather than truth.

"And because of this, I am also announcing today that we are launching an investigation into the potentially prosecutorial and police misconduct in the Faria investigation. During the course of my investigation into Betsy Faria's death, I came across information that could potentially lead to criminal prosecution. Broken down into two simple parts, the allegations in the federal petition for the violation of Mr. Faria's civil right were largely corroborated by our investigation. It is clear to me that investigators made up their minds early into Betsy's death, and that they never once considered Pamela

Hupp as a suspect, despite overwhelming evidence.

"The prosecutor [Leah Askey] jumped to a rush to judgement and came to their conclusion too early. Their investigation was mismanaged from the beginning. Russell Faria was the primary suspect in Betsy's death, yet he had four alibi witnesses, no blood on him despite a gruesome murder scene, cell phone towers along with video evidence in two separate locations put him elsewhere at the time of her death. His alibi was collaborated by this evidence. Most concerning, however, is that information came to my attention from three separate and independent sources that witnesses were asked to lie on the stand by the prosecutor in that case.

"Shortly after the acquittal, it came to my attention, during our investigation, that a destruction order had been drafted by the sheriff's office shortly after the acquittal of Russ Faria which would have destroyed all the physical evidence in this case. This is very troubling to me. I believe in transparency and the citizens of Lincoln County need to know that no one here is above the law. Not prosecutors, not police officers. I will be conducting this investigation along with Sheriff Harrell. We expect that we will finish this internal investigation by early December [2021]. I cannot stress enough how important it is that we have full and complete transparency. Because after that, after my investigation is final, the sheriff and I will produce a report on our findings and release them to the public. At that point, it is possible that criminal charges could be filed. I don't know where this investigation will go but I will take it wherever it leads me. My only goal here today is to establish confidence and to restore faith in the Lincoln County justice system."

In a follow-up question from a reporter to PA Mike Wood, it was asked why specifically he was seeking the death penalty for Pam Hupp? Mr. Wood's reply was:

"One of the aggravating factors was obviously the fact that she murdered for the insurance money. I will specifically say that this case struck very deep to our souls and our conscience with a level of depravity not regularly seen. We have a person who not only murdered her friend, then mutilated the body, staged the scene, testified against an innocent man, and then once he was acquitted, went and murdered someone in St. Charles County to prevent herself from being considered a suspect. If I can't pick a case more depraved than this...this is it."

It seemed the wheels of justice had been turning before this press conference convened. In August of 2018, both Prosecuting Attorney Leah Askey [now Chaney] and Judge Mennemeyer—who sat the seat during Russ' first trial—were voted out of office. Rumors of other mishandled criminal trials by the judge began circulating. According to Mike Wood, none of the officials under suspicion that were involved with Russ' trial now remain in the Lincoln County judicial system. It should be made clear that not all of the investigators on Russ' case were involved in tainted evidence, perjured testimony, or other allegations now under investigation. Some of the team members came forward to blow the whistle on what had happened.

New Findings

In the five-page Probable Cause Statement, a new bombshell was revealed about the mysterious blood and placement of Betsy Faria's socks on her feet as she lay dead on the floor. The statement said:

"The transfer pattern on the knife and light switch plate in the master bedroom appear to have been caused by the socks on the victim's feet. The blood stains on Betsy's socks resemble impressions of fingers and not toes. The position of the socks on the victim's feet suggests they were placed on the victim after she expired. The transfer pattern of blood on the back of the victim's right heel supports this theory. The killer left that transfer pattern on the victim's heel by holding her foot to place the sock on it. Investigators believe the killer placed the socks on his/her hands after the murder occurred to plant evidence onto the crime scene and then put the socks back on the victim after accomplishing his/her goal. The heavy saturation of blood in some areas of the socks did not appear to have seeped through the material and onto the victim's feet if the victim would have walked through a significant amount of blood. The heavy amount of blood on the socks occurred as a result of the perpetrator transferring blood from the victim's body to the knife and slippers while holding those objects with the socks, and then dipping the objects into the blood."

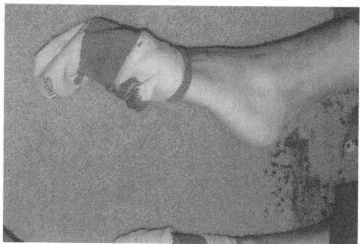

Betsy's blood-stained socks as they appeared on her feet. There was no blood transfer from the socks to her bare feet like there would have been if she had been wearing the socks and gotten blood on them. It appeared someone had removed them, dipped them in her blood and possibly used them as gloves to transfer blood on the knife handle, Russ' slippers and the light switch.
Crime scene photo courtesy of PA Mike Wood.

Russ's blood-stained slippers tossed in his master bedroom closet.

Other salient points made in the probable cause statement were Pam's strategic phone calls to her husband Mark and to Betsy's mother Janet Meyer that night to establish her alibi. She called Mark at 7:04 p.m. when she and Betsy arrived at the Faria home and put Betsy on the phone to say "Merry Christmas and Happy New Year!" to establish at that time Betsy was alive. Pam called Janet Meyer at 8:52 p.m. to say she was worried about Betsy not answering her phone and called Betsy again at 9:07 p.m. to show she was still trying to reach her friend.

The Probable Cause Statement also pointed out that the fake document planted on Betsy's laptop at the tennis courts, laying out murderous intents for Russ Faria, was uploaded one day before the trip to the Winghaven Library to change Betsy's insurance proceeds into Pam's name. Four days later, Betsy is dead.

Another statement opined that the Tuesday Betsy died was significant:

1- It was the first Tuesday after Betsy signed over her insurance proceeds to Pam.

2- Tuesdays were the nights Russ was always away from home at Game Night.

3- Betsy always had chemo on Tuesdays, so she would be in a weakened state. The calendar hanging on Betsy's wall shows the word "chemo" scribbled on each Tuesday of December but one.

Betsy's December 2011 calendar with "chemo" listed on each Tuesday. It also shows the trip to Branson Dec. 17-19, and a DJ gig on December 31st for New Year's Eve.

The Probable Cause Statement also shows that Leah Day tried to call her mother Betsy that night three times to have Betsy approve the new cell phone charges while Leah was at the phone store. She called at 7:21, 7:25, and 7:27 p.m. that night. We know Betsy's phone was lying face down and blood-stained on the family room floor and that it "rang continually" when crime scene investigators were there. If Betsy didn't answer it as early as 7:21 p.m. when Leah called, was she already under attack, or already dead? Whichever scenario, she didn't answer the phone at that time and she and Pam had only been home since 7:04. If, as Pam told detectives, Betsy turned on two lights, let the dog out, went out to the car to get her chemo bag, and took Pam to the master bedroom to show her the jewelry armoire Russ gave her for Christmas, she must have barely laid down on the couch when the attack occurred. That's only eleven minutes after she and Pam walked through the door.

Due to the majority of the knife wounds occurring on Betsy's left side, it is believed she was lying on her right side with the blanket pulled up to her chest, possibly holding her cell phone, awaiting Leah's call. The wounds were primarily to the left side of her head, neck and torso, with only a few on her back. The wounds to her torso punctured several major organs.

Finally, it was pointed out in the Statement that, among other things already established, Pam, through her testimony, placed herself in every room of that house where potential evidence might have proved she was there: the family/living room ("I turned on the living room light"); the kitchen ("I turned on a light in the kitchen"); and, the master bedroom ("Betsy wanted to show me the jewelry stand Russ gave her for Christmas. It looked used.")

Pam's call to Betsy at 7:27 p.m. to say "I'm home!" fooled no one. Her cell phone showed she was within three miles of Betsy's house, or possibly still there. Pam later amended it to say, "I'm home free!" meaning she was out of Troy and knew her way around now and was headed home.

We know Pam was afraid of the Faria's dog. It's natural if Betsy let Sicily out when they walked in, not only to go to the bathroom, but because Pam was afraid of the dog. Russ found the dog still chained outside when he got home at 9:37 p.m. We also know that sometime during the crime scene investigation, one of the detectives let the dog in, possibly feeling sorry for it due to the cold, or it may have been howling. A bloody paw print was found on the back of Betsy's pants and there was blood on the dog's leash.

Prosecuting Attorney Mike Wood had thrown down the gauntlet in his July 19, 2021 press conference. He was going after Pam and the investigative team who, in a nutshell, set Russ Faria up for murder. He mentioned at the end of the press conference, in answer to a reporter's question, that Pam's arraignment to appear on murder charges in the Betsy Faria case, might be "as early as next week." Her arraignment was held on July 27, 2021, and the local news crews were there to get a glimpse of Pam Hupp. She had been hidden away in prison and all were curious to see this enigmatic woman.

The Arraignment for the Death of Betsy Faria

On July 27, 2021, Pam Hupp stepped from a prison cell and into the limelight again as she was brought before a judge Tuesday morning in a case that's made national headlines for a decade. This time, she would be charged with the murder of Elizabeth "Betsy" Faria.

Hupp walked the same path Russ Faria had taken when he was facing criminal charges against his wife ten years earlier. Pam walked into the Lincoln County courthouse with three officers surrounding her. The COVID-19 pandemic allowed her some anonymity as she appeared wearing a face mask and glasses. She clasped her hands in front of her with pink handcuffs on her wrists.

The press crews were waiting for her. It was the first look at the convicted murderer in nearly two years since she was sentenced to life in prison without parole in the murder of Louis Gumpenberger in St. Charles County. The only sound as she walked across the courtyard was that of the chain between her shackled feet.

Hupp had wanted to waive the arraignment hearing, saying she could stipulate her answer of "Not Guilty" in writing and forego the perp walk in front of cameras, but Judge Greg Allsberry refused. So, she was brought from a prison in Chillicothe to the Lincoln County Courthouse where Allsberry could read the charges of First-Degree Murder and Armed Criminal Action to Hupp in person.

"It was on the record so there's no question that it took place because she might come back later and deny that she ever understood she was charged with those two counts," said Assistant

Prosecuting Attorney Dulany Harms. He and PA Mike Wood were in attendance, along with members of Betsy's family.

Hupp's attorney's only declaration during the short hearing was to ask to waive Hupp's right to a bond review hearing Tuesday, because no bond will be set, given that she's already in prison for Gumpenberger's murder.

Hupp sat without speaking during the hearing, and in a span of about two minutes, it was over.

Lincoln County Prosecutor Michael Wood stated earlier in a press conference that he's going to seek the death penalty against Hupp.

Wood said he agreed with the judge's decision to force Hupp to appear in court to hear the charges against her.

"It's rare for a judge to do that but it's not uncommon with a case that's as infamous and that's garnered so much notoriety," he said.

Pam Hupp appearing in court to answer to the murder charges against Betsy Faria.

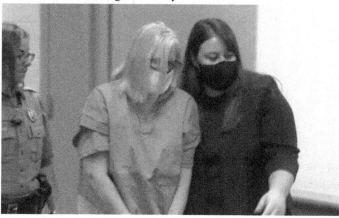

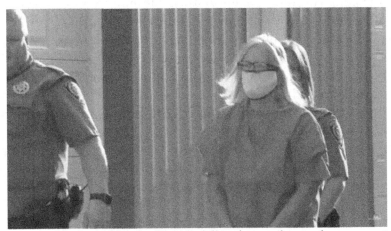

Pam crossing the parking lot from the jail to the courthouse; the same route Russ Faria walked.

When Pam began her 'perp walk' across the parking lot to enter the courthouse for her arraignment, her nemesis was there with his film crew. Chris Hayes with *Fox 2 News* yelled out to her as she walked by, "Pam? Would you like to say anything to Betsy Faria's family?" Pam looked straight ahead. One has to imagine her lips behind the mask were pressed in a look of fierce irritation as Hayes enjoyed the moment.

Melissa Massman, Constituent Services Manager with the Department of Corrections told this author how Pam Hupp may be spending her days in Chillicothe Prison in Missouri.

"Ms. Hupp would be the best person to answer your questions about her daily life," Massman wrote. "I can only tell you in general that offenders have access to a library and a law library, recreation time indoors and outdoors with games and activities available, three meals per day in the dining room, religious services and chapel activities, education and vocational classes, job assignments, visiting with loved ones on the weekend, etc."

Due to Pam Hupp's attorneys recent request to forego a speedy trial in the Betsy Faria murder case, Hupp may not sit before a judge until 2022 for a Preliminary Hearing. At the writing of this book, that hearing is set for April or early May of that year, with a murder trial occurring possibly not until 2023. Hupp's attorneys wanted time to look over all the evidence Prosecuting Attorney Mike Wood and his Assistant Prosecutor Dulany Harms handed over in the form of "discovery." The prosecutor is happy to give it the time it needs. Mike Wood and his investigative team have given it all they have to make sure it is done right this time and that all the evidence available has been gone over with a fine-tooth comb.

Chapter Twenty-One
The Future

As Pamela Marie Hupp remains behind bars, the investigation continues into the murder of Betsy Faria. At the writing of this book in December, 2021, Detectives Bill Wilcox and Mark Ehrhard are at work in their War Room at the St. Charles City Police Department. Prosecuting Attorney Mike Wood and Sheriff Harrell are putting the polishing touches on their case against Pam Hupp for Betsy's murder. New DNA evidence is currently being looked at, new interviews, and fresh eyes are looking over the evidence of this case that was almost destroyed. Weary relatives and friends have to relive it all over again, as their recollections and insights are gone over.

Detectives Mark Ehrhard (l) and Bill Wilcox in the Betsy Faria Murder Case "War Room." Tables and charts of evidence are shown. Betsy's photo is on the whiteboard to the left. Photo courtesy of Bill Wilcox.

Detectives Mark Ehrhard and Bill Wilcox in the "War Room" at the St. Charles City Police Department. Photo courtesy of Bill Wilcox.

Mark Hupp, Travis Hupp and others may be deposed to collect their testimony. They were closest to Pam and investigators are culling any new evidence they can find. In a circumstantial case, without the smoking gun or evidentially finds, it is ultra-important to have the best iron-clad case you can find. In the case of Betsy's murder, the new prosecution team has the daunting job of undoing past evils, mismanaged evidence, outright lies, and leads that can run cold after ten years. This author's close-up view of how hard these investigators are working is heart-warming. There are still good men and women who believe in an honest justice system and strive to keep it that way.

The case of Shirley Neumann's murder is called "an open and on-going investigation" although the St. Louis County Police Department has stated they don't believe anything will come of it. They are accepting any new leads. Perhaps the future will find some closure for that case as well. To date, Shirley's coroner's report says "Undetermined."

A chilling question remains: could rumors of perhaps another victim from a different state be true? At the writing of this book, this author, along with the detectives working the Betsy Faria case are looking into that. They have been kind enough to allow me to do a little digging and some possibilities have come to light. It's too early to tell.

One thing is for sure…there will be a sequel to this book. There's a Preliminary Hearing coming up next Spring and a tall author with a penchant for mysteries will be there. There's a major murder trial looming that so many have waited a decade to see. And, there are hints of more revelations to come as far as findings of evidentiary value in Betsy's murder. Save a place in the bookcase for Part II of this book.

In a twist straight out of Dickens, Russ Faria announced in May, 2021, that he and the lady Pam Hupp lured into her SUV that day in August of 2016, with the intentions to kill her and frame Russ, are now a couple. Russ and Carole McAfee (Alford) have found happiness together. "Out of all this bad—and this bad, bad evil person, I mean she's evil incarnate—if it weren't for her [Pam Hupp], I wouldn't have met this lovely lady here," Russ told *Fox 2 News* reporter Chris Hayes. "I think we both make each other pretty happy."

Carol McAfee (Alford) and Russ Faria, May, 2021.
Photo courtesy of *Fox 2 News*.

As a tribute to Elizabeth "Betsy" Faria, I'd like to end this book with a tribute her daughter Mariah posted on *Facebook* a few weeks ago, in October of 2021:

For Betsy

"It's the end of summer in the 2000's. I'm "helping" my mom DJ at one of her end of summer pool parties. She is dancing to songs she's danced to a million times and still enjoying it like it's the first. I'm sitting in the car being a spiteful teenager and I look over to see her doing the car wash moves with her hands over and over and over again. I smile, because she looks so goofy but I know she doesn't care. I didn't even have to hear the song to know what she was dancing to. Fast forward to today and I can listen to a song that brings me back to moments like those. I miss those moments but I still forever cherish them and hold those memories dear to my heart." --Mariah Day

Betsy Faria doing the 'car wash' moves.
Photo courtesy of Mariah Day.

Mariah also shared that there is something wonderful happening next Spring, 2022. A week ago, she revealed on *Facebook* that the baby she is carrying is a girl! That little girl is due on Betsy Faria's birthday in March. When Mariah asked this author if I felt it was a sign, I said without hesitation, "Of course it is!"

And if a full moon happens to occur during a "Guilty" verdict at Pam Hupp's upcoming trial for the murder of Betsy Faria, it may be a sign as well. Eventually, shadows fall away and the truth is revealed.

Appendix A

Pam Hupp's Countdown to Murder

Betsy Faria:

1- Pam meets Betsy at State Farm in 2002. They work together until 2003. Betsy leaves but returns and is with Pam Hupp in 2005. Somehow, Pam gets Betsy's 2005 IRS 1099 form.

2- Pam has a head injury in 2009 and quits working. She is denied disability. She and Betsy have lost touch but reconnect in 2010 when Betsy finds out she has breast cancer. Suddenly, Pam is with her throughout her chemo treatments.

3-Summer of 2011, Pam is now spending almost every day with Betsy, taking her to chemo and going on walks. In October of 2011, Betsy finds out the cancer has spread to her liver and it's terminal.

4-Pam and Betsy create a fundraiser for another friend with cancer.

5- Betsy's friend Rita Wolf claims Betsy is tiring of Pam's constant contact.

6-In November, 2011, Russ and Betsy go on a "Celebration of Life" cruise with their adult family and friends. Pam is not there.

7-Betsy goes to Branson, Missouri with her cousin Linda one week before the murder. Pam claims she was invited, but her husband said, "No." Had she been invited to Branson or the cruise? Was she feeling Betsy distancing herself?

8-In the two weeks leading up to Betsy's murder, Pam tells detectives Russ began putting a pillow over his wife's face; that Betsy thought her Gatorade at the gym tasted funny; that Russ was talking about how much money he would get when Betsy died; and that he had become so verbally abusive to her that friends stopped coming over.

9-Pam is at the gym with Betsy the week prior to the week Betsy is murdered and "witnesses" the tainted Gatorade bottle.

10-The Thursday before Betsy's murder on Tuesday of the following week, Pam accompanies Betsy to the tennis courts. It is here a letter is uploaded from Betsy to Pam, documenting Russ's behavior and wanting Pam to be her beneficiary. It is later discovered the letter was uploaded from a different 'author' while at the tennis club.

11- The next day, Friday, Pam and Betsy go to the Winghaven Library to have a change of life insurance beneficiary form witnessed. Betsy is putting Pam Hupp as the beneficiary of her $150,000 life insurance and removing Russ.

12-Pam and Betsy go directly to the Post Office to mail the signed form to State Farm Insurance.

13- Betsy spends Christmas weekend with Russ and family.

14- Monday, December 26, Betsy spends the night with her mother in Lake St. Louis to be closer to her chemo appointment the next day.

15- Pam Hupp texts Betsy at 1:15 p.m. on Tuesday to tell her she will be over to pick her up from her mom's and take her to her chemo appointment scheduled for 2:00 p.m. Betsy texts Pam back and tells her she has a ride with her friend Bobbi Wann who is visiting and they want some "one-on-one time." Pam texts back, "Bummer."

16- At 1:30 p.m. Pam arrives at Betsy's mother's house, even though Betsy has told her not to come. Janet Meyer tells Pam "They have already gone." Unbeknownst to Pam, the 2:00 p.m. appointment was moved up.

17-Pam shows up at the chemo appointment anyway. Bobbi states that Betsy was "surprised to see her there." Bobbi also says that the three of them talked about Betsy's idea to ask Russ to move to Lake St. Louis and live in her mother's old house. Betsy and Pam were to tell him when he returned home after Game Night that night.

18- Betsy and Bobbi go to Lion's Choice for an early dinner. Had Pam wanted to go and Betsy said, "No?"

19-Pam goes home to have dinner with her husband Mark.

20- Pam arrives at Janet Meyer's house at "5:15-5:30 p.m." to pick Betsy up to take her home. Betsy has Pam wait until she, her mother, and Bobbi finish playing a board game. Betsy's daughter, Mariah, is sick on the couch with the flu. During the game, Rita Wolf calls Betsy and during the call, Betsy exclaims that she has forgotten her keys. She tells Russ and he leaves the door unlocked for her.

21- Pam and Betsy depart for the Faria home in Troy at 6:30 p.m. Betsy calls her friend on the way to cancel a tennis date the next day. Her white blood count is low and she is not feeling well after the chemo treatment.

22- Betsy and Pam arrive at the Faria home around 7:00 p.m. Pam puts Betsy on the phone to Pam's husband Mark at 7:04. Pam states the house is dark and the front door is unlocked.

23-They enter the house. According to Pam, Betsy turns on the foyer light and the living room light. Pam states she also turned on the living room light and the one in the kitchen. Betsy lets the dog out and puts it on a chain. She goes out to the Nissan for her chemo bag.

24- According to Pam, Betsy takes her to the master bedroom to show her the jewelry stand Russ got her for Christmas.

25- Betsy lies down on the loveseat and has a blanket pulled up to her chest. She is expecting a call from her daughter Leah any minute to approve a cell phone rate change.

26-Leah calls her mother at 7:21 p.m. and receives no answer. She calls two more times, the last one at 7:27 p.m....no answer.

27-Pam leaves the Faria home to return home and calls Betsy at 7:27 p.m. to let Betsy know she is "home free." When it is later proven that she could not have traveled the thirty minutes home and still have called Mark earlier at 7:04 from Betsy's home, she changed her story to say she meant to say she was "home free;" meaning she was out of Troy and on the way home.

28-Pam states she returned home, texted her son Travis, watched TV with Mark, took a shower, and called Betsy and Janet Meyer. She was concerned that Betsy may be mad at her for not staying and was not answering her phone. Cell phone records show Pam texted her son much later—at 9:09 p.m. Unless she returned home an hour and a half after leaving Betsy's, she is lying about her phone log sequence.

29-Janet Meyer calls Betsy and then Russ, receiving no answer from either of them.

30-Russ Faria returns home from Game Night at 9:37 p.m., and finds his wife lying on the floor. He calls 911 at 9:40 p.m.. He is taken to the police station for questioning.

21-Pam Hupp is questioned by detectives the morning after the murder and begins her string of accusations against Russ. She also points out that she has disabilities resulting from a fall into a filing cabinet. Her back, hip, and leg are compromised. Her clothing she wore the night before is requested and she hands it over. The detectives do not process her car or her clothes, despite the fact she is the last known person to see Betsy alive, is benefiting $150k from her insurance policy, and has taken two showers since returning home from the murder scene. They take a buccal swab of her mouth

but never process it for DNA,
22-Russ Faria is convicted of his wife's murder and spends 3 ½ years in prison.

Shirley Neumann:

1-Pam is known to have a contentious relationship with her mother Shirley Neumann. It was said Pam was closer to her father.
2-Pam moves back from Naples, Florida in 2001, after her father passes away in 2000, supposedly to help out with her ailing mother.
3-Shirley Neumann is placed in an assisted living center, after the family "sold everything she owned" to afford the hefty $5,000/month living fees.
4-Pam mentions to Detective McCarrick in June of 2012 that she will get $500k when her mother dies. In another interview in 2013, Pam mentions her mother has been falling a lot.
5-Pam takes her mother to a doctors' appointment on October 29, 2013 and has her mother spend the night with her.
6-On the afternoon of October 30, 2013, Pam delivers her mother back to the assisted living center around 5 p.m., just as the residents' dinner hour begins. Pam leaves shortly after and tells the staff her mother will not be down to dinner nor breakfast. If she is not down by lunch, to please go and check on her.
7- On October 31, 2013, one of the housekeeping staff checks on Shirley at 2:30 p.m. She finds water running and the balcony door ajar. She peers over the third-story railing and sees Shirly Neumann lying below on her back. The police are called. Shirley is found with 8 times the amount of Ambien in her system than normal. The autopsy report lists the fall as "accidental." It is later changed to "Undetermined" after Pam is arrested for Louis Gumpenberger's murder.
8-Shirley's investment money is distributed between her four children. Pam receives around $100k. The death benefit of a little over $10,000 is distributed and Pam gets $3,593.
9- About three weeks after Shirley's death, Pam puts $100k into a revokable trust fund for Betsy Faria's daughters to satisfy the need to show she is giving them money, only five days before Russ Faria's trial. She later revoked the trust after he was sent to prison.

Louis Gumpenberger:

1- Russ Faria is acquitted of murdering Betsy Faria in late 2015. His attorney Joel Schwartz makes it clear he is going after Pam Hupp for Betsy's murder.

2- 2015, Pam Hupp buys a gun. The 2015 Owner's Manual is in her nightstand drawer where she keeps the gun.

3- Spring of 2015, someone calls the *Fox 2* Newsroom to say Russ Faria is at a beauty salon in Lake St. Louis waving a gun and threatening a hair stylist there. Chris Hayes, the reporter who has been a thorn in Pam's side with his media coverage, is called up to the phone. He is handed a note stating the name of the caller (who had been reluctant to tell it) and a phone number that had been pulled from Caller ID. Chris calls the number and is surprised to see Pam Hupp's name pop up. Feeling apprehensive about the whole thing, he decides not to go out to the salon.

4-Several months after the fake call to the *Fox 2 News* station, Pam Hupp begins driving through an O'Fallon trailer park and stops to speak to a woman who is outside her trailer. She tells her she is a *Dateline NBC* producer named Cathy and will give her $1,000 if she will come with her and do a 911 reenactment. The woman goes with her but changes her mind and has Pam take her back home, where her security camera catches Pam, her car, and her license plate.

5- Having lost her chance with the woman, Pam next approaches a landscaper mowing the lots and offers him the same deal. He turns her down.

6- Six weeks later, Pam drives through the Cedarwood Apartments and sees a young man sitting out on the patio. She calls him over to her car and offers him the same deal. He gets into her car, and they drive toward her home about 17 miles away.

7-A security camera in front of a bakery along the route home captures an image of Pam's car with Louis Gumpenberger in the passenger seat.

8-They arrive at Pam's house where she will later tell police that Louis was dropped off at the bottom of her driveway by a speeding car with a driver that looked like Russ Faria. Louis jumped into the passenger side of her car, held a knife to her throat and demanded that she take him to the bank to "get Russ' money." Pam tells police she knocked the knife from his hand and ran into her house through the open garage with Louis right behind her, threatening to kill her. 9-Pam dials 911 twice, but disconnects. She grabs her gun from her bedroom nightstand and dials 911 again, this time staying on the line and yelling that a man has broken into her house. A series of thuds and Louis' muffled voice is heard as Pam repeatedly shouts "Help!" Suddenly, five gun shots are heard. The smoke alarm begins squealing.

10-Pam tells the dispatcher she is exiting the house to wait outside for the responders. She is found in her driveway with her one-year-old puppy on a leash.

11- Responders find Louis Gumpenberger shot to death just inside the garage door, outside Pam's bedroom. He has a perfect cluster of gunshot wounds to his chest. He is lying on a carpet swatch.

12-In Louis' pocket is found nine $100 bills and a note describing how to kidnap Pam, make her go to the bank to get Russ's money, then bring her back and stab her in the neck like Betsy was found. The note also described the address of Russ' mother's house.

13- The O'Fallon police quickly put two-and-two together and realize this is the same Pam Hupp involved with the Betsy Faria murder years earlier in Troy. Suddenly the name "Russ" makes sense, even though Pam denied knowing a Russ.

14-Pam goes to the police station and answers questions. They take her shoes and her cell phone. Her cell phone data puts her at Louis' apartment only minutes before he is found murdered in her home. They also find the receipt for the Dollar Tree where she bought the knife Louis supposedly used against her, the notepad and the pen used in the note found in Louis' pocket. $100 bills are also found in Pam's nightstand that match the serial number sequence of numbers found on the nine $100 bills in Louis' pocket.

15-Pam is seen with her husband Mark removing things from their house in a white garbage bag the morning after Louis' murder. In the white bag are found Shirley Neumann's private papers, her will, etc. Betsy Faria's 1099 form from 2005 and her death certificate are also found, along with bank statements and personal files on Pam's family. A search warrant of their home finds an empty safe.

16-Pam Hupp is arrested for Louis' murder. In order to avoid the death penalty, Pam enters an Alford plea deal that will give her life in prison instead of death row. She later tries to retract the deal but was denied due to missing the filing deadline.

17-Pam Hupp awaits trial for the murder of Betsy Faria where the death penalty will be on the table. That trial will probably fall in early 2023 or sooner.

At the writing of this book, some leads are being looked at for a possible homicide associated with Pam Hupp in Florida during her stay there. This is in the early stages and based on second-hand information.

As mentioned in the Prologue, I have posited questions throughout this book for your consideration. If you would like to state your opinions about the case on the Facebook page created for *Countdown to Murder: Pam Hupp (Death "Insured")*, you can do so at https://www.facebook.com/Countdown-To-Murder-Pam-Hupp-105295738563694/. Please do not denigrate any of the family members concerned with this case, use foul language, or put down other's opinions. Courtesy is appreciated.

Appendix B

Pam Hupp Meets Hollywood

Renee Zellweger, two-time Oscar winner, will portray Pam Hupp in an upcoming NBC series, scheduled to air February 22, 2022. "The Thing About Pam" is a six-episode series based on the *Dateline NBC* podcast of the same name. *Dateline NBC* reportedly did more episodes on the Pam Hupp saga than any other story.

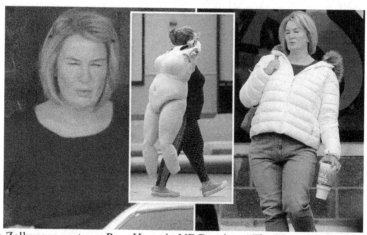

Rene Zellweger portrays Pam Hupp in NBC series, *"The Thing About Pam©."* The middle picture is of the 'fat suit' Zellweger wears to emulate Pam Hupp's proportions.

"The Thing About Pam" will be Zellweger's broadcast television debut. Besides Zellweger, the show will star Josh Duhamel as Russ' attorney Joel Schwartz, Judy Greer as Prosecutor Leah Askey, Katy Mixon as Betsy Faria, Gideon Adion as Mariah Day, Sean Bridgers as Mark Hupp, Glenn Fleshier as Russ Faria, Suanne Spoke as Betsy's mother Janet Meyer, and Mac Brandt as Detective McCarrick. Renee Zellweger is also Executive Producer for the show along with developers *NBC News Studios* and *Blumhouse*.

The actress and producers were ridiculed for choosing to have Renee wear a 'fat suit' rather than choose an actress with Pam Hupp's ample proportions. In an industry that has consistently relied upon make-up and prosthetics to create believable real-life personas, it seems a feckless point to make. Case in point is that of actress Nicole Kidman wearing a fake nose to disappear into her portrayal of writer Virginia Woolf in the movie *"The Hours."*

Nicole Kidman dons a false nose for her portrayal of Virginia Woolf for the move *"The Hours."*

Renee Zellweger wearing a 'fat suit' and prosthetic nose in portrayal of Pam Hupp.

The number of podcasts covering this case is myriad; each weighing in with cited evidence and possible scenarios. If Pam Hupp does indeed fall under the definition of a serial killer, she will join the ranks of an exclusive club. A serial killer is "typically a person who murders three or more people, usually in service of abnormal psychological gratification, with the murders taking place over more than a month, and including a significant period of time between them." Female serial killers account for only 11 percent of all serial murder cases in past history. In more recent decades, it's fallen to just 5 to 7 percent.

Pam Hupp will remain front page fodder for years to come. It is the heinousness of her crimes and the unmitigated audacity of her lies that causes so much sensation around her. All who worked on the cases outlined in this book had the same comment: "Pam thought she was smarter than everybody."

Tim Lohmar, the prosecuting attorney in the Louis Gumpenberger case, who was instrumental in putting Pam behind bars, talked with *Dateline NBC* reporter Keith Morrison in one of the program's episodes on Pam. Lohmar told Morrison the murder plot against Louis Gumpenberger was something "a middle-schooler could come up with." Morrison grins and says, "She won't like that you said that." Lohmar smiles, "She probably won't."

Appendix C

Recommended media and books on the Pam Hupp case:

1-For **YouTube** videos on all the coverage of these cases by *Fox 2 News* investigator Chris Hayes, please go to:

https://www.youtube.com/channel/UCn_4eDvPzNxhlBYj12LWoF g or look for Chris Hayes on YouTube and subscribe for up-to-the-minute reports on the breaking news for this case.

Chris Hayes will be releasing a book of his own covering Pam Hupp in the near future: ***"Through the Killer's Eyes: The Pam Hupp Investigation."***

2-**"The Thing About Pam"**: *Dateline NBC* podcast: 6 episodes covering the case as it stands at the time of the writing of this book. It can be downloaded from Apple Podcasts, Spotify, Google Podcasts, and Stitcher. Keith Morrison narrates.

3-**Bone Deep: Untangling the Betsy Faria Murder Case** by Charles Henry Bosworth. It's available on Amazon.

4-**"The Unimaginable, Infamous Case of Pam Hupp"** by Jeannette Cooperman, a *St. Louis Magazine* featured article from February 2017. It's available on Amazon with the caption "Somebody else is going to die."

5-Myriad podcasts and YouTube documentaries.

6- NBC mini-series, *The Thing About Pam*, airing March 8, 2022, starring Renee Zellweger as Pam Hupp.

Other books by Rebecca F. Pittman

<u>Non-Fiction:</u>

<u>History & Haunting series</u>:

The History and Haunting of the Stanley Hotel,
1st & 2nd Editions
The History and Haunting of the Myrtles Plantation
1st & 2nd Editions
The History and Haunting of Lemp Mansion
The History and Haunting of Lizzie Borden
The History and Haunting of Salem: The Witch Trials and Beyond
The History and Haunting of the Palace of Versailles

<u>Countdown to Murder:</u>

Countdown to Murder: Pam Hupp—Death "Insured"
Countdown to Murder: Harold Henthorn—A Date for Murder
(2022)

<u>Business Books:</u>

How to Start a Faux Painting and Mural Business,
1st & 2nd Editions
How to Start a Scrapbooking Business,
1st and 2nd Editions

<u>Self-Help</u>:

Troubleshooting Men: What in the WORLD do they want?

<u>Fiction:</u>

T.J. Finnel and the Well of Ghosts (Juvenile Fiction)
****

Lizzie Borden Paranormal Card Game
(Available at www.rebeccafpittmanbooks.com)

Rebecca F. Pittman is a bestselling author. Her *History and Haunting* series of non-fiction books have been spotlighted on numerous television, radio, and podcast programs. Based on the Top-10 Most-Haunted Venues in the world, the books offer a comprehensive history of the person, place, or event. It was while writing *The History and Haunting of Lizzie Borden* that Ms. Pittman found her second calling—that of armchair detective. She was responsible for finding new evidence in the famous 1892 murders in Fall River, Massachusetts. Rebecca created *The Lizzie Borden Paranormal Card Game* as a companion to the book. It's a rummy-style card game featuring crime scene photos, evidence, suspects, alibis, and a few paranormal twists. It's available on her website at www.rebeccafpittmanbooks.com, along with her portfolio of books.

Countdown To Murder is Ms. Pittman's newest series. It will cover some of the most-famous, as well as breaking news, true crime investigations. It premiers with *Countdown To Murder: Pam Hupp-Death "Insured."* Ms. Pittman was honored to share some findings with the prosecutor's detectives as they put together the final pieces, including what she found while interviewing key players in the Pam Hupp case, and while researching the crime scene evidence.

Her book *Troubleshooting Men: What in the WORLD do they want?* is based on her former television talk show of the same name. She is also listed with Simon and Schuster for her books on how to start businesses in the creative arts.

Rebecca makes her home in Colorado.

www.rebeccafpittmanbooks.com to sign-up for the *Ghost Writings* newsletter for all updates on upcoming books, signings, & events.

Made in the USA
Las Vegas, NV
29 March 2022

46541424R00213